T3-BNK-853

My Oxford, My Cambridge

My Oxford, My Cambridge

Memories of University Life
by
Twenty-four Distinguished Graduates

Edited and introduced by
Ann Thwaite and Ronald Hayman

TAPLINGER PUBLISHING COMPANY
•
New York

First published in the United States in 1979 by
TAPLINGER PUBLISHING CO., INC.
New York, New York

Printed in the U.S.A.

Illustrations by Sylvia Hall and Ruth Mantle

Library of Congress Cataloging in Publication Data

My Oxford, My Cambridge.

First published separately as My Oxford, edited by A. Thwaite, and My Cambridge, edited by R. Hayman.
1. Oxford. University–Reminiscences, memoirs.
2. Cambridge. University–Reminiscences, memoirs.
I. Thwaite, Ann. II. Hayman, Ronald
III. Title: My Oxford. IV. Title: My Cambridge.
LF523.M92 1979 378.425'74 79-14003
ISBN 0-8008-5468-3

9 8 7 6 5 4 3 2 1

Contents

My Oxford

INTRODUCTION

In an agreeable letter turning down an invitation to contribute to this book, Lindsay Anderson looked back at his time at Oxford and wrote, 'I haven't particularly golden memories of the period—and I am not altogether in favour of perpetuating the Oxbridge myth.' Of course, this book *is* full of stories, of myths. J. I. M. Stewart attached a note to his piece saying, 'At least it's a monument of veracity: not a fib from beginning to end', but it is rather difficult to believe in the Provost of Oriel and his use of Sir Thomas Browne and the badger to speed his parting guests. Nor am I entirely convinced by John Betjeman's Lecturer in Spanish who did not think Spanish a language worth studying. Did C. S. Lewis really wonder whether Coleridge's pants were woollen or fur? Did J. M. Barrie really crawl out of a fireplace? Is it a fact that the Bywater and Sotheby Professor of Byzantine and Modern Greek had once been an electrical engineer in Chelmsford? (The Bywater and Sotheby Professor of my own day is now, far more probably, the Greek Minister of Culture.)

But many stories have the ring of truth: the Lord Chancellor of England being called a saucy boy, Rudyard Kipling timing the Balliol boat at Henley, the Hertford don declaring 'I do not lecture to *undergraduettes*'; so too have Nina Bawden's strange tea party with Richard Burton and her argument with Margaret Thatcher. And Angus Wilson goes out of his way to dispel a myth, to explain how it came about that a don's wife said to him recently, 'I hear you spent nearly all your time at Oxford dressed as a woman.' We are perpetuating myths and telling good stories; we are also communicating some truths.

One truth that hardly needs stating is that everyone's Oxford is different. As things turned out, I have ended up with three Balliol men among my contributors and a rather excessive number of historians. Lord Boothby and Raymond Massey were up at the same time, so were John Betjeman and J. I. M. Stewart, and so, in the mid-'thirties, were Angus Wilson and Jo Grimond. But one would hardly guess this from reading their pieces. Their Oxfords were each entirely distinct. At any one time, there are circles in Oxford which never touch or overlap. I did try not to give the impression that Oxford produces nothing but politicians and professional writers, and I'm glad to have an actor and a lawyer. But it is a pity I could not persuade a scientist to contribute.

People's memories are strange things: there are bound to be odd errors and falsifications in this book, as well as exaggerations and deliberate distortions. In Peter Quennell's recent autobiography he says how flattered and amazed he was to read Graham Greene's tribute to his schoolboy prowess on a horse: 'Quennell always rode a far more spirited horse than mine, galloped faster, jumped higher.' 'In fact,' says Quennell, 'the hack I rode was by no means spirited; and I have seldom taken a jump if it could possibly be ridden round.' I am sure there are examples of this sort of thing in these pages.

This is in no way a comprehensive study of Oxford from the end of the first world war to the present day. There are many gaps, in time and activity. One such is sport. There is a good deal of rowing but not much else. I myself can do little to remedy that omission. Table tennis was the only game I played for my college. I did once see Oxford play the New Zealanders at rugby but my most vivid sporting memory is of hearing, from inside St Hilda's, the roar that went up from the Iffley Road sports ground the moment that Roger Bannister broke the four-minute mile. I never saw Colin Cowdrey play and I didn't particularly want to meet him after reading, in his *Isis* Idol, that his chief hobbies were sleep and eating oranges.

There are a number of names I would have liked to see in these pages. Others recur often. F. F. Urquhart, Dean of Balliol, crops up again and again. I was amused to read in Anthony Powell's *Infants of the Spring* that my contributors are apparently guilty of a solecism. Powell writes sternly that it is 'not Sligger Urquhart, as now sometimes altogether incorrectly rendered, but either Sligger or Urquhart.' After reading the varied descriptions of Urquhart in these pages, it might interest anyone to know that his alleged vices apparently excited Evelyn Waugh to shout in the quad at dead of night: 'The Dean of Balliol sleeps with men!'

It is the dons, of course, that give Oxford its continuity. The undergraduates come and go very quickly but a don may be there, in one form or another, for more than half a century. R. H. Dundas was already Senior Censor at Christ Church in the 'twenties. Thirty years later he was still, in Boothby's phrase, 'asking undergraduates rather intimate questions about their private lives'. College servants, too, give continuity. The chef at Magdalen, referred to by Lord Boothby, was living in retirement in Cowley Place when I was up. His name was Mr Duke and he would remember with affection Oscar Wilde and the Prince of Wales, Lord Boothby and Mr Hodder (of Hodder and Stoughton). My fiancé and the present editor of *The Times Literary Supplement* had rooms in his house, and it was Mrs Duke who insisted on serving them such mammoth breakfasts (porridge, kippers, mashed potatoes, liver, bacon and eggs, etc) that they were forced to deposit packets of unwanted food each morning in the litter basket on Magdalen Bridge.

Lord Boothby's conversation with Sir Herbert Warren is also the sort of thing to fuel the anger of anyone who thinks of Oxford as a den of nepotism, privilege and gracious over-eating. In the 'fifties, at least in the limited circles in which I moved, we had no hang-ups about the ancient universities. We knew anyone could get in who had the brains and determination. Certainly no one I knew avoided them for egalitarian reasons, as the young do nowadays, opting very often for Sussex or York or the University of East Anglia, as being in some mysterious way more like real life. Of course, the new universities did not exist. The alternatives were Bristol, Leeds, Manchester and so on.

I was going to Cambridge, and had indeed already accepted a place at Newnham, when the St Hilda's offer came and I decided, in a flash, that I would rather go to Oxford. I rationalized the important decision in various ways: Newnham was large and had television in one JCR (both cons), St Hilda's was small and was on the river. Moreover, St Hilda's had the formidably impressive Helen Gardner, whose combination of T. S. Eliot and the metaphysicals pleased me. (I had by some extraordinary oversight not realized that *she* was to examine me when I presented as part of my entrance papers a feeble version of her own *Art of T. S. Eliot.* Nor had I really taken in the fact that Eliot, or indeed anyone later than 1830, played no part whatsoever in the English Schools syllabus at the time.)

More cogent really than these outward reasons was the effect of some recent reading: most particularly Spender's *World Within World* and, inevitably, *Brideshead Revisited.* (I was surprised when re-reading that recently to find how much of it is not about Oxford.) Auden and Louis MacNeice were my favourite poets. Of my interview visit to Oxford (sunny, crisp, where Cambridge had been misty, moist), my strongest memory is of my pleasure in finding a signed copy of MacNeice's *Plant and Phantom* in Blackwell's. Antonia Fraser's Oxford is closest to my own. I went up in her last year. I belonged to the Experimental Theatre Club and wore black gaberdine trousers and a black polo-necked sweater. I carried a Goray skirt with my gown in my bicycle bag ready for a quick change before dining in hall. The great thing was to avoid bearing any resemblance either to the earnest females in 'hairy woollens and shapeless tweeds' of Christopher Hobhouse's Batsford book on Oxford (how we hated his description of the women's colleges) or to the 'twittering and fluttering' female intruders of *Brideshead.*

We were not like that at all. There were ten of us reading English at St Hilda's in our year and it included two really beautiful girls: Gillian Palmer and Sally Philipps. In a recent profile of her husband, Michael Frayn, Gill was described as 'once an Oxford belle', a phrase to make anyone shudder and Gill most of all. She has remained, for twenty-five years, one of my closest friends. Both Gill and Sally had more than beauty. Charisma is, I suppose, the current word for it. Sally became the wife of P. J. Kavanagh and, after her early death, *The Perfect Stranger* of his book. Sally's mother was Rosamond Lehmann, then at the height of her fame as a novelist. Her father was a communist, Wogan Philipps, then heir to Lord Milford. By strange coincidence, through the CP, he had known Ruth Mitchell's father, a shop steward in a West Midlands factory. Ruth was perhaps the dominant figure in our group (a word we used before Mary McCarthy's novel)—atheistic, argumentative, touchy, loyal and kind, she went on to marry first a bisexual mathematician who killed himself and then a black civil rights lawyer in Los Angeles. She never did do things the easy way.

Like Angus Wilson, like most people, I had my social horizons widened by Oxford. Like him, I had rarely met anyone before from north of Watford. Although I had not led a particularly sheltered existence, I now found myself for the first time talking to Etonians, homosexuals and Bradford chemists. Beneath the shimmering surface—the white wine in punts tied up beneath the willows, the black Russian cigarettes (the same kind Stewart bought thirty years before) smoked by firelight in old rooms—I became aware of dark things affecting people I knew: abortion, betrayal, suicide. When I saw for the first time that startling epitaph in the abbey at Dorchester just outside Oxford, I knew that what I often suffered gladly was the burden of 'excessive sensibility'. For me it brought not death but a mild rebuke from my Principal, Miss Mann: 'One's first summer term often goes to one's head.'

Our mantelpieces were loaded with invitations—printed, crested, comforting. They came from men in suits. Many of them, like Martin Amis fifteen years later, were spending a lot of time not getting girl friends. When they did get them, they were not always sure what to do with them. In Philip Larkin's preface to *Jill*, he recalls walking down the High after the war, seeing an undergraduate in a sky-blue cloak with hair down to his shoulders, and realizing that all that was starting again. Perhaps he had seen Ken Tynan, who had gone down before I went up. 'Never wear a tweed coat and flannel trousers,' Charles Ryder had been told. And there was George MacBeth in a neat suit with *spats*. Velvet corduroy jackets were all right, and many people wore coloured waistcoats with brass buttons from Halls, close cousins of the ones Angus Wilson mentions. Tweed sports coats were only for the trogs, like the college scarves Antonia Fraser mentions. I actually bought a college scarf before I realized it was not the thing. I don't think I ever wore it at Oxford but it comes in very useful now on occasions (many) when I prefer to be warm rather than elegant. What a snobbish lot we were. Our snobbery had nothing to do with money or birth but everything to do with intellect and style.

I saw George MacBeth in my first week at Oxford, at the first meeting of the Poetry Society. He was Secretary, and stood on the platform beside Dylan Thomas in the packed, enthralled Rhodes House. Alan Coren says of his time, 'Poetry, or Dom Moraes as it came to be called . . .' In my time, poetry had many names. I found a note in my 1953 diary predicting the four poets of our generation. (Four because we always thought of Auden, MacNeice, Spender and Day Lewis bracketed together for the 'thirties.) 'Geoffrey Hill, Thom Gunn, Anthony Thwaite and Alistair Elliot,' I wrote. I had not then heard of Ted Hughes, who was at Cambridge at the time, like Gunn. There were plenty of other contenders: Alan Brownjohn, Adrian Mitchell, Edward Lucie-Smith, George

MacBeth, Jonathan Price. No women. I stopped writing poetry (and my diary) soon after this.

I was eventually Treasurer of the Poetry Society. It was not a sinecure. In fact, it still owes me £20. That was a lot of money at a time when the Regency, Long John's restaurant in St Giles, served an excellent dinner at a maximum price of nine shillings. It was an impossible task balancing subscriptions against the cost of providing quantities of terrible sherry for the pre-meeting party, meals at the Café de Paris, and a poet's bedroom at the Mitre. Sometimes there were disputes about whether we should pay for the poet's wife or mistress as well. Our bank balance was swelled by Spender and Claire Bloom at successive meetings. For her we even had rugby players queuing up to pay their subscriptions. But other occasions, such as the visit of Jocelyn Brooke, and John Wain on 'Deadlock in contemporary poetics,' were definitely for the minority.

Apart from parties and poetry, for me there was *Isis* and the theatre. I wrote a lot for *Isis* and spent much time in the little office in Alfred Street, deciding on type-faces and pasting up galleys. I ended up as Features Editor. Jo Grimond writes very casually that he edited it. In our day, it was certainly a major commitment. Tutors had to give permission and expected no essays that term. As for 'theatre', we were invited to read in plays all the time: *Edward II* at New College one night, *The Way of the World* at Balliol another, *Juno and the Paycock* at Trinity, *Rain* at Pembroke, *Dear Brutus* at Univ. It was not surprising that I soon felt acquainted with a fair proportion of the undergraduate population. There were more nerve-wracking debating invitations too, supporting Jeremy Isaacs at Merton, opposing Nemone Lethbridge at Lincoln. But acting was best.

When I was Myra in *Hay Fever,* Vernon Dobtcheff described me in *Isis* as 'witty, mature, sepulchrally enjoying a dumpy languor'. I wasn't quite happy about the dumpy languor but 'witty, mature' . . . what better false impression could one want to give? Robert Robinson came down from the *Sunday Times* and thought the whole thing most stylishly done: 'It lent authenticity to the current Oxford maxim that it is smart to act.'

One long vac we toured Germany with *St Joan* and a damp verse play by Christopher Hassall. Among my fellow actors an editor of the *Spectator* (now an MP), the editor of *The Good Food Guide* and the editor of the *New Statesman* later emerged. In St Peter's-in-the-East, for the Poetry Society, one of my fellow Women of Canterbury was Maggie Smith. Smartest of all was the masque we did for Princess Margaret, *Porci ante Margaritam,* Swine before the Pearl, produced by Ned Sherrin in a panama hat.

Angus Wilson deplores the young who use their time at Oxford to further their careers in the outside world. Would that dashing blond, Michael Heseltine, have become Mr Heath's Minister for Aerospace and Shipping if he had not been President of the Union? It certainly can't have hindered him. My own careerism was purely Oxford-centred. In the outside world my ambition was limited (I wanted to work in a bookshop and learn to write). But the world was very interested in Oxford. *Encounter* and the *London Magazine* both began while I was up, and Stephen Spender and John Lehmann did a lot to encourage undergraduate contributors. The *Spectator* carried regular undergraduate articles. The poets were published in the weeklies as well as the little magazines. Revue sketches were transplanted to the West End. John Wood, whose splendid OUDS *Richard III* I remember, recalls it resulted not only in glowing reviews in the national press, but also in contract offers from the Old Vic, the Stratford Memorial Theatre, H. M. Tennant and Twentieth Century Fox! The careerists we resented were the undergraduate stringers who eagerly telephoned through to London every crumb of university scandal.

In those days, no women could dine in a man's college. One of our group, now Felicity Taylor, successfully challenged this blanket ruling when she dined as Jeremy Rundall's guest in

Lincoln—disguised improbably as a French boy. The college servants apparently did no more than raise a querying eyebrow. But the story leaked. Someone with his eyes on a Fleet Street career phoned the *Daily Express*. Cowley Place was thronged with reporters and St Hilda's felt obliged to rusticate Felicity until the end of term. Such an innocent prank nowadays would hardly merit a paragraph in the *Oxford Mail*.

'So the fun went on,' as Lord Boothby's did thirty years before. But it was not all fun and games. We thought a great deal about war and peace and the H bomb. Many of the men had already done their National Service. The Korean war ended in my first summer term. My brother had fought there; it had come very close to me. Our *Isis* was full of worried editorials and articles about whether the bomb should be banned or not: these were the first stirrings of what was later to be called CND. Then there was work. We certainly worked enough (often in the middle of the night) to justify our precious places. '*Paradise Lost* is the most marvellous stuff,' I enthused the day after dashing up to London for the Coronation. I think it was the only time I left Oxford in term time. I could hardly bear to be more than a mile or two from Carfax. I never went to Blenheim or even Boar's Hill. I rarely went further afield than the highest boat-house on the Cherwell or the Eynsham home of the Mellors, who ran the Fantasy Press. (Was that our Garsington?) A few weeks later I wrote: 'I forget much too frequently how much pleasure there is to be found in work.'

By the time, two years later, that I left Oxford I had stopped forgetting. This underlines the fact that not only is every single person's Oxford wholly individual but each person's Oxford is different from year to year, and indeed from term to term. I was ready to leave when the time came, to get married and go to Japan. I certainly did not feel, as Lord Boothby did, that I should never be so happy again. But Oxford had meant a great deal to me. I can understand Harold Nicolson's remark about the name on the jar of marmalade.

ANN THWAITE

Lord Boothby

Robert Boothby was knighted in 1953 and made a life peer as Baron Boothby, of Buchan and Rattray Head, in 1958. He was born in 1900 and educated at Eton and Magdalen College, where he took his B.A. in 1921. He was Unionist MP for East Aberdeenshire from 1924 to 1958. He was at one time Parliamentary Private Secretary to Winston Churchill, and Parliamentary Secretary to the Ministry of Food. He has been Rector of St Andrews University, Chairman of the Royal Philharmonic Orchestra and President of the Anglo-Israel Association, and has done a great deal of broadcasting. He has been married twice.

I was commissioned in the Scots Guards on or about Armistice Day, November 11, 1918. Soon afterwards I was sent for by the Colonel of the Regiment, at his headquarters in Wellington Barracks. He said: 'You have passed well out of the Household Brigade Officer Cadet Battalion, and we have a good report about you from Captain Oliver Leese. I have now received orders to offer you a permanent commission in the Regiment. Alternatively, you are to be demobilized the day after tomorrow. I am sorry that you have only twenty-four hours to decide your future career, but that is how things are these days.'

'What am I to do?' I asked.

'Go away and think,' he said, 'and come back tomorrow morning with your decision.'

I had no one to consult. I spent a sleepless night. Then I went back and told the Colonel that I wanted to be demobilized, and to go up to Oxford. After all, had we not just fought 'the war to end all wars'? There seemed, at that moment, to be no future in the army.

I chose Magdalen (it was a happy choice), and sat for my college examination early in 1919. Somewhat to my surprise, for my Latin was very rusty, I got through, and shared digs for the summer term with my old friend Roger Senhouse, who had been with me at Eton and Bushey (the Guards' equivalent of Sandhurst), and was also at Magdalen. I bought a motor bicycle called a Radco, and settled down to enjoy myself.

Oxford after the First World War was a strange place. Not many of the undergraduates who had been there before the war came back. Nearly all of them had been killed. And most of the few who survived understandably could not face returning to Oxford. There were no 'freshmen'. We were all equal. And our job was nothing less than to re-create the university. On the whole we succeeded. For example, someone remarked one day that before the war there had been a thing called the Gridiron Club, where the food and the company were good. We formed a small committee, and started it up again at the top of the High. It was a tremendous success.

In the summer vacation I went, with my three closest friends, Roger Senhouse, Michael Llewelyn-Davies, and Clive Burt, to a 'pension' at Saint-Servan in Brittany, owned and run by Madame Baron, whom I reduced to helpless laughter whenever I tried to talk French, which I frequently did. Roger was an eccentric, with infinite charm. He was no soldier. We shared a tent at Bushey, and one day the whole Company was marched through it to see how a tent should not be left. He was never really happy until he went to Bloomsbury and there, amongst the writers, developed his own literary flair, and became a successful publisher. Lytton Strachey, who loved him, left him his library. Roger's rooms were always a shambles: priceless books scattered all over the floor and two deep on the shelves. But he knew exactly where they all were; and, as Jeffery Amherst has told us in his autobiography, never failed to find a bottle of gin, though sometimes only after a prolonged search. When I got into political difficulties in 1940 because of an allegation that I had failed to declare a personal interest when advocating the repayment of Czech assets in this country to their owners, and had to defend myself in the House of Commons, it was Roger who came to my flat and took me there. Afterwards I said to him: 'I have helped to enable thousands of Czech refugees to start a new life in freedom; and it is the best thing I have done in politics.' He replied: 'You are right.' We went back to the flat, where we found John Strachey. And there we drank a toast—to myself, and to Magdalen.

Michael was one of the five Llewelyn-Davies boys whom J. M. Barrie ran into in Kensington Gardens one day, and by whom he was immediately captivated. Their father was an impoverished barrister, their mother a daughter of George du Maurier and sister of Gerald. Without any legal fuss Barrie took them all over, sent four of them to Eton, and one into the Navy. I used quite often to go and talk to Michael in Adelphi Terrace and sometimes, after about half-an-hour, a tiny figure with black hair and glowing eyes would crawl out of the deep recesses of the enormous fire-place. It was Barrie.

Michael was the only one of my contemporaries at Oxford who seemed to me to be touched by genius. There was nothing he could not do, with effortless ease, except swim. I can still see his face disappearing beneath the waters of the river Rance, where we used to bathe, while Roger tried to hold him up. Barrie said that one day the flags of his college would fly for him; but I could find in him no trace of worldly ambition. '*You* can be a success, if you want to be,' he once said to me, 'provided we can keep you on the rails.' His own genius was purely creative. Apart from an intense admiration for Mr Lloyd George, he was uninterested in politics. Lady Violet Bonham-Carter, who heard of him, tried to get in touch with him. 'Who is this Mrs Carter?' he said to me indignantly. 'What does she want with me?' I think he might have become an artist like his grand-father (he was brilliant in pen and ink), or a writer like his cousin Daphne du Maurier, or both. That he would have done something pretty great I have no doubt. Instead he was drowned at a weir near Oxford, on a lovely summer afternoon. It profoundly affected the lives of his friends, certainly my own. I have a notion that Edward Marjoribanks, the brilliant half-brother of Quintin Hailsham, who wrote me a desperate letter, would never have taken his life if Michael had been alive.

As for Barrie, the fires of a grief to which I know no parallel scorched all the dross away, and drove him to the peak of his achievement—his Rectorial Address on Courage at St. Andrews University. After that he did nothing more.

Clive Burt got everything at Eton, where he was a scholar. Every colour, every prize. Success never went to his head. By nature he was sunny, gay and modest. Everyone loved him. When he left Eton he was, without question, the star of the school. At Oxford he had many friends—I was, I think, the closest; but his career was undistinguished. It was the same when he went on to the Bar where he was popular but never went very far. Gradually he faded. This was perhaps inevitable. If you reach the heights at Eton (I myself reached the bottom), you are bound to feel that life has no further achievements to offer which are worth having. I have seen it happen so often. Indeed, I can think of only two exceptions to the rule, Alec Douglas-Home and Hugh Kindersley.

While we were at Saint-Servan, we used to walk or take a tram to Saint-Malo, only a mile or two away, almost every evening. There we sat outside a café, and drank green chartreuse, and talked as only undergraduates can talk. We also found a casino with 'Boule'. It was my first introduction to gambling. We played nervously and cautiously with five-franc pieces; and I shall never forget Michael's delight when he won. Then we went to Paris for the Peace Procession. At evening, when we got there, the Champs Elysées was already crowded. We climbed a tree, and sat there all night. At ten o'clock next morning the procession began, headed by the three French Marshals, Foch, Joffre and Pétain, riding alone. After that it was poilus, in their blue uniforms, all the way. Haig, with his five Army Commanders, rode by in a single line. They were hardly noticed. The crowd kept on shouting: 'Vive les poilus!' Then, at last, a company of the Scots Guards appeared. Together we shouted 'Vive Bradshaw!' to the stalwart officer in command. He heard, and looked up, startled. We had a marvellous dinner that night, and then sadly broke up.

I went back for the autumn term to find that I had been given rooms in college. My 'scout', Messenger, was first class. The chef at Magdalen, a plump man with a beaming pink face, was the best I have ever come across in my whole life. Pre-war prices prevailed. We drank hock from the Emperor of Austria's cellars at seven shillings and sixpence a bottle. The life of the college hinged round Gynes, who had an office under the Junior Common Room where he dispensed a variety of good things to eat and drink, and also good advice. He might have been a millionaire. He was a great friend of William Morris, later Lord Nuffield, who kept a bicycle shop in Holywell before the war, and asked him to join him. I am sure that he had a happier life running Magdalen.

I had decided to read History. I took the shortened war course, which meant that you took three subjects out of five, and were not classed. You either got an Honours Degree, or you failed. I was warned that the standard was pretty high. I went to Grant Robertson's lectures, which I greatly enjoyed, but otherwise didn't do much work. I soon found that there were far too many other things to do. As I had rowed at Eton, I took up rowing at Magdalen, where we had two blues in the Oxford Eight, Sebastian Earl and A. T. Durand. For a time I stroked the Second Eight. Then Earl said to me, with truth: 'You are not pulling your weight.' He took me out in a dinghy, and we rowed together. 'Keep the boat straight,' he shouted to the cox whose name, if I remember right, was Hoskins. 'I can't,' came the reply. 'He's pulling you round.' I much enjoyed this, but came to the conclusion that the whole thing was far too strenuous for me, and gave it up. This was a disappointment for my cousin R. C. Bourne who, before the war, had stroked Oxford four times to victory.

I turned to golf. Here I was at a disadvantage because I had an inferiority complex. My father's handicap was plus two, and I never came within sight of beating him. Hopefully Roger Wethered asked me to play in the trials for the Oxford team at Frilford. I lost my nerve, and played worse than usual. I then decided that the best thing to do about golf was to enjoy it, and this I did. In those days amateur golf in Britain was dominated by two giants, Roger Wethered and Cyril Tolley; and I was fortunate enough to be a friend of both. In 1921 my father was Captain of the Royal and Ancient Golf Club of St Andrews. When the Open Championship was played there I went up to see it. I walked round with Roger, who had not yet been heard of. To begin with we were alone together, with a dog. It was a windless day. 'Talk to me about anything except golf,' he said. So I remained silent as I watched him put the ball on five successive greens round the turn—an almost unparalleled feat—and hole out in three at each. He would have won the championship if he hadn't accidentally trodden on his ball when he went to look at a line to the green. As it was he tied, and lost the play-off to Jock Hutchinson. Cyril Tolley later won the Amateur Championship at Muirfield.

Life in college was almost unbelievably good. We usually lunched in our rooms, and dined in hall, off superlative food and drink. John Strachey, then a high Tory, was there. We became Joint Editors of the *Oxford Review*. Lord David Cecil was Literary Editor, and Eddie Sackville-West Musical Editor; and we published William Gerhardi's first short story. Gerald Gardiner was also there. Though his academic career was undistinguished, he made his mark as a strong personality. He had great charm, and was an extremely good actor. He devoted most of his time to the Oxford University Dramatic Society, and I am quite sure that, if he had gone on the stage, he would have got to the very top. He chose instead to become one of England's leading counsel, and ultimately Lord Chancellor. Others I knew well were Gladwyn Jebb, who was extremely good-looking, and also good at games, but rather aloof; Kyrle Leng, a son of the famous Dundee newspaper proprietor; and Guy Warrack, our musician. Then, suddenly, Compton Mackenzie burst upon the scene, and overwhelmed us all. Here was a dazzling figure, still at the height of his powers and fame.

It is difficult to describe the spell he cast. I have known only three other men who have equalled him in this respect—Lloyd George, Birkenhead and Beecham. Like them he was marvellous company, and dominated any company in which he found himself. He had been at Magdalen, and adored it. One evening he came to dinner with me, and afterwards we punted, with two or three friends, down the river. I couldn't punt. As we went round in circles, bumping into a moored punt first on one bank then on the other, he laughed so much that he nearly fell into the water. Thus began a lifelong friendship which I have perhaps valued more than any other.

Guy Warrack said I should take my voice seriously, and it was through him that I met Freddie Grisewood, who was teaching singing in the university. He told me that I had the makings of a very good baritone voice, and asked me whether I wanted to be a singer. I said I thought I wanted to be a politician. 'You can't be a politician *and* a singer,' he said, 'but I can teach you something that may be of use to you—voice production. How to breathe, and how to pitch your voice.' He did, and it has stood me in good stead ever since. Freddie went on to make a career all his own in broadcasting.

Then I turned to politics. At that time there were only two undergraduates whose names commanded public attention—Leslie Hore-Belisha and Beverley Nichols. Both became President of the Union. Both were extraordinarily good speakers—Beverley, if anything, the better of the two. Neither fulfilled his early promise. Belisha was a strange man: highly intelligent, but hardly able to do anything for himself. All memoranda, despatches and letters had to be read aloud to him. Even his boots had to be laced up. He brought Liddell Hart, too late, to the War Office; but the Generals hated him. Shortly before he was sacked as Secretary of State for War, he asked me to dine with him alone. He told me that he was very worried about the position in France. His reasons were cogent, and his fears were soon proved to be fully justified. Towards the end of his life he spent much of his time in a monastery. He will be remembered for beacons, which he introduced when he was Minister of Transport.

Beverley was too gentle for politics. I no longer think, as once I did, that he could have stood the roughness of political life. He became a highly competent journalist, but he did not make as much money as Godfrey Winn did, under the guidance of Maugham. Anthony Eden was unknown. He was a recluse, with a small circle of friends who called themselves the Dilettante Society. He played no part in university politics, but he got a First in Oriental Languages.

Edward Marjoribanks introduced me to politics when he invited me to read a paper to the Canning Club, the most select Tory Club in the university, which met in different colleges at regular intervals to the accompaniment of an enormous punch-bowl, which belonged to the club, filled with mulled claret. I had the audacity to choose as my subject 'The Conduct of Naval Operations during the War of 1914–18.' My home in Scotland was near Rosyth and, as a boy, thanks largely to the kindness of Admiral Arthur Leveson, I had seen a lot of the Grand Fleet. I got away with it, and was later elected Secretary of the Canning Club. This enabled me to meet some of the leading statesmen of the day. Soon afterwards Churchill (Colonial Secretary) and Birkenhead (Lord Chancellor) came down to speak at the Union. Victor Cazalet gave a small party for them in his rooms at Christ Church, to which I was invited. Churchill was in full spate, and harangued us all for about twenty minutes. Suddenly he paused for breath. In the ensuing silence Lord Birkenhead, who was sitting in a corner, said in sibilant tones: 'Shut up, Winston. It's not as if you had a pretty voice.' Churchill remained silent for the rest of the evening. I think that Birkenhead was his only friend on absolutely level terms. Churchill was rather frightened of him. In his account of Birkenhead in *Great Contemporaries,* he wrote: 'People were afraid of him and of what he would say. Even I, who knew him so well, refrained from pushing ding-dong talk too far when others were present lest friendship should be endangered.'

Lord Birkenhead was perhaps at his best with undergraduates. He always made us feel not only that he preferred our company to any other, but that he was himself still an undergraduate. He came often to Oxford. One day he arrived with a straw hat on the back of his head, and a large pink carnation in his buttonhole, looking about thirty-five. He told me that when he had asked for a glass of beer at Paddington Station at ten o'clock in the morning, the barmaid had called him a saucy boy. 'I suppose,' he said, 'that it is the first time the Lord Chancellor of England has been called a saucy boy.' I said that it was one of his greatest achievements. On another occasion, when he was prevented from dining with the Canning Club by an unexpected summons to the Peace Conference in Paris, he offered to come to breakfast instead. I viewed this proposal with some misgiving; and my apprehensions seemed to be fully justified when he arrived and sat in sombre silence for several minutes. Finally, he turned to me with a visible effort and said: 'Except for one melancholy occasion at Ten Downing Street, this is the first time I have breakfasted in company for twenty years; and I hope to God it is the last.' I ordered a tankard of draught cider, which revived him, and he made the usual brilliant impromptu speech. I owe my friendship with Lord Birkenhead entirely to Oxford. Later on, when I became a Member of Parliament, I always consulted him when I was in difficulty with my Party, and invariably got good advice. He once said to me, prophetically: 'You will always be in and out of trouble; but if you stick to your constituency, and they stick to you, no one will ever be able to break you.' Shortly before he died I asked him what he really thought of Lloyd George. He replied, laconically: 'I have not yet discerned his equal.'

I never stood for office in the Union; but I spoke there pretty frequently. My college, which was rather snobbish, did not approve of this; but I persisted. In 1922 Austen Chamberlain, the Leader of the Conservative Party, came down to a dinner given jointly by the Canning and Chatham Clubs and made what was, for him, an impassioned speech in favour of the continuation of the Coalition Government. We all agreed with him. Unfortunately the meeting of Conservative MPs at the Carlton Club in the autumn took a different view. They got rid of Lloyd George, Chamberlain, Churchill, Balfour, Birkenhead, and Horne in a single afternoon. The decline and fall of the British Empire then began. It did not take long.

So much for politics. The dons under whose influence I fell were 'Sligger' Urquhart, the Dean of Balliol; R. H. Dundas, a distant relative of mine, who was Senior Censor at Christ Church; A. T. Carter, tutor in Law at Christ Church; and L. B. Namier, tutor in History at Balliol. Urquhart's influence was the widest, and extended far beyond his own college. The reason for this was, I think, a simple one. He genuinely liked the young, he was the kindest man I have ever known, and he was always out to help. He had a chalet above Saint-Gervais in Haute Savoie, where he used to invite a certain number of undergraduates for reading parties during the summer vacation. He asked me to go there, and I did. The climb to the chalet from the railway station was long and stiff, and when you got there the life was pretty spartan. Simple food, white wine in moderation, mountain walks and work were the order of the day. He then arranged for a few of us to walk round, and finally to climb, Mont Blanc. Among the party were two great friends of mine, Peter Rodd and Charles Mathew. At that time all three of us were wild. Sligger put me in charge, and gave me the necessary money. All went well until we got to Courmayeur. There Peter found a casino, and that was the end of the money. After that we lived on tick. I didn't much like climbing Mont Blanc. But the hut where we slept near the summit was extremely comfortable, and the view next morning magnificent. Then we came down the Mer de Glace very fast. So fast indeed that the Swiss guide, who should have roped us, couldn't keep up and was sick. We were told afterwards that to jump the crevasses unroped, as we did, was extremely dangerous. Fortunately we did not know it. At Chamonix we had the first good meal and the first bath for several days. I then decided that it was better to look at mountains and glaciers from the bottom rather than the top, and have stuck to this ever since.

Peter Rodd was an infant prodigy. He looked sixteen, was a perfect linguist, and talked non-stop. This didn't matter because, if you were bored, there was no need to listen. Once, when he was talking to me about the Tuareg tribes of North Africa, he paused and said: 'You are paying no attention.'

'Not the faintest,' I replied; and he went on about the Tuaregs.

He had great qualities. He was loyal, affectionate, sympathetic and brave. He also had an extremely good, if rather disorganized brain. A remarkable career was predicted for him. It did not happen. I was his best man when he married Nancy Mitford. The marriage fell to pieces, as indeed did everything he touched. But she remained very fond of him to the end. So did his friends. Nobody who knew him well could help being fond of him. Some of us hoped that he might find scope for his undoubted talents, and also himself, in war. He didn't. His friend Basil Murray, the son of Gilbert Murray, who was also gifted but not, I think, a very good influence, went the same way to nowhere. Their only claim to fame is to have provided material for Evelyn Waugh, who made good use of them both in his novels.

After Oxford I did not see Charles Mathew for thirty years, until I went on a Parliamentary Delegation to the Far East. I sat next to him at a dinner in Kuala Lumpur given by the High Commissioner and found, to my astonishment, that he was Chief Justice of Malaya. He was quite unchanged, and greeted me as if we were still at Sligger's chalet.

'Is it fun?' I asked.

'That is not a question,' he replied, 'that is usually put to a Chief Justice, but I am enjoying myself.'

Robin Dundas was, from all accounts, a good scholar and an excellent tutor. He was apt to ask undergraduates rather intimate questions about their private lives. A few found it embarrassing, most were relieved to unburden themselves. I enjoyed it enormously, and invented answers which I thought would please him. He spoke and wrote in short brief sentences, always to the point. His postcards (he seldom wrote a letter), always signed D, were written in a clear but minute script. He told Maurice Bowra that he was, at heart, 'a motherly soul'. And so he was. He asked me often to dine with him at High Table in Christ Church. There I met F. A. Lindemann, later to become Lord Cherwell, and Churchill's closest adviser before and during the war. We took an instant dislike to each other, which the passage of time did nothing to diminish. Churchill knew of this, and later took good care to see that we never met. I regretted his influence over Churchill only because, in addition to his Germanic ruthlessness, I thought he was nearly always wrong.

'Don' Carter, as he was called, another of the dons who influenced me, was the antithesis of Urquhart: a bon viveur, completely cynical, with a rich sardonic sense of humour. I used to lunch with him, on occasion, in his rooms at Christ Church. He had very good taste: beautiful furniture, a magnificent collection of old silver, and an excellent cellar. His food and drink were superb; and his anecdotes, not always kind, were accompanied by a chuckle which I can hear to this day. He told me that long ago, before the turn of the century, he had asked one of my father's sisters to marry him. I asked my aunt if this was true, and she said it was. 'I was tempted,' she said, 'because he was such good company. But I couldn't marry him because he had eyes like a snail.' He was a great friend of Birkenhead, who admired his mind with professional legal appreciation, and made him a King's Counsel.

So the fun went on. I have never enjoyed myself so much. Two other close friends of mine were Cyril Radcliffe and Maurice Bowra. They were certainly the most successful. Under

Wilfrid Greene, Cyril was soon acknowledged to be one of our greatest lawyers and, at an early age, was promoted straight from the Bar to the House of Lords. During the war, as Director-General of the Ministry of Information, he established, with Brendan Bracken, the best relationship between a Minister and the Permanent Head of his Department that I have ever seen. After the war two of his colleagues told me that, as a Law Lord, he might have shaped our common law in a decisive fashion and in the tradition of some of his greatest predecessors, if he had wished to do so. He preferred to become chairman of a number of royal commissions and public enquiries, some of whose reports have made history.

A good deal of nonsense has been written about Maurice Bowra by people who did not know him half as well as I did. He was quite uncomplicated; he was a complete extrovert; and he had a marvellous capacity for putting undergraduates, especially shy ones, at their ease, and then for bringing them out. He was disappointed when Gilbert Murray did not recommend him for the Regius Professorship of Greek. But he was far better placed as Warden of Wadham, where he made his name and fame. I think he was also disappointed when he wasn't asked to do anything in the war, for he was a great administrator as well as a great scholar. (Lindemann could have put this right, but didn't.) I was glad to be able to give both Bowra and Radcliffe the honorary degree of LL.D. when I became Rector of St Andrews. I think it pleased them. In proposing the toast of the university at the Rectorial Dinner, Cyril made the best speech I have ever heard—and I have heard a lot.

Then there was Peter Ralli. He came up to New College with what was then a small fortune, and spent almost all of it on entertaining his friends. He looked, as Maurice Bowra said, like an old-fashioned Dutch doll. He gave delicious dinners in his candle-lit rooms in Holywell, with pink champagne. Some were for what he called aesthetes, and others for 'hearties'. Happily I was included in both. Maurice has described him as 'wonderfully perceptive and entertaining, and a most rewarding waster of time'. Among the hearties was Douglas Jardine. He was gentle and charming: but he regarded cricket not as a game but as war. When, as captain of the English Test team, he took Larwood out to kill the Australians, there was, as I predicted, quite a serious rift between the two countries. Peter never thought of work or games. When he took his History finals he answered, I think, only one question. It consisted of a single sentence, in his enormous handwriting: 'Her subjects wanted Queen Elizabeth to abolish tunnage and poundage, but the splendid creature stood firm.' When he came to London he spent the rest of his fortune on entertaining his friends at the Embassy Club, and then died. In his short life he had, again in Maurice's words, derived and given enormous pleasure.

I have read somewhere—I think in Montgomery Hyde's review of Christopher Hollis's book—that the new fashion in Oxford clothes was started by Harold Acton. This is not true. Harold was one of the generation which succeeded mine, and made his own impact. The new fashion was started by me, with the help of Hall Brothers in the High: brightly-coloured shirts without stripes, soon to be complemented by what became known as Oxford bags. As it was my sole creative achievement at the university, I must claim it.

One day I saw a ponderous solitary figure standing in the middle of Balliol quad. It beckoned to me, for Lewis Namier was not one to move unless it was necessary. When I reached him, he said: 'You have been living a life of pure pleasure. I am not against that. But you have done no work. I'm afraid you will not get your degree.'

'What can I do?' I asked.

'It is too late for reading and writing,' he said. Then he gave a deep sigh, and went on: 'There is now only one hope. Talking.'

'To whom?' I asked.

'To me,' he replied.

I went at once to see the President of Magdalen, Sir Herbert Warren, and told him that I wanted to go to Namier.

'On the face of it, this is a reflection on our History tutors,' he said. 'Fortunately for you, I was at Balliol myself, and Mr Jowett once told me that your grand-father was one of his favourite pupils.'

'He was my mother's god-father,' I interjected.

He beamed. 'Well,' he said, 'I would not let you go to any other college, but you can go to Namier. I think Jebb would like to accompany you. If so, I will let him.'

So Gladwyn and I went to Namier. It was one of the richest experiences of my life. With the possible exception of C. H. K. Marten, of Eton, he was the best teacher I have ever known. Our special subject was the French Revolution. He could bring the whole sweep of it into the compass of a single hour. 'You are bound to get a question about Danton,' he said. 'There are two views about Danton, one orthodox, the other unorthodox. I will give you both.' We got the question. I chose the unorthodox view, and I think this is what got me my degree. Anyway, thanks to Namier, I got it. I was asked to give the Address at his Memorial Service. I ended by saying: 'Of the man himself I would say only this. He gave affection, and needed it. He found it not only in the love of his wife, and of a close circle of friends, but in the deep admiration of a host of pupils now scattered all over the world; in greater measure, perhaps, than he himself ever realized.'

When I left Oxford for good, in 1922, I had a compartment in the train to myself; and sat alone, thinking. I came to the conclusion that, despite the stunning blow of Michael's death, I should never be so happy again. I was right. I never again escaped the influence that A. E. Housman had over all my generation.

'They say my verse is sad: no wonder;
Its narrow measure spans
Tears of eternity, and sorrow,
Not mine, but man's.

This is for all ill-treated fellows
Unborn and unbegot,
For them to read when they're in trouble
And I am not.'

Raymond Massey

Raymond Massey was born in Toronto in 1896. His brother was Vincent Massey, one-time Prime Minister of Canada. He was educated at school in Ontario, at Toronto University and at Balliol College (1919–1921). He has been awarded honorary degrees from seven different universities. He served as a lieutenant in the Canadian Field Artillery in France in 1916 and was wounded. In the Second World War he was on the staff of the Adjutant General of the Canadian Army. He became an American citizen in 1944. He first appeared on the professional stage in 1922 and has since appeared in hundreds of plays, films and television episodes. He co-starred as Dr Gillespie in the long-running television series 'Dr Kildare'. He has been married three times and two of his children are also well known on the stage.

In the Michaelmas term of 1919, I went up to Balliol College. At that time, Balliol was the undisputed intellectual focus of the university. I believe it remains so to this day. I never could understand why I was in such an environment, and the college and I did not really come to terms. I believe the fault was almost all mine, except that my brother was an enthusiastic Balliol man with persuasive powers.

Balliol is the second oldest college in Oxford University, founded in 1263 by a flourishing Norman noble named John de Balliol and Dervorguilla, his wife. During the following centuries, Balliol College was joined by some thirty-three later foundations. In 1870, the Fellows of Balliol College elected Benjamin Jowett, Doctor of Divinity, as Master. It was a significant appointment. Hitherto, the colleges of Oxford had proceeded on a more or less even tenor of academic quality. But the new Master had definite ideas about the future of Balliol. An owlish, shrill-voiced little man, Jowett was a rare combination of scholar and activist, not only a don renowned in his classical field and the definitive translator of Plato, but also a determined and practical Master whose obsession was to make Balliol the intellectual leader of the university.

This he succeeded in accomplishing by unashamedly recruiting the best brains from leading public schools. He had an uncanny ability in spotting not only intellect but character in the young and he had representatives or scouts everywhere. Everybody knew Jowett and he knew everybody. He was the outstanding academic figure of the Victorian age.

Within a generation of Jowett's death, Balliol had produced men pre-eminent in nearly every phase of English life: prime ministers, churchmen, cabinet members, judges, pro-consuls, ambassadors, leaders in letters and the arts and every manner of public life. The University Honours List each year sparkled with Firsts attained by the college. There was a fierce loyalty and pride deep-set in Balliol men, usually concealed in British reticence, but expressed with emotional extravagance by Hilaire Belloc, who went up in 1892 and so had had two years of 'The Jowler':

> *'Balliol made me, Balliol fed me,*
> *Whatever I had she gave me again;*
> *And the best of Balliol loved and led me,*
> *God be with you, Balliol men.'*

My brother, who had been up in 1912 and 1913, had filled me with Balliol lore. I must admit that I went up to the college with a feeling that perhaps I was misplaced. I never overcame this apprehension.

Oxford had been hard hit by the war. Two thousand and seven hundred Oxford men had been killed, an academic generation virtually wiped out. The university was generous in the extreme in the accommodation of ex-servicemen. We were excused all examinations but the final Honours Schools and even these, if we wished, we could take on a so-called shortened course. I could in six terms write for my degree. Jowett must have turned over in his grave.

During the year 1919, some hundred and seventy-five of us came up to Balliol, just out of the army or navy. Most of us were a few years older than the usual undergraduates; yet we faced with equanimity, even with pleasure, the restrictions that a wise and ancient institution saw fit to impose on us 'junior members of the university'. After all, it was rather cosy to be regarded as still youthful.

On my staircase was Frank Sandford, a commander in the Royal Navy, who had taken the first submarine through the Dardanelles minefields in 1915. In the Zeebrugge Raid in 1918, he had rescued the crew of the blockship commanded by his brother, who won the V.C. My next-door neighbour was Andrew Rothstein, lance corporal in the Royal Engineers, and later London correspondent of TASS and director of the Information Department of the Russian Trade Delegation in 1921–24. He informed me that in the coming revolution, I would be the first to be put up against a wall and shot. Rothstein was the first Communist I had ever met. He was indignant that I had visited Siberia with a military force intended to interfere with the revolution, and I lost no opportunity of goading him into a rage.

There were six of us occupying rooms in this staircase which looked out on St Giles. It was one of two seventeenth-century buildings in the inner quadrangle. With the exception of a small, fourteenth-century Gothic library, these two buildings were the only ones to escape a devastating renovation in the nineteenth century. The new dining hall and chapel of Balliol, built sometime about 1860, are examples of the Victorian style of which John Ruskin had been the supreme advocate. The chapel, with its horizontal stripes of dark and light brown stone, is particularly offensive.

Oxford conjures up pictures in most minds of oak-panelled rooms, glowing fireplaces, upholstered wicker chairs, pipe smoke and endless, enlightened talk. Such pictures are true but not totally.

There was in my time no inside plumbing at Balliol. In the late eighteenth century, the college had received the gift of some twenty-four water closets from a thoughtful and generous noblewoman, the Lady Elizabeth Perriam. These facilities were housed in a flat-roofed building known as The Perriam against the wall bordering Trinity College and at a minimum distance of one hundred yards from all the staircases. It is proper that all the inevitable graffiti inscribed on the walls of this Balliol structure have been in impeccable Greek or Latin verse.

It was gracious living but with chamber pots. Since my Oxford days, I have acquired a collection of chamber pots, ranging from cloisonné and Spode to the simplest china with ribald inscriptions. I possess some twenty-five of these treasures to remind me of Balliol.

The hardest-worked men I have ever encountered, with the exception of coal miners, were the college scouts, who had to carry huge ewers of hot and cold water up as many as four storeys for 'sitz' baths and then carry the waste down again. They had to serve the breakfasts and clear away the debris, clean the rooms, make the fires and quite often serve luncheons in the rooms of their young men.

The scout on my staircase, Number IV, was an old fellow named Bliss. He had been a scout at Balliol for over forty years. In the long summer vacations, he used to work as a waiter in a hotel at Lynton on the north Devon coast. I had met him when I was there with my family in the summer of 1912. He told me much about Balliol, where my brother had been the previous year. Bliss said that his work at Mr Hole's Cottage Hotel at Lynton was a perfect rest after serving six young gentlemen on staircase IV. I saw his point seven years later.

The high point of Bliss's career was serving the future Marquess of Curzon in 1878, when he was living in the rooms I later occupied in the college.

In my time, none of the occupants of Number IV staircase matched the elegance of Lord Curzon; but with the departure of Rothstein in my second year, the tone was considerably improved. He was replaced by my old school friend from Appleby, John Harlan, who came up to Balliol in 1920 as a Rhodes Scholar. This made the number of future lawyers four out of the six of us: Mr Justice Harlan of the US Supreme

Court; Lord Evershed, Lord Chief Justice of England; Mr Justice Barry and Bertram Bevan-Petman of the Inner Temple. The last, named 'B-P', had been in the Indian Cavalry six or seven years. When I knew him at Balliol I was able to understand the gold standard perfectly. B-P's finances were entirely based on an 18-carat gold cigarette case. All I remember now about his involved but sound theory is that 'it has to be a very good cigarette case'. I also recall that he sometimes pawned the case. Such emergencies he referred to as 'recessions'.

Normally one spent the first two years living in college and the rest in lodgings. But as most of us were up for a shortened course of six terms, we remained in college all our time.

No resident of the college could leave it after nine in the evening or re-enter after midnight. Huge wooden gates were locked with enormous padlocks at 9 pm, the only entrance being by a tiny postern gate. I was relieved of this restriction by the generosity of a friend, Harcourt Johnstone, who bequeathed me a large key to the rear postern gate in St Giles when he was sent down in the Hilary term of 1920. I also had a room looking out on St Giles and the Martyrs' Memorial. It allowed ingress through a window from the top of a hansom cab driven up on the pavement. Several hansoms were still plying in Oxford largely for this purpose, I think. I myself never used this means of entry, preferring the key. One night, about 1 am, a tap on my window from a cabby's whip summoned me to open it. Four merry friends were passed into my room, where for several hours they continued a party they had just left at Magdalen.

Lunch and tea could be served in one's rooms when requested and it was a popular form of hospitality. Late in my first term, I invited two friends from Worcester College to lunch. As I had been entertained well at Worcester, I was anxious to prove that you could have good food at 'that dreary hydro on the Broad,' as Balliol was often referred to by other colleges. Bliss had set the table and brought the wine up, a bottle of sherry and some claret. I thought I would give my guests mulled claret, a popular drink in those days. I set a bottle on the trivet in front of a good hot fire.

No young bride ever fussed about her first meal for her in-laws more than I did for these guests of mine. I straightened the knives and forks, dusted the glasses over and over and finally came to rest standing with my back to the fire.

I was looking at my watch when the explosion took place. I had forgotten about the bottle coming to the boil on the trivet. Luckily, I was wearing a pair of heavy corduroy trousers and the glass didn't penetrate them. My guests and I picked up the fragments scattered all over the room.

Bliss brought up another bottle. 'Try it at room temperature, sir,' he said. 'Mr Curzon always did.'

Oxford learning was based on the tutorial system. Each scholar or commoner in the college was assigned to a tutor, perhaps to two or even more, in the 'school' for which he was reading. My school was Modern History, my tutor Kenneth Bell. He was not only a brilliant scholar but a remarkable human being, kindly, witty, humorous and understanding; we became close friends. He had lectured in Toronto University for three years and, during four years' service in the Royal Field Artillery, had won an M.C., been wounded and commanded a battery. Now he was back at Balliol as one of three History tutors. As Junior Dean of the college, he was in charge of the discipline.

Six or eight of us would go to Kenneth for tutorials twice a week and sometimes I would have a little extra time. These sessions were informal, no two of them alike. The aim of Kenneth Bell was not to impart knowledge but to make us think. History was to be approached in a legalistic, analytical manner. We had to speak up in those tutorials of his. If we were silent, it was evidence of not thinking and that was failure. I realized almost at once that my fellows in the tutorial were just plain better than I was, better prepared and more articulate. In my second term, I asked Kenneth point blank, 'I'm in fast company. Can I make the grade in Schools?'

'You're mentally lazy,' he answered directly. 'Possibly it's timidity. But Schools are not competitive and, as far as the college is concerned, we can do with a leavening of intellectual vagrancy.'

For the first two terms, I went to the Dean, Francis Fortescue Urquhart, once a week for another tutorial. He was known as 'Sligger' and his sessions were just as easy-going as Kenneth's. Sligger was a devout Roman Catholic who spent many of his vacations on a round of visits to the houses of recusant nobility. A good tutor, he dealt with the political philosophy of Modern History, which entailed the reading of such enchanting works as Hobbes's *Leviathan,* John Locke and John Stuart Mill. Even Sligger, who had a pretty wit, could not alleviate my boredom with Mill.

The Master kept tabs on us by requiring an occasional essay. I have one that I submitted in the Hilary term of my first year. It is entitled, 'The Separation of the Functions of Government is the Greatest Discovery of Political Science'. I have read it again after fifty years and I find it has not improved with age. I have this satisfaction: my essay must have bored the Master as much as a lecture of his on 'The Poor Laws in England in the Nineteenth Century' bored me. This was the only lecture I went to at Oxford. Attendance at lectures was voluntary and I found I could borrow the notes of friends and avoid the crush of eager women undergraduates who thronged these gatherings. Lectures were the only university activities in which the sexes met. I convinced myself that the written word was more compelling than the spoken; at least it was less liable to be mislaid.

The Master was a cobwebby little man with a high-pitched voice. His name was A. L. Smith. A formidable scholar, he was steeped in the tradition of maintaining Balliol's intellectual supremacy. Beyond a couple of ritualistic tea parties at the

Master's lodgings and the submission of my essay, I saw little of him until my last term.

A curious phenomenon of Balliol was the singing or moaning of a strange ditty called 'Gordooley' on every conceivable occasion, by any number of Balliol men, drunk or sober. It had a simple libretto of two lines and the tune was reminiscent of a mournful bugle call such as 'The Last Post'. The words were: 'Oh, Gordooley—got a face like a ha-a-am. . . . Bobby Johnson says so and he ought to know!' That's all there was to it. Who or what Gordooley was, nobody ever knew, except that apparently he was no rose to look at. As for Bobby Johnson, his identity is shrouded in mystery. For the previous hundred years, no member of the college had been so named. The chant was used nocturnally, as a rallying cry like an American college yell; or, in spite of its lugubrious, wailing tone, as an outburst of elation or just to annoy our next-door neighbours in Trinity College.

Since most of us undergraduates of the post-war years were older than the usual run of students, less 'youthful exuberance' might have been expected of us. In fact, we were as boisterous as previous generations. I remember two enthusiastic outbursts with pleasure.

The British government, in December, 1919, had distributed a vast number of captured German weapons as war trophies to cities, institutions and villages. Often these obnoxious relics were resented and consigned to the nearest pond or dump. Balliol was included in this governmental generosity. After the Christmas 'vac' that year, we found a large German minnenwerfer squatting in the centre of the Fellows' garden. It was an ugly contraption mounted on two wheels like a gun, weighing eight or nine hundred pounds; an unpleasant memento which, it was unanimously agreed, would have to go.

No plans were made. But a few nights after term began, there was, for no accountable reason, an unusual call for the doughty college ale in hall. Shortly afterwards, the sad strains of 'Gordooley' drifted from the Fellows' garden like a tocsin.

Gowned scholars and commoners swarmed to the ramparts. No orders were given. It was the will of us all that this metallic insult should be passed over the fifteen-foot wall into the gardens of Trinity. Where there's a will there's no weight; in a few minutes, the damned thing was on the roof of The Perriam, all eight hundred pounds of it.

There was now only about six feet of wall to carry. Trinity was offering some resistance, flowerpots coming over in a kind of barrage. But we were close to success now and twelve of us managed to get a hold. With a shout of 'Look out below, Trinity!' over it went. There was a crash of breaking glass as a cucumber frame in the Trinity president's vegetable garden perished.

The operation closed with three triumphant 'Gordooleys' and the happy discovery that Kenneth Bell, the Junior Dean, had joined the group on the Perriam roof, which had given the final heave. There had been no police brutality and academic freedom had been preserved.

In the next term, the university was visited by Princess Mary, the Princess Royal, who honoured Balliol by planting a tree in the Fellows' garden where the Hun mortar had been. The whole college witnessed the little ceremony and HRH was heartily applauded.

That night after hall, the Communists and radicals of the college, about fifteen of them, tried to dig the tree up. They were driven off with light casualties by a small band of royalists and conservatives. A picket was left to protect the tree.

About an hour later, the attack was renewed, both sides having been reinforced, and in this engagement, the tree suffered some injury. The attackers were again driven off and the tree was placed in protective custody in my rooms. It was replanted with splints applied to its fractured trunk by a small party of conservationists early the following morning.

This highly successful exercise in political science had an unfortunate culmination. The Junior Dean, who had performed so commendably in the affair of the German mine-thrower, appeared in his academicals and gated us for a week for interfering with college property. This decision resulted in the confinement to college at night of five loyal monarchists, including two future High Court judges. But, even if somewhat scathed, the Princess's tree survived.

The day I came up to Balliol, I became a rowing man, and in my six terms I never missed a day on the river. Those early autumn days were lovely and relaxing, and I thought how wise I had been to have chosen to row instead of wallowing about a rugger field in the muddy grass.

Rowing was more than a sport at Oxford, it was a cult. It was ingrained in the university, a great deal of the coaching being in the hands of dons. My first days of 'tubbing' in a heavy clapboard, four-oared contraption with fixed seats were directed by an antique don who apparently had come out of the woodwork. He wore a frayed, faded Leander cap, which meant he must have been an old Blue, a trials man or have rowed in a Head of the River boat. The Leander Club is exclusively restricted to such heroes of Oxford and Cambridge. His instruction was, I gathered, faithful to the orthodoxy of Oxford and Cambridge rowing, as developed at Eton, which has always supplied the universities with good oarsmen. Rowing, he explained, was an art in which the oar was moved through the water by the legs and the swing of the back: the arms were merely the connection of the back with the oar. This made the 'English' method of rowing a rhythmic movement of beauty.

He warned us that there was in being, in actual practice, a deplorable heresy preached by a man named Steve Fairbairn, an Australian, in which the back was disregarded in its proper emphasis and the arms were used to finish the stroke. This Australian had taught his baleful ideas to the crews of Jesus College, Cambridge, with the sad result that Jesus had gone Head of the River on the Cam before the war. Fairbairn had also taught the Jesus style to the Light Blue or Cambridge Eight with disgustingly successful results. He had even imparted his revolutionary ideas to a tideway rowing club which had done depressingly well at Henley in 1914. Fairbairn was quoted by the old don as having said, 'It's better to go fast than look good!' The blasphemy was whispered to us.

With due reverence for tradition and style, a very sore behind from the fixed thwart or seat on which we slid in those horrible heavy fours, and a savage determination to excel as a galley slave, I was weaned from the tubbing.

I was lucky enough to be in the winning four in some time tests and in the last week of term was picked as number three in the second Torpid for the bumping races in the Hilary term.

The winter had set in; it was late November and a time to try our souls. The Torpid boat was a heavy barge-like vessel with the same agonizing fixed seats as the four. We never missed a day at the Balliol Boat Club. Sometimes with chapped hands, ice in our hair and blood-stained shorts, we would return from an hour's workout and try to thaw ourselves around the tiny stove in the barge.

After the Christmas vac, Kenneth Bell took over the coaching of the second Torpid, or 'togger'. In the dictionary, torpid is said to mean lacking in energy, vim or vigour. Some Victorian don with a sick sense of humour must have given the winter term races the name. It was not appropriate for us. Though we may have lacked style, we certainly possessed vim and vigour.

When Trinity term started, I found to my astonishment that I had been picked as three in the college first Eight, which I held down for the Eights Week races. We rowed in a new *Lady Dervorguilla* shell with sliding seats, and my days of pain were over. With two Blues and several old Etonians in the boat, we weren't too bad. The college started the week in third place with Christ Church and Magdalen ahead of us. That's the way we finished.

Magdalen, with four Blues in her eight, went Head of the

River by bumping 'the House' opposite the Christ Church barge on Monday and Balliol rowed through every night—the word 'night' was always used instead of day in reference to both Torpids and Eights Week. We did gain on the House (so-called because of its Latin name 'Aedes Christi') by half a length almost every one of the five nights but couldn't pull off a bump.

Eights Week was a lovely sight that year. The weather was perfect and every day the barges filled with pretty women in bright summer frocks. The towpath opposite was a contrast with howling mobs following each boat, and signal pistol shots and shouts of 'You're going up, Merton,' 'It's a canvas, Trinity!' And of course, 'Well rowed, Balliol, well rowed!'

After Eights Week in 1920, the University Boat Club persuaded six colleges to send their First Eights to Henley Regatta. Oxford was making a determined effort to swamp the expected Cambridge invasion. Magdalen, Christ Church, Trinity, Exeter, Merton and Balliol were set to go, and Oxford had entries in every event in the Regatta. We were to row in the Ladies Plate, a race for colleges and public schools. The captain of the Balliol Boat Club was an Australian Rhodes Scholar named Hugh Cairns. A Blue, he had rowed in the Oxford boat the previous March and had rowed at seven in the college eight. He took himself out of the boat in order to coach us. We still had one Blue, Stanley O'Neil, at number six.

Hugh was a gentle, gregarious man, with many friends, among whom was Rudyard Kipling. Hugh brought him to our training table in hall one night before we left for Henley. Mr Kipling appeared much interested in rowing and our chances at Henley. After dinner, some of us adjourned to Kenneth Bell's rooms, Hugh and Mr Kipling along with us. It was a cheerful evening with much good talk, and Mr Kipling fitted in smoothly with the group.

A hero to us all, Kipling might have been just another don

as he curled up in a big chair with his mug of Balliol ale. He listened, talked a bit, laughed a lot and seemed to have a good time, whether he heard about the merits of swivel rowlocks, the virtues of the newest *Lady Dervorguilla,* the shell we were taking to Henley, or the usual small talk of training table. By the time we broke up, it had been arranged that Mr Kipling would accompany us to Henley. We had adopted him in a peremptory manner. He complied cheerily. Hugh Cairns said the house the college had rented for our two weeks at the Regatta would accommodate Mr Kipling in addition to the fourteen of us (Hugh was taking five substitutes as well as the eight).

Two days later, we made our first appearance on the river at Henley. There were thirty-five eights and twelve fours, to say nothing of pairs and sculls entered, and the course had to be reserved for time tests. All day long, one or another of the eights, fours, pairs and single scullers would be rowing a 'course', with a coach and followers with stop watches, all on bicycles, making the towpath as perilous to a casual pedestrian as Fifth Avenue or Piccadilly.

Mr Kipling was all attention, a stop watch concealed in his pocket, timing the crews who were rowing 'courses'. Since he could see starts from the Leander Club enclosure opposite the finishing post, he was able to time all our likely competition in the first two or three days. Nobody knew what he was doing. He was as furtive as a Newmarket clocker at early-morning gallops. He said the only other spy he detected was a bishop whose pink Leander cap clashed so violently with his purple bib that nobody in the enclosure could take their eyes off him. This chromatic disturbance fascinated Kipling. Greatly impressed with the influx of rowing clergy, he was convinced that a superb and stately crew composed entirely of bishops and deans, who were members of Leander, could be put on the river for a five-hundred-yard display.

After ten days at Henley, the Regatta opened with Balliol in fairly good shape. We won our first heat against the Royal

Military College by a length, but in the draw for the second day, we had been told the bad news. We were to row against Eton on Thursday. Although Eton was a public school, its crew was almost always better than the average college. This year was no exception. We faced an eight that had been superbly trained and was a good five pounds per man heavier than we were. Mr Kipling had timed them over a trial course at 7′ 17″, exactly their time in the heat against us. They won by a length. It was a galling defeat. We were rowed out. I couldn't breathe and held my head down between my knees. As we drifted under Henley Bridge, I remember a kindly cockney voice calling, 'Good old three—don't worry, you'll live!'

We paddled back to the boathouse and carried *Lady Dervorguilla* to her rack. Hugh Cairns and Mr Kipling appeared. They had watched the race from the umpire's launch and looked far from dejected.

'You rowed well, the best form you've showed,' Hugh told us. 'Now take it easy and about half-past seven tonight I'm going to put you over the course again, against the clock.'

We relaxed until about seven o'clock that night, then we took the shining shell out and paddled up to Temple Island. There we did some starts and short bursts of rowing. One of the substitutes got in the starting punt and steadied us for a start. Hugh called from the bank: 'I'll start you with a gun ... COME FORWARD . . ARE YOU READY? ... THE SHOT!' We were off. Arengo Jones, our stroke, set us about forty the first minute and then he settled down to what seemed about thirty-five. Something astonishing had happened. The boat was moving forward without our effort. As we came forward, she seemed to slide ahead of us. It was an extraordinary sensation of smooth movement. I felt I was slacking but I dared not press for we were, for the first time, completely together in a rhythmic cycle. Arengo was giving us great length and maintaining the rate of stroke. From the bank, Hugh Cairns on his bike shouted, 'Oh, well rowed, Balliol!'

We were passing the 1500-yard post. I could hardly believe we had come that far. Kimber, the cox, cried, 'Give her ten, Balliol!' and counted us through, Jones bringing us up to forty. We were nearly at Phyllis Court now. We could hear an orchestra playing. It was so easy. Good Lord, there's the enclosure on the Bucks side. Again Kimber shouted, 'Now row her in, Balliol, give her ten!' Ten good long ones we gave her, and it was over. 'Easy all, Balliol!'

From the bank by the Leander enclosure, now empty in the dusk, came Hugh's delighted words, 'Well rowed, Balliol, oh, well rowed!' Mr Kipling was shouting the time, but we couldn't hear him. We paddled back to the boathouse and, as we lifted the *Lady Dervorguilla* over our heads and placed her on the rack, Hugh, Mr Kipling and the substitutes came into the boathouse. We heard the good news that our time had been 7′ 10″—three seconds better than Eton's in the morning. It was the best row I ever had, practically in the dark, racing against the clock, with no one to see us except Hugh Cairns and Rudyard Kipling.

In October, 1920, back at Oxford, I was in the thick of activity. The number of clubs, societies and organized groups within the university was prodigious. I belonged to the Raleigh Club, a collection of imperialists whose interests may be indicated by the toasts at the annual dinner in 1920—'The Empire of the Bretanes', 'The Dominions', 'India', 'The Crown Colonies'; and by the speakers, who included Lord Milner, Lord Meston and my brother Vincent, who had been president in 1913. All this was only sixty years ago, but there was not a sign of Tanzania, Volta, Ghana, Zambia or any of the newborn states that have replaced the Crown Colonies. The Empire was still a reality. South Africa was a staunch and loyal Dominion, of which Lord Milner had been the architect. Only over India was there a cloud in the sky and it was a little bigger than a loincloth. The war seemed to have made the

Empire more solid than ever, at least so it seemed to me after every meeting of the Raleigh Club.

The Brackenbury Society was an old and informal institution. It met periodically for discussion of some timely subject, often with a distinguished visitor. The club had about thirty members, most of whom attended meetings in the old Senior Common Room. At one meeting, T. E. Lawrence came to us. It was a disturbing occasion. I am always ill at ease in the presence of cold intellect. Sheer brain frightens me. Lawrence was bitter and brilliant. He had been allowed to make commitments and promises to the Arabs which were not kept by the British. But the sad fact is that in 1920, he foresaw exactly what is now happening in the Middle East. I have never forgotten that evening with an extraordinary man. We had the privilege of meeting other great men at 'Bracker' meetings: Lord Asquith, a Balliol prime minister, was one of them, but there was never another like Lawrence.

As I joined every club, society, group or faction that would have me, except the Communist Party, I soon found myself a member of the Union. This was the university debating society. Its sessions were modelled closely on those of the House of Commons; and for more than a century, future statesmen, prime ministers and members had learned the ways of the House by debating motions, grave and frivolous, in the Union. The four principal speakers wore white tie and tails, as did the Speaker. A sergeant-at-arms was in attendance and sometimes he was not only ceremonial but necessary. Following the tradition of Westminster, all speeches were extemporaneous, even notes being unfavourably regarded.

Those were still the days of rhetoric and eloquence in public life: before the prepared statement and the speech-writer appeared, before the idiot cards and the teleprompter. The young men who spoke at the Union were worthy followers of Gladstone and Asquith. I remember Anthony Eden, who made quite a reputation for himself as a speaker in 1920 and 1921.

It was my misfortune to speak against a motion that had just received Eden's eloquent support. My friend from Balliol, the future writer Beverley Nichols, was in the chair as Speaker. As he 'recognized' me, there was a look of kindly pity on his face. With something approaching horror, I remember those minutes I stood in a crowded Union and tried to take Eden apart. The funny thing is, I haven't the foggiest recollection of what we were talking about. I spoke again several times but only after careful preparation; my attendance at the Union was primarily to hear my fellow members perform.

It is probably unfair to judge the Oxford University Dramatic Society by its activities in 1919–1920. The OUDS, in abeyance since 1914, had started up again after the war with an entirely new membership. I joined as soon as I could, and this was not so easy as it might have been. The society, which occupied some rather austere rooms in George Street, was run in the manner of a social club. Naturally I knew none of the members to propose and second me. The president, Maurice Colbourne, decided to waive such formalities in view of my obvious enthusiasm for the theatre. He exercised his presidential authority to make me a member forthwith. Other than myself, I think, he was the only member of the OUDS of that year of its revival who became a professional actor. He certainly was one of the few who gave performances of professional competence in the Society's first production.

The programme of the OUDS had never been ambitious: a few casual visits to the society's rooms by critics, managers, writers or actors, evenings of questions and mulled claret; the annual production in the Hilary term. I remember only Harley Granville-Barker coming for an evening's session, a great experience for me. It was my first encounter with a great professional theatre man. He was a Renaissance character—the actor, producer and playwright combined. As a playwright, he could write any kind of play from a farcical comedy like *Rococo* to *The Madras House*. As an actor, he couldn't help writing good dialogue.

It always puzzled me that Granville-Barker undertook the job of adapting or rather editing Thomas Hardy's *The Dynasts*. We played it at the New Theatre. John Drinkwater directed the production and about forty young gentlemen of the OUDS had speaking parts. I doubt if the best professional cast in the world could have handled Hardy's leaden verse. And we were amateurs. I played Caulaincourt in a brief scene of Napoleon's abdication before exile to Elba. I still remember my one speech. You don't forget a decisive defeat. I don't remember who played Napoleon. I had my own problem. It was deeply personal and I faced it in the best amateur tradition, without regard for my fellow performers. Eight times I spoke those deathless lines in front of an audience:

> '*We should have had success. But fate said no.*
> *And abdication, making no reserves,*
> *Is, sire, we are convinced, with all respect,*
> *The only road.*'

The choice of play was unfortunate. The war of a hundred years ago was not the most intriguing theatre fare for people who had lived through 1914–1918. The next year, the OUDS returned to the traditional Shakespearean production with a professional star in the leading feminine role. *The Dynasts* had been cast from the vast number of dons' daughters available for women's parts. In 1921, the committee selected *Antony and Cleopatra* with the beautiful Cathleen Nesbitt as Cleopatra. Cathleen afterwards married Cecil Ramage, who played Antony.

I dropped out of the OUDS during my second year and, with a college friend, Guy Vaughan-Morgan, organized a small play-reading club of fifteen members, mostly from Balliol. We met about every fortnight to read a play. We had about ten readings—plays by Ibsen, Galsworthy, Granville-Barker, Shakespeare, the usual selection of the eager and stage-struck. The 'performances' were sometimes quite effective in what was soon to become a radio technique. One thing is certain: we got more out of our nameless little group than the OUDS ever offered.

London was only an hour and a half away by train and matinees were possible without applying for leave. A night away from college was a different matter. All colleges were stern about such leaves. James Morris's excellent book, *Oxford,* tells of an undergraduate applying for an absence to attend the funeral of his uncle. The reply of the dean of the college was, 'Oh, very well . . . but I wish it could have been a nearer relative.'

Sometimes I am inclined to ridicule the caricatures of Victorian male attire which many of the young and would-be young of today have adopted, particularly for evening wear. But I curb my taunts when I think of my own garb when I went down to London for a day or an evening in '20 and '21. I had two suits, both pin-striped, a dark grey and a brown. White spats or a pair of grey-topped, black-buttoned boots always called for an agonizing decision. Light-coloured waistcoats and broad, striped club ties were in order, and good loud shirts. The ensemble was not in the least conspicuous at that time, nor did it lead my fellow passengers in the third-class carriage to expect that I would shortly produce a deck of cards.

Like a great many undergraduates, I was soon caught in the web of credit. Booksellers, shirtmakers, bootmakers, tailors, even the college stores, flaunted credit at you. In my first term, a Mr Stratton called at my rooms with a bag of cloth samples, a measuring tape and an agreeable personality. I ordered a suit of clothes from his firm, Messrs Lesley and Roberts of 16 George Street, Hanover Square. I was to have a fitting when I could come to London. The suit was to cost £8.8.0 as a trial and the subsequent charge would be £10.10.0.

I thought this fairly steep but the suit worked out very nicely. The cutter, Mr Robinson, was excellent. I thought so then and I've thought so ever since. In 1970, he cut a suit for me as Tom Garrison in *I Never Sang For My Father,* which I played at the Duke of York's. Old Tom was eighty years old in the play and Robbie was persuaded by me to cut the suit loose. It nearly broke his heart. He hadn't changed a bit since 1920 but the price of the suit had.

As the Michaelmas term of 1920 progressed, I continued to live Oxford life to the full. It was a life crowded with meetings of clubs, societies and groups, of luncheons and dinners, and through it all endless talk. I had ears as well as a tongue. But I could not escape the spectre of the 'Schools' that lay ahead, now only a few months away. My work was far behind schedule. The vacations had not produced the required solid reading that I had planned. Not that I wasn't up to the job. My misgivings that I was not up to Balliol standards were just self-pitying hypocrisy. I had done well at school in Canada. I had a fair mind and anyway the examinations were held by the university and not the college. The truth was I lacked the self-discipline that the Oxford system demands. At school, work had been constantly scrutinized, tested and disciplined. I thrived on that method. But without the whip crack, I lay back on the traces. It's a sad admission.

About mid-November, I submitted to Kenneth Bell a 'collection', which was an informal examination on the basis of a Schools paper. By informal, I mean that it was written in my own room without the stress and strain of regular examinations. These were held in an awesome hall called the Examination Schools and candidates were required to wear a dark suit and a white dress-tie. The Schools also included an oral examination, or *viva voce* questioning. It took the courage of F. E. Smith, later the Earl of Birkenhead, to put the *viva* in its proper place. When gently admonished for his obvious lack of preparation on a certain subject, F.E. answered, 'I am here to be examined, not to receive unsolicited advice.' Alas, there are few F. E. Smiths, and I was not one of them.

My 'collection' was handed back to me by Kenneth, with the following notation in red ink: 'One good and interesting answer on the Elizabethan drama; an unfinished answer on Elizabethan archbishops, and that is all! It is most important that you revise a term's work and force yourself by an act of will to write in an examination. I'm sure in your case it is the will which defeats you.'

I spent an evening of contrition, resolution and Scotch with Kenneth, ending in our singing a few 'Gordooleys', my tossing flowerpots into Trinity, and Kenneth donning his gown and gating me for a week. His parting admonition had been: 'It's our purpose here to make you think rather than know, but please remember that in order to think, it is necessary to know!'

My pursuit of knowledge in the long vac had been somewhat impeded by the pursuit of a young lady in Cornwall, to say nothing of the fishing, and this quest seemed at the time to have ended in failure. Now a letter from my father brought bad news of my stepmother, whose health had been poor for some time. I made arrangements to leave for California at the end of the term. In 1920, the trip involved eleven days by ship and trains. My plans for concentrated reading during the vac went out the porthole of a second-class cabin of the *RMS Aquitania*.

I found my stepmother very ill and my father desperately worried. Her condition was breast cancer, which in those days was terminal. After five days, I felt callous leaving them, and I never saw my stepmother again.

In the Hilary term of '21, much of that Oxford life I had been so strongly urged to follow by my brother was dropped. I 'sported my oak' most evenings; that is, bolted the heavy oak door of my room and did my damnedest to catch up with the reading I had neglected. There were two or three London trips that neither helped my work nor my bank account.

Having a chaperon was still the custom for a theatre or dinner dance. That meant the cost of a foursome, no small burden for an undergraduate with a bank book frequently incarnadined. But after some hard work in the Easter vac, admittedly in London, I made progress in my studies.

At the beginning of the Trinity term, five weeks before my Schools in June, I felt fairly confident. Kenneth Bell wasn't quite so sanguine He still thought I should have a dry run at Schools and wait another term for a real try. I assured him I no longer had the jitters. It was my unfortunate sense of immediacy, I suppose. Everything looked fair for a degree in June, a low degree perhaps but an Oxford degree. True, I was rowing in the college eight again, but that was a wise precaution against Oxford torpor, and anyway, my tutor was coaching us.

There came a day about a month before the Schools when I found myself walking up and down the quad with A. L. Smith, the Master. He was patient and kind. There were questions about my work, how it was progressing and what I felt to be my chances in the Schools.

After about half an hour of traversing the quad under the scrutiny of the whole college, the little man paused and said quietly, 'Perhaps it would be best for you and best for the college if you were to go down without facing the examiners.'

'Master,' I asked, 'am I being sent down?'

'No . . . no . . . that decision I leave to you.'

Then and there, I made the decision.

'What about rowing in the eight, Master?'

The man who had rowed at bow in the Head of the River Eight in 1872 answered, 'You may continue to row in the eight.'

As I look back to my Oxford days, my regret that I decided to leave Balliol increases. I had a good but lazy mind. I had frittered away my two years, mistaking information for knowledge and failing to exercise the self-discipline without which Oxford is a waste of time. The Master was a wise old man, and knew that only I could make the decision.

John Betjeman

John Betjeman was born in 1906 and was educated at Marlborough and Magdalen College. He was knighted in 1969 and became Poet Laureate in 1972. He is a frequent television and radio broadcaster on subjects including architecture, Victorian hymns, and topography. He has won many of the major literary prizes, and his Collected Poems *have sold in large quantities. His other books include* A Few Late Chrysanthemums, High and Low, *and* Summoned by Bells, *a verse autobiography. There are two records of him reading his own poems:* Betjeman's Banana Blush *and* Late Flowering Lust. *He married a daughter of Field Marshal Lord Chetwode.*

For me, there were two Oxfords. There was the Oxford of 1916, when I was a boarder at the Oxford Preparatory School (as the Dragon School was still called by old folk) and there was the Oxford of 1925–28 when I was up at Magdalen College.

There was hardly anyone about in my first Oxford. Everyone was away at the Front. We were sent to visit the wounded soldiers who were occupying Somerville and the other women's colleges in bright blue flannel, and we knitted gloves out of string for the sailors on the minesweepers. At that time, the school seemed almost in the country—north of Linton Road there were manifold allotments; east of us, across the narrow Cherwell, were misty meadows and distant elms. To the south, hawthorn hedges made fields between us and Lady Margaret Hall. The way into the shops was westwards. The city was further than we went on foot. The nearest shops were in North Parade—'N.P.', we called it—Gee's, and Twinings the grocers, and Ora Brown, the cheerful lady who sold us sweets.

There was very little traffic then. The infrequent wartime buses down the Banbury Road were worked by gas, housed in a balloon over the top deck. We went everywhere, when we were free, on bicycles, and I spent many a summer evening bicycling round 'the square', as Bardwell Road, Charlbury Road, Linton Road and Northmoor Road were then called.

Most of us could bicycle with our hands in our pockets, slowly zigzagging past the railed-in gardens where tamarisk and forsythia grew; or we would lean against the cream-coloured lamp-posts with their terra-cotta coloured gas-lamps which were placed at infrequent intervals down all the leafy North Oxford roads.

The school was in the redbrick Anglo-Jackson part of North Oxford, which only burst into full beauty when the hawthorn and pink may was in flower. The inner North Oxford—Crick Road, Norham Gardens, Norham Road and the magic, winding Canterbury Road, the cottages and stables by North Parade, and those ecclesiastical-looking houses gathered round the motherly spire of St Philip and St James ('Phil-Jim')—was more haunting, and more daunting. Bicycling down those 'Phil-Jim' roads whose fenced-in gardens had speckled laurels and 'Beware of the Dog' and 'No Hawkers' on their gates, one could glimpse the front-room windows where the widows of Heads of Houses and famous professors sat writing letters in crowded, gaslit rooms. Flowered papers were on the walls and served as backgrounds to photographs in Oxford frames. Hansom cabs still trotted down these roads, taking the aged inhabitants to the dentist in Beaumont Street, or to one of the two railway stations, or shopping at Elliston and Cavell.

In all the wide-roaded silence, the deepest quiet was on Sunday afternoons, when I would bicycle to No. 4 Chalfont Road. There my father's Aunt Lizzie and her husband, John R. Wilkins, ever generous with tea and rock cakes and jam puffs, lived a life entirely unconnected with the university or the school, but closely bound up with the town. My great-uncle was architect to one of the breweries, and did some nice little public houses in a free, Tudor style. He also restored the Clarendon building, and supervised the construction of Professor Dicey's house on the corner of Bardwell and Banbury Roads on behalf of Colonel Edis.

The OPS, or Lynam's as we called the school, prided itself on its freedom. The boys did not have to wear Eton suits on

Sundays and walk in a crocodile, as did the benighted pupils of Summerfields, further up Banbury Road. We could bicycle into the city and look at colleges. Together with my friend Ronnie Wright, the son of a barrister of Tractarian opinions and of a mother who had recently been converted to Rome, we bicycled off to Oxford churches, noticing their liturgical differences. My favourite was St Peter-le-Bailey, which was always empty and always open. I preferred it to the arid Norman revival of St Andrew's Church, which was also very evangelical. We usually ended our explorations at St Aloysius, the Roman Catholic church, where in a side chapel there was a relic of the True Cross, surrounded by candles, polished brass and jewels, which seemed to me very sacred and alarming, as, indeed, did the whole church, with its apse of coloured saints and its smell of incense and many *dévoués* crossing themselves and looking back at us while on their knees. One of our schoolmasters, Gerald Haynes, who had a passion for church architecture—if it was medieval—took us bicycling round the village churches near Oxford, and listened to our accounts of colleges we had explored and chapels we had visited in the university. He liked to take photographs of Norman features in churches, and it was from him that I learned to think that Norman was the only style that mattered, and that Iffley Church was far the most interesting building in Oxford or its vicinity.

Five years later, Oxford—outwardly very little changed, except for an increase in the number of motor cars, so that one had to look to right and left before crossing the Banbury Road or Magdalen Bridge—was a city of pleasure. Schoolfriends from Marlborough had gone to Oxford ahead of me, among them John Edward Bowle, the historian, who had won a Brackenbury Scholarship to Balliol. I was much affected by his outlook on Oxford. He regarded it as an infinitely superior place to Marlborough—and so did I. Dons were to him—as to me—

cleverer and more learned than schoolmasters. He thought Balliol the cleverest college, and the Balliol dons therefore the cleverest in the world—I did, too.

I was at Magdalen, and had beautiful panelled eighteenth-century rooms on the second floor of New Buildings. From my bed I would hear the Magdalen bells 'sprinkle the quarters on the morning town'. They led the chorus of quarters chiming from Merton and New College. I would wait until the fourth quarter had struck and the bell announced the hour, before getting up. This was usually ten o'clock, and so I was too late for breakfast. That did not matter at all.

My tutor was the Reverend J. M. Thompson, a shy, kind, amusing man, and a distinguished authority on French history. Rumour had it that he had been defrocked for preaching in Magdalen Chapel that the miracles were performed by electricity. I later found out that he was an early modernist in theology.

By now I was more interested in the type of churchmanship in a church than in its architecture. I had no Ronnie Wright to accompany me on my expeditions; instead, one of my closest friends was Lord Clonmore (now Wicklow), who was an ordinand at St Stephen's House, Norham Road. We were both Anglo-Catholics. Through the offices of the Reverend Frederic Hood (who was then on the staff of Pusey House under the celebrated Dr Darwell Stone), I was instructed by the Reverend Miles Sargent in the Catholic faith, which was nothing like the abbreviated Matins I had enjoyed daily in the school chapel at Marlborough.

When I left the gentle charge of the Reverend J. M. Thompson, my tutor was C. S. Lewis, who was then in what he would have called his 'unregenerate days'. Breezy, tweedy, beer-drinking and jolly, he was very popular with extrovert undergraduates. He found the liturgy very funny, and delighted in pointing out *non sequiturs* in it; moreover, he ruined Coleridge's 'Kubla Khan' for me by wondering whether the pants in the line 'As if this earth in fast thick pants were breathing' were woollen or fur. Now I knew dons were cleverer than any schoolmaster, even than a headmaster, I realized that when Lewis asked me to read three books of 'Paradise Lost', he had not only read them all himself, but had enjoyed them and even knew what they meant.

Oxford was divided for me into two groups; hearties and aesthetes. Hearties were good college men who rowed in the college boat, ate in the college hall, and drank beer and shouted. Their regulation uniform was college tie, college pullover, tweed coat and grey flannel trousers. Aesthetes, on the other hand, wore whole suits, silk ties of a single colour, and sometimes—but only for about a week or two while they were fashionable—trousers of cream or strawberry-pink flannel. They let their hair grow long, and never found out, as I never found out, where the college playing fields were or which was the college barge. Aesthetes never dined in hall, but went instead to the George restaurant on the corner of Cornmarket and George Street, where there was a band consisting of three ladies, and where punkahs, suspended from the ceiling, swayed to and fro, dispelling the smoke of Egyptian and Balkan cigarettes. Mr Ehrsam, the perfect Swiss hotelier, and his wife kept order, and knew how much credit to allow us. I was an aesthete.

The chief Oxford aesthete when I went up in 1925 was Harold Acton who, with his brother William, was at Christ Church, but was never seen inside the college in my day. He was a frequenter of restaurants, and his own lodgings were somewhere in the High. Michael Dugdale, another aesthete and a friend of mine at Balliol, always used to walk into Brasenose—an entirely athletic college—with the aid of a stick and limping, because he knew that the athletes would be too sporting to attack a lame aesthete.

Aesthetes used to gather at the very fashionable sherry parties—largely attended by Anglo-Catholic and a certain number of Roman Catholic undergraduates—given on Sundays at noon by George Alfred Kolkhorst, lecturer in Spanish at

Exeter College and later Reader in the university. He had been born in Chile, which would explain why he knew Spanish, as I cannot imagine him ever taking the trouble to learn it. We nicknamed him 'Colonel' Kolkhorst, as he was so little like a colonel. He was very tall with a slight stoop, and had rooms on the first floor at No. 38 Beaumont Street. When he first came up as an undergraduate, the Colonel had been known as G'ug—the apostrophe, he thought, implied deference, and gave the impression of a slight yawn when pronounced. He wore a lump of sugar hung from his neck on a piece of cotton 'to sweeten his conversation', and at some of his parties would be dressed in a suit made entirely of white flannel, waistcoat and all. Though people never got drunk at the Colonel's parties, it was a habit to form a circle round him and slowly gyrate, calling out 'The Colonel's tight, the room's going round!' And we used to stick stamps on his ceiling by licking them and throwing them up on up-turned pennies. After one of his merrier sherry parties, the Colonel accompanied Robert Byron and Lord Clonmore and some other undergraduates to the top of St Mary Magdalen's Tower in the Cornmarket, where they sang hymns and began spitting on the people on the pavement. The Proctors were called and waited at the bottom of the Tower for the delinquents to descend, which they eventually did, headed by the Colonel in his white suit. As a graduate of the university and lecturer in Spanish, he was immune from punishment, but the others were fined.

The Colonel disliked dons, believing that they took themselves too seriously. He regarded Spanish as hardly a subject at all, and not worth learning. He thought Cervantes the only outstanding Spanish author, though he liked the Nicaraguan poet Ruben da Rio, whose name we would pronounce at sherry parties with a tremendous rolling of 'r's. The one thing the Colonel detested above all else was research. It might be justified in reputable subjects like 'Literae Humaniores' and biology and the physical sciences, he said, but in Modern Spanish, a subject with very little literary history, research meant nothing but scratching around inventing subjects to increase the self-esteem of examining professors, and did no one any good.

If anyone talked about their subject or held forth with a lot of facts at his parties, the Colonel would open his mouth to simulate a yawn, tapping his upper lip as he did so. He carried a little ear trumpet for 'catching clever remarks', but would swiftly put it away and yawn if they were not clever. I never heard of anyone seeing him in Exeter College, and it was a frequent practice of his friends to ask at the Lodge whether the Colonel had been in lately.

Magdalen College, to which I was admitted through the kindness of the President, Sir Herbert Warren, had been the best college—in the social sense—because Edward VIII had been an undergraduate there when Prince of Wales. It had a very famous steward of the Junior Common Room, named Gynes, who saw to it that the undergraduates had the best food and wine when they entertained in their rooms. I remember giving a luncheon party at which constant glasses of Tokay were the only drink from the hors d'oeuvre to the coffee. I must have seemed an impossible person to poor C. S. Lewis, but he had his revenge, for he wrote me a reference when I was trying to become a private schoolteacher which was so double-edged that I withdrew it after my first unsuccessful application for a post.

However, the best college in my time—it probably still is—was Christ Church, known as 'the House'. There, blue blood prevailed; it was the Mecca of all the socially ambitious. Indeed, one undergraduate who had rooms in the college backing on to a public highway, would let down a rope ladder from his windows after the bell in Tom Tower had finished striking its one hundred and one notes—which meant that all college gates were closed. This undergraduate allowed people from other colleges to use his rope ladder if they were acceptable to him. Thus it was said that he had climbed into society by a rope ladder.

There was always an atmosphere of leisure surrounding Christ Church undergraduates. They gave the impression that they were just dropping in at Oxford on their way to a seat in the House of Lords, shortly to be vacated on the decease of their fathers, or that they were coming in for a term or two, but mostly staying away from college in country houses. They hunted, fished and shot. They may even have rode. But I never heard of them playing football or hockey, or even cricket, though cricket was sometimes played in the grounds of country houses within motoring distance of Oxford, and men from 'the House' might have been called upon to swell a village team. Then it was not unusual for a rich undergraduate, and there were many such at the House, to chuck out the Bursar's furniture and all the humdrum college fittings in his rooms, and have the whole place redecorated at his mother's advice and expense. Edward James, for instance, had rooms in Canterbury Quad whose ceilings were black and whose walls were gold, and around the frieze in Trajan lettering ran the words 'Ars longa, vita brevis'. They outstayed Edward's tenure of the rooms.

Of course, there were also ordinary lay undergraduates—that is, those who were neither peers nor very rich—at Christ Church. There was the clever, bespectacled historian from Cornwall, A. L. Rowse, whom I was not to know till later. My chief friend among the laymen was a tow-haired boy from Greshams called Wystan Auden, who was reading English and was tutored by Nevill Coghill of Exeter College. Coghill was an inspiring tutor who rendered Chaucer into readable English, and was a keen producer of Shakespeare at the OUDS.

There must have been dons at Christ Church, too, though apart from Professor Lindemann (later Lord Cherwell, the scientist, and friend of Winston Churchill), and Gilbert Ryle the philosopher, and J. C. Masterman, the senior censor and historian, I do not remember them . . . except for Roy Harrod, a young don who looked about my own age. He, as junior censor, was in charge of undergraduates' behaviour.

Balliol was, as I have mentioned, the cleverest college, but it was more ascetic than aesthetic. Balliol was associated with brains. Our hero Aldous Huxley had been there in rooms papered plain grey, looking out on frosty stars above the Waterhouse block's Scottish baronial turrets. The whole tone of the college was Scottish and frugal, but like all things Scottish, it had a side of unbridled exuberance, reserved for parties. Lampoons would be sung outside the rooms of dons. Fortunately the dons at Balliol were far friendlier to undergraduates than at most other colleges. The don who dominated Balliol was 'Sligger' Urquhart, who held court in summer on a lawn of the garden quad near the dining-hall. He liked people to be well-born, and if possible, Roman Catholic, and he gave reading parties in Switzerland. I only knew him well enough to touch my hat to him, or to give him an oily smile.

Balliol had good scouts, the undergraduates gave good luncheons and teas in their rooms, and it was the college where I had the most friends. Balliol people whom I knew were, like me, not college men, and therefore were to be found in restaurants and other people's rooms. As well as John Edward Bowle, there was Wyndham Ketton-Cremer, Norfolk squire, Old Harrovian, and a gentle pastoral poet much admired by Bowle. An old distich (by Dennis Kincaid, a Balliol wit who was the life and soul of the Colonel's parties) hath it:

'John Edward Bowle
Had a superflux of soul.
He was more beautiful than Rima,
But not as beautiful as Ketton-Cremer.'

Exeter College was for me the headquarters of Anglo-Catholicism, and I had many friends there, too. The dons were mostly approachable and encouraging, like Professor R. M. Dawkins, who had rooms on the ground floor, and appeared delighted to welcome anyone who called on him, whatever his real feelings about the intruders. He preferred, however, tough sporting men to aesthetes. He was an unconventional man with a red walrus moustache, freckled bald head and gold wire spectacles. He was exactly one's idea of the absent-minded professor, yet nothing escaped him. He was generally called 'Dorks', and was reputed to have known Baron Corvo, though he never mentioned him to us undergraduates. The fact that he was Sotheby and Bywater Professor of Byzantine and Modern Greek was a matter of childlike wonder and delight to him. Although he was the son of a land-owning family with military traditions, he was the least military of men. He had been put into the electrical engineering business in Chelmsford, but had carried on with modern Greek, regardless. How he moved from electricity to a Fellowship at Emmanuel College, Cambridge, is a puzzle. He always thought of himself as a Cambridge man even after Oxford had made him a Professor. He once told me you could never depend on the aesthetic opinions of classical scholars or philosophers—scientists were far more reliable and humble-minded.

That was my second Oxford. It has lasted long. Still the colleges retain their individuality. I could have gone on through every college in Oxford and the halls and theological colleges, but time and the patience of readers press. I must conclude with a mention of what has always been my favourite college—Pembroke, where Dr Johnson's teapot was preserved in the library. In my day it was still a college you could enter if the dons liked you. Examinations were not all that important. Mr Drake, who was the senior tutor, was the greatest authority on port in England, and Pembroke had the best cellar. The last Lord Pembroke was at the college in my day and wrote excellent racing news for the *Cherwell* when I was an editor. I don't think he bothered much about exams. The Master was the great Dr Holmes Duddon, the most successful of all Vice-Chancellors. He had been a popular London preacher at the fashionable and beautiful Holy Trinity Church, Sloane Street. He and Mr Drake and Mr Salt, a High Churchman and Bursar, and dear old Doctor Ramsden, a scientist who kept silkworms on the mulberries in the Fellows' Garden, made the Pembroke Senior Common Room the most enviable of all. Clipped ivy still grew on the walls and in summer the window boxes were filled with pink geraniums, the college colour. Pembroke retained, of course, its barge when all the 'withits' were building boat houses of brick. With its creeper-hung walls, intimate quads and rich Chapel decorated by Kempe, Pembroke was the best-maintained and most romantic Oxford survival. Even today its new buildings have involved the restoration of little streets adjoining, and no flashy additions. Hurrah!

J.I.M. Stewart

J. I. M. Stewart was born in 1906 and was educated at the Edinburgh Academy and Oriel College, where he took a first class degree in English language and literature in 1928. He lectured at the University of Leeds, was Professor of English at the University of Adelaide from 1935 to 1945, and Lecturer at Queen's University, Belfast from 1946 to 1948. He returned to Oxford as a Student of Christ Church and university lecturer in 1949 and became a Reader in English Literature in the university in 1969. Under his own name he has published fifteen novels, and under the name of Michael Innes more than thirty detective stories. He married in 1932.

In the year 1900 (which was a quarter of a century before I went up to Oriel) there appeared a volume called *Memories of some Oxford Pets by their Friends*. The Sub-Rector of Lincoln, William Warde Fowler, explains in a preface that these essays have been brought together by Mrs Wallace 'to win something for the sick and wounded in the war which has made the past winter such a sad one for us', and that her aim will be the easier to achieve in that 'Mr Blackwell has most kindly consented to undertake the work of publication without any profit to himself'. Warde Fowler urges upon hesitating browsers in Mr Blackwell's shop the consideration that 'animal life is assuredly worth study'.

Numerous persons eminent in their day contribute to this publication. The Right Hon. Professor and Mrs Max Müller report upon their dachshunds; a Mull terrier called Skian is the recipient of an important letter from Dr Birkbeck Hill, greatest of all Johnson scholars; Tom of Corpus is celebrated in an English elegy by Sir Frederick Pollock and in a Latin elegy by Mr Plumer; a poodle called Puffles is commemorated in both verse and prose, and so effectively that in my own time as a senior member of the university his name had been transferred to a distinguished member of the higher clergy, the Suffragan Bishop of Dorchester.

One might expect *Some Oxford Pets*—a descendant of the

keepsake books of the earlier nineteenth century—to contain a good deal of the sentimental and the facetious; in fact it exhibits humour, wit, vivacity, and an unforced lightness of air, and may be regarded as a small document of authentic significance in the history of Oxford taste at the close of Victoria's reign. It pleases me that pride of place in it is given to Oriel Bill. The only illustration, a frontispiece, is a handsome photograph of Bill provided by Mr Soame, who was still in my undergraduate time photographing (gratuitously) those of my contemporaries who were achieving precocious fame at the Union or on the river, or even within the Examination Schools of the university.

Bill was a bulldog, the property (or friend) of A. Wootten-Wootten of Headington and Oriel, with whom he lodged for a time at 15 Oriel Street. When Mr Wootten-Wootten attained to the B.A. degree and departed into the world Bill lingered on amid the scenes and faces he had come to love. In his later years, like other retired Oxford worthies in Headington and similar purlieus of the town, he became a little chary of too frequently dropping in on his old college. For long, indeed, he turned up only for the greater festivals: a habit which unfortunately resulted in a growing addiction to the pleasures of the table. But he continued to know every member of the college, and would go with an Oriel man anywhere, while to all others turning a deaf ear. Having earned a just celebrity not only with the learned and investigating classes but with the citizenry at large, he was at all times able to hail a hansom cab when he required to be driven home. He earned high distinction on the stage when undertaking the part of Launce's dog in an OUDS production of *The Two Gentlemen of Verona.*

The memoir of Oriel Bill—written in Charles Lamb's *Elia* manner and not much below Lamb at his best—was contributed to Mrs Wallace's volume by the Rev. L. R. Phelps, later Provost of the college, one of the first acquaintances I made when, a misdoubting Scottish youth, I entered within its curtilage. Dr Phelps was a hospitable man, who faithfully discharged his duty of entertaining the junior members of his society in bunches and on a systematic basis. Being a good conversationalist in a somewhat allusive mode, however, he took particular pleasure in tête-à-tête occasions with juvenile interlocutors possessed of sufficient miscellaneous reading to know what he was talking about. I must have filled this bill quite well, since I can't recall ever having been in his presence in the company of another undergraduate. And since I was very shy, the Provost may moreover have judged me (fallaciously in fact) incapable of convivial association with my contemporaries, and have been the more inclined benevolently to take me up as a consequence.

Dr Phelps was a venerably bearded man, very liable to inspire even more than an appropriate awe, and when I went to tea with him in the Lodging it was frequently to find him entertaining some scholar more venerable still. At one early tea-party it was the great Dr Paget Toynbee, then regarded in Oxford as the first of living authorities on Dante; and Dr Toynbee received a tremendous dressing-down for having turned up on a brief visit to the university without having included dress clothes in his stock of attire. The tea ceremony was itself intimidating, rather in the fashion that a later generation associated with the receiving of that civil refection from the hands of Miss Ivy Compton-Burnett. The equipage included china which had perhaps belonged to the Provost's grandmother. Certainly he cherished it very much. He began by letting fall into each saucer, with a maximum of precision, a single drop of hot water from a heavy silver jug held in an aged but well-poised hand. I supposed this hydrostatic performance to be in aid of fractionally increasing friction or adhesion between saucer and cup, thereby minimizing the risk of humiliating misadventure on the part of a guest doing a balancing act on his knees.

But the Provost, although adept at giving an appearance of leisure to social occasions, was not by nature of a sedentary habit, and he had developed numerous resources for speeding the departure of those young men (always a majority, whatever their background) who were unable to get to their feet and take their leave. Thus at tea-time he would lead the conversation towards some athletic topic, from this to the college games field, and from this again to the subject of badgers—which he would aver, quite baselessly, to have established a set endangering the cricket pitch. He would then recall Sir Thomas Browne's holding in debate whether or not badgers have longer legs on one side than the other, this the more readily to scamper round hills. Next, he would suddenly recall that a portrait of a badger hung somewhere in the Lodging, from which the truth of this matter might conceivably be verified. The picture would be located after a walk through the ramifying house; the badger would be seen to be equipped as other quadrupeds are; and then one would discover that the picture hung beside the Provost's front door, which stood open before one. The proper words would be spoken, and one was out in the triangular public space which the college was later going to persuade the municipality to give a name to as Oriel Square.

Dr Phelps's after-dinner technique was simpler. He would wait until, from the adjacent Tom Tower, Christ Church began to bang out the hundred-and-one peals with which—with some justification immemorially antique—it assaults the city nightly at five minutes past nine o'clock. The Provost would thereupon stand up and shamelessly declare: 'Ah, my dear boys! The witching hour of twelve has struck.'

I have said that the Provost was no sedentary man. He was in fact a formidable pedestrian, and he marched me over as much of the countryside round Oxford as I have ever traversed since. On Sundays, however, his favourite walk was merely up the hill to Headington, where at that time there was situated what I imagine was still called the Workhouse. He had sat on the Poor Law Commission of 1905–1909, and in vagrancy in particular he maintained a keen interest. So we would set off of an afternoon for a chat with the tramps. The walk through Oxford could be slightly embarrassing, since the Provost was given to greeting totally strange passers-by as a squire might greet his cottagers. To men he would raise his blackthorn stick and call out 'Good day to you, my master!' and to women he would touch the brim of his large speckled straw hat. On these Sunday expeditions I felt I ought to wear a hat myself, and as there was no time to doff it to every female thus encountered I was reduced to the brim-touching technique too, and self-consciously felt it to be extremely ludicrous. The tramps, however, were enormous fun, since Dr Phelps possessed the art of drawing them into a free if not very articulate conversation. There was one, from Yorkshire, who claimed to remember the Brontës—and who, it was evident, did authentically remember legends about them.

Dr Phelps was himself good at remembering, and on the walk back to college might entertain me with what I was required to receive as first-hand reminiscences of Matthew Arnold and John Henry Newman. There was frequently a satirical slant to these, particularly when he was dealing with Arnold. One story, much detail of which I forget, was of Arnold's driving out to Blenheim to call on the Duke of Marlborough, entangling his boot inextricably with some patent unfolding step of the conveyance, and writhing helplessly before a line of frozen flunkeys, with the duke himself looking on, equally immobile, at the top of an enormous flight of steps. It was not, I think, the Provost himself who told me how, as a very junior fellow of the college, he was despatched with a group of more senior Anglican clergy having the delicate task of congratulating a former fellow on becoming a prince of the Holy Roman Catholic and Apostolic Church. Young Phelps broke the ice by advancing upon the new Cardinal of St George in Velabro with outstretched hand and the words, 'Well done, Newman, well done!' I believe anecdotes like this a little startled me, Arnold and Newman standing in my mind as the chief glories, by no means thus to be frivolously dealt with, of the not particularly distinguished college in which I found myself.

Phelps and his successor in the Provostship, my moral tutor

W. D. Ross, a much more intellectual man, are the only dons I can remember taking much account of. Ross told me at some brief beginning-of-term interview, when I had no doubt been talking pretentiously about my reading and opinions, that it seemed to him that a great deal of nonsense was written about literature. Because he said this at once diffidently and with authority (a not impossible combination) I received it as a maxim at once, and have applied it with great benefit in my dealings with critical expatiation ever since.

The undergraduates of the 1920s belonged as definitely to a pre-revolutionary era as they did to a post-war one. It had been widely believed that such a cataclysm as the Kaiser's War would be bound to bring radical changes to Oxford. In some colleges the dons held a nervous fear that a returned young soldiery, of whom there were bound to be many, must prove unruly and licentious. They even recruited, under various academic disguises, officers from the Brigade of Guards as experts in disciplinary action. But in fact nothing disruptive occurred. The demobbed warriors proved, if anything, more orderly and industrious than the boys straight from school. There was a general disposition simply to get things going again, to pick up old threads. Within a few years everything was re-established and as it had been. The Oriel I entered a few days after my nineteenth birthday in 1925 can have differed in no marked particular from the Oriel of twenty years before. The social composition of the place was the same: preponderantly public school, and taking the manners and assumptions of gentlemen's sons for granted. It was also taken for granted that, although there were menservants around to empty our slops and carry meals and coal-scuttles up to our rooms, we were essentially schoolboys still, and to be governed accordingly. We were segregated from the other sex both by sundry regulations and on a curiously matter-of-course basis which was a hang-over from the way we had been put through school. 'Womanizing' of a low sort classed a man as unspeakable; romantic attachments and even cautious physical experiments—but all preferably disastrous—with girls in distant places and during vacations were admitted and occasioned mild awe; but one risked ridicule by a bare mention of the women's colleges already flourishing in the university. We were locked up at night. We had to attain a fixed quota of attendances in the college chapel under penalty of being punished in various annoying and trivial ways. There was a further odd segregation when we dined in hall, the clever men having to sit at one table and the other men at others. In the main, I suppose, this last ordinance led to people the more readily finding themselves in congenial society. But it enhanced the notion of scholars and commoners being races apart, and its application in individual cases could be absurd. I can recall Ronald Syme, a mature student from New Zealand who was later to become Camden Professor of Ancient History, having thus to associate nightly in a sort of dunces' gallery exclusively with callow youths whose conversational range was confined to matters of athletic or social concern. In this instance, indeed, the result was pleasingly comical, the future Sir Ronald being unable to conceive of any human being as other than passionately interested in classical antiquity—and talking uninterruptedly, with brilliance and charm, in the confidence of this fond persuasion.

My own acquaintance were a mixed lot in point alike of ability and temperament, but rather fell down in terms of any broad social spectrum. Oriel didn't much go in for the sons of very wealthy people, and it did harbour the sons of a good many very poor ones. This latter fact, admirable in its way, I suspect to have been of the Provost's contriving. One of his unlikelier stories was of the college's Governing Body once having contemplated pursuing Thomas Hardy for libel on the ground that a vignette on the title-page of *Jude the Obscure* seemed to represent our front quad, and might thus suggest that it had been by one of his own praepostorial predecessors that Jude Fawley had been insolently repulsed. Dr Phelps was himself a Carthusian, and Carthusians were prominent among the public school boys who formed the bulk of the college's undergraduate population. But his interest in what used to be called the 'social question' (and rather more a deep charity hidden away in him) made him vigilant to have some genuinely poor scholars around. I remember one contemporary of mine who, having written to him artlessly and from an obscure situation to inquire whether residence at Oxford could be managed on (I think) £30 a year, found himself railroaded into the college at once. He attained in later life to a distinguished position in the profession of letters.

Oxford, like every ancient university, began as an informal association of poor scholars, and for centuries there was almost nobody else around. Later, when the colleges turned substantially into preserves of the prosperous, the penniless lingered on as sizars and the like, and finally as boys living on small scholarships and exhibitions and charitable grants. This didn't in my own time make any sort of edifying spectacle. Considerable gifts of the spirit and intellect are required to counter severe economic disadvantage within a community, and in Oriel as in every other college there were a few young men whose poverty cut them off from too much that was going on. A marked amelioration in this state of affairs has been one of the major gains of the mid-twentieth century. Plenty of people are hard up. But below a certain minimum of subsistence nobody is depressed. If you are poor you at least have plenty of company.

In 1925 it didn't much help those without money that money went a long way. The majority of us, living on modest allowances from fathers in the professions and services and so on, pursued a course of life which would now be regarded as within the reach only of the opulent. We treated each other to quite elaborate luncheon parties in our rooms; dined at the George (where there was the excitement of watching the current celebrities, headed by Harold Acton, come and go with considerable exhibitionistic flair) or drove out to the Spread Eagle at Thame, where Mr John Fothergill afforded us a grand sense of *grande cuisine,* with bills to match. We spent quite a lot of time (it seems incredible today) in expensive clothes, and our shoes came from a superior shop in the Turl. We smoked cigarettes rolled in black paper, or tipped with gold, or in some similar way distinguished from the Gold Flake of the common herd. The pictures on our walls had been done one at a time by artists favourably noticed in sixpenny weeklies. For most of us, of course, there was an honest shoe-string element in the hinterland of all this magnificence. I myself used to get by on the strength of purchasing Francis Meynell's latest Nonsuch Press books in Edinburgh at the end of a vacation and selling them eight weeks later for a larger sum to Mr Sanders in Oxford High Street. The profit paid for a railway ticket home, and there I'd sit down and do some of the work I'd neglected amid the pleasures of university life. This just kept my chin above water as what an earlier generation called a reading man. And all this was very normal and unremarkable.

I sometimes wonder why I don't look back on that life with more affection. One reason must reside in the simple fact that the undergraduate's is in many respects a difficult condition: a state of affairs doubtless constant from generation to generation, and connected with the general ignominy of growing up. One can get awfully glum. Norman Cameron, whom I had known on a neighbourly basis at home, and who had rooms across the staircase from mine in Oriel's front quad, had a habit of breaking in on me in the small hours, making enough noise to wake me up. He would then simply stand and gaze at me in unfathomable dejection. I had no difficulty in matching this mood at once, and after some five minutes of such mute communion Norman would shamble away again, closing the door very softly, as if I were still asleep. His depression may have been enhanced because his scholarship was in some way connected with a Bible clerkship, which meant that he had to appear regularly in the college chapel for the purpose of reading the lessons. His perception of the world's sadness at times a little seduced him from wholly temperate courses, and there was an occasion upon which he advanced to the lectern and pronounced the words, 'Here beginneth the Gospel according to St George.' The Provost from his stall helpfully ejaculated, 'John, boy, John!' But Norman, almost as if he were a scholar in the most senior sense, was reluctant to admit error in a matter of fact. 'Here beginneth the Gospel according to St George,' he reiterated firmly. 'In the beginning was the Word . . .' And he read on in the rumbling sleepy voice which I can still hear when I read his verse.

Twenty years after going down from Oriel I returned to Oxford as a college tutor. Once more a war had ended in a recent past; once more there was a general air of picking up the threads again; once more the returned warriors were of serious and industrious mind. This time, however, radical changes were evident—and it was evident, too, that radical changes were going to continue. As with a largely devastated city, the fabric of British society had to be built up again; much of it would not be as before; to such transformations as came, the university would have to respond. As might be expected amid so much entrenched tradition and assumption as obtains in Oxford, some of these responses were not of the briskest. For example, who was now to come to the place? The colleges, being richly endowed self-governing and self-perpetuating corporations, were inclined to regard this as their own affair, and the university (which could still be viewed as little more than the colleges sitting round a table) was slow to increase the say it had in the matter. Eventually it took some action. There was no need to change the formal position, since already a college could take into residence only persons whose educational qualifications the university deemed adequate. By discreetly moving this test a little away from near-zero the university eventually gained a larger control of the situation, and to the effect of very significantly raising the standard of entrance. Other factors no doubt contributed to this. Among the younger dons now around there were many whose minds had been formed within new climates of opinion; and the competitiveness fostered by a collegiate system began to exercise itself in comparatively new fields—the old talent-scouting techniques being modified to achieve effective operation in schools hitherto regarded as totally obscure. As a result of all this—it may be bluntly said—no men's college is any longer noticeably cluttered up with hopelessly thick or even incorrigibly idle youths from privileged homes. Looking back on the 1920s—I hope with not too jaundiced an eye—I am convinced that here has been a large change indeed. And as universities are places of learning and education it is an important change too.

It is quite as important, certainly, as the change in sexual *mores* ('the sexual revolution') which so frequently arrests the attention of newspaper moralists. Here is a tricky field, all the same, and towards the many young people who demand fresh liberties upon it (and they are indeed numerous, although I doubt whether they would get far on the brute basis of majority rule) three fairly distinct schools of thought would appear to have formed. The first is the forthright Christian one, which requires no comment. The second inclines to the view (for it talks like that) that sex is a good thing, since it has a composing effect when achieved, and returns a man refreshed to his books. The third says that sex is a bad thing—or bad in the context being considered—since it is at best distracting and a waste of time, and at worst productive of nervous break-down and even total failure in the Examination Schools.

Both these latter ways of thinking seem to me trivial and absurd, but I admit this with diffidence, having no more sage comment of my own. I very much doubt whether my tutor at Oriel, an immeasurably deep Elizabethan scholar who was seldom clear about my identity, ever gave serious thought to my sexual life. *Ne sutor* (he would have said with the air of inexpressible erudition he could lend to the most banal quotation)—*ne sutor ultra crepidam.* Who goes with who, the bedclothes say—or, rather, the whole spirit of the age determines; and the matter is perhaps one which teachers within their colleges had best leave alone. It is sometimes averred that Oxford tutors today are inclined to go along with their pupils in overvaluing facile sexual activity. I don't know whether this is in fact so. But to assume that if a young man or woman is unhappy or depressed or not working well it must be because of the failure of some sexual nutrient, so that it is one's duty to the young person to suggest, if only by subtle implication, that it is his or her business to go out and do a quick shop around: to act thus must be to risk doing mischief in a gratuitous way. Rather than that I'd myself prefer to take up an uncompromising Victorian point of view.

The cautious stages by which young men of twenty-one or twenty-two were relieved from the indignity of being put under lock and key at night differed, I imagine, from college to college. In Christ Church in 1949 I was still collecting an irregular sort of gate-money as a consequence of the survival of this antique practice. One of my windows gave on a garden easy of access; it was my wholesome habit to leave the upper sash of this window open at night; and through it would jack-knife young men whose small change tumbled from their pockets in the process. Since they seldom paused to pick up the coins, these were still there when I came into college in the morning. It is my hope—but memory grows dim—that I applied them to some charitable purpose. Eventually this source of revenue dried up, no doubt upon the discovery of some more amusing and hazardous way of climbing within bounds. The business of locked gates was partly a matter of normal security such as any prudent householder would observe, but it was also bound up, of course, with the problem of ladies in college. At what hour does a female presence become indecorous; at what stroke of the clock does virtue waver and libidinousness grow bold? Serious men, charged as deans or senior tutors with the harrassing responsibility of preserving both good behaviour and good feeling among several hundred closely stacked-up youths of vigorous enterprise and spirit, have been obliged gravely to perpend these ludicrous problems.

The minor problem of compulsory chapel-going was easier to solve, and again, it is to be supposed, the solution came about piecemeal round the university.

'Be wise,
Ye Presidents and Deans, and to your Bells
Give seasonable rest; for 'tis a sound
Hollow as ever vex'd the tranquil air . . .'

Wordsworth's vigorous injunction, written in 1805, was heeded at last, with what consequences for the devotional life of the university it would be hard to determine. Nobody could any longer be constrained to listen to a Norman Cameron or a Provost Phelps, speaking with those angelic tongues lent to them by the Prayer Book and the Authorized Version of the Bible. People now sought out these things only if they spontaneously wanted them. In Oxford, the clergy apart, it had become difficult to be religious without enthusiasm.

The quality of undergraduate life 'then and now' is a topic that can be very variously pronounced upon by elderly persons in reminiscent mood. Mr Christopher Hollis, who went up to Balliol in 1920, has lately expressed the opinion that his contemporaries at Oxford lived fuller and more enjoyable lives than their successors can be observed to do today. I incline to the opposite view, while feeling at the same time that we may both err in positing any significant change between one generation and the next. I seem to recall another contemporary, Mr Anthony Powell's Nicholas Jenkins, reflecting that the undergraduate condition is characteristically somewhat melancholy at any time. This may well be the truth. The undergraduate's, after all, is the period of Yeats's

> '*distress*
> *Of boyhood changing into man.*'

Angus Wilson

Angus Wilson was born in 1913 and spent part of his childhood in South Africa, his mother's home. He was educated at Westminster School and Merton, where he took a second class degree in Modern History in 1935. The following year he became a librarian in the Reading Room at the British Museum, and after working at the Foreign Office during the war he was deputy to the Superintendent of the Reading Room from 1949 to 1955. He began to write in 1946 because, he says, he had 'decided he needed an extra interest in life'. His many novels have been translated into sixteen languages, and one of them, Late Call, *was successfully serialized on television. He has been Professor of English Literature at the University of East Anglia since 1966. He reviews and lectures widely.*

None of my family had been to Oxford. Nor to Cambridge, for that matter. Save in the expression 'Cambridge blue', I do not remember to have heard that university mentioned until I was sixteen or seventeen. No other university, of course, was ever spoken of. We were essentially the sort of middle-class family that reposed upon 'good' English public schools. My grandfather had come to one all the way from Scotland in the 1850s, and my father in the 1870s. All my brothers, save my delicate third brother, had been at such schools between 1900 and 1917. The first thing my family asked about any man was what school he had been at. With a decent public school behind you and what they called 'a little social pull', a man could get an equally decent post in the City or in the colonies, and of course service officers had no need of universities. If a boy was especially brainy, or there was a tradition in the family of going into the Church . . . Otherwise a good public school was all you needed.

The whole of this middle class has, I suppose, now entirely disappeared. Already, by the time my brothers came back from the Great War in 1918, a public school education by itself, without a little capital, was ceasing to be such a miraculous passport. Public schoolboys, including two of my brothers, acted as supers on the sets at Elstree or sold Electrolux vacuum-cleaners from door to door. After 1930, one of the tragedies of the Depression, as seen from Kensington and Eastbourne (my family viewpoints), was that public schoolboys were coming to be 'almost a drug on the market'. Luckily for me (in this respect only, let me hasten to say) my mother had died in spring 1929 when I was fifteen and so, in the Michaelmas term of 1932, when I was just turned nineteen, I went up to Merton College, Oxford.

The connection of events seems fortuitous but was direct. In the first place, had my mother been alive, her small capital (diminished by endless loans to my brothers and gifts to my father) would have been needed for her support. In the second place, her colonial pride in her father's self-made success, usually played down after decades of Kensington and South Coast rentier snobbery, would have probably asserted itself against the idea of my going to Oxford on a private income, even if it could have been afforded. She might have scraped and saved (as only she knew how) to send me there had I secured the closed scholarship from Westminster to Christ Church for which I entered. But I failed to satisfy the examiners. If I try now to recall how, I remember only that I may have made in my viva what I thought witty but what must have been insufferably superior remarks about these very South African maternal ancestors of mine to Patrick Gordon-Walker, later a Labour Cabinet Minister but then a young Christ Church don. And so I only got to Oxford as a commoner at Merton by the aid of my mother's capital which she had left me in her will—reasonably, since she had already helped my elder brothers and I was thirteen years younger than the youngest of them.

Through the enmeshment of family trustees and unpaid family debts to my mother, the sum that I finally received was a good deal smaller than she had reason to think she had left me; but it was enough to give me £300 a year at Oxford on top of my tuition fees, my college payments and my expenses in vacations. It was as my second brother, a headmaster of a preparatory school, who would dearly have loved to have been at Oxford himself, quite rightly said, a good income. I used, in later days, remembering the chronic impecuniosity of my family, to congratulate myself on having left Oxford with no debts. It was a self-deceiving congratulation, since £300 a year for term-time pleasures alone, in the deflation of the mid-'thirties, allowed me to live in a way almost deserving the popular description 'like a lord'.

Perhaps I should briefly describe this manner of living, since it formed the rather pleasurable material basis of my three years at Oxford. Some part of it was derived from what years of living with my father had taught me was 'a good life'. This principally consisted in eating out at restaurants and having 'good food' as often as possible. I think that I ate in college only in the first two weeks of those three years—and that out of a fear of the consequences of not doing so. This fear was part of the general fear of communal college life that I felt in my first term, for, as I shall describe, coming from a London day school, I half-seriously clothed college life at first with all the terrors of boarding school life that I had derived from stories describing Eton under Keate in the 1820s, or, at best, Rugby under Arnold in the 1850s. In fact, I *was* acting against college regulations by not fulfilling a certain number of dinners in hall; but, as I never 'signed off', I paid in full for dinners every night of my three years and consumed none of them, so the college authorities were the richer by some hundreds of dinners not eaten but paid for. It might have occurred to me that *this* was an example of inherited prodigality, but it never did; I saw it as the only way of avoiding 'the too appalling food and company'. In those first three weeks I had seen people throw bread at each other and had anticipated that before term was out this would have ended in bodily assaults. I had also received a garbled account of 'sconces'. I had not understood that these were forfeits by which you had to pay for other people's beers (something I should like to have done) but I thought rather that they were penalties in which beer was forcibly poured down one's throat. In any case the food, by the standards my father had given me from the Café Royal and the Trocadero, was vile, worse than that served at my brother's prep school, which was the nadir of my father's scale of feeding. After the first three weeks, I ate out in restaurants.

My closest circle, especially in the early days, was a number of friends from Westminster—some at Christ Church, some at New College and elsewhere. It was natural that we should eat together as often as college regulations allowed. We soon found that the best food was at the George—it served that sort of good semi-French cuisine that still existed in the best English provincial restaurants before the war, before ignorant and pretentious 'international' menus based on deep freezes had led to our present sad state of affairs. But whereas I think my friends ate out only on those evenings when they did not have to pay for college hall, I ate out every evening, often sitting by myself, elaborately consuming Sole Mornay and Meringue Chantilly with a book propped up against the vase of flowers that ornamented the table. I (and the others) could not by any means regularly afford the George and we ate at assorted restaurants, cafés and 'ladies' tearooms'. I remember no other place that seemed 'good' save a restaurant in the Cornmarket where for a time they served excellent asparagus omelettes. As to drink, my father had years ago foresworn alcohol as a result of near cirrhosis of the liver, and I therefore knew little of wines. Only one of our circle, coming from a wealthier family, was used to drinking wine at all regularly. I think this lack of regular wine drinking was much more common in middle-class homes of some pretension in the inter-war years not only than now but than it had been in late Victorian times. At restaurants we drank normally gin and tonic; and, in our own rooms, a great deal of dry sherry (a peculiarly disgusting habit, I think now). On occasions of evening celebrations and parties we also drank, as I remember, port and liqueurs, especially cointreau. This curiosity becomes explicable when I reveal that the cocktail for smart parties—we drank it in large quantity on my twenty-first birthday—was a White Lady (gin and cointreau in suitable proportions). Later—from the summer term of my first year—when I had come to know the life better and had no more fears of college, I used to give luncheon parties in my rooms. The food for these was very good. I got to know the college chef, who understandably liked appreciation. His speciality was a first-class crême brulée. With these luncheons I provided wine—by whose advice I can't remember, it became habitually 'Liebfraumilch'.

On top of this rather extravagant expense upon food, I smoked regularly about thirty-five or forty cigarettes a day, very costly small flat Turkish cigarettes called Melachrino, which I carried about with me in tins of a hundred. Occasionally I tried to economise by changing to Abdullah. But these seemed very ordinary, even though I smoked them in a long cigarette holder from which the stubs could be ejected by pressing a little button—so far as I know, a new amusing device. From my second year on, I also purchased from Hall Bros. in the High Street a good number of canary-coloured woollen waistcoats with brass buttons, a lot of foulard spotted scarves, and a pleasing selection of bottle green, maroon and dark crimson velvet ties (ordinary ties, not bow ties). These added a touch of elegance to my regulation undergraduate grey flannels, sports coats and umbrellas, that deceptively might have suggested to a stranger that I belonged to a smart Oxford set. There was, however, no intention of deceit in these sartorial accessories; it was simply that for the first time I could buy the clothes I wanted and I knew that I wanted these. The rest of my money went on books from Blackwell's—a good number both new and second-hand—which I paid for on account at the end of each term. I do not remember to have paid anything towards furnishing, save for a pair of hideous orange and apricot shot silk cushion covers which I had made because my rooms 'lacked colour'.

All this must sound, and is, very small beer; but I state it because I remember my Oxford years always against a sense of pleasing material sufficiency and comfort. It would not have been so, I think, if I had gained that scholarship and gone to Christ Church, for then I should fairly quickly have made friends far richer than I was and rapidly have got into debt. As it was, I only came to know a few such people much later when I joined the OUDS—by which time my pattern of life was set and they were merely a handful among a varied circle of acquaintances. At Merton, I was probably financially better off than most of the undergraduates, and could make my own standards. I count this as one of the most important of the many advantages Merton gave to me.

At first I didn't feel it so, however. All my Westminster friends were at other colleges. There *was* a very small rich set at Merton, and in my first weeks they made a great deal of drunken noise on many nights. As, with my father's assistance, I had chosen some excellent rooms over the Junior Common Room, I noticed this noise particularly. It seemed the blood-curdling prelude to heaven knew what roastings and defenestrations. I was very 'pansy' in manner and I was very conscious of it. The other new people who seemed out of it all were different. They came from various parts of the North and Midlands of England. A few of them were to become my close friends. But in those first weeks, I could as easily have confessed my loneliness and alarms to them as a warthog can communicate his fears of lion to a herd of zebras. Such people as visited me in my rooms came to ask me if I intended to play this or that athletic game—something I had never been expected to do in my last years at Westminster. Of course, I was not really expected to do so at college, but it all added to my feeling that I had joined Stalky and Co.

I remember that for some weeks I did not dare to stay in my rooms in the afternoons for fear I should be identified as an aesthete or a swot. I went for long and tedious walks into the countryside, and, only after one desperate and frozen visit to the pathetic little Oxford zoo, did I settle down to a programme of browsing the early afternoon away at Blackwell's, followed by china tea and walnut layer cake at Fuller's tea-room. Apart from my evenings spent with my Westminster friends, that first term was hell, in particular because I had greatly looked forward to unlimited reading of medieval history and now I found that because I had to take Pass Mods, my days were spent in elementary classes in Latin and Economics that seemed to have transported me back at least two years in time to the school world before School Certificate.

It was not surprising that, with my lifelong capacity for psychosomatic illnesses, I went down with jaundice after Christmas and most ungratefully told my father and my brother that I didn't want to return to Oxford. However, they nobly persuaded me against their financial interest, and I came back to what were to be uniformly happy (though not ecstatic) years.

I must digress here for a paragraph or two to say how mysterious I find that kind of permanent identification with Oxford and Oxford things that so many men appear to make. When I read of the Oxford days of Cyril Connolly or of Evelyn Waugh, I stand in amazement at the hypnotic effect that the university had upon them. It might have been so for me, too, I suppose, if I had been at Balliol. I had already been much influenced by one very Oxford-struck Balliol man, the historian John Edward Bowle, who had taught me history in my last two years at Westminster. He, I think, has never been wholly content away from Oxford, where he now resides. Other friends of mine, often successful and distinguished, seem to look forward to frequent visits to Oxford to regale themselves afresh with high-table gossip—happy those few of them who have All Souls Fellowships or dining rights at their colleges. Such lasting enchantment is clearly not confined to Oxford, for the very type of such men seems to have been E. M. Forster at King's. Nor is it wholly to do with the more celebrated or grander colleges. I count these friends happy in this curious pleasure. Clearly they are more discriminating than those who live for visits to their old schools. But I don't at all understand how their affections became so fixed. I was flattered and pleased when the Warden of Merton invited me to dine at High Table a few years ago; I was also delighted to be invited to speak at Westminster School. I live quite a lot in the past and to visit at intervals places which bring memories alive gives me great pleasure; but I greatly dislike an exclusive call upon my affections or loyalties of any one of these past places—Sussex, South Africa, Oxford, Kensington, Provence, Bloomsbury, East Anglia and so on—over the others. Yet for many people Oxford clearly has a magic that never leaves them.

It may be that a great part of these men and women had hoped or intended to become Oxford dons and make their lives there. I notice that they have in common with my Oxford don friends a kind of mythology that underlies their general gossip, in which the names of Oxford 'figures'—Bowra, Sparrow, Berlin, David Cecil, Rowse, Trevor-Roper and many others—play a continuous part, standing all the time for something mysteriously more than the remarkable men who possess them. This is, of course, to be expected if you are part of the Oxford set-up, but if, in fact, your contacts are confined to a certain number of visits a year, it seems strange. It is not just gossip, it is the sense such people, who have known Oxford's magic, convey that 'thought' and 'civilization' and the 'real world' are inextricably bound up with the university. I had no idea or hopes of becoming a don. I aimed, at first, rather vaguely at schoolteaching and then later, more definitely, at getting a job in the British Museum. In any case, until I was forty, I suppose, I could not have imagined the centre of my life outside London. Therefore I never saw Oxford at any time as other than a place of temporary sojourn. I talked a great deal and listened to a great deal of talk about politics and literature and history; but, as I shall show, it had little to do with what was being thought in serious academic circles in Oxford. Dons were either the few who had things to tell me about English history that interested me, or the many more whose first lectures in the term I attended to be reduced to painful suppressed giggles by what seemed to me the immensely comic quirks with which they delivered their boring discourses. I had to leave a lecture of the Regius Professor because my laughter set rattling the form on which I was sitting. Anything interesting I could find in books. The idea of knowing dons socially never entered my head. There was a famous university figure at Merton called Garrod who entertained undergraduates. I was clearly not the sort of undergraduate he entertained, for he never invited me; but I also am clear that it never occurred to me to get myself invited to his famous teas. I had met both John Sparrow and Maurice Bowra when I was a schoolboy, through John Edward Bowle, and had found them charming and entertaining; but, once again, I do not think that I even remembered that they were connected with Oxford when I was there.

Some part of this failure to respond to Oxford's importance I am pleased about. I was not an ambitious young man, using the university and its contacts for worldly advancement. When I meet such young men occasionally—presidents or secretaries of this or that—I am repelled and saddened, for they seem to be wasting their youth in exploiting it for their adult years. At least, my life at Oxford, however small and self-satisfied and over-glib, was enjoyed every minute for itself. But there was great loss in it. Not the loss of not having known famous dons, but something that this implies—a lack of humility before knowledge, and more still a lack of capacity to listen to difficult thinking, a protective irony and frivolity that lost me more in power to reason and evaluate than they saved me from boredom and pretension and intellectual snobbery. I was right, as were my friends, to think that we could supply sophistication and wit and elegance of living as good if not better than these distinguished dons could provide. But to see this was to see only the superficial. What I missed was the capacity to think hard and painfully; to have learned this would have been worth supporting a great deal of the cult-nonsense that surrounded Oxford's famous men. Ironically enough, the failure of my undergraduate life at Oxford which irks me most is something quite else. It is the fact that the architectural beauty of Oxford largely passed me by. I attended, I remember, a series of fascinating lectures on architectural history delivered by Goodheart Rendel at the Ashmolean, but it never occurred to me to look for what I had seen on the lantern screen in the streets and quads. I was not wholly damned, for I always felt a visual excitement in seeing the Queen's College, and I was quite right. I remember moments of transported joy in combined architectural and natural scenery—walking in the Botanical Gardens, in Addison's Walk, sitting one hot day preparing for Schools beneath the walls of Merton Fellows' Garden. But, in general, Oxford's visual beauty passed me by. Yet in fact this was not so serious, for twenty years later architecture began to exercise an increasing spell over me, and now a stay in Oxford is a continuous visual delight. To think about difficult things and listen to difficult thinking, let alone to express it, I shall never now learn.

I must content myself with the thought that I probably never could have done, and had I tried to do so at Oxford I should simply have crushed such originality and capacity for *aperçus* as I have beneath a dead weight of received thinking. Perhaps so, probably not. One thing offers some explanation. Oxford in the early 'thirties was not in that sense, I think, a 'great' time. Of all the people I associated with in the OUDS only Sir Terence Rattigan and Peter Glenville have been figures of real influence in the theatre; most of the other actors and producers have faded out. Although I debated politics privately endlessly, I was not a Union man, beyond attending some famous debates. Yet I do not think that any of the undergraduates of my time have achieved political fame, unless it be John Freeman, whom I knew quite well, but I don't think he had political ambitions then. There are probably many well-known people who were Oxford undergraduates whom I never knew; but of my friends of those days the best known are most certainly women—Barbara Jackson (then Barbara Ward), Sally Chilver, the Principal of Lady Margaret Hall.

The high 'twenties of Waugh and John Betjeman and Cyril Connolly and Harold Acton were behind us. The 'thirties poets of the Left, too, had gone down by the time I arrived. Only the war itself, in fact, lay ahead. It is against this background that I must briefly sketch the various positive ways in which I gained from Oxford. My London sophistication and my Westminster schooling and my camp carry-on attached me to the OUDS and past Oxford; Merton and the friends I made there from working-class homes in the Midlands and the North attached me to politics and the Left. The latter because it was a new experience was the more important; yet by now I should find it hard to say how much of either is left in me in the form in which I received them then. Very little, I think.

The central thread of my university life began with the small group (three or four) of Westminster friends at other colleges and remained with it to the end. We knew each other's families before we went up. We stayed at each other's houses in the vacation. We continued to know each other into adult years; and the only other survivor of the group, D. P. Walker, the eminent scholar of the Warburg Institute, is still a close friend of mine. Three or four other undergraduates became part of our group, although none of them, in fact, through me. Two of us were historians; two studying French and German literature; two medicine. None, and it was a serious intellectual loss to me, philosophy. Otherwise, this mixture of subjects was good. It led me, for example, to read a good deal of French, and even German, literature which I should not otherwise have done; and started, in French at any rate, a lifelong habit. It gave me some acquaintance with the current problems in biology and medicine. As we none of us studied English literature, this (and in particular the English novel) became our lingua franca. I read a prodigious number of the great English novelists. For all this I am very grateful, although it can hardly have helped my concentration on my history studies. We spent evenings reading plays together over port or madeira. The standard of intelligence among our small group varied greatly as did our centres of study. One friend, in particular, who died in the war, had a strong personality but rather small reasoning powers. Humour, therefore, and above all humorous gossip and amateur psychologizing, inevitably loomed large, for they dissolved any mental disparities. We were a civilized, old maidish group, whose genuine wit was incommunicable because it was so inturned. I gained so much from the group, and it was so much part of my life for so long, that I cannot easily stand away from it. I think we had a lot of laughter and interesting talk, but I think we were inevitably rather smug—more than justifiably sure that Jane Austen had been right in basing her insights upon the compass of three or four families.

I was, however, the rover of the group, more naturally sociable, finding communication with all I met not only easy but almost unavoidable. I thus lived a strange life—as one of a very tight little group, from which I suppose I received nothing that I had not known before I went to Oxford, save for the independence that we all had of being at last away from our families; and also as someone who knew a number of sets of people or individuals—some very well—quite outside the little group, and quite unlike it in background or concerns. Two or three of these I shall write something of, for I could not have met them had I not gone to Oxford. They altered my outlook quite considerably, and, I think, they are not unrepresentative of the changing Oxford of the early 'thirties.

I think I can safely say that, until I went to Oxford, I had never known anyone of working-class background. There had, of course, been my London promiscuous sexual encounters. Many of these had been with cockney working-class young men. But this life which had begun before I was sixteen was a world as separate from my daily life as were my dreams (I dreamt and do dream a lot). It was to be many years before I began happily to connect the two lives, and certainly Oxford was for me something quite apart from active sexual life. Apart from that, the only working-class people I had known were servants—and, given my family's near penury, these were not many. I had never known anyone well who came from north of the Home Counties; and, apart from one visit with my father to Scotland to revisit his boyhood home in Dumfriesshire, I had never penetrated into England north of Hampstead. I think this is literally true. The glory of Merton was that by the natural course of events, simply through casual encounters, and more still through shared tutorials, I found myself among a group of people whose backgrounds were in varying kinds what I had been brought up to call 'working class' and who came from various parts of the Midlands and North. I was so class-bound that I was not very class-conscious. Thus it came about that I knew these very agreeable and interesting men merely as my fellow history students, and only gradually realized that their backgrounds and assumptions were so entirely different from my own. It was the very best way that it could have come about and I am deeply grateful to Merton for it. Of course, after a time, out of this agreeable and interesting group, there emerged two who were more agreeable and much more interesting to me. I owe them both a lot.

The first was a very small Jewish man from the Midlands with very expressive eyes and an irony of approach which fitted well to my own. It was with him that I sat talking, first about the history we were studying together, and then about life in general, until my scout (a very paternal man) expressed great concern that each morning the ashes of my fire were still glowing because I had sat up so late. I think those night-long talks were some of the most pleasing things of my Oxford time (and they had to be for me to endure being awake after midnight, something that all my life I've avoided since so much of my childhood was made miserable by my family's habits of very late hours to which I was monstrously expected to adapt at a very early age). I do not remember what Norman's father worked at, although it was in a factory; but the family were good solid Labour people. I had for some years, through the influence of well-to-do socialist parents of school friends and of left-wing masters at Westminster, vaguely professed Labour views. It was only now when I listened to Norman that these acquired meaning. It wouldn't be true to say that he did not propagandize, but only in so far as he could not bear to see someone intelligent that he liked so totally ignorant of the life that he knew so well. I think that I too felt a need over and above communication to convince him of the reality of middle-class and London life of which he was equally ignorant. We presented our lives and our worlds to each other, however, always in an ironic and absurd light. It was probably the only way that either of us could have accepted the reality that lay below the exaggerations.

His scepticism about Oxford and his determination not to allow it to penetrate his Staffordshire Jewish self was complete. We used to go together to Labour Club meetings and took part in occasional demonstrations. But he felt and he conveyed to me that this was all a kind of playacting of the real thing as he knew it at home. And of course he was right. As a result, we had as often to leave the Labour Club meetings because of our uncontrollable giggles as we did the history lectures. In particular, I remember going from a lecture of Dora Russell's on her school because we had woven a fantasy throughout her speech that she was Mae West in disguise sabotaging the Labour movement. This contemptuous approach to undergraduate politics meant, of course, that I never knew the aspiring politicians and famous left-wing dons of my time. The most prominent of these dons was Dick Crossman. Judging by his arrogance and cultural myopia when I met him in later years, I did not lose as much in this as I did, in general, by my failure to meet famous Oxford figures. In two different vacations I visited Norman at his Bilston home. His family were all very small people like him and his parents were Orthodox Jews. This lent a certain exoticism for me to their very pleasant household. He and his brother and sister had enjoyed a greater education than their parents, to whom they were devoted, but their parents were both highly intelligent people. This gave to the exotic quality of the home a sense of familiarity also, for my father, whom I equally loved, was also a less educated man than I and also highly intelligent. The only thing, in fact, about Norman's family that fitted my stereotyped image of working-class life was that they lived in a council house. I emphasize this because once again I acquired a sense of a world totally different from my own without any debasing self-conscious sense of 'getting to know the workers'. I was simply making some new unusual friends whose loyalties were very stoutly declared for the working class. I was also seeing Bilston, Darlaston and Wednesbury as they were at the height of the Depression, and this was most educative of all.

In return Norman came to stay at the house of my very impoverished, extremely chi-chi Catholic brother Pat, who was at that time trying desperately to run a tea-room at Pevensey. He got on with my brother as well as, I hope, I got on with his family. And I think he may have learned something from that visit also. I have seen him only once since the war. But I was told recently that he concluded from my writings that I had not changed at all since Oxford. This I know to be absurd. Recently I saw him on television speaking on behalf of Manchester Labour City Council. He seemed to me not to have changed. This is probably equally absurd.

In my second year I got to know Denis. He always spoke as though he was a working-class boy; but his father was in fact, I believe, an Inspector of Education in Manchester. Yet I suppose that he and his brother were the first two university-educated boys in the family. Denis has remained a close friend. I owe to him a different widening of my outlook. He was conventionally and stoutly Labour and had the habitual irony of all my friends. But he had a very confident attitude towards society and his future. He meant to succeed and he did, becoming a very top civil servant. Although I had no confident ambition, he gave me the sense that men who meant to be at the top were not people with whom I could make no communication—a first step to my later greater social confidence. He was also a thoroughly assured heterosexual. Had I gone to

Christ Church, I think that with the numbers of South of England public schoolboys there, I should hever have made such friendships. I am again grateful to Merton.

But not all Merton men were Northern or Midlands working class. Next door to me and a year senior was Stuart, the very epitome of a Byronic public schoolboy. Tall, handsome, enormously charming, with a wide Oxford social range, an easy culture, he seemed to me a figure out of a book. But he proved to be a very kind and friendly senior. And I in turn, I think, a good neighbour when he returned on occasion late at night from what I thought of as a gilded Oxford, rather helplessly drunk. Perhaps it was this relationship, or perhaps it was his having some musical instrument, I think a mandolin, but I always saw him as Steerforth, which, despite Dickens's overt moral disapproval of his character, is for me a very high compliment indeed. I think that he wondered why I should lead such a mousy life and have such mousy friends, and he persuaded me into a smarter Merton set—first to act in *The Doctor's Dilemma* in the Merton Floats and then to be a member of an exclusive dining club, The Myrmidons, where we wore special violet evening coats and violet ties. The dinners were most agreeable and delicious. And, once again, I am grateful to him for this entry to what still seems to me a direct Victorian survival with its deliberate intention of intoxication, its witty drunken speeches and its patronizing chaffing of the scout who waited on us. It could have been Dickens once more—Pip and the Finches of the Grove. Perhaps it was for this reason that I never felt I quite made the grade in the smart Merton world for, if it was sophisticated, it was also determinedly manly in the old Regency sense of the word.

I came to another Oxford world of sophistication, by chance, because Peter Glenville, the theatrical producer, had rooms next to a friend of mine at Christ Church. He, too, urged me into a wider life, which meant the OUDS, where I played in Marlowe's *Dr Faustus*. But my greatest success was in a smoker to which Peter brought Ivor Novello and (against the OUDS rules) Gladys Cooper. Here I did a skit of a well known débutante (I think) who had played the heroine in *Faustus* with a coy song, 'I won't be kissed on the lips', and represented one of the deadly sins in a chorus. How 'nineties our views still were may be seen by the fact that I represented the sin by wearing flame-coloured pyjamas and carrying a madonna lily. I enjoyed all the OUDS life, including the Sunday breakfasts, very much, and through it went to a number of sophisticated parties at which my camp wit went down rather better than among the Myrmidons. As to the aura of wickedness that still hung round the OUDS from the 'twenties, it never seemed to me to go further than 'daring' talk and camp flirtation. From my background of London promiscuity, I thought it all rather absurd. But now I'm inclined to wonder. Despite my gay chatter, I did carry a governessy aura around with me at Oxford and, for all I know, as soon as I left the parties everyone may have relaxed and started to have it off.

Finally I owe a debt to another group of three men at Merton, very intelligent, public school, sophisticated and dissipated. They were a year after mine, and perhaps this is why—sign of things to come—their greatest friends were all the most intelligent girls from Somerville. The smart Christ Church set, for example, went on in the old way and knew no women undergraduates, only debs from London and the shires. My friendship with these young women was a very enjoyable aspect of my Oxford life. From Barbara I borrowed the clothes I wore in the smoker. With the assistance of Sally I dressed up as the stepmother of one of our friends and completely spoofed the middle-aged parents of another at a tea-party. I can remember now how, dressed in tweeds and looking, I imagine, rather masculine, I leant forward to the conventional middle-class father and, cutting out his wife, said, 'You and I are rather more up to date, aren't we? We can appreciate Cézanne.' And his gallant, flirtatious agreement.

I mention this absurd episode because based on it, I believe, has grown up the sort of legend that always overtakes fact. An

Oxford don's wife said to me recently, 'I hear you spent nearly all your time at Oxford dressed as a woman. What fun those days must have been.' Such is how legend overtakes the very simple original which I have tried to set down here—an original much too shy to be in the smart set anyway, despite my continuous amusing chatter, an original who was pleased enough when his name got once or twice into the *Cherwell*, but who, in the main, enjoyed an Oxford that might have been any other place that allowed one lots of time to do just what one wanted. I am a little surprised, looking back, however, that I didn't want to do rather more.

Jo Grimond

Jo Grimond was born in 1913 in Scotland and was educated at Eton and Balliol College, where he took a first class degree in politics, philosophy and economics. He practised as a barrister until the war, when he served in the 2nd Fife and Forfar Yeomanry and on the staff of the 53rd Division. He has been Liberal MP for Orkney and Shetland since 1950 and was leader of the Liberal Party from 1956 to 1967, and again briefly in 1976. He has been a director of the Manchester Guardian *and* Evening News, *Rector of both Edinburgh University and Aberdeen University, Chancellor of the University of Kent, and Chubb Fellow of Yale. He is married to Laura, daughter of the late Sir Maurice and Lady Bonham-Carter (Baroness Asquith of Yarnbury).*

My first sight of Oxford was the row of gabled Victorian houses which decorated the road to Henley. I approached the sacred city to take a scholarship examination. To me it was indeed a sacred city. I experienced some emotions faintly like those which it is said Luther experienced when first seeing Rome. Part of the troubles of university education today, it seems to me, stems from the fact that the romantic excitement of universities has departed.

Everything about Oxford appeared new, interesting and unexpected. I remember the peculiar mixture of the couple of days or so I spent at Balliol: the austerity of the rooms with their greenish walls and iron bedsteads and, on the other hand, the extreme agreeableness of 'Sligger' Urquhart's hospitality. F. F. Urquhart, the first Roman Catholic to be made a Fellow since the Reformation, was then still Dean. He was a leading example of a type of don now rare and much missed. He lived not for promotion nor by writing articles or books, but for the students of Balliol. He had his favourites. But he spread through the college a feeling of good-will. He combined relaxation with authority—authority flowing not from discipline but from his personality and the standards of behaviour which he exemplified. Why he was called 'Sligger' is uncertain but unlike many nicknames, particularly those bandied about in the press, it was the common way of referring to him. I remember, too, reading Robert Louis Stevenson's essays, but of the examination I have no memory. However, I got a scholarship.

My expectations of Oxford when I went up there were high and on the whole were not disappointed. All this was perhaps rather strange: in many ways Eton must be the public school most like a university. Yet the change from school to university seemed to me vast.

My first impressions of Balliol were not mistaken, for it remained a curious mixture. Its discomforts were typical. The only baths were a steaming inferno presided over by a one-armed man of great charm when one got to know him, but at first sight reminiscent of one of the keepers of the Underworld. These baths were some hundred yards across country; so were the lavatories. The staircases were stone and perpendicular. As an ingenious torment the lights would stay on for only a short time. This time was insufficient for the older members of college to reach the attics. I am told that a distinguished German refugee of advanced age was frequently found in pitch darkness half-way up the stairs waiting for someone at the bottom to switch the light on again.

On the other hand, there was the blissful sense of freedom—the joy of having one's own rooms: two rooms, not one; and also there was the hospitality of the dons who lived in college—again, at the head of these was 'Sligger'. By that time he was an old man and ill, but his rooms were still open when he was in college to almost anyone who wished to call. There he sat, pale and silent; nevertheless, people still liked his company and however painful it might have been from time to time he at least gave the impression of being inexhaustibly keen to see undergraduates.

Roger Mynors, who later became Professor of Latin at both Cambridge and Oxford, was another who kept open house. Friendly, amused but firm, he was the archetype of the best dons.

The great difference which distinguished the style of teaching at Oxford from that I had known at school was the assumption that you were of course deeply interested in the subject taught; that you were capable of infinite comprehension and, indeed, of making a contribution to it. Along with this went a fairly stringent examination of any opinions which one put forward. The first pure draught of Oxford life came to me when I went to a tutorial with Humphrey Sumner. After it was over he thrust into my arms two tomes which, with his charming diffidence, he suggested I might find interesting to glance through. On closer examination they appeared to be a detailed study of the Russian railway system as it had affected their military dispositions on their Western frontier. Part of the volume was, I think, in French, and I rather believe that some of the footnotes were in Russian, but it never occurred to Humphrey that everyone was not as clever as he. Then there were tutorials on mediaeval history with Vivian Galbraith, who lived in rooms of startling austerity. It was rumoured that he steadfastly refused to teach any history after 1600, but up to that fatal date he was a very stimulating teacher, and extremely funny. Rocking gently on a chair said to have been inherited from Tout, he was a great favourite of my contemporaries.

Political philosophy was taught me by the admirably clear John Fulton, philosophy by Charles Morris, later Vice-Chancellor of Leeds University. As he rolled about like some stranded dolphin, I had for the first time the alarming experience of being asked what the words I used meant. This type of examination was the hallmark of Oxford philosophy. A. J. Ayer was teaching the new dogmas of logic positivism, but even among the older schools this meticulous examination of meaning, if not actual grammar, was endemic. In the hall of Corpus Professor Pritchard lectured on morals with stupendous contortion of mind. Not only did he have to go back to the very beginning of his endless paragraphs whenever the Corpus clock struck (I believe he eventually had it stopped from striking), but on one famous occasion, after making sixteen false starts on some proposition, he petrified a girl who was sitting in the back by announcing that either she could wind her watch or he would lecture. It was said that a distinguished rugger player who had never considered that he had a mind was rather startled by Pritchard crying out during one of his essays, 'Stop, stop, if you go on reading that stuff you will ruin your mind.'

Mr W. M. Allen, who taught me economics, was another new experience. He had a genius, also found in some other Oxford teachers, for attaching the most erudite meanings to any stumbling propostion which one put forward. This was immensely heartening. If one ventured some such remark as that prices depended upon supply and demand, Mr Allen would leap upon it with delighted surprise and expatiate upon the genius with which one had hit off one of the more complicated new theorems of the Austrian school.

It is easy to laugh at the word-splitting of philosophers or the incurable optimism of dedicated dons, but there is no doubt in my mind that they were the making of Oxford. I wonder if they exist to the same extent in the modern university?

'Excellence,' the universities chant; 'centres of excellence,' they proclaim, demanding ever more money from an unsympathetic world. To me Oxford was indeed excellent. The jargon of 'elitism' had not been invented—the word being reserved chiefly to describe very non-elite cafés. The excellence subsisted not in the labs, splendid as these may have been, nor in the buildings (some of breath-taking beauty, some hideous, most of them uncomfortable), nor in the amounts spent or the number of earnest committees earnestly manned. Excellence subsisted first of all, in the quality of the dons; and then in the enormous variety of opportunities open to the student. I had begun to hear about Atheism and Communism (which in those days were mildly unorthodox); I listened to queer psychological doctrines expounded by Professor Soddy; I was stimulated by the OUDS; and above all I was exposed to all those traditional

Oxford conversations that go on almost all night. I learnt from my contemporaries.

On my staircase were Jasper Ridley, killed, alas, in the war, the most brilliant of us, with a mind like a beautiful Clapham Junction through which ideas slid off at every sort of tangent, and Norman O. Brown, later to achieve fame as the author of *Life against Death*. I lunched off repulsive dishes with Ridley and Con O'Neill, then, believe it or not, even more pessimistic than he was in middle life and already with a major resignation to his credit. I find my contemporaries exceedingly difficult to write about. Jasper and Guy Branch were killed when very young, so no list of achievements is possible. Nor indeed would it be appropriate: their genius lay in being rather than doing. The expectation of seeing them was infinitely agreeable. Jasper was an excellent companion, equable, critical, eccentric, and materially undemanding. He was ahead of his time in suggesting the possible beauty of shaven heads—though he recommended them for some girls as well as for some film stars. Guy was also generous, eccentric and always in a good temper. His eccentricity took a slightly more flamboyant form, his sociability was more orthodox, running to parties and expeditions of all sorts. We were, I think, much more interested in people than are modern students. We discussed the inmates of the university, the hunger marches, the Spanish War, Baldwin (whom we rather admired) and Great Philosophical or Political Questions, on which people read papers to clubs.

The sort of excellence which Oxford dispensed depended on a two-way traffic. We actually *liked* the university. We were charmed into ecstasy to have so much provided for us; we did not yearn to organize the kitchen; we *enjoyed* dining with Tom Boase, the Dean of Hertford, or eating crumpets in the JCR and drinking beer in the buttery. We did not yearn to be premature civil servants engrossed in tedious administration and sabbatical jobs. I edited *Isis* for a term. I did it very badly (unlike Tony Woozley and Stuart Daniel and Paul Dehn, who edited *Cherwell* and did it brilliantly—the exploits of Pornographa Lady Purple-Passage were much funnier than anything now in *Punch*). In those days we did it in bits and pieces, between lectures and tutorials. Now I suppose all the staff would be taking a sabbatical year and would require a budget and a university printing works.

I was interested in politics, but I was never a member of the Union. Over this I have no regrets. To have attended its debates I would have had to give up something else. It is absurd to generalize about the effects of the Union—its great figures have been of many types. But it could—I put it no higher—encourage that view of politics which expresses itself in clichés suitable for speeches or articles. It has been a little responsible for the superficiality of much political comment, the sneering, the desire to appear to be on the inside and claim a spurious intimacy with political figures even if you have never exchanged a word with them. On the other hand, some of the best House of Commons performers in the traditional style—Lord Boyd Carpenter and Sir Derek Walker-Smith—no doubt owed something to it, though I suspect their native abilities and training at the Bar contributed more.

There is no point in creating expensive universities unless those who go there enjoy them, unless the interplay between dons and students goes on all the time. A university is not like big business or the army. In my day 'career structure' was a name unknown. No Fellow of a college cried himself to sleep because he was not a Professor. In St Andrews, where I was brought up, Professor D'Arcy Thompson sailed through the sacred town in an enormous billowing gown for over sixty years. He presented me with a stuffed hawk when I was six. That's how Professors ought to behave. But now when the siren blows the poor wretches scurry off to complete their endless articles on more and more abstruse subjects, or to sit on the joint inter-departmental committee on the control of mice in the gymnasium. I notice it is often the products of Oxford and Cambridge—those wicked haunts of elitism—who give up their evenings (and their pocket money and their wives' time) to entertaining their pupils, thereby showing an admirable social conscience.

What difference did Oxford make to me? What warts or dew did it leave upon me? There was a certain amount of rubbing-off. This influence seems to me underestimated in the innumerable reminiscences of Oxford figures, though I would not say now that to go to Oxford or Cambridge was an experience not to be missed. For that matter I would not say that to go to a university at all was essential to the good life. I nearly joined a firm instead of going to Oxford which would have despatched me to Buenos Aires. I wonder what then would have happened. I do not know. But I can make certain guesses.

The university of Oxford—and for that matter those of Cambridge and Glasgow and Edinburgh and, less certainly, Birmingham and Manchester—turns the thoughts of its students away from industry and commerce. No doubt many of those who haunt the plushier buildings of London's City and the neighbourhood of Charlotte Square in Edinburgh have university degrees, but the climate of our universities—especially Oxford—encourages rather commitment to the professions, or what is somewhat peculiarly called 'public service'. The 'rub-off' is in that direction, and it has done the country much harm. The richest and the most expensively-educated of my generation certainly did not grapple with problems of production.

I do not mean that more students from my day should have studied engineering (though they probably should) or business management or brewing, baking or candlestick-making. I do not mean that Oxford deliberately taught them that these were ignoble arts. On the contrary, all intellectuals deeply revere navvies. But that is just the difficulty. Intellectuals revere *navvies*, not entrepreneurs to engage them in new and useful enterprises. And it is reverence—not a desire to participate—which moves intellectuals. Professor Pritchard generously assumed that the rugger player had a mind, and was willing to expend great gobbets of his time and intellect in grappling with that intractable opponent. Should he not have said, 'How excellent you are as an athletic, simple, shrewd man. Do not attempt the higher reaches of philosophy. Production, action, expression, are far more important'? Better still, should he not have asked several of his Firsts in Greats to go out and bend their talents to industry or trade? After expending their abilities in their business during the day, they could have devoted their evenings to high thinking. And that thinking should have included how industry, economics, politics and morals were to be blended. As it has turned out there has been little or no blending. The thinkers have been speakers and publicists, not doers.

The universities have largely failed to live up to their name. The point of combining diverse subjects in one institution is to get those who practise them to discuss the universality of knowledge, of human experience, of the human situation. Specialized research into medicine or engineering or law should be carried out in separate and specialist institutions. That is what happened in the seventeenth and eighteenth centuries in England, when there were only two universities, and both were commonly judged to be sunk in sloth and ignorance. Yet it was the golden age of English science. The greatest of English historians, Gibbon, never read History. There was no such School. The great English lawyers did not learn their law at Oxford and Cambridge. Today the French Grandes Ecoles make one wonder if universities are necessary. The justification for universities must be that they offer a fully-rounded education. They should be breeding grounds for something better than bureaucrats devoted to the narrow claims of their particular subject. They should teach science and technology against the background of morals. They should care for the future and cherish the past. From the universities should flow an informed public, capable of judgement, and with some notion of the common good.

This goes far beyond not only science or medicine, but the mere study of philosophies or language or history or sociology or economics. Greats and Modern Greats at Oxford, and the Humanities in the Scottish universities, were the schools which came nearest to teaching the methods of *civilization*. Yet efforts to introduce something like Greats or Modern Greats into the new universities have not been a success. Nor has there been any greater understanding of science by non-scientists. I believe much of this is due to the Faculty/Department tradition, which has not really been changed by the introduction of Schools. For Schools too, though they may increase the number of subjects taught in each division, still emphasize the division of learning, still depend upon the old organization of the university into compartments.

What we need is not a dilution of effort by having, for instance, a first year in which several subjects are studied superficially. On the contrary, every student should have his mental capacities stretched and sharpened by being made to study seriously one of those subjects which can properly be called disciplines, such as medicine, the established sciences, Greek, or philosophy. But the university should also insist on a general training in what, for want of a better description, I will call moral philosophy. This should include some history of civilization and institutions, some teaching of general morals, some introduction to the presuppositions of law, politics and economics, and some acquaintance with European literature.

The Oxford of my day did not provide this type of education within the curriculum, but the college system went some way to correct this. The denizens of a college to some extent educated each other by exploring together the freedom which the university offered them. The luckier among them were in and out of each other's and dons' rooms talking of many things beside the subject in hand. Innumerable societies existed, as they still do. But, of course, the great difference between the

Oxford of the 'thirties and today was not only that it was truly collegiate—the colleges being much more than hostels in which we ate and slept—but that it was part of a different world.

Universities are sometimes said to be ivory towers but this is at best only a quarter true. The good-humoured complaint in my day was that the dons were always in the potteries lecturing for the Workers' Educational Association. As I have said, hunger marches, the Spanish War, strikes up at Headington, the activities of the Oxford City Council, kept many dons and undergraduates involved in other people's affairs—more involved perhaps than today. No students, as far as I know, went to fight in Vietnam.

The Oxford of Tom Tower and Peckwater, of the Radcliffe Camera and the Codrington Library: the Oxford of punts on the Cherwell, blossom, carols from Magdalen Tower and crumpets in Magdalen rooms on a misty autumn evening with deer among the fallen leaves of the park—these are the Oxfords of nostalgia. They evoke careless, unhurried days. Certainly one or two such memories remain: an expedition to a pub on the Thames below Wittenham Clumps; a drive through the summer night to Suffolk in which the countryside seemed a reincarnation of Keats's England—eglantine, vast elms, deep hedges and villages of white-washed houses where farm workers drank beer outside the pubs. But the background to Oxford was work. Though I never learnt to apply my mind, or for that matter my pen or my eyes, for long, my conscience drummed away at me none the less, and I was sufficiently ambitious to mind what class I got.

Much of Oxford was depressing. Certainly in those days before John Betjeman had come into my life the beauties of North Oxford or of Victorian Gothic were not to me apparent. Even now my rapture for them is modified. I have always believed that universities should be in the middle of towns so that I cannot complain too much about the suburbs—but these in any case were off-set by the bustling and to me heart-raising clamour of Elliston and Cavell's and St Aldate's. Over Oxford life too hung the clouds that shadow any life; Oxford, too, had its share of dissatisfaction and boredom; of foggy afternoons with a smell of cabbage cooking.

After two years living in college I went into digs in Beaumont Street with Jasper Ridley, Mark Pilkington, Lionel Brett, and John Pope-Hennessy, and later in South Eaton Place with William Douglas-Home. I was lucky in my digs: they were agreeable, faded, comfortable, unexacting places where we gave small dinner parties and were admirably looked after. For all the convenience of life in college, most people who could find it—and afford it—preferred an unpretentious house outside. A room in such a house seems to me the ideal way to spend a year or two, but, alas, such houses are now difficult to find, expensive to keep up and depend upon a race of house-keepers which no longer exists.

If Oxford was independence compared with school, Beaumont Street was independence within Oxford. I suppose there were rules but I have forgotten what they were. As Finals were drawing near I spent much time in the Codrington and Radcliffe Camera libraries—and very irksome it was. But Beaumont Street was a base to which I would return with the same companions, with pleasure.

Oxford was the centre of our world during term. I went to London to eat dinners in the Middle Temple, but London was not the magnet it appears to have been to previous and subsequent generations. We went to few parties and fewer dances. Girls came occasionally, and female undergraduates aroused excitement from time to time when they appeared at lectures or the occasional meal. Academic dress becomes nearly all girls, and their value was increased by their comparative rarity. But during term we lived largely in a male society. And even in the holidays expeditions were seldom mixed—indeed, it would have been thought scandalous by most of our relations. These expeditions in ancient cars bought for a few pounds or borrowed from parents must be counted part of Oxford. They were nearly the best part. I remember Zarauz and Madrid, the terrifying, empty, scorched plains of Spain, more vividly than much of Oxford blurred in Thames fog. I went to the famous chalet of 'Sligger' Urquhart above Saint-Gervais and below Mont Blanc. I found myself with Con O'Neill in Germany on the night of the long knives when Hitler carried out his first publicized murders. We gave a young man a lift who insisted on lying hidden under our coats in the back of the car and asked to be let out when we got near to the French Border so that he could cross unseen. We were inclined to laugh at him but when we were well into France we were overtaken by the French police who searched our car from top to bottom for no apparent reason. Perhaps he was someone of importance in danger after all.

Another expedition started from Cliveden with David Astor and Adam von Trott, and ended in Vinagradoff's rooms in the old *Guardian* building in Manchester where he was Foreign Editor—the first time I was ever in it. In particular, I remember the lift, crowded as usual with the restless inhabitants of a newspaper office, a peculiar hazard to von Trott who had contracted a boil on a vulnerable spot.

I mention these matters, unimportant as they may seem, because my more vivid memories are eccentrically trivial rather than significant, and certainly not flamboyant. The parents of my friends were more flamboyant than we were. When William Home and I went to dine with one of his elderly Lambton cousins we were dressed in unobtrusive dinner jackets, he in a suit of crimson velvet. Sober we were (or, if drunk, not often; drink for my contemporaries has been a middle-aged vice), concerned about life and philosophy and literature and death. Death figured quite largely. It seems strange now to have suffered a pang on realizing that 'of my three score years and ten' not 'twenty' but actually twenty-one would not come again. Forty-nine to go seemed very few.

Beauty and Oxford are oddly conjoined. It has beautiful buildings but it is not as beautiful a place as Cambridge, nor as grand. Art, music and literature were admired and their appreciation encouraged. It would be wrong, therefore, to accuse the universities of being unaesthetic, yet of late they have put up some spectacularly ugly buildings. Nor do I remember any great awareness of beauty in most Oxford rooms—either of dons or students. Looking back, it seems odd that artistic effort was so infrequent. Some of my contemporaries played instruments, a few painted. The urge to create seemed weak. Why should it have been otherwise? Scholarship does not imply creativity.

'Bald heads forgetful of their sins
Old, learned, respectable bald heads
Edit and annotate the lines
That young men tossing on their beds
Rhymed out in love's despair
To flatter beauty's ignorant ear.'

I look back on Oxford with pleasure, yes, but with no great desire to repeat the whole experience. Its education was excellent. It certainly formed and stretched whatever minds were open to it. But perhaps the education was unreal. All education, of course, is unreal, in that boys and girls are rarely taught the skills of life: to type or mend a motor car, to cook or read a balance sheet. There are few more unreal places than those gorgeously-equipped laboratories in our schools where girls are taught to cook and boys to work at wood with tools they will never see the like of again. But the unreality of Oxford lay in the gap between the world of humanities taught there and the values of the world in which we lived. No one proposed that we should behave like the Greeks yet their philosophy and poetry were displayed for our admiration. Economics were remote from ordinary decisions—indeed the very dons who taught economics and advised governments did not appear to think that governments should act according to the rules. I am not saying that Keynes and Henderson, Hayek and Pigou did not have an effect on official thinking. No doubt too, Greek discipline enabled lawyers and administrators to marshal and deploy a case with economy and elegance. But the way of life was largely unaffected. Now we could perhaps do with some assertion of Greek values and pure economics, indeed, as I have mentioned, of theology and moral philosophy. We discover, however, that endless hours spent in memorizing Horace, passing examinations in the 'General Theory', going to chapel or discussing the views of Pritchard, Joseph, Collingwood or Joachim (all professors in my time), have left hardly a mark behind. The efforts to bring the benefits of Oxford to a wider public, the WEA and Ruskin College seem to have led to no great flowering through the nation of the spirit of reason and the wide view; nor indeed to any great improvement in our critical faculties or values. It may be that it was the education for a ruling class which has hung on miraculously well but is passing. At any rate, of its sort it was good.

Nigel Nicolson

Nigel Nicolson was born in 1917, the younger son of Harold Nicolson and Victoria Sackville-West. He was educated at Eton and Balliol College, where he took a third class degree in History in 1938. He served with the Grenadier Guards in the African and Italian campaigns in the Second World War. In 1947 he co-founded the publishing firm of Weidenfeld & Nicolson with George (now Lord) Weidenfeld, and he is still a director. He was Conservative MP for Bournemouth East from 1952 to 1959. He has written a number of books, including Portrait of a Marriage *(1973). He has edited his father's diaries and letters, and also the letters of Virginia Woolf. He lives at Sissinghurst Castle in Kent.*

The school chapter in an autobiography can by tradition be a pretty gloomy record, but by the time the hero reaches university, he is expected to show by selective anecdote and deft allusion to names which subsequently became famous, that he was at last in the swim, and that the university meant for him a sudden flowering of talents and lifelong influences and friends. For me such deception would be outrageous. I made a mess of Oxford, and Oxford did not make much of me. My three years (1935–38) began in disillusionment, continued in despondency, ended in a third class degree in History, and left not a single intimacy and little affection behind. I write this confession in order to exorcise a memory, and to explain to myself how it happened.

It was not Oxford's fault. My present ingratitude is caused entirely by wasted opportunity. Where you do not succeed, you cannot love. Periodically I return to Balliol, pace its quads, climb my old staircase, and each glimpse of a scarcely-altered scene reminds me of humiliation and idleness. 'He was unhappy at Oxford.' Not quite true. There were moments of exhilaration when I felt myself sharing, if not generating, triumph—on the river, at the Union, late at night. But these moments were rare. More often I retreated hurt, disconsolate and envious, for a university is the period when envy takes precedence of admiration, and self-approbation alternates unpleasantly with self-distrust. My dominant mood was depression, but I was damned if I was going to confess it. I have re-read for the first time the letters I wrote to my parents during those years. Even at this distance of time I know that they conveyed a deliberately false impression. I made the most of small successes, magnified acquaintance into friendship, and exaggerated the frequency, length and stimulus of undergraduate discussions, describing an atmosphere of youthful abandon, and concealing my melancholy and loneliness. How often did I sit miserably by a miserable fire, hitting with a poker at the coals, and hearing distant shouts of friend to friend, and the banging of doors that signified my exclusion.

It was parental expectation that led to this deceit. My father too had been at Balliol. Throughout his life, as he wrote in old age, the name of Oxford, even on a pot of marmalade, quickened his pulses. He had found there a sudden release of energy and spirit, discovered the joys of literature and friendship. Surely it must be the same with his son? Balliol, he told me, was a palimpsest of achievement on which every generation writes its new chapter. To him it was still the Balliol of the early 1900s, and before that of Jowett and Curzon. There was a tradition of disdainful pride, of effortless superiority. The rest of the university, we were led to believe, envied us. We were the centre, with the highest standards, the greatest charm, the most Firsts. Captivated by this legend, even I would answer when asked for the name of my college, 'As a matter of fact, I'm at Balliol.' But outward pride was not matched by inner confidence, and privately I wondered where the magic was of which my father had so often spoken. Had it really been so glamorous in his day? Did he never endure pangs of indolence and inadequacy? Was he not recreating a myth?

I have found the letter which he wrote to me on the eve of my first term:

> 'The main thing to remember is that it is half a school and half not a school. In other words, you cannot treat it

exactly like a hotel, and yet you need not treat it as a Summer Fields boy would treat Eton when he goes up for a viva. . . . Balliol does not care overmuch for the extent of a man's knowledge: it cares dreadfully for his state of mind. They would far rather that you were ignorant than that you were silly. If you do not know something, and say so, they will not care in the least. But if you pretend to know something which you do not know, they will care very much indeed. Remember that what they want to find out is whether you are *intelligent,* not whether you are *learned.* They judge intelligence by the extent to which you avoid saying something stupid rather than by the extent to which you manage to say something bright.'

Now that was all very well. So anxious was I not to say anything stupid, that I never said anything at all. I was desperately shy, and shyness at nineteen may be a pathetic quality, but it is not particularly endearing. On arrival I found an invitation to lunch with a senior Fellow, Roger Mynors. I knocked on his door with the sort of knock that tries to be casual, but only succeeds in conveying timidity. He greeted me affably, even warmly, but I noticed a quick glance at my eyes for some indication of intelligence, and my heart sank. My fellow-guests were the two Pope-Hennessy brothers, John and James, both undergraduates, but with social and intellectual gifts that soared beyond my own. The conversation soon turned to Piero della Francesca, of whom I had heard, just, but could think of nothing to add to John's amazing flow of erudition and analysis. James took all this in his stride, poking his brother's fire with caustic comment, while I sat silent. Eventually Mynors turned to me.

'What have you been reading lately?'

'*Emma.*'

There was a slight quickening of interest. 'And what did you think of *Emma*?'

'Rather snobbish,' I said.

They resumed their discussion of Italian art.

I knew the right note to strike, but not how to strike it. I found the attitude of the dons, half-masters, half-colleagues, intimidating. They were living symbols of that glorious past. A row of baits was dangled before me, but I spat them out. At school there had been insistence that one be in certain places at certain times to carry out definite tasks. At Balliol nobody seemed to care what one did. In other people, I observed, this sudden freedom led rapidly to conceit. We were being treated as adults. The mere fact that the crudities of converse at school were succeeded by the politeness of university intercourse persuaded them to identify that politeness with admiration. It was so startling to find 'Oh my God, Nicolson' replaced by 'Hullo, Nigel, have a drink', that it was tempting to attribute the alteration in manner to some hitherto undiscovered prowess in oneself. An assumption of disapproval became overnight an assumption of approval, and to many the change was intoxicating. But not to me. It was as if water-wings had suddenly been snatched away, and I was afloat unsupported at the deep end. My efforts to adopt the Balliol manner were floundering and embarrassing. I had never known time go so slowly. After two days it seemed that I had been there a fortnight. I felt myself to be under constant scrutiny, and that opinions were being formed about me which were unflattering, irrevocable and true. Panic seized me. I allowed something of it to leak into my letters home, and in a rare burst of confidence, recorded this verbatim conversation with my tutor Humphrey Sumner:

H.S. (sharply the whole time): 'You were at Eton?'

N.N. 'Yes.'

H.S. 'Where did you spend your last holidays?'

N.N. 'At Tours.'

H.S. 'Nice place. Where did you go when your parents were in Persia?' (He seemed to know all about me.)

N.N. 'I stayed with my uncle in Devonshire.'

H.S. 'Nice uncle?'

N.N. 'Not too bad.'

Really, I felt, this is absurd, and rather cruel. But what was Sumner doing except fishing for an interest, a character, a peg on which to hang something? He was a difficult, admirable man. Tall, wiry, pipe-smoking, he had a prodigious capacity for work, and set his pupils unattainable standards—his own. He distrusted generalization, and disliked epigram. He elicited opinion, but seldom expressed one. Once he asked me, after I had read an essay on Napoleon, 'Do you like Napoleon?'

'Quite,' I said.

'I hate Napoleon.' There was a dead silence: at last he had committed himself. His unsolicited answer became famous, and so, momentarily, did I. I was the man to whom Humphrey had said that he hated Napoleon. His austerity was strange and frightening. He asked his pupils to call on him whenever they wished, and a fortnight later I did so.

'Have you come to talk about something special,' he asked me, looking up from his work, 'or just to talk?'

'Just to talk.'

'What about?'

I could not catch this ball. It required an experience beyond me, and after a few unproductive remarks, I shambled out, self-confidence lowered by several more degrees. For all his kindness, he was a terrifying man. There seemed to be nothing that he did not know. We tested it; it became a game. A friend of mine, with an impertinence I envied, was marooned in Bergen for a few days, and spent his time learning all he could about Norwegian football teams, with the sole purpose of confronting Humphrey with knowledge that Humphrey could not possibly possess. On returning to Oxford he worked the conversation round, with some difficulty, to his newly-acquired speciality. He began by touching lightly on the tactics and prospects of Lillehammer and Trondheim, only to find himself immediately challenged. Humphrey was conversant with every statistic, the name of every star player. After that, we never tried again.

With so much discouragement under the guise of encouragement, so much freedom, such an excess of opportunity, I grew lazy, which I had never been at school, and spent hours staring out of the window at the St Giles traffic, bustling importantly to the library to find unnecessary quotations or through the Junior Common Room looking right and left as if in search of someone with whom I had an appointment, but only hoping to be hailed. It was weeks before I discovered where the bathrooms were (steamy catacombs where no bathrooms should be), being too shy, and as time passed, too ashamed, to ask. I sat in hall, always in the same place, scarcely speaking to my neighbours, and they began to look curiously at me, for I seemed, alone among my contemporaries, to have no fun, and not to desire it. Do I exaggerate my loneliness? I do not think so; and I believe that my experience was, and perhaps is, far more common than undergraduates dare admit. One needed psychological counsellors, but Balliol was too proud to provide them. After all, the place, in the most civilized way, was highly competitive, and you had to learn for yourself to use its tools. I experienced no unkindness, no form of ostracism, but simply mounting despair. How untrue it is that memory retains the pleasures of life, to the exclusion of its pains!

That was the first year. The second was better. It was impossible that things should not improve for someone who, after all, was not a natural misanthrope. I slowly made friends. One was a jolly Portuguese, Peter Bon de Sousa Pernes, who teased me out of my moroseness; another was Rohan Butler, who gallantly fought down the handicap of a painful stammer, and with him I engaged in earnest discussions, but he was a cleverer man than I was, a potential, and later an actual, Fellow of All Souls, and our friendship was not destined to last. A third, and the most important, was James Pope-Hennessy. I owed more to him than to anyone else, don or undergraduate, for he took me by the scruff of the neck, declaring my solemnity absurd, and forced me to bicycle with him through Normandy one long vacation. I think that was the turning-point. I learnt to laugh with him, to quarrel and forgive, to enjoy excess, and he taught me that in nine cases out of ten a person dislikes you only because he imagines that you dislike him. James seemed made for Balliol, with his cleverness, companionableness and charm, his slenderness, black hair, and willowy walk, but he was one of the few among us who did not last the course. He left Oxford after two years, without taking a degree. He thought the place stuffy. There was the occasion when a delegation waited on him (it now seems incredible) to complain that his gaudy ties were giving the college a bad name. There was his essay on constitutional innovations in the reign of Queen Elizabeth, which turned out to be a discussion of the Queen's personality in terms of her dress, starting with her slippers and mounting to her jewelled hair. He was told to do it again, properly. Although he remained throughout his life boyishly irresponsible, he was already too mature for Oxford. While I found it too free, he found it too restricting. His departure was a terrible blow to me, but his example left much behind.

Stars circulated in our small firmament, a few young men who embodied all the qualities which I recognized to be central to Oxford's purpose, and I knew some of them peripherally. The most brilliant constellation was formed of three who were killed in the war—Jasper Ridley (we called him 'Bubbles', a singularly inappropriate childhood nickname which he had never managed to shake off), Guy Branch and David Wallace—and three who survived to attain the eminence expected of them—Stuart Hampshire, John Pope-Hennessy and Jeremy Hutchinson. The centre of their élitist group was 7 Beaumont Street, lodgings which I later occupied myself with less galactic companions. When allowed to, I sat literally at their feet, on the floor. Ridley, discovering me there for the first time, leant down to ask, 'What do you think of Tuesdays?' a question which today I might manage to laugh off, but which then crushed me into silence. Branch was kinder. Two years older than me, he had been my hero at school, and still was, and in an attempt to break down this most inhibiting of all relationships, he took me to his room, which was furnished and carpeted entirely in white, with the first white telephone I ever saw, and told me how unhappy he had been when he first came up to Oxford. I don't think I believed him.

Women were lacking from our lives. Of course we knew that they were around, but somewhere in the outer suburbs, convents loosely linked to our great monastery, but unvisited, and from which no visitors came. In all those years I never once entered a women's college, and never knew a single girl well enough to call her by her first name. Perhaps, even for Balliol, I was exceptional in this, but I do not think so. We took our cue from the dons, who discouraged heterosexual love, it now seems to me, as irrelevant to our purpose in being there, and treated girls as blue-stockings who could not be expected to understand our male society. There was a don at Hertford whose course of lectures on Edward II I was advised to attend. About fifty of us assembled for his first lecture, including six girls. He looked down the hall, wrapped his gown protectively around him like a toga, and declared: 'I do not lecture to *undergraduettes*' (the word was expelled with mordant sarcasm, heavily italicized). 'I will not begin until they have left the room.' Spontaneously we all rose and walked out. Next week we returned, including the girls, and he surrendered. Now this may seem in retrospect a splendid demonstration of university solidarity, but it was more a gesture of romantic chivalry on which we greatly flattered ourselves, and a noble excuse for avoiding a lecture which we expected to be dull. None of us ever spoke to the girls whose champions we had so unexpectedly become. There were no Zuleikas among them. In fact, in the whole university there was only one who could lay even approximate claim to that title, and she was a White Russian. She was called Tatiana Voronoff. Ignoring the taboos which the women's colleges accepted as their sad lot, Voronoff thrust herself into our monastic world, filling our rooms with heavy scent and sexy Caucasian-Parisian laughter. There must have been some who loved her, for she was very beautiful, but in most of us she confirmed an incomprehensible prejudice. She had heavy artificial eyelashes, apparently dipped in tar, and was much rouged. She wore fluttering silks. Her long white fingers were ringed in amethyst, and tapered to lacquered nails. I hated her.

Such were my glimpses into unattainable worlds. So was the world of politics. Once I spoke in a Union debate, late at night; and once with Niall Macdermot I attempted to organize a university branch of the National Labour party, and we invited down from London a leading member of the party, Kenneth Lindsay, to address our inaugural meeting. Four people came. On that terrible evening I realized, not for the first time, that I did not possess the charismatic gift. Nor did I recognize it in others, for which there was little excuse, since among my Balliol contemporaries were Edward Heath and Denis Healey. I knew both of them slightly, but ask me to describe them as they then were, and I find the focusing difficult: too many later impressions have supervened. Of Healey I recall his gift for mimicry and comic ballads, and his rubicund amiability, but nothing of the ruthless courage with which he is credited today. Heath is sharper: his way of laughing until his whole body shook, his undeviating gaze, a touch of puritanism, and his passion for music, for he was our Organ Scholar. But when he became President of the Union he swam out of my reach. I was not yet deeply interested in politics. The Spanish War was for me little more than a serial story in the newspapers: the Hitler crises—although I spent two holidays with anti-Nazi families in Berlin and Göttingen—recurrent excitements. I would like to claim despair, or at least apprehension, at what was about to happen to my generation, but I cannot. We did not want war—particularly as the most agreeable Rhodes Scholars were German—but the thought of it did not appal us. It would rouse us from lethargy, we thought, and make us short-cut heroes, while the idea of an early melodramatic martyrdom nurtured our self-esteem. There were no pacifists among my friends, except one, Douglas Young, a formidable Greek scholar, stiffly bearded like a youth on an Attic vase, and saintly in his gentleness and humour. We called him God, and when required to act the word 'dog' in a word-game, we carried him into the room upside down.

The upshot was that there was no group into which I naturally slotted, and that was distressing for someone so desperately anxious to slot. So I took to rowing, hoping that the unison of an eight would link me to at least some of my fellows, as in a chain-gang. It worked. I much enjoyed rowing. The Balliol eight was drawn from all parts of the college, including two Americans and a Canadian as cox, and we were good enough to be awarded our oars one summer, and to row at Henley. The companionship was pleasant, and so was the exercise, for the rhythm of a well-trained crew has no parallel except perhaps in dancing, and the implements of our sport were as beautiful as its river setting, eight identical oars cupping the water simultaneously each side of a long light shell in which we perched and slid, floating forwards, lunging back, in silence except for the rumbling of the slides and the piping injunctions of the cox. I spent happy hours on the Isis, but the best was Henley. There we were in competition with the finest crews of several nationalities, and at no moment in my life have I experienced so *sustained* a wish to excel. For those few days we lived in dread of the next race, discussing tactics, grooming the boat, eating enormously, sleeping long—and then the last terrified backward glance at the course before the race began in distant privacy to end ten minutes later between banks of parasols and tumultuous acclaim. Those were ecstatic moments.

But work? Surely I worked? Yes, in spasms timed to the climax of the weekly essay, and the less thought I had given to it, the lengthier were my last-minute plagiarisms. This was the temptation of easy access to great libraries where one could find obscure books which even Humphrey Sumner might not have read, but he always had. I worked, but I did not study. I would take up an eighteenth-century novel with the excuse that it gave me 'period-feel' when I should have been acquiring solid information or digging deep enough into a subject to reach its subsoils and justify me in differing from a scholar's opinions. To lose time at Oxford was good: to waste it was a crime, and I wasted all too much of it. I would take on holiday to Venice Stubbs's *Constitutional Charters*. Stubbs remained unread, but Venice was ruined by his reproachful presence. There were days, however, when I felt myself gripping something, and I associate them mainly with the Codrington Library at All Souls, the loveliest, coolest room in Oxford, to which I was given privileged entrance. The long hall was almost empty except for book-filled shelves, but alcoves sheltered us, and we read in silence. There was no escape, except in humiliation. Having paced the length of that marble floor, one could not decently retreat along it until many hours had lapsed. Under pressure of confinement, I began to learn what study is, the joy of documents, the mean pleasure of finding experts wrong, and to form, gradually and intermittently, an attitude of my own. Then I could test it against Sumner's pouncing mind, argue my point-of-view, and feel the muscularity of his response.

Too late. I sat my final examination with apprehension, memorizing each night my past essays in the hope that the same subjects would recur, learning by rote quotations which might fit in somewhere (oh, the shame of it), and then scribble, scribble in the Examination Schools, gowned and bent, envious of neighbouring scribblers, twisting questions to admit prepared answers, trying to deceive but knowing all the while that deception of this kind is always detectable, as it was.

I aimed for a Second. I achieved a Third. The news reached me in Glasgow. I was on my way to the Outer Hebrides to spend a fortnight on some uninhabited islands which I had just bought with a small legacy, and I took with me Rohan Butler. It was the year of the International Glasgow Exhibition.

We decided to separate at the entrance, and meet again three hours later at a designated spot to compare impressions. When Rohan returned, he was carrying a copy of *The Times*. Casually I asked him if the Schools results had been published. He said they had.

'What did you get?' I asked.

'I got a First.'

'And what did I get?'

'You'd better look.'

I looked. I searched expectantly down the Seconds list, failed to find my name, and then the Thirds. It was there.

'Get in,' I said. We drove an hour in silence. Then he said, 'Do you realize that we're going the wrong way? We're driving south; it should be north.'

'Yes.' I reversed. Gradually the blood began to recirculate. I thought, 'Here is this man, my friend, in ecstasy. Here am I, his friend, in despair. Why should I spoil his pleasure?'

He was infinitely kind. We camped on my island, never mentioning the contrast that was in both our minds, and quarrelled only once, about forks. He insisted on civilized behaviour. I ate with my fingers from the tin.

That for me was the end of Oxford, for him almost the beginning, for he is still there. Oxford, I felt, had condemned me, and I deserved to be condemned. When I return there now, I may avoid Balliol because it has every reason to be indifferent to me, but with each visit I find things which I never bothered to discover as an undergraduate. Last summer I climbed to the cupola of the Sheldonian, looked across the pierced view and downwards onto flat roofs, and sighed to think how much I had missed, wishing myself nineteen again, but without reproach, except self-reproach. Now my son is nineteen. From shame, and because I hope to enjoy vicariously a new deal, I am sending him to Cambridge.

John Mortimer

John Mortimer was born in 1923 and educated at Harrow and Brasenose College (1940–1943). He has written five novels and a number of plays, including The Dock Brief, The Wrong Side of the Park *and* A Voyage Round My Father. *He has also written numerous film scripts and television plays. He was called to the bar in 1948 and became a QC in 1966. He now lives with his second wife and small daughter in Oxfordshire.*

I was at school when the war started, dark days for Europe and, I was finally convinced, for me. The bastions of freedom were falling, the lights going out all over the place, and we stood in the Speech Room singing the school songs, 'Five Hundred Faces and All So Strange', 'Jerry a poor little fag', those fiercely nostalgic evocations of Victorian boyhood. An ancient and quavering voice was added to ours, the sibilants slurred as from too much brandy or ill-fitting teeth. Mr Churchill, not yet Prime Minister, had come down in search of his distant youth. After the singing was over he was helped onto the platform and peered at us like a misty-eyed tortoise, his hand trembling on the ivory handle of his stick. He said a few words which I didn't find easy to hear or to understand. 'If they ever put *him* in charge,' I said to my friend Oliver, 'then we're all goners.' Shortly after that Mr Churchill took over the war and I went to Oxford. I was seventeen and had I not written poems about Spain at my prep school? Had I not been the sole occupant of a Communist cell at Harrow? I must surely be top of the Nazi black-list; and when they crossed the Channel they would inevitably make a bee-line for me.

I went to Oxford, therefore, in expectation of imminent death.

My going there at all was a late decision of my father's. Old, blind and brilliant, his income had increased with the call-up of younger barristers. 'I think we might run to Oxford,' he said, 'provided you fall in and read Law.' I fell in, but after Oxford what was to happen to me? My mind was continually changing; should I become a pilot? Or even, and it seemed at times the most courageous alternative, a pacifist? 'The best place for you is the RAF groundstaff,' my father told me. 'Avoid the temptation to do anything heroic.'

I wondered why he chose Oxford. He'd been at Cambridge himself and Brasenose was a college which he'd only heard mentioned, in an apparently disparaging way, by someone in his Chambers many years before. But as he offered me Oxford like the sausage and scrambled eggs of the condemned man's breakfast, I felt it churlish to refuse. I presented myself, accordingly, for an entrance examination.

Whenever I hear now of the appalling efforts, suffering and anxiety of those who are trying to get their children into the older universities I think of my entrance examination with a pang of guilt. I went to Brasenose and was led up some stairs by a college servant. After a long solitary wait a bald-headed man wearing carpet slippers and carrying a large dictionary of gastronomy under his arm came shuffling in. He handed me a passage from Lucretius, told me to translate it and shuffled away. I sat for a while puzzled by the complicated stanzas describing the nature of atoms and then another door opened. Through it came my friend Oliver also carrying a book. 'There's a shop on the corner,' he said, 'and I went out and bought this. I think it might be a help.' It was a Latin dictionary and he had slipped out unnoticed and acquired it at Blackwells. With its help we wrote out a translation and went to find our examiner. He was having lunch, reading a recipe from the book propped up on a stand in front of him whilst he feasted on—what was it—dried egg, spam salad perhaps? He took our work without a word and later we discovered we had passed into Oxford. I never saw the bald gastronome or, indeed, very much of Brasenose College again. It was taken over by the War Office and they sent us to Christ Church.

Oxford after France fell, as the black-out was pinned up in the Buttery, as Frank Pakenham, history tutor at Christ Church, drilled dangerously with the Home Guard in the Meadows, was at the end of an era, and I was at the end of my extraordinarily secluded middle-class, 'thirties education. Although Harrow is a stop on the Metropolitan line we never used it except to sit, jeered at, dressed in a top hat, pearl-grey waistcoat and carrying a stick with a blue silk tassel, for our annual visit to Lords. We weren't allowed to speak to the boys at the bottom of the hill, although the Prefects occasionally gave one of them sixpence to carry a suitcase up at the beginning of term. The only women we saw were elderly and fierce matrons. We were waited on at table by footmen in blue tailed coats and settled down for the night by a butler called George. Our homosexuality was therefore dictated by necessity rather than choice. We were like a generation of diners condemned to cold cuts because the steak and kidney's 'off'.

I can't say I came out of this bizarre hothouse and met the real world at Oxford. That encounter, intoxicating, painful, invigorating, hilarious and tragic, was held from me for two years until, in the company of GI's, cameramen, electricians, aircraft workers with their Veronica Lake hairdos tied up in scarves, script girls and infantrymen, I stopped being educated and came, belatedly, to life. Meanwhile I lay becalmed at Oxford.

The Oxford of the 'twenties and 'thirties was still there, like college claret, but it was rationed, on coupons, and there was not very much of it left. The famous characters still behaved as if they lingered in the pages of *Decline and Fall*; indeed, they were famous for nothing except being Oxford characters: once they left their natural habitat in Magdalen or the House they grew faint and dim and ended up down back corridors in Bush House or as announcers in Radio Monte Carlo. They had double-barrelled names: Edward Faith-Peterson, Tommy Motte-Smith. By day they lay naked in their rooms listening to Charles Trenet or Verdi's *Requiem*. By night they would issue into the black-out, camel hair coats slung across their shoulders like German generals, bow ties from Hall's settled under their lightly-powdered chins, to take the exotic dinner (maximum spending allowed under the Ministry of Food Regulations—five shillings) at the George Restaurant. What did it matter if the steak was whale (Moby Dick and chips) or the wine rationed Algiers or even black-market Communion? They still talked about Beardsley and Firbank and *Point Counter Point* and how, sometime in the summer vacation, they had been spoken to by Brian Howard, supposed model for the Waugh heroes, itching in his A. C. Plonk's uniform in the downstairs bar at the Ritz.

So at Oxford after Dunkerque the fashion was to be queer. It seems that it was only after the war, with the return of the military, that heterosexuality came to be completely tolerated. As it was, my own sporadic adventures with WAAFs and girls from St Hilda's, my grandly-titled 'engagement' to a student of book illustration at the Slade, were subjects I preferred not to discuss with Tommy Motte-Smith when he invited me and my friend Oliver for whale steak at the George.

The high life of Oxford, of course, was something I had never encountered when I moved into my rooms in Meadow Buildings. To my dismay I found I was sharing them with Parsons, a tall man with bicycle clips and a pronounced Adam's apple who tried to lure me into the Bible Society. One night my friend Oliver and I tried the effect of boiling up Algerian wine, college sherry and a bottle of Bols he had stolen from his mother's dressing-case, in Parsons's electric kettle. Oliver's mother was an ageless South American who moved in an aura of patchouli and poodles round a series of rented flats with white wrought-iron furniture in the area of Charles Street. Perhaps for this reason Oliver saw himself an an eighteenth-century English squire and this extraordinary brew was meant to be punch, or hot toddy, or whatever eighteenth-century squires drank in the evenings. When I recovered from the draught I found Parsons wearing cycle clips and kneeling over me in prayer: I also heard from down the corridor Brahms's Fourth Symphony like music from some remote paradise.

In fact, my memory of Oxford seems, looking back over a vast distance, to consist almost entirely of Brahms's Fourth Symphony, a piece of music of which I have become decreasingly fond, as I have lost the taste for bow ties, Balkan Sobranie cigarettes, and sherry and Bols boiled up in an electric kettle. But that music came from the room of someone who really did affect my life and of whom I still think with gratitude and bewilderment, remembering his serene life and extraordinary death.

My father, to whom I owe so much, never told me the difference between right and wrong; now I think that's why I remain so greatly in his debt. But Henry Winter, who slowly and with enormous care sharpened a thorn needle with sandpaper to play Brahms on his huge horned gramophone, became a kind of yardstick, not of taste but of moral behaviour. He had no doubt whatever about the war: he was against it. He looked forward to the call-up, the refusal, the arguments with the tribunals and the final consignment to Pentonville or the Fire Service with amused calm. He read classics, I mean actually *read* them. He would sit in a squeaking basket chair, smoking a pipe and giving me his version of chunks of Homer and Euripides which up to then I had been trained to regard as almost insoluble crossword puzzles or grammarians' equations with no recognizable human content. I was born of tone deaf parents and, in the school songs, I was instructed to open and shut my mouth soundlessly so that no emergent discord might mar the occasion. Yet Winter slowly, painstakingly, introduced me to music, and the pleasure I now take in it is due entirely to him.

Winter's rejection of violence, and what seemed to me the extraordinary gentle firmness of his moral stance, was no result of religious conviction. He was courageously sceptical, fearlessly agnostic, open and reasonable, with none of the tormented Christianity of my ex-room mate. Parsons had applied for a transfer after the desecration of his electric kettle and left me in solitary possession of a huge Gothic sitting-room and a bedroom the size of a waiting-room at St Pancras, with a chipped wash basin in which I kept a smoked salmon caught by my aunt in Devon and in defiance of rationing.

I suppose Oxford's greatest gift is friendship, for which there is all the time in the world. After Oxford there are love affairs, marriages, working relationships, manipulations, lifelong enemies: but even then, in rationed, blacked-out Oxford, there were limitless hours for talking, drinking, staying up all night, even going for walks (how many years is it since I went for a walk?) with a friend. Winter and I were emerging from the chrysalis of schoolboy homosexuality; and the girls we preferred were notably boyish. Veronica Lake rather than Betty Grable, and Katherine Hepburn in *Philadelphia Story* who, Frank Hauser told us, was the natural bridge into the heterosexual world. At first the girls we loved were tennis-playing virgins, posed, like Proust's androgynous heroines, forever unobtainable against a background of parks and carrying string bags full of Slazengers. There is nothing like sexual frustration to give warmth to friendship, which is why it flourishes in prisons, armies, on Arctic expeditions and did well in wartime in Oxford. Winter and I became inseparable, and when, as time went on, I began to do things without him, I felt, for a moment quite strongly, guilty twinges of infidelity.

I had the more time for friendship as I did find learning law enormously dull and spent as little time at it as possible. I have always held the view that law has no existence whatever until people become involved in it, and that knowing a great deal of it is a hindrance rather than a help to the advocate in Court. Nevertheless, to fulfil my bargain with my father I acquired a working knowledge of Roman law and after about a year I would have been able to manumit a slave, adopt an elderly senator or enter into a marriage by the ceremony of 'brass and scales', skills which I have never found of great service in the Uxbridge Magistrates Court. Roman law was taught by a mountainous grey man who, like the Royal Family, had changed a German name for an old English one, who peered at me through glasses thick as ginger beer bottles and who was forever veering away from Justinian's view of Riparian ownership to Catullus' celebration of oral sex, a change of course which I found very welcome. Returning to Oxford by train from a legal dinner, he mistook the carriage door for the lavatory and stepped heavily out into the black-out and onto the flying railway lines just outside Didcot. After his death I gave up Roman law.

Other subjects I found encased in a number of slim volumes: *Tort in a Nutshell, The Basic Real Property, All You Need to Know about Libel and Slander.* I read them listening to Winter's gramophone, or as we punted down the river and the ATS in the long grass on the bank whistled, 'Keep smiling throo, Just as you, Used to doo, Till the good times come again one sunny day'. If these were not good times I was deceived by never having known anything better.

Oxford acting was good in those two years; but the universities had not yet become the natural training ground for the West End Theatre. Michael Flanders, not only alive then but upright, handsome and walking, played Pirandello's *Henry IVth* and gave me an admiration for that play which survived almost thirty years and was only shattered by actually seeing it again. Frank Hauser, who sat in rooms in Christ Church decorated with fleur de lys so that he seemed to be ever awaiting the imminent arrival of Joan of Arc, played Noel Coward on the piano and talked endlessly of the bit players in old Hollywood movies. He directed plays I had never heard of by Strindberg and Jean-Jacques Bernard, productions which I can still see in my mind. Peter Brook, ignored by the OUDS, made a film of *Tristram Shandy* with Tommy Motte-Smith playing Sterne. I acted a series of minor Shakespearian villains, but I always enjoyed the parties and falling hopelessly in love with the ladies-in-waiting, more than the performance. Finally I was cast as Rosencrantz and stopped going to rehearsals.

The war was also a time for poetry, perhaps the last time when poems were widely read; before the popular verse market was captured by folk singers and pop groups. I tried to write modern ballads heavily influenced by Auden, and was very proud when one or two got into the *Cherwell*. Since those days I haven't attacked a poem and I hope poetry is for my old age, like brewing home-made wine and spending every day in the garden. John Heath-Stubbs was a remarkable poet and Sidney Keyes a war poet about to meet a war poet's appropriate death. When twilight fell over Peckwater, pale, dark-haired Michael Hamburger, moving through the shadows with a heavy but always gleeful despair, used to come and read me his superb translations of Rilke and Hoelderlin. He was also besotted by the tennis-playing girls and seemed in constant fear that one might surrender to him, thereby breaking the spell of Gothic gloom in which he moved so happily.

Winter was a year older than I and was about to face his Tribunal. There was a man named Charles Dimont, then a character of great eminence in the pacifist world, who would give Winter a lesson in how best to put his reluctance to kill people to a bench of ex-officers and patriotic magistrates. Winter told me that a favourite question was, 'What would you do if you saw a German raping your grandmother?', to which he intended to reply, 'Wait until he'd finished and then bury the dear old lady again.' We went to Boars Hill, where Charles Dimont lived, by bus. When we got there he had a bad cold and was in a dressing-gown; there seemed to be a large number of small children about, one of whom was dropping jam onto *The Bible Designed to be Read as Literature*. In the corner was a dark-haired woman of remarkable beauty who said nothing and looked as if she was heartily sick of the tramp of bright young conscies through her sitting-room. Charles Dimont told Winter that it was very difficult to persuade the Tribunal that you really didn't like killing people unless you believed in God. He offered us a cup of tea, but the pot was empty and anyway we had to go.

As we waited at the bus stop I had no idea that Charles Dimont was about to change his mind and obtain an infantry commission. I had still less idea that in some distant peace I would marry the dark, silent Mrs Dimont and bring up those numerous children, but that, in fact, is how it turned out. About one thing, however, I was certain. I was going to take my father's advice and sign on for the RAF groundstaff.

Star-struck by poets, Michael Hamburger and I used to travel up to London. Drinking beer in the Swiss Pub in Soho we might even be spoken to by Dylan Thomas or Roy Campbell. When the pub shut we went to a terrible cellar called the Coffee Ann where a huge Alsatian lay on a billiard table chewing the ivory balls: over the loo a verse was pinned which read: 'It's no use standing on the seat, the bloody crabs can jump ten feet'. One drunken lunch-time Dylan Thomas, telling us he was searching for a girl with an aperture as small as a mouse's ear-hole, led us to the offices of *Horizon* where Stephen Spender and Cyril Connolly, large as life, were sitting drinking tea with a girl wearing wooden, hinged utility shoes.

Later I went to visit Winter in the Pacifist Service Unit he had been sent to in Paddington. He never rebuked me for my election of the RAF groundstaff, was duly impressed by my having met Stephen Spender, although I had had to hurry from the tea-table to dispose of the quarts of brown ale we had drunk at lunch-time, and told me that he had decided when the war was over to become a doctor. He was working as a hospital orderly and the fact that he would, as a classical scholar, have to start from scratch with elementary science, disturbed him not at all. I noticed that the Pacifists quarrelled violently about whose turn it was to do the cooking, and even about the size of their portions of vegetable pie. Only Winter remained imperturbably calm. After supper we played 'The Brahms Fourth' again: and Winter told me he had fallen in love with a girl whose head emerged from a cigarette kiosk on Paddington Station. He planned, as soon as possible, to get to know the bottom half of her. When I returned to Oxford it had become, I thought, rather dull.

I did my best. I went to the Slade School (evacuated to the Ashmolean), I sat in the life class before large nude ladies who were pink on the side nearest the radiator and blue and goose-pimpled on the other. I tried to draw them. Occasionally the teacher, a small grey-haired man in a bow tie, smelling faintly of Haig and Haig, would come, sit beside me, do a perfect drawing of the radiator side and leave without comment. I met a girl at the Slade and we became 'engaged'. She was very gentle, very quiet, came from Wales. I took her and her mother out to dinner at the George and, overcome with excitement and too much Algerian wine, seized a silk-stockinged leg to fondle under the table. I looked up to see the mother was glowering at me over the dried egg omelette: I had chosen the wrong leg.

My engagement, like my enthusiasm for Oxford, wilted. I had been for a medical and was rejected, even for the RAF groundstaff: but Jack Beddington, son of a barrister my father knew, was in charge of films at the Ministry of Information.

Mr Beddington, many years before, had seen me do *Charley's Aunt* in my puppet theatre and I had apparently just the talent needed to help film the defeat of Fascism. I got a war degree in the shortest time available. It was given with no ceremony. and, luckily for me, there were no classes. It was just one utility B.A. A degree in a nutshell. I left Oxford station for the last time and went up the line to London, scene of all excitement, the Blitz and the Swiss Pub, the Coffee Ann and the book shops in Charing Cross Road, Winter's Pacifist Unit in Paddington, the Ministry of Information with the silver barrage balloons in the blue sky, long trips with cameramen and electricians, leaving to write dialogue and scenes about a war which wouldn't stay still to be photographed. I was away a long time, but now I go there often; because my son's at Oxford, with the time, and the talent, to do it all properly.

Michael Hamburger became a distinguished poet as well as a translator of the German Romantics. Peter Brook did a thousand times more for the theatre than the Oxford theatre did for him. Frank Hauser stayed at Oxford and gave it plays to enlighten and stimulate generations of undergraduates. My friend Oliver joined a Guards regiment, fell in love with the Regimental Sergeant Major and was asked to leave. Later he married one of his mother's friends and went to live in Portugal.

And Winter? Henry Winter took his science exams after the war and became a country doctor, with a practice in the West Country. From time to time, when I wanted to know the difference between right and wrong, I would visit him and drive with him on his visits. In the evening we would drink beer and listen to Brahms and wonder what had happened to everyone we knew at Oxford.

I went to see him less and less and then one day he called on me in London. He had fallen desperately in love with a married hospital cleaner and wanted my professional advice about a divorce from his wife. What happened next I only read about in the papers. The hospital cleaner refused to live with him, they quarrelled and he killed her with a shot gun. He drove his car into a wood and swallowed most of the drugs in his medical case. It was some while before they found his body.

I think about it so often and still I cannot explain it. All I can suggest is that Henry Winter suffered terribly from not having taken part in the violence which was waiting for us at the age we went to Oxford.

Nina Bawden

Nina Bawden was born Nina Mabey in 1925. She was educated at Ilford County High School and Somerville College. After leaving Oxford, she worked for a short time in town and country planning. She has been a Justice of the Peace since 1968, and reviews novels regularly. She has published sixteen novels; the most recent title is Afternoon of a Good Woman. *She has also written nine children's books, of which several, including* Carrie's War, *have been adapted for television. The latest,* The Peppermint Pig, *won the 1975* Guardian *award for children's literature. She is now married to Austen Kark, Controller, English Services, BBC.*

In 1943, Oxford was a university restored by war to a strange and timeless silence. By edict, no bells rang and there was almost no traffic; the uncluttered curve of the High, the spires and towers of the colleges, slept in the clean, moist, quiet air as in some old don's dream of peace. After three years as an evacuee in the dusty confines of a Welsh mining valley and a final school term spent dodging flying bombs and sleeping in sandbagged shelters in London, I felt I had arrived in Arcadia.

I went to Somerville for my interview wearing my grammar school uniform; navy gym slip, red blazer, and hat. Two girls were already waiting outside the Principal's study, talking in high, neighing, upper-class accents. The pitch of their voices and a kind of expensive glossiness about their hair and their skin made them seem like healthy young mares. As soon as I heard them and saw them I knew it had been presumptuous folly to imagine I might be allowed to join this exclusive society. I told myself I should have known that the educational ladder I had climbed so laboriously would turn into a greasy pole as I reached the last rung. While the girls chattered breathlessly on I stared proudly ahead and smiled secretly. They went into the Principal's room one by one, and, when their interviews were over, clung to each other. 'Oh my *dear,*' they wailed, 'wasn't she *terrifying*. Of course we haven't an *earthly*.'

I was much more intimidated by them than by the prospect of meeting the gorgon who clearly lay in wait for me in the study. I knocked and went in. Helen Darbishire rose from her chair by the fire and held out both hands. She said, 'Come in, dear child. I have been so looking forward to meeting you.'

For a second I thought there must be someone else in the room for those two, superior girls to have been so alarmed, but there was only this small, rosy woman, beaming at me with a kind, grandmotherly air. We sat by the fire and she asked me about my family, my parents and brothers, and what I hoped to do 'after Oxford'. I said (timidly) that I wanted to write and (rather more confidently) that I intended to do something to make our country a better place to live in once the war ended. I told her about the people in Wales I had lived with; the unemployment in the valleys throughout the 'thirties, the miners with silicosis, the children with rickets. I feared as I spoke that my indignation sounded naive and affected but she listened with an interested expression as I unfolded my master plan to set the world to rights and, when I had finished, it seemed only polite to show interest in her in return. I asked what was her special subject? She told me her great love was Wordsworth. I said I had read him 'of course' but found him rather indigestible. Too wordy, I said, too sentimental. And all that romantic tosh about Nature! Helen Darbishire, the great Wordsworth scholar, heard me out patiently. She said I should try reading him again in a year or so and I might find I felt differently: the age at which one 'came to' a poet was very important. She smiled and gave me a chocolate. She said, 'Dear child, we will be happy to have you and I believe you will be happy with us.'

The *tone* of that interview is what I remember most clearly from Oxford; a sweet note of courteous respect for one's callow opinions, followed by a gentle suggestion that one might, perhaps, think again. This slyly effective educational method takes time and, in that fifth year of war, there was time in abundance. There were so few undergraduates and, proportionately, so many dons. I was taught mostly in single tutorials and, to begin with, found this concentrated exposure alarming. Enid Starkie, with whom I read French for two terms, was less tolerant than Helen Darbishire. I read her a long, pompous essay on Baudelaire. She looked at me with her astonishing eyes, like blue fire, and said, 'Nina, tell me. Do you know anything *at all* about sex?' Then, when I changed schools to read Modern Greats, I was sent to Lord Lindsay, the Master of Balliol, to be taught Philosophy. This was meant as an honour for me but it turned out a dismaying experience for both of us. He had not taught girls before and could not believe I had never learned Greek. He seemed convinced (although he was too polite ever to say so) that I must be concealing this simple and fundamental skill out of some mysterious modesty. He was very kind, comforted me with hot, milky drinks, and tried to explain about Bishop Berkeley. Unfortunately, what was so simple to him, the flowing order and clarity of his beautiful arguments, became, as it dripped through the sieve of my ignorance, bewilderingly muddled and murky. I began to feel as if I stood on the threshold of a brightly-lit room but a locked door barred my entry. I went to Helen Darbishire and asked if I might change my tutor. I said I was too stupid for Lindsay. She laughed and kissed me and sent me to Dr MacKinnon of Keble, a large, untidy, engaging man who rolled on the floor and played with the coal in the scuttle, sometimes chewing a lump (with frustration, presumably) while I read him my essays.

One evening he said, when I finished, 'What you have said is profoundly true. . . .' I waited, holding my breath—had the door opened at last without my perceiving it? The fire hissed. He sighed and shook his heavy head. '. . . And profoundly unilluminating.' I said I was sorry. He offered me a sardine sandwich with his coaly fingers and I was brave enough to explain about the locked door. He gave a relieved shout of laughter. 'All you need is a key!' He suggested a pupil of his, a young don from Glasgow who taught me, very slowly and patiently, the basic words, the first principles; coaxing me into the sea of philosophical method as one might coax and encourage a nervous swimmer until one day I realized, with detached surprise, that although I was out of my depth, my head was safe above water. . . .

Ungrateful memory cannot supply that kind young don's name, nor the names of others who taught me. Only faces, voices, remain. There were two refugee European Professors. One wrapped me in a rug (Oxford, in wartime, in winter, was damply, bone-achingly cold) while he read Hobbes aloud in a Viennese accent, or flirted with me, saying I reminded him of a squirrel. 'You are so shy on the ground but once safe in the tree you chatter and chatter.' The other, a whey-faced giant with large, dangling limbs that seemed only loosely tethered to his vast frame, tried to persuade me that darning his socks was a more suitable occupation for a young girl than learning statistics. And there was a small, gallant Englishman who had been dropped into France during the Resistance and occupied our tutorial hours very pleasantly by telling me how interesting (though alarming, of course) his experiences had been, and showing me how to light fires without kindling, using neatly-folded newspaper fans. I cannot remember what else he taught me, any more than I can remember the contents of the lectures I occasionally attended. All that comes back, try as I will, are small things. G. D. H. Cole's red carpet slippers. And Lord David Cecil's more neatly shod foot gyrating in circles, his sweet, elfin face wildly grimacing as he read a paper to a literary society I sometimes attended.

There were so many societies. Standing in front of the notice board my first term, I was dazzled by the delights that they all (with the exception of the Bell Ringers and the Rowing Club) seemed to offer. I had only to join this, or that, for a whole new world to open before me, a glittering world of agile and civilized argument, of brilliant occasions at which I would shine, and, most important of all, meet young men. I longed for young men in a way that was not consciously sexual, nor even romantic. At my girls' grammar school I had often felt isolated; been laughed at for 'odd' ideas and opinions. This had made me nervous of my own sex and a first look round my fellow pupils at Somerville had not suggested I would fare any better at Oxford. Like the girls at school they seemed to fall into two distinct groups: the plain ones, with their damp, eager smiles, drooping skirts and wrinkled stockings, and the beautiful and self-sufficient young goddesses who were already, while I eyed them cautiously in the early days of that term, greeting each other in hall and Common Room with confident affection and laughter. I did not want to be trapped by the first group and I feared that the second would never admit me to their exquisite company. Men, I told myself, would be easier to get on with, more tolerant, as well as being more interesting. Once I knew some young men everything else, the social and intellectual excitements I longed for, would automatically follow.

This approach had its pitfalls. By the time I discovered that some of the plain girls were amusing, not all the goddesses quite unapproachable, and that the ideas some of my school friends had found so extraordinary were almost distressingly common at Oxford, I had spent a great deal of time doing things that secretly bored me, like watching rugger, or drinking beer, or discussing Wittgenstein. I joined the Welsh Nationalist Society in pursuit of a Welshman; painted flats for an Experimental Theatre Club production of *The Dog Beneath The Skin* because I admired (alas, from afar) a second-year medical student at Magdalen. Although I had no real desire to join the Oxford Union (the standard of debate was so low, most of the speakers so deep in youthful self-love they made me feel old and tired as I listened) I threw pamphlets and balloons from the public gallery in support of a motion to admit women because the President invited me to. That was Tony Pickford who, with his frail, beaky good looks, his style and intelligence, seemed to me the only exemplar in the whole university of what I had expected Oxford to be; the fact that he was known to be suffering from a fatal disease gave him an added, and awesome, romantic attraction.

Tony was 'so mature' we said to each other at Somerville. Maturity was a quality we prized very highly because most of us so conspicuously lacked it. We had come straight from school, our call-up deferred; the sprinkling of undergraduates over nineteen were either, like poor, clever, doomed Tony, and later, Ken Tynan (clever but silly we dubbed *him* at Somerville), unfit for the services, or refugees from battle-torn Europe, or even older wars. There were several aristocratic and charming Chinese with whom I celebrated V.J. night in London, one of whom claimed to have walked out of China across the Indian frontier 'disguised as a peasant'.

Our war barely touched us. It was there, in the background, but we had grown up with it and were used to it, grumbling on over our heads like so much tiresome, adult conversation. In the vacations we worked on farms and in factories, and during the term we were detailed to help the war effort for a fixed number of hours a week, but since my particular duty was listed as 'Entertaining American soldiers' I found it no hardship. All I ever did for those polite, bewildered young men, kicking their heels in the camps outside Oxford, was to serve as a waitress at the Red Cross Club in Beaumont Street. Although I knew other girls did more—it was clear that one undergraduate, who changed from her drab working clothes into butterfly garments made from home-dyed cheese cloth when she left college at six every evening, was not just setting forth to cut sandwiches—an obscure prudishness stopped me admitting it. Fellow students gossiped and giggled. I maintained that if this particular girl was more generous with her time and her company than the rest of us, it was largely because she understood the Americans better. She was studying sixteenth century English literature and it was well known that the American language was closer to Shakespearian than to modern English. It wasn't only a matter of accent, but of the way words were used. When this argument was received with coarse laughter, I backed it up by quoting the Master of Balliol. His war work with our allies consisted of taking occasional Philosophy seminars and he had told me that he sometimes found communication difficult. A statement like, 'Well, I guess I swing along with Berkeley here,' was, he said, a fair example of how two nations could be divided by a common language.

We were divided by more than that. These Americans were new to war; pampered, peace-time children with smooth, milk-fed faces, whose fledgling innocence about the kind of minor privations we were accustomed to, amused, astonished, and shocked us. Working at the Red Cross Club, we were often appalled by the amount of delectable food left on plates and casually thrown away.

Not that we were ever really hungry. We were rationed to two ounces of butter a week but college meals were adequate if dull, and cheaply supplemented by British Restaurants, by the Taj Mahal in the Turl where you could get a good lentil curry for ninepence, and by the Cake Factory at the end of the Banbury Road. Since men and women were not allowed in each other's colleges before lunch or after six in the evening, tea was the meal to which we invited each other and the Factory cakes were standard fare. Wholesome enough to begin with, they went stale very rapidly, and there were girls at Somerville who claimed to measure the strength of their host's affections by the freshness of the buns he offered them. If they were still moist, he cared enough to have risen early and bicycled to the Factory before they had sold their supplies for that day. However much he protested his passion, if his cakes had already acquired that familiar, desiccated texture, disintegrating drily on the tongue, he could not be considered really 'serious'.

This kind of innocent, romantic conjecture occupied a great deal of our time and attention. Most of us were virgins, though we often affected not to be, out of pride, and we yearned for love. During the vacations we sometimes fire-watched in the museums and libraries and, although I remember one eerily unpleasant week, spent sleeping on a camp bed between a mummy in a glass case and a stuffed alligator, what chiefly comes back, when I recall the part I played in the defence of my city, is sitting on the roof of the Bodleian Library playing planchette with an upturned glass and a circle of letters, trying to coax from the Fates the colour of my true love's hair.

I find I remember, not the important occasions, but the unimportant, private ones. I remember V.E. night, the tumbling bells, the joyful streets full of people, but chiefly because I met an undergraduate at Carfax with whom I fell in love. And although I can, with an effort, remember being unhappy sometimes, crouched chilly and bored in my room waiting for something exciting to happen, what I remember with ease are the happy times. A dance at Queen's, wearing a black taffeta dress I had bought second-hand; swimming naked in the river with my great friend, Mairi MacInnes, the poet; skating on Port Meadow when it flooded and froze one bitter January; the mysterious, pale beauty of the blacked-out colleges on clear, moonlit nights; evenings at the Playhouse, or the Classic Cinema in Walton Street where they always, invariably, seemed to be showing Hedy Lamarr in *L'Extase*. I remember the pleasure of my small, dull, box-like room where, for the first time, it seemed, I was able to be, or to become anyway, the person I wanted to be without interference except of a kind that only protected my freedom. I never found college rules irksome. To have to be back in college by eleven-fifteen was an excellent way of escaping, without appearing too unsophisticated, from unwanted sexual entanglements. For those who did not want to escape, there was a door into Somerville from the Radcliffe Infirmary that was usually open all night. If it was locked, for some unpredictable reason, there was always the high wall between the college and Walton Street. The only time I climbed it, I sat on the top and saw Helen Darbishire walking in the garden. She looked up and said, 'Who is that?' I was too frightened to answer. Helen had always been gentle with me, but she was not gentle with everyone. Already that term, she had sent two girls down—for idleness, I realized afterwards, but at the time I believed it was for climbing in after hours. But all she said was, 'Oh, it's only you, Nina. Do get down at once, child, and have a hot bath before going to bed. You might get a chill, sitting on that stone wall.'

My affection for Somerville is centred almost entirely on the small, warm, dignified person of Helen Darbishire. Beside her, other dons seemed remote and cold and I was never much involved in the internal affairs of the college. Among my contemporaries the ones I remember, apart from close friends, are those whose paths crossed mine later, or who have achieved some kind of fame. I remember Richard Burton partly for this obvious reason, but I would have remembered him anyway, for one strange, shared experience. He was an RAF cadet, up in my first year, on a two-term short course. He called at Somerville one afternoon to take me out to tea. He arrived, limping dramatically. He had cut his foot, he announced, and was in terrible pain. I was only moderately sympathetic, and it amused me to observe that his limp disappeared as we left college and walked to the tea shop. The shop was closed and we stood on the pavement, feeling hungry and cheated and looking, I imagine, disconsolate. A lady appeared from the house next door and said, 'Were you two young things wanting tea?' She was a small, bright, bony woman with an incisive, cultured voice. We smiled at her foolishly. She said, 'You poor dears, how disappointing. Will you let me give you tea?'

She swept us into her house, up to a first-floor drawing-room full of rich clutter: pictures and books and fine carpets. We sat where she told us, on a silk-covered sofa in front of the fire and eyed this grand room and each other awkwardly. She brought a huge, laden, silver tray and set it before us. She said she had to go out, to a lecture, but we could stay as long as we wanted, take our time over our tea, and just remember to close the front door firmly behind us when we had finished.

We were too amazed even to thank her—as I remember it, neither of us spoke a word. She vanished with a merry wave of her hand, a good fairy in this odd, Oxford pantomime; her heels clicked down the stairs, the door slammed. Richard said, 'Do you think she really belongs here? I mean, suppose she's the maid?' I said she wasn't a servant, you could tell by her accent; she was just kind, and eccentric. But his doubts set my mind working. The tea was delicious, the scones home made and thick with real butter. While Richard talked about the part he was playing in Nevill Coghill's production of *Measure for Measure,* I wondered if our generous hostess might be a madwoman, given to inviting strangers in from the highways and byways and feeding them the family rations. Or worse—a cunning, professional thief who had stolen a few priceless trinkets and was using us as a kind of camouflage screen, while she got safely away. Richard asked me if I would like to spend a weekend with him in London. He knew Emlyn Williams, he said, and we could stay at his flat. I shook my head, laughing nervously. Even if I had believed he knew Emlyn Williams—and I was sure I could recognize a boastful lie when I heard it—I would have been far too preoccupied to consider the offer seriously. As I ate greedily, I listened for the sound of a key in the door, a heavy step on the stair. Any minute now some large, angry man would burst in, accuse us of breaking and entering and telephone at once for the police. Of course they would realize we were innocent *finally,* but there would be a lot of unpleasantness first. And rightly so. We hadn't stolen anything, not intentionally, but we had eaten this tea—scones and jam and several ounces of butter. We would be humiliated, exposed as gluttons! I said I felt sick, and Richard agreed we should go. He seemed apprehensive himself suddenly, though his estimation of our hostess was more charitable than mine. He said, when we stood safe outside, 'She was very trusting, wasn't she? You'd have thought she'd be worried we'd walk off with the silver.'

I may have met him once or twice after that but what rings in my mind whenever I see that coarsely-pitted, middle-aged rake's face on the screen, is that one, awed, boyish remark. He is fixed in my memory at the age he was then as Margaret Thatcher (then Margaret Roberts) is still a plump, neat, solemn girl of nineteen. We came up the same term, both grammar school girls on State scholarships. Our first year college photograph shows us standing, side by side, in the back row, but my only clear memory of her is, appropriately, of a political argument. I was an active member of the Labour Club and it astonished me that she should have chosen to join the Conservatives. I told her so, one afternoon in Storm Massoda's room. Storm had a cold and was sitting with her head under a towel inhaling Friar's Balsam. Margaret and I argued over her shrouded head. The world was changing, I informed Margaret; to cling to the habit of deference towards the 'top people' which was all, to my mind, she was doing by belonging to the Conservative Club, was not only old-fashioned but a clear dereliction of duty. She and I, with our lower middle-class backgrounds, had been lucky to get into Oxford. We should not use our good fortune simply to join the ranks of the privileged but to make sure that when the war ended a new, happier, more generous society would take the place of the bad, old, selfish one. I cannot remember how she replied—I was enjoying the sound of my own voice too much to listen to hers—but sensing, perhaps, that my lofty sentiments were not having quite the missionary effect I had hoped for, I shifted my ground and pointed out that the Labour Club, besides being on the side of the angels, was also more *fun*. All the really lively and interesting people were members—Ernest Gellner, Michael McMullan. Margaret smiled, her pretty china doll's smile. Of course, she admitted, the Labour Club was more *fashionable*—a deadly word that immediately reduced my pretensions—but that in a way suited her purposes. Unlike me, she was not 'playing' at politics. She meant to get into

Parliament and there was more chance of being 'noticed' in the Conservative Club, just because most of the members were a bit dull and stodgy.

Perhaps I felt, briefly, put down. (Storm, rearing her head from her towel, said, 'You lost that round, Nina.') But if some of us in the Labour Club were playing at politics, we were soon playing in earnest. The whole Labour movement was riding on a high tide of hope, preparing for the election of 1945. A contingent of us went to Reading to fight for Ian Mikardo and found ourselves caught up in an extraordinary atmosphere of political excitement that everyone seemed to share—soldiers on home leave, old men in pubs, tired women in bus queues. We canvassed until our feet were blistered and our throats were sore. We slept in the Labour Party Hall, ate marmalade sandwiches at the People's Pantry, marched through the streets singing, 'Vote, vote, vote for Mr Mikardo, chuck old Churchill in the sea.' We were hungry and happy and enthusiastic, convinced that the New Jerusalem was dawning.

When we came back after the summer for our last year the shadows were already lengthening. The war was over and Oxford was changing. The ex-servicemen were returning, the scholars first, under Class B release, and they seemed to our eyes to be older than their actual years warranted; stern, purposeful men with wives and moustaches, taking over our university and reducing us, by their middle-aged presence, to the status of schoolchildren. There were compensations, of course: more excitement, more people—among them, Tony Crosland, John Wain (who published my first short story in *Mandrake*), Henry Fairlie, John Watney, my cousin, Dr Cushing, returning to Balliol—but on the whole we felt displaced uneasy, slightly resentful. Our cafés, our streets, our societies—the whole of our playground was invaded by demobbed soldiers and sailors and airmen; colleges where we had previously known almost everyone were full of strangers; the Radcliffe Camera, so comfortably adequate for its reduced, wartime population was busy as a mainline station at rush hour.

Everything, and everyone, seemed so busy, suddenly. The feeling that one was special, and favoured, was fading; a feeling exemplified for me by the retirement of Helen Darbishire and the appointment of Janet Vaughan as Principal of Somerville. She was a good appointment, an excellent, worldly, efficient woman whom I respected, but I missed Helen's especial quality which was to make me feel loved and valued, not for anything I had done, or was likely to do, but for the person I was at that moment.

Most people feel their generation is unique. I think mine has a real claim to be. The austerity of war concealed social and financial differences. Since we were all poor and shabby, neither poverty nor shabbiness troubled us. Since we expected to be recruited into the services when we went down, we were not fretted by personal ambition. If we worked hard, it was for the fun of working, not to get our feet on the bottom rung of yet another ladder, and that is a rare kind of freedom. We inhabited, in a world at war, a peaceful, privileged oasis, and since in the vacations we worked as postmen or as land girls or in munition factories, we knew how privileged we were. But perhaps the most important thing is that we were so few. People had time, not just to teach us, but to welcome us. Oxford—*my* Oxford—has a distinct personality. When I look back I see, not spires, or sun-baked quads, or famous libraries, but a kind, clever old lady, holding out her hands and saying, 'Come in, dear child.'

Antonia Fraser

Lady Antonia Fraser was born Antonia Pakenham in 1932 and brought up in North Oxford. She went to the Dragon School, and later to St Mary's Convent, Ascot. She was up at Lady Margaret Hall from 1950 to 1953 and read History, in which she got a second class degree. She has since written a number of books, including Mary Queen of Scots, *which won the James Tait Black Memorial Prize in 1969, and* Cromwell Our Chief of Men (*1973*).

I see it all in terms of clothes. Which is odd, as I have not been much interested in clothes as such—more in myself inside them—ever since. Nor were any of us endowed with enough money to be really exotic in our dress. It was just that we were all so obsessed with authority and conformity, that our clothes were the only way we could find to indicate our submission to the former, our desire for the latter. No one had yet heard of a life-style, let alone acquiring furniture or learning cooking as a manner of self-expression. We more or less had to fall back upon clothes. As a result, you could at least tell not so much what people were but what they wanted to be from their appearance. The famous spires were way above our heads. Oxford in my day was a city of dreaming wardrobes.

Again, the desire for conformity was odd, because in 1950 clothes rationing had only just ended. You would think we might have broken out. Yet most men were dressed with a formality I am sure they have never since surpassed. William, for example, wore garments of a solemnity which would not have disgraced a Victorian Prime Minister: it is good to think that he subsequently found the right niche for his wardrobe as the editor of an august newspaper. At least such positive sartorial statements made things simple. Caroline, who was a Communist and most dashing, wore a shirt of solid red. Shirley, who was not a Communist, but was a prominent (now famous) member of the Labour Party, wore a shirt of checked red and white.

Theatrical people, whom I longed to know but was too frightened to approach, wore a great deal of black. The men seemed to have black hair to go with it; in fact a black polo-necked jersey, plus some black hair and eyes to match was an almost certain sign of the Experimental Theatre Club. Members of it appeared to be preoccupied in talk, sophisticated talk by the sound of it, and generally to have a great deal of fun. My lot were, alas, too nervous ever to get involved. Besides, we didn't have the right things to wear.

When I arrived at Oxford, aged just eighteen but already the veteran of the hat department in a Bond Street store, the accounts typing pool of an advertising agency, and a Do-it-yourself, Débutante attempt which failed, my own wardrobe was an amalgamation of all the compliments I had ever received in these varied situations. In particular it was dominated by a colour called Cyclamen Pink. This was because someone had once murmured aloud the name of my Revlon lipstick: Pink Plum Beautiful, and added romantically: 'Which goes for you too.'

That moment marked the demise of Midnight Blue as the prime favourite of my wardrobe. It had enjoyed a long reign—ever since, in fact, my best school friend Lucy and myself had agreed that Midnight Blue brought out the mysterious haunting brilliance of my eyes etc. etc. And of course I was ready to sacrifice Cyclamen Pink in a crime of passion of an instant, if anyone suggested it: I was always one to consider a wardrobe well lost for love.

However, no one was yet ready to accept the humble offering of my appearance. Therefore although the group photograph of Lady Margaret Hall first-year students is in black and white, I know perfectly well that my bat-wing jersey was of Cyclamen Pink. My black and white check skirt, on the other hand, came from Goray and had permanent stitched pleats, which were invaluable for bicycling.

Bicycling . . . It is extraordinary to contemplate an age when one did not have automatic recourse to Marks and Spencer, when cheap clothes were nasty clothes and served you right for being poor. An age without denim, above all an age without trousers. I well remember my first sight of a pair of blue jeans outside a Western film: they were worn deadly clean, rather wide, with neat white turn-ups. The girl who sported them, appropriately named Joy, was sitting on the handlebars of her boyfriend's bicycle, screaming with happiness as she whirled along. Of course one did see the occasional pair of trousers: the women of the Experimental Theatre Club tended to wear them, in black naturally, to match their men. Within Lady Margaret Hall itself they were generally worn late at night, or by those who wished to indicate that they were in an 'essay crisis': I sometimes found putting on a pair of trousers was a convenient substitute for actually getting down to write. But on the whole we tottered along on our bicycles, lower-calf skirts, stockings, suspenders and all. For this was the age of the stocking—I was still in theory darning my stockings at Oxford —an age before tights, before straight skirts, before mini-skirts. Everything we wore inevitably tangled in our bicycle wheels. I lived on a total allowance of £60 a year, which I could only make do by eliminating altogether all shop cleaning and shoe mending. Even today I cannot see oil marks without recalling those endless ravages of the bicycle to which all our wardrobes were subject.

The problem became particularly acute when it came to parties. In those days a party dress *was* a party dress, often of taffeta which needed a frilly petticoat underneath to sustain it: Lady Margaret Hall lurked at the end of Norham Gardens, a great red neo-Georgian dragon, ten minutes from public transport if you wore high heels, anyway my high heels, and that was infrequent. Taxis were beyond most people's means (although of course we did occasionally hire them as with many things beyond one's means). But the real answer was the bicycle. The truth was that our clothes, like ourselves, were romantic but hopelessly impractical for the lives we were supposed to lead.

The same air of unreality attended the love life of my particular circle. The rules of Lady Margaret Hall were strict and rumoured to be implacable: i.e. once you were caught breaking them, you would be put out. There were no late passes after midnight under any circumstances. You even needed permission to go to London; officially nights could never be spent away. No men were admitted to the college before lunch-time, and they had to leave by supper at seven. There were no locks on the doors. I was told that my Aunt Julia's generation at Somerville had been compelled to put the bed out in the corridor when entertaining a gentleman to tea. We did not exactly have to do that. But there was the same air of challenging restriction, obstacles which existed to be surmounted.

For of course we did surmount them. We all went to dances, came back at 2 am and climbed in by whatever the popular route of the moment might be. As our ball dresses were in the same high-flown style of our party clothes, it was fashionable to remove the dress first, before attempting the climb. Whether it was better to throw your dress over *first* and risk sticking on the wall, or count on your escort being able to lob it over afterwards to join you (and then the dress might stick) was the subject of much earnest theological discussion at breakfast. Shattering experiences were discussed. Later we all discovered that the easiest method was to sleep out altogether: in my case I hit on the expedient of returning for breakfast wearing a black veil, as though I had been to early Mass.

We were also wonderful at surmounting problems by assuming they did not exist. It was assumed, for example, that all my immediate circle lived in a state of perpetual virginity, which would not have disgraced St Ursula and her eleven thousand companions, because nothing, but nothing, ever terminated it. It was tacitly understood that one could survive the most delightful experiences untouched: perhaps we were like the

Aga Khan, on whose lips wine turned to water. At any rate what we firmly believed of ourselves, we naturally believed of our best friends. And this, despite all the evidence to the contrary which a life of lockless doors and endless spontaneous borrowing of other people's belongings (from Stenton's *Anglo-Saxon England* to Earl Grey's Tea) inevitably produced. Such incidents, such unplanned interruptions, were never discussed afterwards. Our talk amongst ourselves concentrated on love. We sometimes indicated gently that love might justify the ultimate sacrifice, that we might soon find it hard to refuse. But no one ever batted a cynical eyelid. We were the Romantic Generation.

If sexual experiences were theoretically minimal, social expectations were on the contrary great. Once there was a Drag Hunt Ball just outside Oxford, to which I had unaccountably failed to be asked. I asked God to do something about it, and God recklessly killed poor King George VI, as a result of which the Hunt Ball was cancelled. Not all social problems were solved so cataclysmically. Saturday night, for example. It was awful to be found dining in hall on Saturday night, because it obviously meant that no one had asked you out. Most of us preferred to heat up tinned Scotch broth in our rooms rather than face that. If caught, alone and inexplicably loitering, it was conventional to snatch up a book of poetry (Donne was rather smart) and indicate sudden world-weariness, a preference for *la vie intérieure*. . . .

The total lack of the telephone, and the existence of the college message service, brought a formality to social relationships which suited us very well. There were little notes of invitation, with initials in the corner, and there were occasional anonymous approaches ('I am the man who tweaked your gown impudently at the history lecture') as well as the equivalent of the heavy breather. 'Dear Miss Pakenham, I could not help noticing in the Bodleian Library yesterday that we share a taste for German mediaeval bishoprics. This encourages me to suppose that we may have other tastes in common. . . .'

We all of us swore that we never accepted anonymous invitations, and this may in fact have been true as we all of us also lived in mortal fear of being seen out with anyone wearing a college-crested blazer, or worse still, a college scarf. Blazers without crests were esteemed patrician, but the college scarf rule was absolute, and none of us would have dreamt of breaking it. Thus missing, I have no doubt, the company of almost every interesting man then at Oxford.

As well as being pathetically (or anyway romantically) snobbish, we were of course frightful cadgers. There was no question of paying for one's own meal: they were the men, weren't they? Anyway, we were the young ladies. I think the only man who ever got me to pay anything for myself while I was at Oxford was my brother Thomas, whose time there happened to coincide with my own. And then it was only because he actually walked out of the restaurant, leaving rather more than half the bill at my disposal.

Anne was an immensely popular girl at Oxford, not especially pretty, but with a bright smile which worked wonders of free feeding. I remember one young man telling her bitterly when she was in her third year: 'Anne, you are made of food. Food paid for by other people.' Anne looked absolutely amazed, and temporarily even hurt, before philosophically helping herself to yet more asparagus out of season—we were at the Bear at Woodstock at the time. I certainly thought it the most bizarre remark: only subsequent reflection has told me how true it must have been.

At the time my own peach-fed appearance consisted of long brown curly hair and pink cheeks. I was also distinctly plump, or rather as I put it then and still prefer to put it now, rounded. It had not yet occurred to me that this particular appearance need not necessarily be accepted for the rest of time. It was possible, for example, to choose to be blonde, have short straight hair, and even be a good deal less plump. In my second year, these lessons began to come home to me. In general our appearances improved. Take Melissa, my Oxford best friend.

Melissa was small and sweet, a combination which was ravishingly popular. It also enabled her to overcome, most successfully, the rumour that she was incredibly clever. The rest of us putative scholars had to rely on our incredibly silly behaviour to give the unflattering story the lie.

On arrival at Lady Margaret Hall, Melissa was equipped with princess-line coats and princess-line dresses, made by her mother's dressmaker. I marked her down as a bit of a princess herself, not least when I noted her leaving for Morning Service at Christ Church in a fetching velours hat, presumably made by her mother's hatmaker. On these occasions Melissa was always much fêted, if not within the portals of the cathedral itself, at any rate immediately afterwards, and she never failed to secure at least three invitations to *post cathedra* sherry by Old Etonian members of the college (a coveted combination).

In spite of the influence of *Brideshead Revisited,* allegedly making Catholicism so elegantly desirable, there was no doubt that you got a much better class of invitation at Christ Church Cathedral of a Sunday morning than you did at the Roman Catholic Chaplaincy just opposite. My own attendances at this unremarkable building never resulted in anything better than invitations to go brass-rubbing or beagling from people who had been at school with my brother. And on one occasion I actually had to make do with an invitation *from* my brother (we would both share the costs of petrol to go and see John Betjeman, who was not however expecting us). Disillusioned, I abandoned the Chaplaincy and took to going to a short sharp Mass at St Benet's Hall in St Giles, where there were no rewards to be had, but no disappointments either.

Melissa's numerous admirers were easily marked out by their appearance. A Melissa Man possessed very long legs, encased in very tight cavalry twill trousers, cut quite as tightly indeed as denim now, but I think the objective was different, more *cherchez le cheval* than *cherchez la femme*. Anyway it must have been extremely convenient for bicycling. A Melissa Man had wonderfully thick hair, generally fair, on which in colder weather he reverently placed a tweed cap, the tweed however never by any chance matching the material of his habitual tweed jacket. In really cold weather a Melissa Man added a British warm overcoat. I was expected to mark down Melissa Men, as hunters note the movements of rare animals on the plains of Africa, but I was also expected to keep off them myself. This was comparatively easy, because few of them showed any signs of keeping on me.

For one thing, by my second year I had decided that my style was Vivacious Gypsy. Cyclamen Pink was a thing of the past, and I had acquired a red felt skirt, circular, terminated by black braid; together with a V-necked black jersey (which could be adjusted off the shoulders for quick changes), a black elastic belt and black stiletto heels, this was a uniform which saw me through every conceivable social occasion. I loved my red skirt as a young squire loves his sword, and in order to save it from the depredations of my bicycle, I even took to spending special nights out, out of sheer affection for it. Also, as Nancy Mitford's Lady Montdore believed in the sparkle of diamonds round the ageing face, I now believed in the magnetism of earrings. I had quite a collection. Indeed, had I been a pirate, I would have dazzled the Spanish Main: I often lost one of them on my way out to dinner on my bicycle. It would tinkle down into the leafy gutter of Norham Gardens. I gallantly rode on, wearing the survivor.

In our second year, things were on the move altogether. Melissa was asked out by an Indian (what should she wear?) and the Oxford University Conservative Club card had long ago disappeared from her mantelpiece. The Oxford Labour Club card had never stood much chance on mine: it was there when I arrived, in honour I presume of my parents, both of whom had stood in their time as Parliamentary Labour candidates for Oxford City. Like an unwelcome presentation plant, my membership wilted and finally died. I certainly never paid for it.

We did sometimes dine at the Union as guests: dinner

jackets for men, long dresses for girls. It was an admissible activity, so long as you were careful whom you went with. I once went with David, a licensed eccentric, but apparently his licence did not extend to taking me to the Union. My cousin Henrietta was the most tolerant person I knew, but it was in her other capacity as a remorseless observer of the social scene that she hissed at me: 'You made a great mistake being seen at the Union with David. Everyone says so.' I certainly wasted an evening. I cannot remember one word of the debate. Although it transpires by now that I was at Oxford with most of the leading politicians of our day, that whole side of life passed me by like a dream. Politics at Oxford was not at all what I had in mind. I had had quite enough at school of my father's unconventional Socialist views: 'A *Labour* minister?' someone would exclaim. 'Well, do you know this joke about the Labour government: They're like a bunch of bananas. First of all they're yellow.' Yes, I did know it. I'd heard it before.

By my third year I had got thin and fallen in love. It was lucky that the two processes coincided, otherwise it would have meant not one but two new wardrobes. I also discovered the pleasures of work—a subject, it will be noted, which has been singularly absent from this account: this, despite the fact that all the girls of my generation had to write two essays a week, in contrast to the men who only wrote one. Even with the minimal amount of study, this meant that our work must have taken up an enormous proportion of our time. The fact was that it did not take up the same proportion of our thoughts. Suddenly, in our final year, it was all different. We rediscovered that genuine scholarly enthusiasm which ages before had secured us those coveted places at Oxford. We felt again that pure love for history or literature which had once given rise to the rumour that we were incredibly clever. We regretted passionately that we had so long disproved the rumour by our incredibly silly behaviour.

It was of course rather late in the day for us foolish virgins (as we naturally still were) to trim our lamps. For three years

I shared tutorials with Carol, a wise virgin, who subsequently got the First she richly deserved. From the start her grim grey jerseys and baggy tweed skirts had indicated an insatiable appetite for work, which her behaviour had never belied. Now, at last, my friends and I found ourselves attired in the accoutrements of study. Jenny, my most beautiful friend, with the white face and red-gold hair of a Madonna, took to leaving make-up off altogether. As a result, she looked not so much earnest as consumptive. We were all much impressed by her appearance. Lipstick with us all became a rare occurrence. The object of my love was not at Oxford at all, and you could tell of his potential arrival on a Saturday evening by the fact that I donned a newly-suave corduroy dress of Forest Green—yes, Forest Green was in, its colour showing up the mysterious haunting brilliance of my complexion etc. etc. But I still wore earrings, a pair of dangling earrings with golden bells in them, giving a sparkle to the working face.

I thought a good deal about St Augustine, my favourite saint, and the fact that he too had been a bit of a late developer. How fortunate that I had learned from a novel by Ethel Mannin the correct translation of his famous words: 'Too late have I loved thee . . .'! Not so much too late as 'Late have I loved thee, oh beauty ever ancient, ever new, late have I loved thee'. I was most inspired by this text.

But of course, whatever the good luck of St Augustine, it was actually too late for me. Where our final exams were concerned, we were like very old people, who were nevertheless quite unprepared for death. Surely it couldn't happen to us? We didn't *feel* old. We were certainly not ready for death-by-examination. In fact, by June, the season of Schools, we were just getting into the stride of our work, enjoying it, making little discoveries, this after all was what it was all about, what we had come to Oxford *for*. . . . Why did no one ever tell us?

Too late. The date of the exams arrived. And suddenly the authorities imposed upon us, to our great surprise, something we had totally forgotten: a uniform! This was the so-called academic dress, the sub fusc or black and white clothing which was regulation wear for Schools. Men had to wear dark suits, white shirts and white ties. In girls, it took the equivalent form, black stockings, white shirts, black ties, black skirts. I had my fantasies about it. Sheer black nylons with seams, a white transparent nylon blouse with billowing sleeves, a floppy black velvet artist's bow as tie? It didn't work. The rules were strictly enforced. Ironically enough, it was in academic dress that for the first and last time at Oxford, I succeeded in what I suppose had always been my aim: looking exactly like everybody else.

Alan Coren

Alan Coren was born in 1938 and educated at East Barnet Grammar School and Wadham College. He got a First in English in 1960, spent a further year at Oxford in research, and went to America on a Commonwealth Fellowship in 1961. After two years at Yale and Berkeley, he returned to work for Punch, *where he is currently Deputy Editor: he also has columns in the* Daily Mail *and* The Times. *He was Rector of St Andrews, 1973–6. His books include* All Except The Bastard, The Dog It Was That Died, The Sanity Inspector, Golfing For Cats, The Collected Bulletins of President Idi Amin, *and, for children*, The Arthur Books.

Had I ever kept a diary, there is little doubt but that the entry for October 4, 1957, would have read very much like one of the hotter numbers of the *Anglo-Saxon Chronicle*.

It was that racy tabloid, you'll instantly recall, which first established the link between event and augury on a popular basis, thus laying the foundation for Great British Journalism. No fact was permitted to the record unless the editorial staff could relate it to fraught speculation of the most sensational and catchpenny order. Thus: 'This night, several comets were seen in the sky, and Bishops Aelforth, Aelwyth, Aelstryn all fell down foaming and died. Cattle went mad. A frog in Mercia ate a horse'.

It took the *Daily Mirror* nine hundred years to catch up. Yet even they, as a sift through the relevant file copy will show, did not notice that the moment at which I first alighted upon Oxford station, at 9 pm in the evening, was the exact same moment at which a far Soviet forefinger pressed a button to chuck the first earth satellite into brief orbit, ushering in, according to taste, either a new era of wonderful hope for all mankind or the end of the world.

Either way, it was good to be getting off the London train that day.

You felt somebody.

They were epochal days. Following the Suez triumph of a mere twelve months before, England basked in the high noon of Imperial magnificence. A new Elizabethan age had dawned, and nowhere was its mood more keenly felt than in Oxford itself. We had a radiant young queen—he had the room directly above mine, as a matter of fact—and, in Harold Macmillan, a Prime Minister who brought new meaning to undergraduate cabaret. Vivian Fuchs was belting towards the South Pole, Her Majesty Elizabeth II was rehearsing her very first televised Christmas message, Network Three leapt that winter from Auntie's fecund womb so that henceforth no undergraduate was forced to shave without the accompaniment of Pushkin, and, in general, it was a jolly good time to be British.

It is some indication of the depth and breadth of the general optimism that my only problem, that October, was an *embarras de richesse*. As the world was my oyster, so Oxford was my winkle: the question was, with which of my myriad pins should I attack it?

There was sport.

I had come from a rowing school. Situated as it was in lush council surroundings, School (as the jargon had it) lay no more than half a mile from Oaklands Park, that stretch of rolling chickweed which separates Foskett Bros (Grocers) Ltd from Standard Telephone & Cable, in verdant North London. Each summer afternoon, we day boys—the school being co-educational, many senior couples were given to spending the night in the bicycle shed—would stroll across to the park and buy such hours of boating as the fruits of our mugging would allow.

In consequence of this regular training, I became something of an oar, able quite often to keep both blades in the water simultaneously; and it was therefore only natural that my thoughts turned to the Oxford boat.

It was even more natural, after my first glimpse of the river, that they turned away again. There, in the chill fog, hundreds of young men paddled about in their underwear, their skin tripe-dimpled, their teeth leaving on the icy air the impression of a Flamenco eisteddfod. I, who had never touched oar without first buttoning my herringbone overcoat tightly about me, was shocked: no beer-crates cheered their skinny water-logged shells, no gramophones sang at their sterns, no busts broke the heaving vertical contours! This was not rowing as we that love the true sport know it.

I settled my smart rowing balaclava more snugly over my ears, and walked briskly away. And it was not long after that I determined to remain a stranger to all Oxford sport; for it was not in boating alone that the curious impositions of a cloistered other-worldly community had changed those games in which I was sparklingly proficient into weird unplayable mutants.

Football, to take a further example, was played with an ovoid, a shape calculated to knock out the eye of any centre-forward uncircumspect enough to attempt to head it, while tennis, though played in the correct manner (i.e. knocking the ball against a convenient wall), involved a tiny black pellet that flew back off the brickwork with such speed and incalculability that the risk of having one's cigarette rammed down one's throat far outweighed any pleasure one might have taken in the game.

And as cricket was played by these suicidal eccentrics with a hard spherical rock which, if I'm any judge, would have torn the spade from one's hands and hurled its fragments all over the beach, I quickly abandoned all thought of a sporting career, and turned instead to the stage.

I suppose that neither before nor since that explosion of dramatic talent in the late 'fifties was Oxford as blessed with so dazzling an array of actors, directors, dramatists, and, above all, theorists of theatre. In the twin wakes left by the churning screws of Beckett and Osborne, literally hundreds of brilliant heads bobbed in the choppy water; that all have now sunk without trace points only to the cynical commercialism of the

West End theatre management clique whose bourgeois stranglehold on taste ensures that profit, comprehensibility and pleasure are put before the challenges represented by thrilling experimentalists willing to transmute their nervous breakdowns into wonderful mimed symbolism or dramatize the Marxist view of the Black Death in gripping blank verse tetralogies.

Wadham, in those wonderful mould-breaking years, was the very cockpit of the struggle for expression. Young men whose names were on the tongue of everyone who cared about untranslated Rumanian allegory rightly eschewed the soft options of Shakespeare and Shaw in pursuit of their mission; which was to cull as many dramatic fragments as they could from the pages of very thin German literary magazines and stage them for the delectation of like-minded friends. Such was the dedication of these young producers to the concept of alienation, one would often see audiences running from their productions like field mice from a combine harvester.

This is not, of course, to say that the classical theatre was ignored: I myself sat through a powerful reading of *Charley's Aunt* in a freezing Walton Street hall, the object of which was to elicit the fundamental (yet until then unrevealed) conflict in the play between the heterosexual and homosexual elements in man's character. Spellbound, practically, I came to realize that Brandon Thomas had a message for all of us which, provided it was put across slowly enough, might very well change our entire view of what theatre was for.

As for the young lions who were actually writing original material, their myriad play-titles somehow escape me now, but I give the gist and temper when I say they were called things like *Waiting For Harris, Waiting For Rita, Waiting For Arthur, Waiting For Morrison* and so on, or else reflected the shrewd fancy of the time for Ionesco and Simpson and peopled the college stages with characters who believed themselves to be old beer bottles.

In short, it was a wonderful time to be alive, and encouraged by the general thespian frenzy, I threw myself into the world, nay, universe, of Oxford theatre. Michael Kustow, a Wadham colleague who later wrote a book in which he referred to himself throughout merely as K (a diffidence borrowed, with characteristic skill, to amuse those who knew and loved him) invited me to take part in a reading of *Chicken Soup With Barley*, one of the several thousand seminal masterpieces of the period. The production itself does not stick in the mind, but the preliminaries do; the cast had to lie on the floor of a cell in Somerville and perform a series of eurhythmic contortions which Mr Kustow had picked up from some Actors Studio manual of arms. After our reading from the shared Penguin, which was of course enormously enriched by the isometric vorspeise, I recall that Arnold Wesker sat rapt while Michael explained what the play was about. It was one of those precious moments when youth and age, innocence and experience, Academe and Life, theory and practice, suddenly all fused together into one lunatic whole.

After that, I auditioned for a major big-budget production of Aristophanes' *The Frogs*, designed, as I recall, to bring out both the Freudian undertones and the working-class *ur-politik* inherent in the original Greek. So great an impact did this audition make on the producer that I was immediately assigned the job of organizing the seating. I do not wish to boast, but I have heard it said that men still talk in Oxford about the verve and authority I brought to the hiring of chairs and van alike.

I retired from the theatre soon after that. I used to go to see Oxford productions quite often, though. Even now, almost twenty years on, I am unable to watch Gordon Honeycombe read the *News At Ten* without recalling the magic experience of his Othello. As the trade figures spill impeccably from his lips, I cannot forbear from expecting him, any second now, to break into 'Sonny Boy'.

It was by now the summer of 1958, and in the various waterways around Oxford the punts coagulated sluggishly into log-jams as their polers hove to in order to read aloud to one another.

Through the mists of spiralling gnat, snatches of Salinger and Scott Fitzgerald filtered from boat to boat: the fashions that summer were *The Catcher In The Rye, The Great Gatsby* (resurrected by some nostalgic spirit at the Bodley Head), *Lord Of The Flies, The Alexandria Quartet* (or, rather, trilogy; *Clea* still writhed in Durrell s churning head, accreting metaphor) and *Our Man In Havana.* These were the mass-consumption biggies, though a few rarer souls had forked out their fifteen-bobs on Iris Murdoch's *The Bell* and Angus Wilson's *The Middle Age of Mrs Eliot.* Almost everyone had bought *Doctor Zhivago,* though it would have been possible to put all those who had actually finished it into one punt with no threat whatever to buoyancy.

It was primarily in consequence of Salinger's brush-fire success that some ninety-five per cent of the people one met that summer were writing novels. Why it had taken five years for the book to catch on I have no idea; all I do know is that in Wadham it was impossible to sleep at night for the clatter of Olivettis reverberating around the Old Quad, scattering Jacobean shards onto the unconscious drunks beneath, and I have no reason to believe other colleges were any quieter. All the novels got as far as page forty-one and contained much iridescent description of blackhead and bra-strap; it was as if Salinger were some kind of Pied Piper whose fanatical followers disappeared into the rock at page forty-one.

Wadham contained two energetic typists who actually managed to complete whole novels, and, what is more, get them published: David Caute and Julian Mitchell released their *oeuvres* to a slavering world, and the London agent became overnight a permanent ornament to the Oxford scene. In the embering 'fifties, it was impossible to go to a literary party without finding a pin-striped man from A. D. Peters or Curtis Brown leaning on the mantelpiece with the easy nonchalance that betokens the small fish in an even smaller pool and eyeing the bustier nurses while passionate literati informed him that they were currently engaged upon a revolutionary prose project that would make Henry James stand on his ear.

And then there was poetry, or Dom Moraes, as it came to be called. Dom's success having carried beyond the city limits, he was the focus of much ambivalent admiration: I recall in particular one occasion upon which he rushed in to inform the aforementioned J. Mitchell, who also assumed he wrote poetry, that a London actress—having found herself in the Moraes chambers with their tenant unaccountably absent and possibly escorting some other lady—had torn up all his manuscripts. There came into Mitchell's kindly eyes an odd light that, had it been spotted by le Duc de la Rochefoucauld might well have sent the old aristo scurrying off to write 'Dans l'adversité de nos meilleurs amis, nous trouvons quelque chose qui ne nous déplaît pas.' But, then, he was not there, so the moment will have to be allowed to pass into literary history without benefit of speculation.

It was soon after this that Julian and I went into the movie business together. Seeing himself, I believe, as some kind of Wykehamist Sacha Guitry, Julian temporarily laid aside his various careers as scholar, poet, novelist, journalist and wit in favour of searching for fresh fields to be conquered on. He bought an old 16mm Bolex and several miles of black-and-white stock, and invited me to be the cameraman to the *nouvelle vague* with which he intended to engulf Oxford, and, indeed, the world.

Film had become very big with the intelligentsia by then. It was always referred to unarticled, as in 'That is what film is all about', 'Antonioni has, how shall I put it, a *sense* of film,' and so on, and at the Scala Cinema in Walton Street, anyone who cared anything about film would flock to the latest epic examination of trauma on the Scandinavian foreshore. Directors became currency, as once stars had been; subjects were irrelevant: 'I thought we might see a Bergman and have a curry afterwards' was, by 1959, the most familiar phrase in the English language.

Now, had the good Ingmar never existed, nor Fellini and Buñuel, there is every chance that Mitchell and I might have made quite a decent little documentary about that area of working-class Oxford called Jericho. Indeed, I thought that's what we *were* making: we would potter the streets in Julian's old Morris Minor, whacking away at characterful faces, broken windows, derelict churches, all that fraught stuff, and by the end of the month, I personally reckoned we had enough poignant footage to persuade Cartier Bresson to chuck in the towel and open a tobacconist's.

But when we came to cut the thing and edit it (at a charming Cheyne Walk house gutted to make a film factory by its owner, the excitable Jeremy Sandford), it became clear to me that what Julian had believed we were making was an agglomeration of *Citizen Kane, Le Chien Andalou* and *Alexander Nevski*.

With every pretension complete, it was sent to the Edinburgh Festival, where, according to Julian (I had by this time walked away from the carnage), it was Mentioned. In what terms it was Mentioned I dare not begin to guess, though references to Old Bolex were doubtless rife, if I'm any judge of the low level of cinematic wit.

'Of course, there's always journalism' was a phrase that rang round the neighbourhood, I recall. Its first peal tended to echo the clack as the Olivetti typed 42 at the top of a virgin sheet, announcing that the novel had come to its premature (yet inevitable) end, and its author hurled the machine aside the better to assume the pose of poor Chatterton conked out on his ottoman. Literary snobbery being what it was, is, and doubtless always will be, failed novelists invariably expect that when their Muse gathers her soft skirts and runs, the Fleet

Street whore will slide from her doorway and grab them to her withered dugs with the hungry gratitude of all unloved things.

That this never happens demonstrates only that most aspirant novelists know as little about life as they do about writing. But, in Oxford, at least, their arrogance had a certain naive charm.

'I suppose I could always do the Ken Tynan/Bernard Levin/ Nick Tomalin stuff', the lovely lads would sigh irritably; and would then hightail it into Oxford journalism where they immediately gave evidence that if any subsequent newspaper let them nearer anything more challenging than the local flower show, it could mean only that their father had been at school with the paper's proprietor.

Basically, there were, in those days, three sorts of undergraduate journal: there was *Cherwell,* a news-sheet which misspelt the wrong information and then illustrated it with a photograph of something else printed upside down; there was *Isis,* a literary magazine packed with verse so free you couldn't even give it away and short stories about people staring at cracks in the ceiling while they waited for the abortionist to ring; and there were Little Magazines, called *Boil* and *Fart* and so on, most of which owed so much to Allen Ginsberg that if they ever paid the old fraud back he'd have enough oaths to keep a town the size of Cleveland swearing until well into the next century.

I myself had some considerable success with *Isis* during 1959, mainly on the strength of a donkey jacket I had purchased second-hand in a Folly Bridge pawnshop, an accent that went with it, and a habit I cultivated of cracking my knuckles, narrowing my eyes to slits, and spitting tobacco pips out with no concern for targets. Thus it was that I became an authentic working-class voice, and sold many stories to a succession of gentlemanly editors each of whom was allowed to believe he had discovered Frank Norman alive and well and living in the Thames Valley. That I secretly committed *Brideshead Revisited* to memory while listening to Albinoni in a mustard quilted housecoat was, of course, information that never went beyond the joss-choked dig in which it happened.

There was also at that time a curious journalistic operation in progress, cobbled together by a small group of prep-school japesmiths who had latched on to the immortal truth that if they said 'bum' or 'nigger' often enough, they could make one another fall down and roll helpless on the Axminster. In order to bring this illimitable delight to a wider world, they founded a magazine called *Parson's Pleasure*. It subsequently became *Private Eye*, where it has gone from weakness to weakness.

I seem, here and there in this chronicle of gelded youth, to have hinted that class still ran its fading blue thread through the social woof of Oxford.

And so it did, albeit oddly.

For in these, the immediate post-Angry years, new heroes and new hierarchies had burgeoned, overgrowing the old. New prides were everywhere, which in turn meant new arrogances and vanities, which in their turn meant new pretensions and deceptions. One was constantly bumping into people who referred to themselves as one, blushed, and corrected the offending emblem to *you*. Tall willowy lads with inbred conks and hyphens might be found, in the dead of any night, burning their cavalry twills and chukka boots in lay-bys along the A40, thereafter changing into blue jeans and Marks woollies. They stood before mirrors, abbreviating their drawls and lopping their aitches; they defended, with a heartbreaking desperation, their entitlement to membership of the new order.

Thus:

'Yes, well, I mean werl, my father, that is to say me dad, *did* send me to Stowe, but that doesn't, don't, mean I'm one of your mindless bleeding plutocracy'.

Or:

'I'm not saying the family aren't merchant bankers *now*, I'm only trying to point out that in the early fourteenth century they were all solidly behind Wat Tyler. I mean, bugger me, squire, there's nowt tha can teach me about t'working-class struggle, tha knows!'

And:

'Oh God, roll on my twenty-first, I'll be able to renounce my title and just be plain Auberon Fitzwilliam de Brissac Giles Corkseeping-ffearfful!'

But there were still, you may be amazed to hear, a few glaring class indicants; and the most interesting of these, or certainly the one most fraught with ramification, was sexual. It was a general principle among privately educated male undergraduates that one walked about holding hands with well-born gels whom one planned eventually to marry, but screwed nurses; whereas the rest of us walked about holding hands with nurses whom we planned eventually to marry, and screwed well-born gels. Oxford could be said to divide along a Lord Chatterley/Oliver Mellors line; and it really was the most super fun, as we used to say to the supine ruins as we reached for our shoes and detached the bicycle clips from our fallen underwear. It was like being a member of some sexual fifth column, dare I say crack division, dropped into alien territory to infiltrate and sabotage.

I myself was less conscious than many of the lads of the political implications of pleasure. I have heard that there *were* blokes who, at fever pitch in the cloistered confines of some curtained St Anne's eyrie, shouted to their panting ex-Roedean victim: 'And this one's for Jarrow!', though I cannot swear to the accuracy of the report.

What was certain was that these were interesting sexual times. It was the period of, if you like, the phoney permissive war, a time of promiscuous false alarms, and daring border raids, and wild rumour, and occasional staggering achievements by bold pioneers. Undergraduates could, for example, still be sent down for being caught *in flagrante delicto*, but this did not stop some of them from pulling coups which, had they known about them, would have sent college authorities scurrying to the statute books to seek among the footnotes a precedent for garrotting. I recall one particular occasion on which a Wadham friend, a studious introverted lad with a passion only for (or so we imagined) chess, took two foreign girls from the St Giles School of English to his room in the Wren Building and kept them there for five days. We learned of this ongoing tryst only on the fourth day, when, unable any longer to contain our speculation, we stopped him on what had become one of his regular journeys between the JCR bar and his quarters with teetering platefuls of tomato sandwiches, to enquire the reason for this sudden Vitamin C craving.

He revealed to us that one of the girls was Portuguese, the other Norwegian, and that both of them had enrolled only the week before. None of the three spoke the language of any of the others. I never learned what subsequently became of the girls (the hero returned to his chess and introspection on the sixth day), but I still, even today, occasionally divert myself with thoughts of what they must have made of this induction into English mores.

Do they still tell their goggle-eyed co-nationals of that strange race of pasty troilists beyond the foam who subsist entirely on tomatoes and are content to communicate only from loin to loin?

I do not propose to dwell upon the many deep and meaningful and very, very wonderful relationships I shared, and where I could not share enjoyed, in those distant days. All the girls were, Oxford being the lusty pastoral idyll it was, extraordinarily beautiful, brilliantly witty, by turns tender and inventive, passionate and sophisticated: in short, successive amalgams of Zuleika Dobson, Zelda Fitzgerald, Princess Casamassima and Catherine the Great, particularly a wonderfully vital young seat-trimmer from Morris Motors who was Beatrice to my Dante for nearly a week in early 1960, who had a bust you could stand carriage-clocks on, and who is selected to represent her fortunate sorority in this narrative only because of the interesting sidelight she helps throw upon the shifting moral shadows of the time.

I was living in digs on the Iffley Road that spring, with a Mr and Mrs Fairless, a kind hardworking couple in their late thirties, who had four children and a budgerigar that was encouraged to fly round the breakfast room, walk through one's cornflakes, and enquire at repetitive length what one thought of his prettiness.

The Fairlesses were in the habit of retiring at around 10 pm, enabling anyone with a lissom seat-trimmer on his hands to introduce her to more comfortable premises before the sword outwore the sheath; and for several nights, much that life has to offer had its options taken up in that quiet Victorian semi, the seat-trimmer departing with the dawn.

Except, that is, for the night on which she overslept and, tripping down the hall, fetched up against assorted Fairlesses homing in on bacon. I lay listening to the formal exchanges and the slam of the front-door; no plausible excuses sprang into the mind, so I prepared myself to brazen out whatever lay ahead, washed, shaved, and went in to breakfast.

The meal passed reasonably enough, any stases in the conversation being ably taken care of by child and bird, and it was not until their mother took the children out to hose them down for school that I found myself alone with the landlord. As in some bizarre parody of Victorian melodrama, he paced the linoleum awhile before turning. At last:

'Look here,' he said, 'I think I ought to make it clear that—'

It was at this point that the budgie landed on my head.

'Go away, Charlie,' said the landlord.

'I'm so nice,' said Charlie. 'I'm so nice.'

'Here's a fine do,' said the landlord.

'Go away, Charlie,' I said.

This pre-emptive strike having been taken by the bird, the landlord's iron jut went limp.

'About this young lady,' he said.

'Yes?' I said.

'I hope you're going steady,' he said.

I realize I have said very little about work.

This is primarily because in the matters of study and intent, I doubt that my generation was very different from any other Oxford generation, the undergraduate corps being split into those who looked upon the university as an opportunity for general enlightenment, unshackled to the mundane pursuit of mere honours and qualifications, i.e. those who got drunk a lot and fell off walls after midnight; and those who looked upon it as the finest centre for formal education in all the world where, in the lush environment of scholarship and mature enthusiasms for eliciting one's fullest potential, the brilliant student would become tomorrow's titan, i.e. those who had four ball-point pens of different colours in their white lab-coats and subsequently vanished into ICI.

As a cross-cultural utilitarian bohemian who dreamt of carrying off the Nobel Prize for Literature while at the same time holding down a steady pensionable position with luncheon vouchers, I tended to straddle these schemata, at considerable perineal risk. Fortunately for me, I was reading English, a discipline hardly worthy the title, involving as it did nothing more arduous than sitting under a tree and reading books that one would otherwise have read for pleasure, and, at the end of three years, showing off about them to grown-ups.

There was, of course, Anglo-Saxon, which formed a mandatory part of English Schools just in order to endow the course with a spurious scholasticism; but where others carped constantly at having to wrestle with yog and thorn, I really rather enjoyed *learning* something at Oxford. Especially something with no use, purpose, or practical application whatever. My only sadness in the Old English course came with the discovery that *The Battle of Maldon* was but a fragment: hardly has Aelfwine, son of Aelfric, mounted his counter-attack than the manuscript comes to its mouse-chewed end. What the final score-line was, we shall never know.

In short, then, what Oxford did was train me to understand that true happiness in life attended that man who could persuade someone to pay him to work at something which he would otherwise do from love, anyway. And that, therefore, is the course to which I have cleaved for the past sixteen years, with much joy.

Martin Amis

Martin Amis was born in 1949, a son of Kingsley Amis. He was educated in Britain, Spain and the United States, attending over thirteen schools and then a series of crammers in London and Brighton. He gained a formal first in English at Exeter College. After leaving Oxford, he worked for three years as an editorial assistant on The Times Literary Supplement, *and is now assistant literary editor of the* New Statesman. *He has published two novels,* The Rachel Papers *(1973) and* Dead Babies *(1975), and a number of short stories.*

My Oxford is likely to seem rather shapeless—even rather jangling and unassimilated—compared to reports of it by my predecessors there. This is because my Oxford, the Oxford of 1968–71 (and presumably everyone else's Oxfords thereafter), did not feel like an experience which had shape, point, a clear structural place in one's life. I'd better add quickly that it was, for me, often a terrifying, hilarious and emotionally eventful three years, but I suspect that, for me, those years would have been terrifying, hilarious and emotionally eventful anyway.

Oxford is no longer somewhere with a special focus and a special identity: it is just somewhere that gets passed through by individuals. There will, for example, be no more Oxford 'generations'; eminent contemporaries may emerge, they may even happen to have known each other, but all sense of cultural community is gone, for better or for worse. Socially—in the sense of trying to make friends and trying to fall in love with certain people—it is as easy or as difficult as your social life ever is: with more varied opportunities, but no easier. And intellectually, too, it is for the most part a collection of people sitting alone in rooms, one of whom turns out to be you.

When I went up to Oxford I was anticipating just this—anticipating just everything, really: far and away the most flamboyant and original things about my Oxford were my presuppositions about the place. What the hell would I do? I knew, for a start, that only two types of people ever went to Oxford, and I knew, for a fact, that I belonged to neither. I was not (i) a craven swot from somewhere called Heaptown, so I wouldn't be picking my nails with a compass and drinking quarts of instant coffee in my room all day, joining the Young Trade Unionists, going to Venezuelan films at the cinema clubs, talking about politics, engineering and jobs, and (if I was lucky) getting my terrified girl-friend down from home every other weekend. Equally, I was not (ii) a haughty cretin from one of our public schools, so I wouldn't be motoring my 1898 MG into the country for strawberry picnics, joining the Young Reactionaries, debagging new boys and roasting town yobs, beating the daylights out of the Junior Common Rooms after Cuppers Suppers, putting chamber pots and cars on chapel spires, and falling for the fresher on the next staircase.

No, I was a Londoner, thanks, far too flash and worldly to countenance the pompous hicks and dumb Henries I expected to find in boring old Oxford. For instance, I could account constructively for only *five days* of the traditional mind-expanding nine months between school and university, in which I had worked in my step-uncle's record shop in Rickmansworth—whereas, I imagined, the hicks had all gained key positions in blacking factories and the Henries had all walked from Oslo to Peking and back. Oxford would just be where I went to work, for the almost derisory eight-week terms. I wouldn't need to know anyone; I did not want to act, edit, debate, row or run; I would be a loner, a poet, a dreamer. London would always be there, waiting to be rediscovered by me—and I had even decided coolly to return to it for the first weekend of term.

Underwriting these excitable notions, of course, was an element of candid terror. Originally a child of the lower middle classes, I feared what I so lazily disdained, and in the same over-heated terms. Again, I could see it all. Three years of unsuccessfully dodging streetfights, waking up on the quad lawn in my underpants, getting my velvet suit slashed and my tiny hi-fi stomped in, hiding under my sofa as, outside, loutish Yahooism raged along the staircases. Or alternatively, three years of waking up every morning dangling naked from the chapel rafters, my head shaved, my balls blackened with shoe polish, and a sign reading 'Yaroo—College Squit!' suspended from my neck. And—anyway—would I be *clever* enough . . . all those wizened ghouls on *University Challenge*—they may have looked like Bamber Gascoigne's uncles, but boy did they know their shit. I'd obviously have to work like an idiot to avoid instant disgrace and expulsion, never mind girls, friends, London, meals, sleep, anything. I imagined myself studying away in dour and dusty solitude, while the rest of the world clamoured gaily somewhere out of doors, coming to my ears like the sound of street footfalls to children sent to bed early in summer.

As if in deft reply to these academico-social misgivings, I checked in on the Saturday before term started at Exeter College, Oxford—to find that I was sharing rooms with an Old Harrovian who said 'Pardon?' when he meant 'What?'! Everything about this arrangement mortified me: the matching desks symmetrically flanking the bar heater in our large and uncompanionable sitting-room (no truly humane scholarship, surely, could ever be done there); the matching, cream-walled bed-cubicles leading off it (no Oxford girl, surely, could ever be successfully entertained there); and the goofy horror of my 'room-mate' (as disgusted by my presence, surely, as I was by his). If I was going to suffer, I thought to myself, I wanted to suffer on my own, not with a fellow-dud lurching and fumbling alongside me. Anyhow, three weeks later, having completed a gauntlet of routine grotesqueries—eighty-four hours with Roget on my lap writing my first essay, lone sconce-dreading dinners in hall (i.e. college), a begowned sampling of lectures and libraries, tentative, don't-mind-me sorties into the town—I got a credulous Classicist to swap his room for my half of mine. Then I started to look round about me.

Although more fragmented and less corny than I had expected, there *were* types of people at Oxford, and like all types they elected to stick together. In some senses, also, my slanderous fancies about them had not been altogether without foundation. Galumphing Henries with diagonal pock-marked faces (people who would starve to death if locked in a fully-equipped kitchen) were well enough represented; my Harrovian room-mate said that, on his visits to Oriel, he felt as though he had wandered back to Harrow, such was the incidence of closed-scholarship dunces who groped and blinked through its quads. And the out-of-towner owls were very much about the place too: at the end of a gluttonous college breakfast (one of the real joys of Oxford life), during which I had talked Talleyrand with an unsmiling rustic, I asked him why he was filling his pockets with marmalade rolls. 'For the girlfriend,' he said, gesturing with his head to indicate the hungry room where she damply cowered.

But there were more types than I had thought there would be, and they weren't, in my view, sufficiently well-defined or demarcated types, and I wasn't quite clear which type *I* was or how I could change types and become one of their types even supposing I wanted to. Which type, anyway?

There were political people (you seemed to need a ginger beard to be one of them); they came to your room for talks or tried to sell you scabrous hate-sheets in the quad; they fought for valorous reforms like having breakfast served fifteen minutes later, and they picketed the innocuous Matriculation ceremony (one cleverly ironic graffito at the time was MATRICULATION MAKES YOU BLIND); they also staged an angry meeting about the invasion of Czechoslovakia in my first term, which I angrily attended. There were a few God people left—another dying breed; they came to your room, too, but with such queasy diffidence that you could quite often just tell them to go away. There were sport people, who seemed to keep themselves agreeably to themselves, apart from self-destructive rampages after some important date in their calendar.

There was a great deal of what were called 'gnome' people; almost brazenly repulsive in dress, demeanour and visage, these humble clerks of the new literacy stuck in groups of four and five, attended lectures during the morning and libraries in the afternoon, invariably enjoyed dinner in college (legend told of a gnome who never once signed out for dinner in his entire four-year course), and, still in a clump, quaffed Bournvita well into the large hours. And then there were the 'cool' people (a fairly recent type, I should think), the aloof, slightly moneyed, London-based, car-driving, party-throwing, even vaguely intellectual butterfly elite; I say with confidence that they had among their number all the cockiest and best-looking youths in Oxford; they drank alcohol and took drugs, and they were as promiscuous as anyone well could be there; in many ways they seemed to be having the best time.

Oddly, incongruously (and probably not at all, really), I seemed to straddle these last two types. I had no friends, no friends whatever; a potent qualification for gnome membership. I did indeed drink a lot of instant coffee, spending in aggregate (I would guess) the equivalent of a term crouched over my electric kettle. I always ate in hall and always tried to stay close to my old room-mate and his new one, a delightful pair. I, of course, had no girlfriend. All I had was a room. In fact, even during my relatively in-demand periods at Oxford, most of my life there was to consist of me alone in a study, reading books pressed calmly out on the blotting-paper, or writing malarial, pageant-like, all-night essays, or listening to records, or playing moronically simple forms of patience, or having soul-sessions, or having crying-jags. And, however self-pitying I was about it at the time, this segment of my life I regret not at all: a relative late-comer to literature, I was a contrite pilgrim on the path towards its discovery. Many poignant and humbling moments were passed with assorted masterpieces staked out on my lap; over those three years 'the friction, the sense of pregnant arrest' which accompanies fresh intimacy with an *oeuvre* (the glamorous phrase is F. R. Leavis's) was a regular guest at Tower 1, my romantic room facing the stained glass of the chapel windows ten yards opposite, which were warmly illuminated from within at dusk.

And yet—come, come—I wanted a good time too: and there I was, in my black velvet suit, my snakeskin boots and eagerly patterned shirt, a relative tike by Oxford standards, with quite a few metropolitan girlfriends and one metropolitan love-affair under my belt, a famous Oxonian father, hardly a perfect stranger to human contact, not unpleasing (though small) to look at, a £9-a-week allowance—and nothing to do. I wanted friends, and I wanted to be loved, same as any other undergraduate. I wanted friends because I wanted a girlfriend. But I couldn't have a girlfriend because I didn't have any friends.

So most of my leisure during the first term was single-mindedly devoted to one activity: not getting a girlfriend. I spent several hours every day of the week all over Oxford not getting a girlfriend. In the bookshops I would not get a girlfriend by wandering along the shelves, standing as near as I dared to them and not engaging them in conversation. In the streets I did not get them by walking silently past them. In the libraries, not getting a girlfriend took the form of sitting opposite them and not sending them notes. I joined the Poetry Society (thinking, for some reason or other, that Poetry Society girls would be, by definition, both beautiful and sexually undiscriminating) and did not get a girlfriend at the few meetings I attended, during which plain persons of both sexes unblushingly read out their own verse, or unblushingly sat about while others read out theirs. (In addition, and equipped with similar motives, I joined the Humanist Society, which was also very horrible, and particularly good for not getting girlfriends at.) Least taxing of all, perhaps, was not getting a girlfriend in the lecture hall; one just stared across it at them.

Two things about Oxford girls seemed immediately clear: first, that you could never be happy there without one, and, second, that there was no means of ever getting to know one.

And by 'Oxford girls' I mean all the girls in Oxford, not just those clever, serious, independent students, the ones with more O-levels than freckles on their faces, who looked as if they had just cycled 'up' from Cheltenham or Tunbridge Wells, and who (one imagined) would not take to being stuttered at in the streets. As I staggered through the town on those hollow autumn afternoons, directing my gaze impartially at town and gown alike, it was not for a Zuleika Dobson, nor even for a Jill, that I craved: what I craved for was a girl—or someone who knew one, or someone who knew someone who knew one.

Which posed problems for Oxford's reply to Albert Camus, the Kafka of Carfax, who had serenely redirected the few offers of companionship he had received. After half a term at Oxford I think I am right in saying that, throughout the entire borough, I knew one human being—not counting my ex-room-mate (by now I had abandoned my former haughtiness and perpetually ached to be by his side), my 'scout' (or cleaning-man—a menacing and thyroid-eyed Welshman), and my tutor (urbane, pooh-poohing Jonathan Wordsworth, the distinguished nepotic scholar). This other human being I knew was shy, at Balliol, and, incidentally, was the son of the then Minister of Defence, now custodian of our economy. *He* already had a girlfriend, a metropolitan one whom I vaguely knew, who in turn knew another female human being, an Oxford-based one, whom I sometimes came across when I saw them together. With this young lady giving me nothing whatever in the way of encouragement—save that she showed no sign of unrealistically abrupt dislike—my prolix and gawky approach-work began.

My introductory period at Oxford, then, was given over (a) to work for preliminary exams, and (b) to not getting this particular girl. The first was solitary, satisfying, sane; the second expensive, nerve-racking, and wealthy in embarrassment.

We saw films two or three nights a week and—to my secret boredom—attended the odd meeting or discussion or talk (a nomadic sampler of secretarial courses at the time, she later went on to read Philosophy at London). I held her hand now and then. We ate in College whenever possible, because it was free, or we ate in a friendly Wimpy Bar opposite St John's, because it was cheap. On a few occasions she suffered me to kiss her goodnight at the bus stop. Things continued not to improve. One night in her flat she went through the pockets of my jacket (under my supervision) in search of some matches. I died a little as she accidentally produced a wallet of contraceptives instead. 'Well, you never know your luck,' I said.

And I certainly never knew mine, throughout that Michaelmas term—though I remained deeply convinced that this was all somehow better than nothing. I called at the lady's London home once or twice during the Christmas vacation—which I divided between hard work, light revelry, and sitting about waiting for her passionate, Lawrentian, slightly pornographic (and actually non-existent) letters. In London I assume I cut a rather more attractive figure, what with my stepmother's smart yellow car and my own relative aplomb in the metropolis. But Oxford, the true locus of both our lives then, was the place in which the battle would be lost or won, and I was impatient to return there, after the yawning six-week recess, in the new year. (I later learned, interestingly, that my non-girlfriend had beguiled the vac by having an affair with someone else—and someone who everybody agreed was much nastier, thicker and uglier than me.)

Early on in my second term the election for the Oxford Professorship of Poetry was held. My father, as an M.A. (and an implacable foe of Yevgeny Yevtushenko), had come up to vote for Roy Fuller, whose son John threw a party. I was asked along—and I sexily invited my non-girlfriend along too. She embraced this opportunity to make her indifference known, and I returned to my room *à un*, realizing that after half a year in this life-enhancing, character-building, horizon-expanding place, I now had no one, nothing. The famous skylines I could see from my window, the stained-glass hagiographies of the chapel opposite, the Songs and Sonnets of John Donne laid out tenderly on my desk—suddenly all this was second-hand, mere leftovers, junk. I sat there for several hours, and when I couldn't bear sitting down I stood up, and when I couldn't bear standing up I sat down. About 9 o'clock there was a tap on the door. It was she, bearing apologies and a persuasively-worded invitation to return with her to her flat. Intimacy (with the author in rather less than colossal form) took place, and a happy few months began.

As against this—and hardly less rollickingly—I was working with paranoid verve for Prelims, unpleasant and meaningless exams which befall the student at the end of his or her second term. The five papers include one on Old English grammar, all indecipherable inflection changes and vile vowel movements, and a Latin paper, requiring from the candidate two translations from Books IV and VI of the *Aeneid*. (Both these papers have been superseded; mine was the last year to sit them, for which many thanks.) In my Oxford entrance papers, my attempt at the Latin unseen had consisted of a single word, mistranslated: I had rendered *igitur* as 'the general', whereas I gather it in fact means 'therefore'. Well, *igitur* I now took the precaution of memorizing literal translations of these two books in their entirety. (This would raise only two dangers: not recognizing the passages, and not knowing, as it were, when to stop translating them.) Towards the end I worked practically round the clock. I used to leave notes by my alarm—often set for 4 or 5 am—saying things like *Oh Really Get Up* and BLOODY GET UP! in case I merely slapped the button and returned groaning to my cot. I worked far, far too hard, and passed with jittery ease. When the exams ended so, for some logical-seeming reason, did my interest in the girl whom I had courted and squired for nearly a year.

And that's how it went on, I'm afraid. I was lucky enough to get another girlfriend, a connection which bestrode the (traditionally quite idle) second year and flourished well into the third. Under this girlfriend's auspices—she was a History freshwoman whom I had known a bit before she came up—my social needle's-eye expanded somewhat, and I tasted some of the conventional sweets of Oxonian life. Punting drunkenly up the Isis to a hostelry at evening, being tweely offered a choice of Malvern Water and tonic at a 'drinks' party on the beautiful lake-side lawn at Worcester College, walking round the place with my father (all husky with nostalgia—but then he had a Generation to talk to when he was there) on his infrequent visits, stealing the odd drug from the trusting, ponderous pushers at Hertford, rather shining in classes with my derivative and journalistic essays, going to many films many times, smuggling the St Hilda's scholar past the scout on my staircase, feeling superior to new boys, getting a bigger room, having more interesting periods to study . . . till Finals loomed.

Nobody can be forced to work at Oxford, but things are made easy, pleasant and stimulating for those who want to work. And just as there is the time for pleasure, there is the time for boredom and neurosis, which only work can fill. At the beginning of my third year, owing to an impetuous scheme to share a house in the country with unstable and profligate friends, work was fatally eased out by pleasure, most of it pleasureless, and for my last two terms I radically readjusted—i.e., over-readjusted, as usual.

In short, I re-embraced the life of a gnome. Leaving the house and the girlfriend in equally disgraceful circumstances, I moved into the Annexe of my college, a grim bastion of gnomery on the unattractive Iffley Road. It was a large flat house that smelled of locker rooms and lavatory spray, a suspended, echoic warren of shuffling caretakers, winded cats and dozens of progeriac postgraduates, who resembled very old ladies and who made fantastically elaborate meals for themselves three times a day, and sat about all the time discussing those meals, either anticipatorily, or with the evaluating calm of hindsight. It suited me perfectly.

Here I went again: I rose at 6 am, drank a great deal of

coffee ('real' coffee by now), worked until 8, went into college for breakfast, took my seat in the college library by 8.45, worked until 1, had lunch in college, took my seat in the college library by 1.45, worked until 7, returned to the Iffley Road, worked until 9, prepared for myself a Vesta Beef Curry or a Vesta Chicken Supreme or—best—a Vesta Paella (not a single item of genuine nutriment, I can safely boast, passed down my throat at Exeter House), returned to my desk and worked until 1 am. I rose at 6 am . . . At this rate, I was going to look a bit of a bloody fool if I didn't do very well indeed. The nine three-hour papers came in a heroic blur. I got a formal First, coming third in that year.

The unique freedom of Oxford—now more than ever, probably—is that you don't have to account for more than, say, ninety minutes a week for eighteen weeks a year. That's about three days out of three years of your life. Conventional ways of filling that time are gone; it is all yours now. It doesn't happen to you before and it never happens to you again. Perhaps once is enough—but not more than enough.

My Cambridge

INTRODUCTION

My Cambridge? Retrospectively, yes, my Cambridge is as different from everybody else's as the memoirs in this book are from each other, though at the time I could hardly have felt less possessive about the place or more grateful to feel possessed by it. Part of the pleasure was in imagining that the Cambridge experience had always been the same: that for hundreds of years undergraduates had been wearing the same gowns, shivering in the same draughty rooms, carrying on flippant conversations across the same long wooden dining tables under the same lofty, church-like ceilings, climbing over the same walls with the same trepidation when they came back to college after midnight. Many of my clearest memories centre on things that have changed little over the centuries—the lawns, the buildings, the bridges, the river, the trees and the fact of having so many friends and potential friends of the same age all within walking distance. Isaac Newton, William Pitt and Wittgenstein must all have heard the same bells, looked up at the same patterns of light and shade on the same spires, and—if punts existed by the time of the Civil War—talked with the same frivolity as they punted between the same weeping willows.

An individual can do little to alter the city or the university; how much can Cambridge do to alter him? We all change very rapidly as we move reluctantly out of our teens and into our twenties. Possibly the idea of becoming an adult is even more frightening to those without the privilege of what one union debater called 'three years of premature retirement'; possibly the undergraduate changes more slowly than the boy or girl who goes straight from school to paid employment. But can any Cambridge graduate know whether he'd be noticeably different today if he'd been an undergraduate at Oxford or Hull or Southampton? Or not gone to university at all? Or been at a different Cambridge college or read a different subject or had a different circle of friends? One can speak only for oneself, and for my part I know I can't measure the effects or the after-effects of Cambridge with any certainty of being accurate.

I still possess a copy of an old *Granta* (8 June 1954), edited by Nicholas Tomalin and Karl Miller, publishing the results of a questionnaire they'd circulated to Thom Gunn, Frederic Raphael, Michael Winner, Leslie Bricusse, Ronald Bryden, Stephen Haskell and me. Most of the questions were jokey: 'Who did you give up for Lent?' 'Do you count your imbecilities?' 'How do you make friends?' ('I don't,' answered Thom. 'They make me.') There were also some ostensibly serious questions. 'What is civilization?' ('Croissants and café au lait,' suggested Frederic Raphael) and 'What is success?' 'A Guggenheim,' answered Ronald Bryden. My own definition of success now seems alarmingly symptomatic of a determination which must already have hardened: 'To write without starving, pot-boiling or taking a job.'

To the question 'What is the function of a university?' Thom answered 'Education?' and Ronald Bryden 'Cynicism.' I said: 'To select people, bring them comfortably together, and give them a great deal of time to do nothing in but talk.' Twenty-two and a half years later I can't remember all that much comfort but I do remember that the conversation seemed to be having more of an educational effect than the lectures. With a limited amount of space and an unlimited number of candidates, selection is obviously inevitable, but if I were answering the question today, I would be more conscious and more critical of how it was done, and if I were in a position of power, I would agitate for selecting the boys and girls who seemed most likely to influence each other towards realizing the best of their potential—intellectually, creatively and sexually. It is more obvious now that it was a mistake then to assume that the three forms of fulfilment were not interdependent.

What Cambridge seemed to be offering in the early 'fifties was time, space and freedom. I knew I had been given an opportunity to find out who I was. If three years later I was still unsure, it was partly because I hadn't gained enough self-confidence, in spite of having been able to try out poses and affectations as if they were fancy dress. But the clothes that seemed rebellious then—purple corduroys and black shirts—would pass unnoticed in Charing Cross Road today. The word privilege may now be used more often and much more pejoratively, but permissiveness, the democratic conscience and the multiplication of universities have played their part in emancipating a very large group of young people into the kind of self-expression which then seemed to be one of the most important privileges available to a very small, very favoured minority. The freshman who arrives at Cambridge today cannot have anything like the same sense I had in 1951 of being admitted to an elite. After eighteen months of organized time-wasting in the RAF, I did not feel guilty about being fortunate. I did feel constantly incredulous. One of the problems, for me, was that after so much hard work and eager anticipation, so many years in which parents and teachers had talked as if the two senior universities were combining to situate Heaven in England, the fact of arrival seemed less like a beginning than a happy ending.

So why did I attach so much importance to my black shirt and my purple corduroys? It couldn't merely have been a matter of celebrating my liberation from grey-blue uniform, so what did I imagine myself to be asserting? I was by no means alone in making sartorial gestures of what seemed like defiance, but English social history was soon to make them look pathetic.

The underprivileged teds, mods and rockers did it all more effectively than we did. They looked no less self-confident, more rebellious, and they got more publicity.

Perhaps the function of a university varies from generation to generation. Probably time, space and freedom are still the most important gifts on offer; probably self-knowledge and self-confidence are still the most valuable qualities to be acquired. But the insecurities of next year's freshmen will be slightly different from this year's and very different from what ours were in 1951. Not that the question of self-confidence is ever simple. Most eighteen-year-olds are liable to look enviously at the apparent self-possession of other eighteen-year-olds. Knowing how to seem more confident than they feel, they keep forgetting that others are playing the same game.

In 1951 the contraceptive pill was not yet available, there were no mixed colleges and there were still only two colleges for girls as against eighteen for boys. (At the end of November 1976 it was announced on the front page of *The Times* that male students will be admitted to Girton College as soon as it is 'expedient'.) I don't know whether greater sexual freedom tends to make for less sexual competitiveness, but in the early 'fifties the male competition for the more desirable Girtonians and Newnhamites was extremely fierce, though it was only one of many competitions that could engage enormous quantities of emotional energy. The sexual drive was inseparable from other incentives to success. The things that seemed to be most worth having were the things that most people would be unable to have—a First, a girl, a Blue, a leading part in a production at the ADC, a profile in *Varsity*. That it was possible not to compete never even occurred to me: nobody ever talked about dropping out, though sometimes the glamour-race seemed paradoxically unglamorous, especially in those heart-to-heart conversations when a friend's vulnerabilities were exposed to the sudden glare of intimacy. That they were so similar to one's own was both reassuring and disconcerting.

What I regret most, retrospectively, is that the dons were

so much less helpful than the place towards providing a perspective in which the emotional and the intellectual experiences could be integrated or at least related. When one felt suicidal, there was consolation to be had from the fact that the buildings and so many of the trees were so extremely old. They must have seen so many generations of undergraduates battling with very similar doubts about whether it was all worth while. So far as I knew, there had been very few suicides. I remember one moment of depression when I was walking down the narrow passage that leads from Trinity Street to Trinity Hall. The weatherbeaten stone walls were far enough from being straight for me to wish fervently that they would bulge in further, squashing everything, the bicycles propped against the kerb, the other gowned undergraduates, and me. But I knew the walls were much too wise and friendly.

The dons were not very friendly. I was interested to find that so many of the contributors to this book had similar negative feelings about them and that the memoirs provide so very little evidence of personal influence exerted by lecturers and supervisors. At school there had been so much opportunity for making personal contact with the teachers—asking questions, chatting, feeling befriended. At Cambridge the lecture halls were more like theatres than classrooms. The don would make his entrance through a door that led on to a platform, where he spoke for an hour from behind a lectern, and then left without inviting questions. We had direct access to just one don for just one hour each week during 'supervisions', when two of us would sit in his room, reading and discussing our essays.

The one name that recurs frequently (even in memoirs written by people who did not read English) is that of Dr Leavis. Some of the references to him are hostile, but for many people he obviously made a major contribution to the experience of growing up. *Maturity* was a word which featured prominently in his classes on Practical Criticism, which he preferred to call 'Judgment and Analysis'. Sincerity wasn't enough. Shelley's lyrical surrender to the tumbling flow of emotionality had been uncritical and unintelligent. So had the rhetorical outpourings of the Victorian Romantics. We learned not to be overawed by the reverential tone that actors and other readers were liable to put on for dealing with the Beautiful and the Sublime. If we got nothing from the verse beyond word-music and a vague sense that the poet himself had been excited, maybe it wasn't our fault but his. That the writer had duties meant that we, as readers, had rights. We were entitled to expect not only that he should give us a lively impression of the experience he was describing, but that he should make sense of it. Inevitably we tried to cultivate in ourselves the virtues Leavis taught us to look for.

What Leavis was doing single-handedly was what the English Faculty—and the other faculties—should have been doing in an organized way. He was teaching us a discipline which was more liberating than constricting. By pushing pretentious rhetoric out of the way, he was creating space for a much greater enjoyment of poetry by John Donne and T. S. Eliot, poetry which put us in touch with an individual voice. If emotional self-indulgence was damaging to literature, it must be damaging to life—incompatible with the critical play of mature intelligence. Not that Leavis could, by himself, do enough to compensate for lack of commitment and understanding in the other dons or for our lack of personal contact with them, but on many of us Cambridge would have had less influence if he had not been there.

If it is true that all meaningful statements about the Cambridge experience must be partly autobiographical, it follows that any account of it will be incomplete, subjective, impressionistic. With a different editor and twelve different contributors, this could have been a totally different book, yielding a different pattern of pros and cons. But in any such book the dissimilarities between the memoirs would be no less interesting than the similarities. No one will ever be able to write a history of the undergraduate experience, and I'm glad that there's so much variety in the experiences described between these covers.

RONALD HAYMAN

Sir Nevill Mott

Sir Nevill Mott was born in 1905, the son of a science teacher, and went up to St John's College to read Mathematics in 1924. Sir Nevill, who had been to Clifton College, Bristol, was not yet twenty-eight when he was appointed Professor of Physics at Bristol University. He held the position for 21 years before he became Cavendish Professor of Physics at Cambridge in 1954. He was President of the International Union of Physics from 1951–7, and in 1955 of the Modern Languages Association. He was chairman of the Advisory Committee for the Nuffield Science Project and has been active on committees advising on science education in schools. He was a member of the Institute of Strategic Studies, concerned with nuclear disarmament, and he organized a Pugwash meeting in Cambridge in 1962. In 1971 he retired from his Cavendish Chair. He is a Fellow of the Royal Society.

For as far back as I can remember, I never had any doubt about what I wanted from Cambridge. My father and my mother had both worked for a short while in the Cavendish Laboratory, as pupils of J. J. Thomson, and so I was brought up in a family which followed Rutherford's work on 'splitting the atom'. When at school I found I had some ability for mathematics, I never questioned that I should try for a scholarship to Cambridge and seek a career in atomic physics. As regards the choice between Cambridge and anywhere else, there were in England only two important schools in physics at that time, Cambridge and Manchester; Rutherford had come from Manchester in 1919 and was vigorously at work in Cambridge when I entered St John's College in 1924. But Rutherford was a far-away giant to a first year undergraduate, and only later was I to be influenced by him directly.

For me the first impact of Cambridge was that it offered complete freedom, freedom particularly from the standards and rules of the peer group which influenced a boy's every action at a boarding school. In Cambridge I had my sitting-room and my bedroom and the 'oak'—the door that one could lock and keep out the world if one wanted to. You could row or not row, just as you liked, go to lectures or cut them and nobody said anything, sit up half the night talking to friends or tell them to go away; and with this marvellous freedom I don't think it occurred to our generation to question the rule that brought us back within the college by midnight, compulsory dinners in hall, or anything else. Freedom to talk, to read, to join societies, to make friends, made that first year at Cambridge a paradise.

I elected to read Mathematics, believing, correctly, that this was the quickest way to get to research in physics. Some of the lectures were not very well delivered, in spite of the distinction of those who gave them, and I don't think I stuck many out to the end. Once a week also there was a 'supervision'; two of us went to a don for an hour, and asked him questions or he asked us questions. One, I remember, said, 'If you've no questions you'd better go away', but others tried to find out what we were up to. Somehow or other, with books, lectures and supervisions one could pick up what was needed for the final tripos examination. And indeed, even the most enthusiastic undergraduate didn't dream of doing mathematics all day, and it wouldn't have done him much good if he had. The experimental scientists, with laboratory work, had much less free time than those of us who read Maths. I would guess that perhaps three hours during the average day, an occasional evening and good deal of vacation work was about what I personally put into it. So there was plenty of time to enjoy the freedom of Cambridge. As I remember, it was mainly reading all sorts of books and talking to friends. One of my friends summed it up by saying that in our first year we talked about God and the nature of the universe, in the second year we talked about politics and in our third year about our worries with the approaching final examination.

In my first year I remember going to a few philosophy lectures, reading Bergson, Bertrand Russell and Shaw, and talking about them far into the night. Perhaps this sounds unduly serious—but often towards midnight the conversation would have turned to matters more personal. Then my second year was the year of the General Strike, so socialism, the League of Nations, economics and societies concerned with these things became our concern. I remember trying to collect a subscription for the League of Nations Union from the Master of my college and being turned away with the remark that he did not believe in that, and also from a young don who refused with the remark that he did not believe in nations. And, just as for the present-day undergraduate, there was the excitement of travel; three of us set off with push-bicycles, and a tent on the back of mine, and we went from Dieppe over the Brenner into Mussolini's Italy, along roads hardly sullied yet by cars, and got as far as Venice. On the way back, after stopping for a while to start learning German, I arrived in Geneva, sold my bike, and got into the League of Nations building to hear the formal admission of Germany, the French prime minister making a splendid speech, throwing away the machine guns and embracing peace.

After my Tripos (the final examination) came a grant from the Department of Scientific and Industrial Research (now the Science Research Council) and we went along to the Cavendish to find out what research problem we ought to try our hands at. I say 'we': there were two of us from the mathematical Tripos, and we wanted to do theoretical physics, which we saw as the use of mathematics to understand the strange facts that Rutherford and his experimentalists were bringing to light.

I must say something about the state of theoretical physics at that time. The electron, the basic unit of electricity, was known since J. J. Thomson's investigations in Cambridge about 1900. Atoms, we knew, contained electrons, but how were they fixed there? In 1911 Rutherford with his co-workers in Manchester found that the atom was rather like the solar system, with a heavy 'nucleus' attracting the electrons to it, and each kind of atom, such as those of hydrogen, oxygen, copper or iron, differed from one another only through the number of electrons that the nucleus could hold. Then in 1913, also in Manchester, the Danish scientist Niels Bohr proposed that, while he agreed that each electron in an atom moved round the nucleus in an orbit like that of the earth round the sun, there were strict rules, formulated in the so-called quantum theory, stating which of all the possible orbits it could make use of. There was no indication why this should be so; one just had to assume it to explain a multitude of experimental facts.

With the end of the First World War theorists in several countries—particularly perhaps Germany, but with Niels Bohr in Copenhagen always an acknowledged leader—set out to perfect the quantum theory and see where it led. It was a small group of men and they all knew each other. The names of Born, Heisenberg, Pauli, Schrödinger and Dirac are some of the most notable. In 1925–6 it first became clear to this group that the quantum theory as proposed by Bohr simply would no longer do, that the orbits did not exist and that the laws of nature had to be rewritten much more drastically. In the new quantum theory which then emerged, a particle sometimes behaved like a wave and a wave sometimes behaved like a particle, and both were subject to the apparent contradictions of Heisenberg's uncertainty principle, but, nonetheless, both were governed by mathematical rules, so that the equations guiding their behaviour could be solved.

It was at this revolutionary moment in the history of science that the two of us from the mathematical Tripos came to the Cavendish wanting to do research. Ralph Fowler, Rutherford's son-in-law, was in charge of theoretical physics. But there was no big school, as there was at Göttingen, and certainly, being very little looked after, we had to stand on our own feet. Quantum mechanics, as the new theory was called, was so strange and so imperfectly understood, that I doubt whether anyone in Cambridge could have chosen the right problem for us. Moreover Fowler was just off to America for a sabbatical year and suggested that we should come back a year later, whereupon my friend decided to abandon physics and to read Law instead; he became a distinguished solicitor.

For my part, my undergraduate years had given me the taste for working alone and I was not discouraged. I spent a delightful and leisurely year with no exams to worry me, trying to learn the new quantum mechanics from the original papers, and learning German at the same time so as to be able to read them, and with almost no one to talk to about it all. Of course I got to know some of the experimental physicists in the Cavendish at this time; they were interested in the new theories, but found them somewhat mysterious. There was tea to be had in the small Cavendish library, and here one could sit among the smell of breadcrumbs and look at the journals and sometimes talk to people. But the perpetual talk that the young scientists have now, the exchange of ideas over extended coffee and tea breaks, was something about which Cambridge theorists had yet to learn. The tradition was that of the natural philosopher sitting and thinking in the seclusion of his college room.

It has been said that of all the professional scientists who have ever lived, ninety per cent are still alive, and now when research is an organized and highly competitive profession, it would be difficult for a young man to start with so little help. But then, once a student had mastered these German language papers on the new quantum mechanics, half the problems of physics and chemistry stood wide open to be fitted into this framework. The ideas of the new theory were difficult, but the maths was easy, the sort of stuff that had been known for a century. Once one had the hang of it, one could ask: how do two atoms of the hydrogen stick together to form the hydrogen molecule? A classic paper gave the answer. Why do some solids conduct electricity and others not? This became clear, too, within about four years of the discovery of the new theory.

I was lucky—I thought of a problem that I could solve, solved it and took it to Fowler, then back from his sabbatical year, and he sent it to the Proceedings of the Royal Society; and then, after a term in Copenhagen with Niels Bohr, I thought of another thing and predicted that the so-called 'Rutherford Scattering Law', on which had been based the nuclear theory of the atom, might not always be right. Chadwick, later the discoverer of the neutron, did an experiment to find out whether it was so, and when the answer was positive, he took me along to see the old man. His comment was: 'If you think of anything else like that, let me know.' This certainly made my day.

Rutherford had not always taken kindly to theorists—'paper physicists', as they were sometimes called; he once said about this time, 'The theorists are getting too uppish and it is up to us experimentalists to bring them down to size.' But my favourite Rutherford story is that, after the discovery of the neutron in his laboratory, a distinguished foreign visitor said to him, 'Lucky man, Rutherford, always on the crest of the wave.' His answer was: 'Crest of the wave, indeed! I made the wave, didn't I?' Which was true enough.

After a year with W. L. Bragg in Manchester, I came back to Cambridge for three years as a lecturer and college fellow. This time is what I remember most vividly of my early days in Cambridge. Theoretical physics had achieved such success, even with Rutherford's beloved nucleus, that we were far more acceptable in the Cavendish, and the crumby tea-room was often crowded. There were more of us, for central European scientists were in and out of Cambridge. Later, many came over for good as refugees from Hitler. George Gamow, a Soviet citizen who left Russia in 1930 to attend a congress and didn't go back, applied the new theories to the nucleus and made quite an impact. Later he wrote *Mr Tomkins in Wonderland*, a successful and popular book about the new physics. The Cavendish, we felt, was the centre of the world of physics, where the most exciting things were happening, even more than in France, Germany and Italy, or so it seemed to us. Two of the exciting things were these: Cockcroft and Walton were the first to use an accelerator to break up the nucleus, paving the way for the giant accelerators of today; and Chadwick discovered the neutron, the long-suspected heavy particle without any electric charge. We theorists rushed in to try to explain all these things. We did not, of course, have the slightest idea in the early nineteen-thirties where the neutron was going to lead—to nuclear weapons and nuclear power; this came later, in 1939. We were just caught up by Rutherford's wave; the nucleus had to be understood—because it was there.

Looking back on that time, from 1930 to 1933, it is hard to remember that this was the period of the Great Depression and of the rise of Nazism, a period even more laden with anxiety than the present, with the apparent breakdown of capitalism everywhere, the inevitable drift towards war and the socialist alternative even then clouded by Stalin's liquidation of two million property-owning peasants. I do not wish to imply that the scientists were unaware of the catastrophic events in the world. I would guess they were as aware of them as most other groups of educated young people. I remember political societies, debates, discussions in the evenings at the houses of colleagues. Nonetheless, the challenge presented by the explosion in our understanding of nature, and the urge to be part of it and contribute to it, is much my strongest recollection of that time, and I believe that most of my surviving contemporaries would say the same. Even later, as 1939 approached and war seemed certain, I remember hoping to get such-and-such a piece of work finished, published and given to the world before the catastrophe, which was envisaged as far more destructive of city life than in the event it turned out to be, at least in this country. It was after the war, knowing what physics had done and could do to the science of making war, that physicists of my generation became really involved, with the Atomic Scientists' Association and the Pugwash movement.

Working in the Cavendish at that time were many contrasting personalities who could not but influence a young man thrown among them. First of all there was James Chadwick, virtually director of the laboratory. Chadwick had worked with Rutherford at Manchester before the war of 1914–18, and was spending a year in Berlin when that war began. He was interned for the whole duration in Ruhleben, an experience from which he never completely recovered. After the war a Fellowship from

Caius College enabled him to join Rutherford in Cambridge. He was to play a major political role in smoothing co-operation with the Americans during the atomic bomb project. I remember him as a rather distant man of complete integrity whose praise or blame was valued. In Ruhleben he had met an army officer, Charles Ellis, and converted him to physics; Rutherford, Chadwick and Ellis were the authors of a famous book on the atomic nucleus, and Ellis and I published a joint paper in which—sadly—we just failed to predict the existence of a new particle (the neutrino), though all the evidence was before us. Then there was Peter Kapitza, a Soviet citizen who boasted that he was the only one of his compatriots who had a passport marked for unlimited journeys to and from his country. Alas, when he went back for a visit in 1934, the authorities there told him to stay, and he did not visit England again till this decade, but in the early nineteen-thirties he had a laboratory on the Cavendish site built for him by the Royal Society. The 'Kapitza Club' met in the evenings once a week in his room in Trinity College and anyone who had some new results subjected them to Kapitza's gay and fluent criticisms, in a variant of English that had to be learned.

C. P. Snow, already riding the two cultures, was a regular member, and told how he asked Chadwick what it was like to discover a new particle (the neutron), a passport to a Nobel Prize and much else—and got the answer: 'I'd like to go to bed for a week.' But that isn't my recollection of this occasion; I remember that as Chadwick outlined all the observations he and others had made, and came to the conclusion that this *was* the neutron about which people had speculated, a note of pride and satisfaction was just detectable in his quiet voice.

Then, also, there was Patrick Blackett, a naval officer in the first war, a man with great charisma and power to win the loyalty and affection of his students and young colleagues, such as myself. He, too, was destined to receive a Nobel prize for his part in the discovery of another fundamental particle (the positron), to advise a Labour government on scientific policy, and to end up as President of the Royal Society. He, as well as Chadwick, carried out an experiment to see whether one of my theories was right, and again it was. In fact these three years led me to understand what I believe theoretical physics to be about. Scientific truth, it has been said, is the consensus of what top scientists believe, and so it changes from time to time. But certainly the most convincing proof of the truth of a theory, the one that is most convincing to others, is its ability to predict correctly the result of an experiment that has not yet been made. This is much more striking than 'explaining', or fitting into a mathematical framework, facts which are already known. So during my time in Rutherford's Cavendish, I came to believe as I have ever since, that theoretical physics has a wider role still than putting the truth in mathematical form; it shows the people in the laboratories the most fruitful experiments to make, in order to understand and control nature for the development of technology.

Rutherford's laboratory was of course strongly oriented towards nuclear physics, but not entirely. Appleton was making the investigations of the electrical properties of the upper atmosphere (the ionosphere) which later led to radar and to the new science of radioastronomy, which gained for the present-day Cavendish the latest of its Nobel prizes just two years ago. Bernal had a group in crystallography, and Kapitza's laboratory worked on low temperatures and magnetism. A contemporary of mine, Alan Wilson, later to become an industrialist and chairman of Courtaulds, turned his attention to the application of the new quantum mechanics to electrons in solids, and was able to explain the true nature of a semiconductor. It is a matter of opinion whether nuclear physics, leading to nuclear power and nuclear weapons, has had a more profound effect on mankind than have semiconductors, which have led to the transistor, to solid state electronics and to computers and thus on the military side to guided missiles. But I think we had neither the desire nor the ability to look into the future in those days. I do not remember that Wilson's work made much impact among those of us who were bound up with nuclear physics. In fact, there was a kind of snobbery which lasted well into the postwar period; nuclear physics was true physics, looking for the unknown; the rest was the application of known principles. Rutherford reputedly said, 'There are two kinds of science, physics and stamp-collecting', by which he meant, if indeed he said it, the mere collection of facts. And many in his laboratory would have interpreted 'physics' as nuclear physics.

The excitement with the atom and the nucleus have led to some surprising delays in our understanding of nature. For instance, since the use of metals by man it must have been known that they were ductile, and so could be bent or forged. It was not however till the immediate pre-war years that anyone asked—in terms of the properties of the atoms of which they are built up—why this should be so. Geoffrey Taylor, another great man of that period who died recently, was the first to do this in 1934. Another very old technology is the manufacture of glass. Glasses are materials in which the atoms are not stuck together in regular arrays, as in crystals, but more or less anyhow like the grains in a heap of sand. It was only a decade ago, when glasses which conduct electricity were being investigated, that scientists suddenly realized that they could not apply Wilson's theory to them and they did not even understand how a material that was not crystalline could be transparent. A flourishing branch of science—electrons in glasses—was thus born, occupying several people in the Cavendish now.

All this is what we now call solid state physics. I have made my career in solid state physics, but I had no interest in it in my Cambridge days. What I did learn was that a theorist should see what were the strengths of the laboratory where he worked, and try to help. When I went to Bristol in 1933, I found some solid state research already in progress, and here found an amply rewarding and at that time perhaps a less competitive field than the nucleus.

When I came back from Manchester in 1930, Ralph Fowler went off to the United States for another period of leave and suggested to me that I should look after his research students. Just as I am glad that Fowler left me alone to find my own problems when I began, so I look back with gratitude to this. One of the great satisfactions of research is setting young men on the road to a successful career themselves, and the lifelong friendships that result. Cambridge was able to give me this experience early. At that time, moreover, I was still a candidate for the Cambridge Ph.D., paying to the Board of Research, and through them to my absent supervisor, Fowler, some £4 a term. At the same time I received this fee each term from each of his students. With a tenured position in the university, it did not seem worth while to continue as a candidate, so I withdrew and did not ever take a doctorate.

Many people have written about Rutherford's Cavendish in its period of greatest glory. It lasted a few years; then some of the leading men left Cambridge to start new schools in the provinces, as I did myself; after 1933 the influx of refugee scientists from Germany gave enormous new strengths to other laboratories, particularly to Oxford. In 1937 Rutherford died, since when the Cavendish has been a very good laboratory among others, but without perhaps the unique position in this country that it then held. But this essay should be about Cambridge, and I must try to place the Cavendish in the early 'thirties in the context of Cambridge at that time. Every don then had two jobs, one with his college, which in my case paid more than half my salary, and one as a lecturer in the university. So in a sense we had two loyalties: on one hand the enormous pull of the Cavendish, a world-renowned centre, probing into the atom, changing our view of nature; and on the other hand the college, oriented towards undergraduate teaching, where the senior tutors were the most important and indeed the best-paid people in the university, and where the natural rival both in sport and exam results was the next-door college, not anywhere outside Cambridge. The college expected its Fellows to teach groups of two students at a time, who brought their puzzles and questions from their work, in my case, for the mathematical Tripos, and I think that this work together with the scholarship examination was in term-time at least a half-time job, leaving the rest and the vacations for research and for lectures in the university. Dons are sometimes accused of neglecting their teaching for research; whether or not this is often true I cannot say, but at this time under the college system it was certainly not so in Cambridge; the whole way of life in the college ensured that it was not.

However, after two years with these two jobs I was offered the professorship of theoretical physics at the University of Bristol, where in the previous few years an impressive new physics laboratory had been built, financed and staffed mainly through munificent gifts from the Wills family. As always I went to Fowler for advice; there was little if anything in it financially and I was not sure that I wanted to leave the Cavendish at the height of its fame. I knew that there was something that I wanted to do in Bristol, namely to build a group of theorists who would work in the laboratory closely with the experimental people, something that Cambridge did not attempt till many years later. On the other hand, I would be leaving the fount of ideas that was Cambridge. Fowler's advice was, as always, good. He, like Rutherford, was a bluff straightforward man, a cricketer, full of vigour and honesty. His advice, like his physics, was down-to-earth and practical. 'You,' he said, 'want to do research. If you stay in Cambridge, and unless you become a professor, which is hardly likely, the college will make more and more demands on you—teaching, committees, administration—and you will not want to refuse. So your opportunities for research in Bristol will be much better than they will soon become here if you stay.' So I took his advice and spent twenty-one years in Bristol (apart from some of the war years) before coming back to the Cavendish chair. 'My Cambridge' of that time before 1933 was thus the place which left me alone in my first years to do what I wanted to do, and later gave me the kindliest advice to get out when pressures began to build up which would have stood in my way.

Lord Caradon

Lord Caradon (Hugh Foot) was born in 1907, the son of the Rt. Hon. Isaac Foot, a Liberal MP and a Government Minister. Educated at Leighton Park School, he went up to St John's in 1925 to read History (he later changed to Law). He became President of the Union. During a distinguished career in the Colonial Service he has been Chief Secretary in Nigeria, Governor of Jamaica, and Governor of Cyprus, where he helped to achieve the settlement that culminated in the island's independence. From 1964–70 he was Minister of State for Foreign and Commonwealth Affairs and UK Representative at the United Nations. He is the author of A Start in Freedom.

The pictures of Cambridge in the nineteen-twenties which survive and emerge and develop in my memory are nearly all closely personal and not at all objective. If I attempted to give a description of the teaching of history, for instance, or of the undergraduate interest in politics or of the standard of Cambridge rowing at that time, I could do so only from a very patchy recollection. And my impression of the undergraduates I knew best is somewhat influenced by what I have known about them in subsequent life. One of my friends was Will Sargant, now one of the best known psychiatrists in the country, but I knew him first as a big bony rugger forward. Another friend in my own college was Stanley Marchant (now Sir Herbert Marchant). He became a leading ambassador, in Cuba amongst other places, but at that time I admired him mainly for his excellence as a high jumper. Selwyn Lloyd, subsequently Foreign Secretary and Speaker of the House of Commons, was my immediate predecessor as President of the Liberal Club, but in those days I respected him mainly as a fast wing forward from Fettes.

I was fortunate enough to have four undergraduate years at Cambridge instead of the standard three. I went to the United States in 1927 in my third year as a member of the three-man Cambridge debating team. I had just changed from History to Law and I needed more time to face my second and final

Tripos examination. For me the extra year was a boon—and I sometimes think that the American system of a four-year undergraduate course has much to commend it. The additional year was specially valuable to me since I had gone up to Cambridge young—too young, I think. I was not quite eighteen when I arrived at St John's College in 1925, and went to my first digs in Bridge Street, looking out from my bedroom window on the entrance to the Cambridge Union. The additional year enabled me not only to go to debate in America but also to take a greater part in university politics, and in my last term to be President of the Union.

I had decided to come to Cambridge rather than follow my elder brother, Dingle, to Oxford because I wanted to escape humiliating comparisons. When I was a small boy I had gone to the same preparatory school as Dingle. He was clearly cleverer than I was—and he did not seek to disguise the fact. I determined to suffer no more from the comparison. So when he went to one later school I went to another (Leighton Park School in Reading) and when he went to Oxford, I went to Cambridge, and when he left his university to enter British politics and the law, I went for a lifetime overseas—and I haven't come home ever since except for short intervals. I have therefore good reason to be thankful to him. And I tell my other brothers, John and Michael, who also with my brother Christopher went to Oxford, that I am sorry for them, condemned as they now are to deal with limited local problems of domestic politics, while I have been privileged to devote my life to the far greater dangers and challenges and opportunities of the wider world and the future of all mankind.

Once when I was the Governor of Cyprus at home for consultations, I wrote a letter to the *Daily Mail*, complaining about a whispering campaign put about, I was sure, by my brothers, that I was their inferior—some sort of wild half-wit, they called me, brought up on the Cornish moors with the gypsies. In my letter I said: 'I wish to protest about all this. I was, I think, the only one of the five brothers to win a scholarship to my school. I got exactly the same university degree as all of them—second-class Honours. Like them I was President of the Union. The only difference was that I went to Cambridge and they all went to Oxford. I would thank them to remember, that except for our father, who is as we all know, head and shoulders above all of us, we are intellectually equal—all second-class stuff. And as to the gypsies—well, I like gypsies. And who wouldn't make for the moors when the alternative was to endure the insufferable superiority of four Oxford brothers?'

I have had occasion to remind them of Abba Eban's famous retort when he was congratulated in America on his Oxford accent: 'Sir,' he said, 'I would have you know that I went to Cambridge—but in public life you must expect to be smeared.'

When I arrived too young and almost too eager to dive into the excitements of university life, I cheerfully set myself three purposes: to row in the Lady Margaret First May Boat, to be President of the Union and to get a First in History. Unfortunately I put the three aims in that order. I did row for the Lady Margaret Boat Club on the Cam and at Henley, but I did less and less study as my four years proceeded.

I failed to get a First. Having got a two-one in the first part of my Tripos in History, I then sank to a two-two, when I switched to Law in my last two years. I gave up too much time to rowing, and a lot of time to university politics, becoming President of the University Liberal Club.

On most days at Cambridge, rowing came first for me. I became an enthusiastic member of the Lady Margaret Boat Club, one of the toughest organizations in the university. It was a brutish life we led. We met early in the morning for a training run. We rowed every afternoon. We dined together in hall at night. Female society was entirely excluded and despised (I cannot imagine that this ridiculous extension of public school prejudice has survived, but certainly in my Boat Club in my time one would not wish it to be known that one had any unmanly association with the segregated inhabitants of

Newnham and Girton). The language of our conversations was startlingly foul. When we were—rarely—not in training, vast quantities of beer were consumed. I had promised my grandfather (for a financial reward) not to drink until I was twenty-one, and so, as the only teetotaller in the Boat Club (until the moment I was twenty-one) it was my special duty on Bump Suppers to see that fellow members of the Club who were unable to get to bed were assisted. My devotion to the Boat Club remains, but I cannot pretend that, apart from the exuberance of intense physical fitness and the recollection of the occasional joy of being in an eight rowing perfectly together, I had much to show for the long hours I spent on the River Cam.

What did arise from my rowing activities was the thought of escape from the prospect of a lifetime in my father's law office. It was fashionable for rowing Blues to go to the Sudan Political Service. The Blues governing the blacks was the jibe. So though I could not claim the supreme qualification of being a Blue, I put my name down in my last year as an applicant for that Service. My motives were vague and not particularly creditable. I knew little about the Sudan. I had some desire for escape and adventure. It would be pleasant to earn money on my own as soon as possible. I was attracted, too, by a picked Service with a fine tradition. But I had no high motive, no dedication, no missionary enthusiasm and certainly no thought at that time of self-government or independence for peoples under British administration.

When I had passed the first few Sudan interviews I was called to the Colonial Office Appointments Department and told that there was a vacancy for a Junior Assistant Secretary in Palestine. Would I like to be considered for it and abandon my Sudan application? A decision must be made at once since the Palestine vacancy could not wait. I went out into London and had a noisy dinner with some of my Cambridge friends. None of them could tell me anything about the relative attractions or disadvantages of the Sudan and Palestine.

Nevertheless, the Palestine offer was a bird in the hand. I went back to the Colonial Office the next morning. Yes, I would go to Palestine. So within two months of leaving Cambridge I was on my way to become the most junior member of the British Administration in Jerusalem.

An increasing amount of my time at Cambridge was given up to politics and the Union. When I first came up to Cambridge the best known names in the Union were those of the subsequent Archbishop of Canterbury (A. M. Ramsey of Magdalene) and the subsequent Foreign Secretary (R. A. Butler of Pembroke); as freshmen we listened to them speak and in our time they were followed at the Union by a red-headed orator from Christ's called Patrick Devlin, a round bustling energetic figure from Clare, Geoffrey Crowther, and Selwyn Lloyd, with whom I went off speaking for the Liberals. When I went to the United States in 1927 in the university debating team, the other members of it were Lionel Elvin, subsequently Head of the Department of Education at London University, and Alan King Hamilton, subsequently the famous judge. So in preparation for public life I was in pretty good company.

Training in public speaking is not to be despised. My father used to tell me to speak to the man at the back of the hall. To throw your voice, make sure to be heard by everyone present, to communicate, get through to the audience, instead of mumbling into a machine. At Cambridge some of us had opportunities to gain some first-hand experience in a healthy tradition of public speaking. The Cambridge Union was a useful training ground. Not only was it necessary to debate rather than merely make set speeches, but we had the benefit of listening to some of the best orators of our time, when orators were not so very rare as they are now.

Lord Birkenhead was perhaps the finest natural orator I have ever heard. After a dinner at which he consumed what we undergraduates thought was an alarming quantity of wine, he made the most eloquent and devastating speech I ever heard in the Union. At one point when he was in full spate, there was a faint interruption from the back of the crowded benches opposite to him. The great man stopped short. We were all terrified by the ominous silence which followed. 'Stand up, sir,' ordered Lord Birkenhead, and at the back of the Debating Hall a small figure rose in a tattered gown. There was another dreadful silence. Then Lord Birkenhead exploded. 'Sit down, sir. The insignificance of your appearance is sufficient answer to the impudence of your interruption.' The anxious tension was broken; the whole House roared its relief and delight.

Lloyd George came to speak at my Liberal Club Dinner, and we delighted in flashes of his quick wit and his vivid imagination. I had heard him once before at a Liberal Rally in the west country addressing a crowd of many thousands in the open air from a farm cart with no loudspeaker but with every word heard all over the great field before him.

I had learnt my early lessons from my father, going round with him to village political meetings in Cornwall. I had done some speaking at school, as well as speaking in the Cambridge Union and the Liberal Club, and I went off one summer with Selwyn Lloyd, a Liberal in those days, speaking from a travelling van in the Liberal Land Campaign. It was good practice to speak in the squares and street corners of west country villages, occasionally to quite large and noisy crowds but more often to a mere handful of curious villagers. When we arrived in a village or country town, we would put down the side of our van, and Selwyn and I would take it in turns to speak first to an empty street or square, endeavouring to collect a crowd. It was useful speaking experience to have to attract a crowd—and equally good for us no doubt when our listeners decided to disperse, leaving us holding forth in salutary solitude.

In America, too, it was good practice. American college debating was serious and formal by our standards. Our American opponents were out to win the debates by the accumulated weight of solid arguments for which points were allotted by the judges. We were more light-hearted, and we liked to reply at once to the previous speaker, without waiting for the rebuttals at the end of the debate (made after an interval to consult card-indexes of previously prepared replies to the anticipated arguments). We were more anxious to score as we went along—and our opponents were shocked that we didn't seem to care whether we won or lost.

These few months on our debating tour gave me a liking for speaking in America, and in subsequent years, whenever I have had leave from my posts in Arabia or Africa or the West Indies, I have sought permission to go off on speaking tours in the United States.

I had come up to Cambridge in 1925 well prepared. I had been very well taught at school and I had a genuine interest in History and in the Classics. At Cambridge I was at once attracted by some of the History lecturers. I had no difficulty in keeping up, and in pacifying my anxious tutor. Life was easy and varied and exciting. But I cannot claim that I made any progress as a scholar, and when I switched to Law in my last two years, although I found the cases of tort and contract fascinating, I was already heavily over-absorbed in other activities.

Looking back, I am amazed that I could get by with so little time and interest devoted to academic effort. There was enough in the History and Law teaching to keep me lightly interested, but no sense of urgency, no realization that to excel I would have to try far harder.

My brother Michael once wrote this about me in the London *Evening Standard:* 'At Cambridge he picked up bad habits that never entirely left him. Over the years it became increasingly evident that he had acquired strange tastes and was ready to indulge in pastimes which the rest of us wouldn't be seen dead at—such as rowing, playing polo, dressing up in Goering-like uniforms and enjoying it, and occasionally, even—at a pinch—placing some trust in the word of Tory Prime Ministers.'

I do not deny Michael's accusation that I learnt bad habits at Cambridge or that I wasted much of my time there. But I had some assets for the career I so casually adopted. I was physically very fit. I had learnt some History and a little Law. I had picked up some experience of politics and public speaking. Most important of all, in spite of many diversions, I had not altogether forgotten what I learnt from my mother and my father. I had not properly digested the family diet of non-conformity, but I had been brought up on my father's quotations from Cromwell and Milton and Burke and Wordsworth and Lincoln, and I had the beginnings of a hatred of tyranny and privilege and injustice and cruelty. I was irresponsible, no doubt, but I had learnt a great deal from my parents, and I did not forget that it was from them that I had what was worthwhile.

Only the beginnings. Subsequently I have become intensely involved in the causes in which I have been engaged in the wider world. I have so often seen and hated the evils of violence —not only the violence of resistance but more the violence of suppression. I have had ample opportunity to witness the dangers of drift—the failure to act while there was still time. I have tried to teach the gospel of the obligation of optimism—to convince people that the rapidly mounting dangers of the world—of conflict in Cyprus, for instance, or in the Middle East or southern Africa or the longer term dangers in the world-wide problems of race and poverty and population, can all be dealt with if we believe that solutions are possible, if we take positive initiatives in time, and if we do not neglect the international instrument for effective action provided by the United Nations

But these strong convictions came later. When I left Cambridge at the age of twenty-one to go to Jerusalem, I was still very raw material.

Muriel Bradbrook

M. C. Bradbrook was born in 1909, and went up to Girton to read English in 1927. She had previously been at Hutchesons' School in Glasgow and Oldershaw School in Wallasey. After a year in residence at Somerville College, Oxford (1935–6), and working from 1941–5 for the Board of Trade, she became a university lecturer at Cambridge in 1945. In 1962 she was appointed as Reader and in 1965 as Professor of English. In 1968 she became Mistress of Girton, retiring both as Professor and Mistress in 1976. Her 20 books include Elizabethan Stage Conditions (*1932*), Themes and Conventions of Elizabethan Tragedy (*1934*), Joseph Conrad (*1941*), Ibsen the Norwegian (*1947*), The Rise of the Common Player (*1962*), Malcolm Lowry (*1974*) *and* The Living Monument (*1976*).

I complete my half century at Cambridge in 1977. In October 1927, the youngest bar one of sixty-eight young women, I came up to Girton from my northern high school to read English. To compare then and now is perhaps the simplest way to define my Cambridge.

Then, as now, to become a member of this little society was to become a citizen of the world. The sixty-eight included Monica Hunter from the Cape, Eileen Traill from the Argentine, Munira Sadek from Egypt. As Professor Monica Wilson, the first is known today throughout Africa as a brave defender of the liberties of all Africans; the second has achieved vicarious fame as the mother of Judy Innes; the third pioneered scientific education for women in her native country.

Today, with Cambridge in a 'steady state' at about twice its pre-war size, the first year at Girton averages 150 undergraduates; from a date as soon as is found practicable after 1978, these will include men. Men can be elected to the Fellowship from 1976.

Fifty years ago, although still without full membership of the university, the Fellows of the two women's colleges had been newly admitted to university posts as teachers and examiners. Girton was still issuing the certificates which it had given its younger members since 1869; so in 1930 I received one stating that I had done all that would have entitled me, if a man, to graduate as a B.A. The university also supplied a degree certificate in which the word 'titular' had been inserted by hand; this came through the post. No procession to the Senate House, no family parties in the Yard. Today, undergraduates kneel to receive their degree from the first woman Vice-Chancellor, Rosemary Murray, President of New Hall.

As freshers, none of these distinctions concerned us at all; we rapidly formed ourselves into little groups known as 'college families'. Every member of the college belonged to a 'family', sat together at meals, met together at night for a collation known as 'jug', and if necessary signed one another 'out of hall'. Every morning and evening we signed the 'marking rolls' to show we were 'keeping nights' as the university required of men (though not of us).

In due course I was invited to meet one of the original five students who in 1869 joined the first College for Women, then at Benslow House, Hitchin; in 1873 it moved to within two miles of Cambridge and was renamed Girton College. Emily Gibson, Mrs Townshend, an exquisitely pretty old white-haired lady of eighty, observed, 'I will give you a piece of useful advice, my dears. If ever you have to go to prison take a change of underclothes, so they will know you are a lady; and say you are a vegetarian—the food is better if you do.' In the cause of women's suffrage, she had spent a fortnight in Holloway jail.

Set in its fifty-two acres of grounds, the college was exceptionally self-sufficient, and had a strong identity. Older members felt themselves primarily members of Girton. The founder had felt it essential to site the buildings at a safe distance, in order to retain the support of ladies who otherwise 'would have been almost ashamed to speak of it.' True, Cambridge was a riotous town, and the Vice-Chancellor had a private prison for prostitutes, which survived to the 'nineties. But the choice of site has proved a handicap in modern times. It was the one fact mentioned by the BBC in announcing the decision to admit men. It is the one fact everyone knows.

For us, a college bus ran in and out, as it still does; college closed at 11.15. As always, climbing in was easy, but it could lead to questions. Rosamond Lehmann had just published her novel *Dusty Answer*, where Girton's restrictions were rather overdrawn in the interests of her beautiful and intensely sensitive heroine. Friendship at Grantchester and betrayal at The Whim put her Judith into the Cambridge of Virginia Woolf, whose style is echoed in the richly evocative set pieces of landscape painting, breathing an odour of nostalgia.

It was the first of the 'older' images of Girton I was to meet; I did not then realize that the story was essentially that of L. T. Meade's novel of the 'nineties, *A Sweet Girl Graduate*. But in my second year Mrs Woolf herself came to visit Girton and Newnham, and spoke to the Odtaa Society (so called from the initial letters of 'one damned thing after another'). 'I hope your society is a great improvement on my sketch,' she wrote to the Secretary; the result was *A Room of One's Own*.

Mrs Woolf contrasted the dreary meal at a women's college with a splendid lunch at King's. But I was told the meal would have been better if Mrs Woolf had not sat so long looking at the sunset on the Backs that she came in long past the dinner hour. On the other hand, even the most opulent college does not serve *crême brulée* every day. We enjoyed Mrs Woolf but felt her Cambridge was not ours.

The university was at a peak of intellectual activity. Keynes in economics, the Cambridge school of anthropology led by Frazer and Jane Harrison, the school of archaeology in classics, the work of Moore and Wittgenstein in philosophy, the new English school led by I. A. Richards and 'Manny' Forbes kept level with the great scientists, J. J. Thomson and Rutherford.

I had come up well prepared in Shakespeare, Donne and the Romantics, but not at all prepared for the intellectual explosion of Modernist poetry and the work of Joyce, D. H. Lawrence, Virginia Woolf. The imaginative grasp of this new work came in the live exposition of our teachers, by direct contact, by hearing the words 'spoken with power', to borrow a phrase from anthropology. I was told that even the great Indian mathematician Ramanujan had known his subject in isolation, but that meeting with Hardy had alone enabled him to develop it.

Cambridge English had separated off from Modern Languages only in 1917, and the new Tripos began in 1926, introducing contemporary and comparative literature, with a good deal of social history, some aesthetics and philosophy. The men who taught it had begun by reading classics or history or moral science. We therefore discussed Aristotle's *Poetics*, read Dante and modern Americans; but above all, the poetry of *The Waste Land* gave us a new world. Once I heard Sir Herbert Grierson read aloud the poetry which, as a young man, he had recited to himself ecstatically as he walked Edinburgh's New Town; and for those moments, listening, I could feel that Swinburne might be a great poet. What Swinburne was to Grierson, Eliot was to us. Major contemporary literature was coming out all the time. To be able to go into a bookshop and buy a new volume entitled *Ash Wednesday* or *The Tower* challenged the revolutionary method of 'Practical Criticism' which Ivor Richards was expounding weekly. 'Bliss was it in that dawn to be alive!'

We met no consensus of opinion. Some lecturers held views very different from those of Richards, whose psychological theory of literary value became for some of his followers something to be accepted as revelation. The creative work being produced at Cambridge in that time was sceptical yet exhilarated. William Empson, with whom I have always been so proud to have been bracketed in the results of the Tripos examination, had first read mathematics; his mathematics was part of his poetry, in 'Legal Fiction', for instance, or 'To an Old Lady'. Kathleen Raine has spoken of his 'contained mental energy, as of a flame whose outline remains constant while its substance is undergoing continual metamorphosis at a temperature in which only intellectual salamanders could hope to live', and of 'that sense of vivid shock his presence always produced'. *Seven Types of Ambiguity* was written for Ivor Richards, who supervised his studies at Magdalene; bits of it came out in the magazine *Experiment*, where Jacob Bronowski was also publishing poetry, and some of Kathleen Raine's early poems appeared. She was in my year at Girton, reading botany. Malcolm Lowry and John Davenport were writing for the same magazine and also composing Footlights Revues for May Week. Michael Redgrave, at Queens', edited another magazine, *The Venture.* Alistair Cooke drew caricatures and wrote verses. I think he read modern languages. He founded the Mummers, the first mixed drama club.

Political debate centred on the Union Society rather than the clubs; one of my 'family' became a friend of the President, Kenneth Adam, the future director of BBC programmes. She was a keen Liberal and a member of the 80 Club; together we sat in the Gallery, for the union was not open to women, and followed the debates. Hugh Foot was President in my third year.

Nor could we at first join the dramatic societies (so I saw Dadie Rylands in feminine roles at the Marlowe Society). The musical world, however, freely admitted us, and two of my 'family' sang in Boris Ord's Madrigal Society, which then, as now, performed in May Week from punts outside King's. In college itself there were many small informal groups, like Odtaa. But the best gift was the right to be solitary and independent if one wished, as Dame Margaret Cole recorded in *Growing up in Revolution* (she came up to Girton in 1911):

> 'My first impression of College was one of freedom—freedom to work when you liked; to stop when you liked, to cut, even, lectures which turned out unhelpful and uninteresting; to be *where* you liked *when* you liked and with *whom* you liked (subject to not making too antisocial

a racket); to get up and go to bed when you pleased and, if desirable, to go on reading, writing or talking till dawn.'

Apart from the lectures (some of which were held very informally in college halls) teaching was still largely a college affair. 'Mays', the first year examination, was a semi-private intercollegiate game, of three groups. Although Richards crowded the largest room of the dreary old Arts School, one had to run smartly from Cat's to King's to Emma to hear Tom Henn, Dadie Rylands or F. R. Leavis. Sir Arthur Quiller-Couch still addressed his audience as 'Gentlemen' and was displeased when he found he had inadvertently awarded the Chancellor's Medal for English Verse to a woman, Elsie Phare of Newnham. He would not accept us at his evening classes on Aristotle's *Poetics*.

However, our college teaching was varied. My don, Miss Hilda Murray, arranged for us to be taught Practical Criticism and the modern period by F. R. Leavis. He cycled up on Wednesday afternoons to the old army hut where classes were held, with unbuttoned shirt and a knapsack full of books. He read us Eliot, Richards and Empson (how many people have been taught poetry written by a contemporary undergraduate?); many horrendous examples came from *The Oxford Book of English Verse*. Besides Eliot, he stressed Walter de la Mare, Wilfred Owen, Edmund Blunden and Edward Thomas. Other teachers were Joan and Stanley Bennett (she taught whilst bringing up a family of four, who sometimes interrupted the supervisions) and the terrifying Dr Pettoello, who taught Dante in a little room filled with copies of *La Libertà* (he was in exile from Mussolini's Italy). Brandishing a poker he would declare 'Firrst, you assassinate [this word was hissed] sommvon in Turin; zen you assassinate sommvon in Milano; and zat undermine zeir *morale*!' He was to be met also in the sixpenny gallery of the Festival Theatre, to which experimental productions of Goethe's *Faust* in both parts, Elmer Rice, Eugene O'Neill, Aeschylus, drew an audience from all over Europe. There I saw *As You Like It* staged in black and white, Rosalind as a boy scout blowing a whistle; *Julius Caesar* in modern dress (which must have delighted Pettoello) and most unforgettably, Flora Robson in *Six Characters in Search of an Author*. The Festival opened just fifty years ago.

In addition to directing our studies, Miss Murray conferred on her pupils the benefit of an Oxford point of view quite opposed to that of Cambridge. She was the daughter of Sir James Murray, editor of the Oxford Dictionary, and had begun her life by compiling index cards for that great work in a 'tin tabernacle' in her father's garden. He used his large family for enforced labour as he had, of course, no public grant. A Cambridge colleague was later to remark that she had 'one of the best memories in Europe'; her knowledge was daunting and her most caustic comments were pencilled upon our weekly offerings in a fair round hand; but 'Have you any manuscript authority for that variant?' she once asked when I made a slip in translating Chaucer. As we trooped into her book-lined room with its colour scheme of blue and orange, we used to practise meek ways of saying 'yes'. But when at the end of my first year my father died, and left a young family still to be educated, she was tenderness itself.

Bereavement and poverty and falling in love, all during the years of depression, made up my life in its personal aspects. The years 1930–6 gave me a taste of extremities which have ever since enabled me to put other difficulties in proportion. After my mother's death, with two brothers still completing their education, I had two years to wait before Miss Murray retired in 1936 and Girton elected me to a teaching fellowship. I was twenty-seven and had published three books. I started at £250 a year. My youngest brother won a scholarship that year. I was at Somerville College, Oxford from 1935–6, and witnessed the acid reception of Dorothy Sayers's *Gaudy Night*.

In 1945 I was given my first temporary university appointment.

I had spent the war years in London with the Board of Trade, a most educative experience, had learnt Norwegian from the Norwegian Navy, and was writing a book on Ibsen. Post-war students were the most brilliant set; an era of intercontinental travel began for scholars. Six visits to North America, two to Australia and New Zealand, two to the Far East, many to Scandinavia, one to India, one to Kuwait, one to Hungary, one to Berlin enabled me to give students from these places some insight into problems of adjustment when they came to Cambridge. The scholars' is the only international society that really works.

Looking at Cambridge now, I see a much larger and more organized English School. With Frank Kermode, Christopher Ricks and a host of lively young people, it is not inbred, and in my view still leads the field. It still remains a college-based subject: each undergraduate may determine his own course (for example the subject of his 'long essay' which replaces a conventional paper), but this has to be centrally accepted. The combination of wide options and growing numbers (at present about 800 undergraduates) means a headache for the university computer at the time of planning examination timetables. Instead of one professor (who spent much of his time at Fowey as Commodore of the Yacht Club) there are now seven professors, four readers, twenty-seven lecturers and assistant lecturers, all reaching for their lawful allocations of leave and mostly spending it much farther off than Fowey. These numbers include the Department of Anglo-Saxon which, after spending forty years in unnatural union with Anthropology, has made a companionate marriage with English. But the total Faculty numbers 130, some living precariously on the fringe. To keep communications open, the forms of the Tripos examination are constantly being discussed, and formally laid down; for it is the subject of intense anxiety, and reassurance is constantly being sought. The present system of public grants links an undergraduate or graduate student's future much more directly to his examination.

The anxiety extends itself to general forms of university life. Changing patterns of relations depend on changing habits. Very few dons reside in college, and yearly the number grows less. Even inflation does not send them back. Those breakfast parties that I remember from the 'thirties have disappeared. It may be the changing form of the college community (most dons are married and without the domestic help of former days) that has led to the demand for mixed colleges; if the generations no longer combine in one community, an alternative is for the sexes to do so.

In the late 'fifties and early 'sixties the arrival of the new colleges for graduates (Darwin, Clare Hall, Wolfson) which were mixed from the beginning, had followed the institution of the third women's college, New Hall, which opened in 1954.

Cambridge seemed to run a steady course through the 'fifties and early 'sixties. In 1966 in California I met the Berkeley students' protest movement, and Marcuse, who was also there. He greatly impressed the impressionable, with his unending flow of clichés. About two years later, Californian attitudes became fashionable in Cambridge, and reforming the university became an alternative to study.

Handicapped by the science students' preference for their labs, and by the lack of a strong social science department, Cambridge was assisted by the strong sense of guilt which such exceptional opportunities and privileges could generate (a form of egoism, of course, if the privileges are taken as being merely gratuitous and not a public investment). A few students created a few incidents, though often heavily reinforced from outside. On one such occasion, when honorary degrees were being conferred, a group began yelling 'Intellectuals in! Adrian out!' outside the Senate House Yard. They had mistaken the Chancellor, Professor Lord Adrian, for an hereditary peer, not realizing that as the discoverer of the D waves in the brain, he had more intellect in his little finger than the whole bunch of them put together. He walked on with the puzzled look of one whose experiment is showing unusual features. But I hated that chant. It had exactly the rhythm of 'Sieg Heil! Sieg Heil!'

Good sense and a sense of humour were not wanting. Among the *graffiti*, the inscription 'Give me back my mind' provoked the retort underneath: 'No—you must find it for yourself'; and 'Is there intelligence left on earth?' was met by 'Yes—but I'm only visiting.'

The relation of senior and junior members has changed much more than the forms of academic study. The ritual of being chased by the Proctor and his 'bulldogs' is being succeeded by the institutionalizing of 'sit-ins' for which, as I understand, a sort of code is being drawn up. The 'Rites of Spring' generally occur in the second half of the Lent Term; the university is not sufficiently settled in the Michaelmas Term, and in the Easter Term other interests take precedence.

For the don, it has become more necessary than ever to listen to the words behind the words. The undergraduates are now of legal age; many have travelled widely; their newspapers are filled with appeals to aggression. 'Shock report slams Tutors', screams the headline—and then somewhere, in much smaller print, the report that only a tiny fraction said they were not proud to be members of their college. Publicity is sweet for the undergraduate (it may mean a cheque and ultimately a job); so the desired image is produced. On the whole, because Cambridge is found enviable, the image will either be that of the old world of privilege (blazers and boaters and champers and *crême brulée*), or it will be Sex Probe at King's. Students are news, and sex is news; both together—!

The attitude of Cambridge to women has always been ambivalent. In 1875 a Cambridge hostess wrote after a dinner party: 'My dear, she was a nice girl, with rosy cheeks and nice manners and nicely dressed, and you wouldn't have thought she knew anything!' In her talk to the freshers in 1927, the Mistress concluded, 'And remember, my dears, the eyes of the Cambridge ladies will be ever upon you!', advising us to don hat and gloves at Storey's Way. As late as 1920, an undergraduate referendum had voted by a majority of 2,329 out of 3,213, to exclude women from full membership. It was thirty years and more after they had gained the national franchise that women were permitted to vote in the Councils of the university; full rights came in 1948. Yet when I was at Oxford in 1936, whilst I had already examined for Cambridge University, I found there ladies much senior to myself who had never so officiated. ('I prefer justice to favours,' one of them remarked haughtily.) Girton and Newnham were built only by the cooperation of Cambridge men, who taught their undergraduates, spoke for them, served on their governing bodies (at Girton, till 1952). In the last eight years, during my Mistresship, men took over our teaching posts, if women were not available—Christopher Morris, a Fellow of King's, for some years directed studies in history; economics is now directed by another member of King's; German taught by a Fellow of Magdalene; and of the two hundred and eighty supervisors on the Girton lists of teachers, the majority are inevitably men, since Cambridge is still predominantly a men's university.

At the end of *Dusty Answer* Rosamond Lehmann wrote:

> 'Farewell to Cambridge, to whom she was less than nothing. She had been deluded into imagining that it bore her some affection. Under its politeness, it had disliked and distrusted her and all other females, and now it ignored her.'

'Of course I am entirely without prejudice,' remarked a committee member once. 'I would always prefer a first-class woman to a third-class man.'

One or two of the Girton Fellows now hold joint teaching posts at other colleges (they are certainly first-class women); at Jesus College Jacob Bronowski's daughter, the first woman Fellow, has been admitted after progressing from Newnham to a Fellowship at Girton, from Girton to King's. Another Girtonian went to Clare, another to Churchill, yet another directs studies and lectures at Trinity. But this is to anticipate the story of the last decade.

I had been Mistress of Girton for about two weeks when in October 1968 a printed note through the post informed us that one of the men's undergraduate colleges was going to admit women at all levels. The motives of senior and junior members did not necessarily or even probably coincide. Pressure for co-residence (co-education already existed) came mainly from undergraduates who evinced a sometimes explicit desire to have more girls about. The fellows were concerned to maintain standards in threatened subjects ('We thought we might get a few good classics,' one senior tutor blandly observed). In general it was favoured by the young and opposed by the older generation of dons.

What happens in the universities is closely dependent on what happens in the schools, but here again stands a big question mark. The boys' public schools are increasingly admitting girls; the girls' public schools have not, to my knowledge, reciprocated. Yet the women's colleges at Oxford and Cambridge have never been dependent on the large girls' public schools, and have always drawn from hundreds of smaller establishments up and down the country. More than two hundred schools every year send in candidates for Girton. What the Ministry does to these will react upon us directly.

It was therefore decided quite soon to introduce a new statute which would offer the chance for Girton to admit men at any time it wished to do so. This enabling statute went through the elaborate procedure of being approved by the Queen in Council, thus freeing the college to decide for itself by a simple vote. The decision of a women's college to admit men is certainly not simply the converse of the men's decision to admit women. No woman can fail to rejoice that the splendours of King's and Trinity are now opening to her sex or conceal the pleasure she feels at seeing the young women look so completely and easily at home. In their search for a new image to replace Castle Adamant, women's colleges will need to develop a creative response which utilizes their own previous experience and blends it with the changing needs of the present and future time.

Among the men's colleges that have admitted women, the different atmospheres have already established a very different degree of popularity in the schools. The academic issue is largely of keeping the balance of subjects to ensure a full community. If the feminine trend to arts is not reversed, we shall end with a polarized society where men read science and women arts. The government asks Cambridge for a fifty-fifty ratio. English, the most popular faculty for women, is already oversubscribed; this is true of other arts faculties, even in terms of the colleges, certainly of the university. Medicine alone has a 'quota'.

Given the present pace of change, Girton's strong feminist image is now part of history. The exasperating stamina of the obsolete image of Cambridge or the obsolete image of Girton may be contrasted with the efforts to fix or establish an identity in the instant universities of the 'sixties. The 'absolute' and intransigent quality of the Girton image has been academic, not social in its origins, and sprang from a conviction that women must prove themselves by following the exact course, be it good or bad, that had been set for men. This was proved more than a hundred years ago, when three young women answered the Tripos papers in the University Arms Hotel, watched by their chaperon. The impulse to iconoclasm is strong, but should be resisted; transformation, not destruction of the image will ensure continuity. 'Girtona Unisex' is too hard to sell.

The Cambridge image is remarkably constant too; from Rosamond Lehmann's *Dusty Answer* of the nineteen-twenties, to Charlotte Haldane's *I Bring Not Peace* of the nineteen-thirties, Andrew Sinclair's *My Friend Judas* of the nineteen-fifties, to the latest manifestation, Frederic Raphael's *The Glittering Prizes*, a return to the same intense recollected image that is an image of the writer's youth, goes with a sense that the student's life is a public role to be played out.

Yet alongside the images, a stream of quiet traditional life flows, which isn't news and never seeks this kind of projection. There are as many different Cambridges as there are graduates, and for some Girtonians, a mixed college may amputate them from their own past. At a gathering of former students, an old lady looked round Woodlands Court with disfavour. 'When I was up, none of this was here!' My placatory 'When I came up, only half of it was here,' produced little softening. So, one of the older Fellows at supper—'All these husbands!' 'Only one each,' I said. My Cambridge, always changing yet the same, like the flowing Cam, presents me with a series of images, not one clear, distanced view. Seasons return. The Fellows of Girton were kind enough to elect me to a Life Fellowship, but I told them I wished it could have been a Research Fellowship, the title I had held more than forty years before. For that represented what I felt it to be for me.

So I am still part of Cambridge, living in a little house between the one where Lord Ramsey, the former Archbishop, was born and the haunted house of the Christ's College Ghost, at the corner of Croft Holme Lane. I can still enjoy Gregorian chants in St John's College Chapel; the insight of a pupil that comes with a shock of delight and instruction to the teacher; strawberries and cream in Neville's Court; the Japanese Society of Visiting Scholars in English; the eights rowing up to Jesus Lock before breakfast through the November mists; the lecture that sends me rushing to the University Library, and then writing furiously into the small hours; the fresh young voice uttering some platitude with awe and wonder; the sight of the Vice-Chancellor bicycling through crowds of shoppers with every lineament proclaiming the need to breast Castle Hill before half-past three; the triple bob major from the tower of Great St Mary's; the old drunk cadging money in Market Square; the hideous proliferation of bogus college or university ties, scarves, tee shirts donned by the most unsuitable visitors.

Doesn't Cambridge make you feel (asked the local councillor at the sherry party) when you go to London, that you are living in an ivory tower?

Raymond Williams

Raymond Williams was born in 1921, and went up to Trinity to read English in 1939. He had previously been at Abergavenny Grammar School. From 1946–61 he was working as Staff Tutor in Literature for the Extramural Department of Oxford University. During these fifteen years he published several books including Reading and Criticism *(1950)*, Drama from Ibsen to Eliot *(1952)*, Culture and Society *(1958) and* The Long Revolution *(1961). In 1961 he returned to Cambridge as a Fellow of Jesus College. In 1967 he became Reader in Drama and in 1974 he was appointed as Professor of Drama. His more recent books include* The Country and the City *(1973) and* Keywords *(1976).*

It was not my Cambridge. That was clear from the beginning. I have now spent eighteen years in the university, in three distinct periods. In each of them I have started by being surprised to be there, and then, in time, made some kind of settlement. But this has always, even in the longest period, felt temporary.

The surprise can be related to the fact that, in each of the three periods, I didn't ask or apply to come here. When I became an undergraduate, at Trinity, it was the first time I had seen Cambridge and I knew virtually nothing about it. My headmaster in Abergavenny had spent a year at Trinity, after taking his degree at Aberystwyth. I took the old Higher School Certificate at sixteen and was awarded a State Scholarship. There had been no talk of university before that time. My headmaster and my father met and talked about it, and the headmaster wrote to Trinity. They said I could come up in October 1939, and that is what happened. Then, since other more important things had been happening meanwhile, I had only two years as an undergraduate, before I was called up into the Army. Just over four years later, in mid-October 1945, I was with my regiment on the Kiel Canal, and next in line on the list of Captains to be posted to Burma. What was then called BLA, the British Liberation Army, was generally translated as Burma Looms Ahead. One morning I was called to Headquarters, and I expected it to be the posting. It was a notification of what was called Class B Release, with instructions to report to Trinity College, Cambridge, where the first term of my third student year had already begun. That period lasted till the following June. I was offered a graduate scholarship at the end of it, and considered staying for research. But I wasn't much interested, and in any case now had a family to support. I got a job in adult education, from Oxford, and that was the next fifteen years. I visited Cambridge only once during that period, to give a lecture at a summer school. I walked around and, though I knew my way, it seemed wholly strange. Then, in the spring of 1961, I went down one morning for the post and opened a letter informing me, in three official lines, that I had been appointed to a Lectureship in the English Faculty at Cambridge: a job I didn't even know was vacant and certainly hadn't applied for. The adult education job had been changing, in ways I didn't like. Over the next two days I had other letters, which had been meant to arrive first and explain the situation. These included requests that I would consider accepting the appointment, but the die had already been cast and in fact I was glad. A bizarre episode followed, in which I visited Jesus College to be considered for a Fellowship. That eventually came through, and so in the summer of 1961 I was back. I shall presumably stay until I retire.

Each of the three periods presented a very different Cambridge. The image of the place includes persistence, duration, stability, and this is obvious enough from most of the buildings. Some spirit also may be said to persist. Certainly I have noticed its radical difference from Oxford, in spite of the obvious similarities. But to see this long-run Cambridge means standing back. I feel it most when I am away, or sometimes when I am showing a visitor around. What comes through then is very general and probably in its own way true. But in each of these three periods I have known the place in quite different ways, from close up and within what I suppose is a sub-culture. These sub-cultures vary at the time and over the years. Some are projected as the essential Cambridge, or as the Cambridge of particular years. I don't know. In these three periods I have found the place quite different. What sticks is what you were doing, and particular individuals and groups. But memories are selective. This is clear even in those cases in which people profess to be remembering a group (it is usually brilliant; it is always unique). What I have noticed about these memories of groups is that they are at least partly determined by what happens to the people afterwards. The successful, obviously, are more easily remembered; the others, equally important at the time, can be made to fade. There is a close parallel in external images of the intellectual life of the university. People talk of the Cambridge of Moore and Russell, or of Wittgenstein and Richards, and so on. Yet at any time such figures are a tiny minority in the whole intellectual life of the university. It is falsifying, in a particular way, to project the place through these few figures, who are as often as not relatively isolated, or quite uncharacteristic. It is the same, though less obviously, with the buildings. Often, when I am showing someone around, I am told how beautiful the place is, and I can stop and look and agree that it is so. But hurrying through and past the same places in the ordinary buzz and rush, it is extraordinarily difficult to see this. Buildings materialize as memories of meetings, or as unwanted appointments. Changed places, changed uses, carry odd mixed memories. And as these change through time, for someone who comes back and works here the effect is bound to be different from the images and memories carried by people who were here for three years and then left. One obvious difference is that when you live here for any time you get to know the town, as a town, as well as the university, and that whole added dimension makes many of the more local memories very different.

When I came up in 1939 the war had just started and the feeling of temporariness was bound to be strong. It was my first view of the place, though my parents had visited my lodgings, in Maid's Causeway, and a box of food—ham, marmalade and honey—had been sent ahead with my trunk. I was told by a porter where to buy a gown, but spent much longer hunting the streets for a lavatory. On the next morning there was an address in hall by the Senior Tutor: scriptural and familiar. Later that day I discovered that though I had come to read English, the college had no arrangements for teaching it. I had to go down the road to Dr Tillyard of Jesus College, who sent me on to Mr Elvin of Trinity Hall. I was given an essay assignment on Shakespeare's sonnets, and a lecture-list. That worked out well enough. There were others in the college reading English, and these were my first friends. I put my name down for rugby, and played a few games. I joined the Union, as a life member, but only after some embarrassment, since I knew no one who could propose me. In this and in other ways, over the first week, I found out what is now obvious: that I was arriving, more or less isolated, within what was generally the arrival of a whole formation, an age-group, which already had behind it years of shared acquaintance, and shared training and expectations, from its boarding schools. I was reminded of a conversation my father had reported to me, from his advance visit. The porter had asked him, rather haughtily, whether my name was already down. 'Yes, since last autumn.' 'Last autumn? Many of them, you know, are put down at birth.' I try to be charitable, and find it easier now. But I remember sitting on the benches in hall, surrounded by those people, and wishing they *had* been put down at birth. There was little personal difficulty or dislike, but the formation was easy to hate—is still easy to hate—and I have to record that I responded aggressively. The myth of the working-class boy arriving in Cambridge—it has happened more since the war, though the proportion is still quite unreasonably low—is that he is an awkward misfit and has to learn new manners. It may depend on where you come from. Out of rural Wales it didn't feel like that. The class which has dominated Cambridge is given to describing itself as well-mannered, polite, sensitive. It continually contrasts itself favourably with the rougher and coarser others. When it turns to the arts, it congratulates itself, overtly, on its taste and its sensibility; speaks of its poise and tone. If I then say that what I found was an extraordinarily coarse, pushing, name-ridden group, I shall be told that I am showing class-feeling, class-envy, class-resentment. That I showed class-feeling is not in any doubt. All I would insist on is that nobody fortunate enough to grow up in a good home, in a genuinely well-mannered and sensitive community, could for a moment envy these loud, competitive and deprived people. All I did not know then was how cold that class is. That comes with experience.

There was soon an alternative, or what seemed at the time an alternative. I was already active in politics, and I joined what was then called CUSC—the Socialist Club. It was an extraordinary political situation. From the mid-'thirties the club had been dominated by student communists, but the CP was now against the war and the coming split was obvious. In those first months of what is now called the phoney war there was in fact less tension than there should have been. The open split didn't happen until later in the year, when the son of a Labour MP wrote to a schoolfriend in Oxford, setting out the plans of a new Labour Club. It seemed very funny at the time that the schoolfriend had meanwhile become a communist. But what mattered more than these inevitable manoeuvres was the intense sub-culture of CUSC. I have seen nothing like it since, even in the days of the strong student Left of the late 'sixties. To begin with, there was a clubroom, which served lunches. This became the effective centre of social life; much more so than the college. It was above what used to be MacFisheries, in a passage off Petty Cury. The room later belonged to the Footlights, and I have seen other nostalgic memories of it. The whole area has been pulled down now, and replaced by a shopping centre. But it is one place I still remember vividly. The lunches through the hatch on the right of the door as you came up the stairs. The posters on the walls, including the inevitable 'Your Courage, Your Resolution . . . will bring Us Victory', altered either by underlining Us or by changing Resolution to Revolution. The wall newspaper, on which I pinned my first political article, done on my new typewriter, on which I could get only the red part of the ribbon to work. But more than anything the films. Virtually the entire sub-culture was filmic. Eisenstein and Pudovkin but also Vigo and Flaherty. Someone said it was only in the 'sixties that under-graduate culture became cinematic rather than literary. In some ways this may be true; the literary culture was then also there. But the lunches and the films were, I now think, the real organizing elements of CUSC, with the Cosmo in Market Passage as an out-station. Much of the politicking was internal: a fairly persistent feature of the Left. But we intervened actively in the Union. I spoke regularly in debates, but in the middle of the first term was suspended for speaking ill of the Curator of the Fitzwilliam Museum, who was on the opposite side in a debate on the rights of women. I insisted that he was not a curator but an exhibit, until the bell stopped me.

One other thing that had happened was the evacuation of the London School of Economics to Cambridge. This eventually affected the politics, making it more varied and considerably more sophisticated, though also more to the Right. One fortunate effect of the evacuation was that I met my future wife, who was an LSE student. She came with a birthday party to a CUSC dance in the Dorothy Ballroom, at which I was taking the admission tickets. I don't know whether it was just that night, but I was certainly then talking with an American accent. It was at about the same time that I dropped out of playing rugby. My last game was for Trinity against the LSE.

There were several magazines, and I contributed a short story called *Mother Chapel* to one of them. In some way that I have never understood it got back to Wales and caused a good deal of embarrassment to my parents, though they were not chapel people. I also wrote a story called *Red Earth*, which interests me now because half of it was a satiric presentation of avant-garde students. All these incidents, now obviously enough, show confusion and division of feeling. But over that whole first year, and indeed the first term of the second year, I was an active student militant, as it is now called, and this took up most of my time, the academic work going along in what seemed like a separate existence; indeed as a sort of routine job, or, put the other way round, a hobby. The special conditions of Cambridge academic life, especially for arts students, seem to produce this situation again and again. When I read other reminiscences—especially now as what other people call a don—I am continually surprised at the relative absence or minor interest of work. Yet some work got done; I found a packet of it recently. Examinations were passed. It was just that all the real life was this other.

In my third term I became editor of the student newspaper, then called the *Cambridge University Journal*, commonly *CUJ*, printed by Foister and Jagg in another building, near the Lion Yard, which has gone down under the shopping centre. It was no term to be an editor. The war became real suddenly, but there was still general surprise that the Proctors banned a debate, which was announced as comic, on a motion welcoming the imminent collapse of Western Civilization. The date was May 1940. I printed summaries of the speeches in the *CUJ*. There was some trouble, but more important things were happening. We left Cambridge expecting invasion, not expecting to come back. In Wales I went with my father to the first shooting practice of what became the Home Guard. There is an infinite capacity, at that age and especially in certain conditions, to live several merely nominally connected lives.

The second year, understandably, was more serious. The politics could not continue as a privileged extension of the 'thirties. CUSC was now in a basement on the corner of Peas Hill and Benet Street; it is a clothes shop today. Slowly, through the year, a different mood became dominant. In my own case it meant mixing more with the group in CUSC who were called the aesthetes. We published a magazine, for which I wrote a story called *Sugar*, and worked hard and, we thought, stylishly, at other writing, and in theatre and film. I still spoke regularly in the Union, and in the Easter Term was elected Chairman of Debates, the wartime equivalent of President. But the most important thing that happened, intellectually, during the year, was that I had to relate the active cultural interests, and the radical theories that seemed to go with them, to my academic work in English, which in the first year had seemed separate and formal, like school. Now, as they say in examination papers, I had to compare and contrast, bring the two kinds of interest into useful relation. I didn't succeed. I could have done with some help, but, unsurprisingly, looking back, there was none available. There was plenty of sound academic teaching, but it had no connection at all with the problems of our own writing and with our arguments about new forms and new audiences. Moreover, in the relatively self-contained and often arrogant atmosphere of our group, we didn't know how to frame questions that might have provoked some answers. We had an activity and an affiliation, and we knew what we thought about others.

At the same time, conditions were becoming harder. Friends back on leave from the Army were contemptuous of the undergraduate life-style which they had shared only a few months before, but while that contrast was obvious, the style itself was becoming more cramped. I think it was at this time that some of us founded, in Trinity, against considerable senior opposition, a college students' union. The flashpoint in the origin of this now highly-respectable body was the appearance at meals of a hitherto unknown meat dish called bitok: a peculiarly nasty kind of rissole. It is curious how persistent this kind of student complaint about college food is, and how very seriously it is taken at the time. I recall also that this was happening to an undergraduate generation which, as a matter of course, assumed an upper-class life style. Parties were like that, and there were regular visitors from literary London and the London theatre who kept up the style. Our group drink, as

I remember, was the especially potent gin and cider. I think I can still taste it, though I have not drunk gin since the war.

As a condition of finishing our year's course we were required to enrol in military training, as officer cadets. I remember Bren gun sessions on the Rifle Range beyond Grange Road. I had now been moved to be supervised by Tillyard. When I came back to Jesus College, fifteen years later, he had recently retired as Master, and we talked on High Table. 'All I can remember about you, Williams,' he said gruffly, 'is boots.' I at once related this to the character of our supervisions, where he was kind and quiet over a cup of tea and I was pushing hard and probably rudely with questions I couldn't properly formulate. Then the memory came back, and the more prosaic explanation. My supervision hour with him came immediately after this weekly drill. I had to rush back on my bike, still in uniform, and clump up his stairs. The slightly comic situation is still symptomatic, however, of the displacement and disconnection which, through no fault of his, were now evident. I was indeed running hard all the time to stay still, or rather, since stillness would have been welcome, running hard, desperately improvising, into the same deep-seated muddle. When I thought I had got out of the muddle, many years later in *Culture and Society* or in *The Country and the City*, I found looking back on that time exceptionally embarrassing and even painful. I came to feel the same way about many of the earlier political naiveties. This has now almost, if not quite, gone. It was so mixed up with problems of personal development, which included every kind of emotional confusion, that I was probably the last person to realize that the tensions and contradictions, messy as they were, belonged to a phase of quite general transition. Certainly that is what many students now tell me, though with the advantage of knowing answers that, to the extent that some are real, were in practice dearly bought. It was this whole experience, and one later experience, in 1948, that I had in mind when, years later, I described

Burke as 'one of that company of men who learn virtue from the margin of their errors, learn folly from their own persons'. I would not put it like that now. I think the angry thrust was necessary, and moreover that it was substantially right. The errors it involved, of a general kind, followed from its insertion into the preformed and only partly connecting world of the public-school Left and the late Bloomsbury avant-garde. Yet these, where I found myself, were the only formed alternatives to the much larger and more dominant public-school Right, deeply embedded in the colleges, and to the depressed academic literary establishment. It took me much longer to get out of the alternative formations; the orthodox formations had, for obvious reasons, never seemed even plausible.

That is to look back. At the time it all simply spiralled downwards. When I left Cambridge, in the June, I sold my typewriter, my gown, my bicycle and most of my books. This was only partly a symbolic gesture. I was in debt, and in a couple of weeks I was going into the Army. But I remember thinking, beyond these practical reasons, that it was goodbye to all that. We read golden reminiscences of Cambridge so often, from the successful, of course. Remembering 1941, and having seen scores of cases since, I have to include this other kind of fact. Cambridge can break you up, to no good purpose: confuse you, sicken you, wring you dry. In the 'sixties, now on the side of authority, I used to see young men to whom this had happened, and always, beyond that uncomfortable figure in the chair, I saw a strange and at least equally impossible young man of 1941. I was once taken, on an academic outing, to a performance in King's College Chapel, on the safe theme of the Biblical writing on the wall. Our party responded aesthetically, but they approved the theme as a matter of course. Outside, on the sacred wall of the chapel, two young men had written, in paint, 'Free Nelson Mandela'. I went to court to give them character references. In the general shock, which I could indeed understand, everyone else had left them to fend for themselves. After this and other similar cases, including going weekly to a prison to supervise a young man unreasonably convicted in what was called the Garden House Riot, I got the reputation—the phrase is still used—of being 'soft on students'. I even had this said to me by one of the former leading activists in CUSC, now a respectable Professor. In the ordinary sense I think I am hard on students; certainly I have found that I am a harsh examiner. But I have good and continuing reasons for knowing that the challenge Cambridge offers is not only to achievement; it is often, necessarily, to dissent. The university prides itself on being liberal to dissenters, and in comparative terms this is often true. But there are kinds of dissent which are beyond its terms: inarticulate, incoherent, and then often raging or messy. It is at times like this that I wonder whether any of my colleagues has ever been young, or young in ways which did not repeat those of their fathers or prefigure their own rounded maturities. My complaint against students, in fact, is that too many of them fade from their tensions, or go whoring after any authority but their own possible futures.

Anyway, it seemed to be over. But then the ironies began. Everywhere I went in the Army I found that Cambridge—not my painful flux, but the clear distant sound of the place—was an admission ticket; indeed, as it used to be called for the families of railwaymen, a privilege ticket. Once, only once, this was because it indicated that I was clever. A future General decided that, having been to Cambridge, I could learn anything, and sent me to train as an instructor on the machinery of a new type of tank; I indeed learned the manual but I am mechanically one of the stupidest people ever born, and the fitters, with their usual loyalty, had to clear up after me. Mostly, Cambridge mattered because it showed I was the right sort of person. Shades of 1941, when a future Peer, then the most active of our Tory opponents in student politics, called out of the window as I was leaving: 'Remember, I'll get you, Williams.' Anyway, to my brother officers on the Kiel Canal, when the release came instead of the posting, the pattern seemed correct: the first words after 'lucky bastard' were that I was 'going back where I belonged'.

It didn't feel like that, in a demob suit in the autumn of 1945. All the familiar centres had gone. I had lost touch with all my previous friends and acquaintances. And the atmosphere had changed, beyond recognition. Eventually, through a chance contact, I found the new alternative sub-culture, which in English but also in Anthropology was the group around F. R. Leavis. I had known virtually nothing of him before, and I was not now to be taught by him; Trinity had a young Indian Research Fellow, B. Rajan. In that whole year I heard Leavis talk once. But I had two close friends who were taught by him, both also socialists, and we spent much time together planning a magazine—it was eventually two magazines—which would bring together *Scrutiny* criticism and Left politics. We also collaborated on other writing projects, and this lasted for a few years after we went down. I lived in my third lodging in Cambridge (Malcolm Street had followed Maid's Causeway): a house at the top of Victoria Road. My wife, until I finished my course, lived with our daughter at her mother's home. It was a quieter, if, in retrospect, no less confused and confusing time. But one of the differences was that I got back to intensive academic work: losing myself for many months in Ibsen and then spending an Easter vacation reading George Eliot against the clock. This is the prototype of the hardworking ex-serviceman student, but there were also the long hours in the Indian Restaurant opposite St John's and the planning of the magazines. When we thought we couldn't raise any money beyond £20, we even considered going to Newmarket and putting it all on an outsider. Eventually, as an ex-serviceman, I got a paper allowance, under the rationing scheme, and we made our way for a time. But what I think mattered most—it would have been strange to that young man of 1941; it is a much more common choice now—was the Tripos. I became extraordinarily involved with the examination itself; emotionally involved. I remember walking down from Victoria Road and across Jesus Green on the morning it started, and all I saw was my home village, which in a strange way now seemed at stake. One of my examiners told me, years later, that mine was one of the two sets of papers she clearly remembered after many years of examining. Certainly I put a strange intensity into what, after all, is a relatively distant and formal exercise. But English Part Two makes more room than any other examination I know for that kind of commitment. My first two books, and parts of others, started with that work. Alongside it the influence of Leavis, indirect as it was, proved extraordinarily invigorating. For some time it seemed a solution to the unresolved problems of 1941, to which it appeared to speak so directly.

Sorting that out, and eventually rejecting it, took the next ten years, and during that period, as for so many people at a distance, Cambridge was Leavis, though with the paradox—which supported much of our indignation, and which was an important element of the affiliation—that Cambridge, established Cambridge, had rejected him. It was very strange, after 1961, returning as a colleague when he was about to retire, and with many of my own positions changed, to get to know him directly for the first time: with a persistent respect, but with the changes rapidly hardening. I wish, looking back, that I had come into contact with him in 1941, when his questions and some of his answers would have been directly relevant. But the moment had passed, and although we tried to talk, very little got said on either side. What I mainly remember is a curious incident when we were sitting side by side in a crowded meeting and our hands were on the table in front of us. The backs of my hands are covered with hair, and I noticed him staring at this, with his marked physical intensity, and then looking at his own very different hands. The trivial incident sticks in my mind because it is a fair enough instance of how deep, when it came to it, all the differences really were.

The return in 1961 was as strange as might be expected. The Lectureship seemed a very good job at the time, though within a couple of years I was being offered Chairs elsewhere. But for reasons that should be apparent, it was very important to me to work out my particular argument in Cambridge. The lecturing of that first five or six years had the intensity of a culmination; also, as was later to appear, of a rapidly deepening isolation. All my friends and acquaintances were now a generation younger than myself. My contemporaries and seniors, some of whom showed me kindness (which was as readily offered), were colleagues at work but in little else, for we were thinking all the time about different things, and in that sense living in quite different places. I took and have since taken rather more than a full share in the business of the English Faculty, but after fifteen years I am intellectually more isolated from it, and from anything at all likely to happen in it, than I was when I came. The key moment, perhaps, was my rejection of literary criticism: not only as an academic subject but as an intellectual discipline. I have argued that case elsewhere; it involves a parallel rejection of the specialization of literature. But nobody quite believes I mean it, and the Faculty, for its own good reasons, has literary criticism as its heart and soul. I spend much of my time in Cambridge writing, and beyond that it is a great crossroads, where I am glad to keep meeting people, especially from other countries. What is formed and forming, at the centre of it, is as alien now as at any time in my life.

This is especially evident in my college. But that began on the wrong foot. I was asked to stay a few days, with a Fellowship in mind. In Cambridge a University Lectureship is the key appointment; to a married man, anyway, a Fellowship is at best a social convenience. What was in mind for me was a Teaching Fellowship, involving direction of studies and up to twelve hours supervision a week. This is paid for, but partly in kind, and one lives, mainly, on the Lectureship salary. Now if in these circumstances a college wants you, the favours, it seems to me, are at least even-handed. But it was not like that. The atmosphere of most colleges, more so then than now, indicates privileged admission beyond the terms of the already achieved intellectual appointment. I was surprised to find, when I arrived, that I had sponsors, and that they were necessary because I had a number of opponents. I was wheeled round to be looked over, by enemies and by the all-important neutrals. I was asked to breakfast, a Cambridge custom I had forgotten, by a senior Fellow who told me, over the toast, that he was himself a 'good Labour man', and that he had for years been trying to persuade the college to celebrate (with a feast) the feast-day of the Old English patron saint of domestic servants, who were quite insufficiently regarded. I replied that I must be a different kind of Labour man, since this would surely mean only more work for the staff. 'Servants we call them here,' he explained, genially. I went out of that and another encounter to tell my sponsors I didn't give a bugger what they did with their Fellowship. But the hours of cross-talking had had a different effect, and I was eventually elected. In the light of later events, with my dropping out of the dining and most of the social life, though I kept up the teaching, I am sure the original opponents believe they were right all along. And indeed I was welcomed back to Cambridge by a front-page editorial in the *Cambridge Review*, written by a colleague and entitled, with a cold acidity that became clearer as it continued, 'Mr Raymond Williams'. Another meeting, I have heard, summoned to discuss my arrival, decided that I was a prime instance of what was happening in State education, where you feed these boys and then they bite your hand. Of course, this wasn't all that happened. When I have been doing Faculty and university business, I have found the element of Cambridge that nobody outside seems to know, and that is in any case obscured by the very different figure of the more public don, as it is or was also invisible to the undergraduate intent on his own absorbing sub-culture: the extraordinarily plain, hardworking, cool centre. That is congenial enough, for business. When I went to my college I found I could manage best by thinking of it as the officers' mess which, in surprising ways, it so closely resembled. In the university it is more like any English public body, and like all English public bodies coping intelligently and efficiently, in local ways, with problems and contradictions so deep-seated that any possible solution, other than hand-to-mouth, goes wholly beyond their terms: their terms of reference, as they would call them, in their essentially incorporated way.

So then, as I look across the fields to this strange city it is both easy and difficult to remember how much has happened to me here, and how important, at different times, it has been in my life. Easy because I still work here, with certain traceable continuities, and with so many places reminding me of past and present. Difficult because, over all these years, it still seems no more than an intersection; never a possession, of or by. There are specific reasons for that, but as I read the history, and the recent history, it seems to me a more common case than is usually acknowledged. So many things have been done here, and so often they have been done quite against the grain.

Donald Davie

Donald Davie was born in 1922, and went up to St Catharine's to read English in 1940. He had previously been at Barnsley Holgate Grammar School. From 1941–6 he served with the Royal Navy, returning to Cambridge in 1946 to finish his degree. From 1950–7 he was lecturing at Dublin University. He became a Fellow of Trinity College, Dublin in 1954. In 1957 he went to the University of California as a Visiting Professor. In 1958 he was appointed a lecturer at Cambridge, and in 1959 he became a Fellow of Gonville and Caius College. He left in 1964 to become Professor of English at Essex, where he was appointed Pro-Vice-Chancellor in 1965. Since 1968 he has been a Professor at Stanford University in the United States. He has published five books of poetry, and his books of criticism include Thomas Hardy and British Poetry *and* Ezra Pound.

From Barnsley, where I was born and grew up, there runs north and south an unbroken chain of squalid little townships, the meanly built and hastily improvised barracks of the Industrial Revolution, all the way from Sheffield up to Leeds and beyond. But west and east it is a different, more hopeful story. Westward in particular—and we lived on the west side of town—the land begins to rise at once, through Dodworth and Silkstone and Hoylandswaine; and then, after a dip into Penistone, which is already a windy upland town, it rises steeply again to become after a few miles uncultivated and largely trackless Pennine moorland. Though coal is mined on the lower slopes, so that Silkstone indeed gives its name to the whole seam, the look and the feel of the country, once you are through Dodworth, is quite different. Hoylandswaine, for instance, is lean and rinsed and raking. There are seventeenth-century farmhouses thereabouts, all the better for being merely bare and solid, the harshness of weather giving no purchase for creepers or lichens any more than the harshness of livelihood could afford Jacobean curlicues. The stone is good, a washed-out yellow in some lights very faintly pink. And in particular, near to Hoylandswaine but off the main road and until lately away from any metalled road at all, there is the vast tithe-barn of Gunthwaite, little known and little visited, still indeed a barn. Going from Barnsley to Hoylandswaine, though it is less than ten miles and one is travelling west rather than north, one moves out of the Midlands decisively into the North, the North Country as I came to know it later in Wharfedale, Nidderdale, Swaledale, and in the poems of Wordsworth and Emily Brontë. To me and to my brother—for I know that on this issue I can speak for him—it has been important that we should define ourselves as Northerners, of that 'North'.

And 'north' is a metaphysical or else a metaphorical place—in this sense: that wherever in the northern hemisphere one writes from, northward is the region of the stripped and the straitened, the necessitous. It was many years later that I realized this, seeing what 'north' and 'northward' meant in the poems of William Stafford, who speaks his poems always from some place on an axis between Kansas and Oregon. And it was years later again that I reflected how odd it must be to be an Australian, for whom the north is, I suppose, a region of tropical luxury. This metaphor of 'the northern' has meant much to me, since as far back as I can remember; what may look in my later life like a considered opting for the spare and the lean—in intellectual style or in literary style—is in truth, I think, only a clinging close on my part to that northern metaphor which I have agreed with myself to trust through thick and thin.

From that North—still literal, though already metaphorical also—I came in 1940 to Cambridge, on scholarships and exhibitions that I had won through fierce competition. It had been for too many years the pinpointed objective of my own and my parents' ambitions; it was impossible that Cambridge, or any other place, should have lived up to the hopes that we had placed upon it. And to this day I cannot tell how much of the rancorous unhappiness which I often feel when I am in Cambridge harks back to the predictable and inevitable disappointment that it was to me thirty-six years ago. I expected too much of that town and its university; and if I still expect flagrantly more than it has to give, that is, I dare say, devious and twisted testimony to the love and the loyalty that I invested in it. But it is with a bad grace, and reluctantly, that I concede so much. For its complacency seems as impregnable now as it was all those years ago. Some time in that span of years I arrived at the diagnosis which I adhere to still: that the Cantabrigian ethos—is it Cromwellian? I persuade myself with some gratification that it is—leaves no margin for *caprice*, for that free-running, freely-associating, arbitrary and gratuitous play of mind out of which, not exclusively but necessarily, art-works arise. This is a diagnosis which undercuts such comfortably intra-mural altercations as Kathleen Raine's with William Empson, or F. R. Leavis's with C. P. Snow.

To a Northerner such as I believed myself to be, or was determined on being—one moreover who, as it happened, had been reared a Baptist—a Cromwellian ethos should have had, and to some degree it did have, obvious attractions. It would certainly appear that Cambridge was more appropriately my university than Oxford (though, needless to say, in the scholarship competition I was happy to settle for either place, and what Oxford might have done for me, or done *to* me, who can say?). Undoubtedly when, in my second term, I was supervised by Joan Bennett in her house at Church Rate Corner in Newnham, the somewhat self-applauding 'stringency' of the Cambridge ethos, and its disputatiousness, were very much to my taste; I felt secure and at home with these modes or fashions of intellectual life. But outside of my studies, Cambridge in 1940 seemed to be peopled or at any rate dominated by exquisites from King's or swells from Trinity; and these were people so far outside the horizons of my previous experience that I regarded them from afar with uncomprehending resentment and alarm. I felt very vulnerable indeed—very far from home, and very much at sea among modes and codes of behaviour of which I had no experience, and to which I had no key. That an unusually stupid member of my college, St Catharine's, should once or twice in hall have tried to snub me, an exhibitioner, as himself a fee-paying commoner, is doubtless an interesting item of social history. But it wasn't fatuities of that sort which dismayed and bewildered me. The cleavage was not along the lines of *class*—I was petty bourgeois, and knew it, and in time came to recognize that many of my Home Counties fellow undergraduates were petty bourgeois no less. The cleavage, the divide, was not social but cultural, in the anthropologist's sense of 'culture'; to give a ludicrous instance, I and my first friend, Arnold Edinborough from Lincolnshire, suffered through many weeks of our first Michaelmas term before we realized that our provincial ritual of High Tea about five in the afternoon could not be reconciled, without digestive discomfort, with the institution of dinner in hall two hours later. In crucial matters like these—and they *are* crucial, since they are matters of daily rhythm, how it is punctuated and thereby ritualized—the Cromwellian university was as alien to us Northern provincials as ever Royalist High Church Oxford could have been.

But it is a far cry back, in time and in experience, from the specious security of such diagnoses, to what it felt like to be, in Cambridge in 1940, walking for the first or the twentieth time across Coe Fen. As always, memory shies at the daunting challenge—what was it like *then*? What was it like *there*?—and runs for cover into recalling instead images of some use to social history or the history of ideas: for instance, the bookshop in Rose Crescent which in those days proffered Stalinist paperbacks to remind us that the university had housed, not many months before, Julian Bell and John Cornford. That crucial difference—between the experience itself, and diagnostic discursiveness about it—was precisely what the Cambridge approach to literature, as mediated to me through Joan Bennett's admirably eager and attentive tuition, and the lectures by F. R. Leavis that I began to attend, seemed in some danger of denying.

Our concerns—I speak for myself and my few close friends, Douglas Brown, Arnold Edinborough, Stanley Lockett—were not political, as they probably would have been only eighteen months before, but, explicitly or covertly, sexual. To Douglas, brilliantly scholarly, devoutly low-church Anglican, ascetic, chaste and pacifist, the rest of our group was, more or less mutinously, subservient. I endured the challenging pressure of his example more constantly, and so in the end more mutinously, than either Arnold or Stanley. Douglas was Cambridge-bred. His home—his parents' home—was in Sedley Tayor Road. And more than one summer evening of 1941 saw the two Northerners, Stanley and me, lagging unwillingly along the privet-hedges of Hills Road and Sedley Tayor Road, heading for the feast of exotic culture—mostly, music on records—that Douglas, eager and impulsive, would have cooked up for us. (Arnold, his eyes already set on the Marlowe Society and devoted to that alternative Cambridge of King's and Dadie Rylands, escaped by that token the Cambridge austerity that Douglas embodied, and presented as a challenge to Stanley and me.) Already at that time I recognized that I was going to join up; that in imagination I was already serving in the war, and that I had only to find how to rationalize my way out of the principled pacifism of Douglas, and of the sectarian society that I had joined without enthusiasm—the Robert Hall Society. Meanwhile my sexual needs were focused, by no means satisfactorily, on the person of a Colchester Baptist's daughter, Faith, from Newnham, with whom I walked out demurely on Sunday afternoons towards Grantchester and Coton.

Sometimes it seems to me that if there is one sort of rhetoric for which I have been fitted by nature as well as nurture, it is the jeremiad. I have made a comfortable career out of crying in saturnine tones, 'Woe! woe!' or 'It is later than you think', or 'Things are going from bad to worse'. And a whole generation of English writers grew up along with me in this modestly profitable skill. The best of us are those, like Kingsley Amis or Bernard Levin or Anthony Burgess, who mock their own gloomy irascibility even as they articulate it. And this is only just; by whipping their own exasperations to comic or farcical fury, such writers very happily belie their own premises. For the elation of comedy is saying hooray for life in its own terms, however incongruous and absurd. But this was not anything I learned from Cambridge, or in Cambridge—where on the contrary everyone was caught still in Matthew Arnold's dilemma: how to find room, in a theory of literature which turned upon 'high seriousness', for the great masters of the comic vision, for Chaucer and Burns, Dickens and Aristophanes. There was, to be sure, Leonard Potts of Queens' College, author of a modest handbook, *Comedy*, which still supplies the best account known to me of why Congreve's dialogue in *The Way of the World* is not just a classic of the English theatre, but poetic also. But in 1940 and for years thereafter one was unmistakably aware that Mr Potts—so easily as he could be disconcerted, so manifestly idiosyncratic as he was in his habits and his bearing—was not to be taken seriously. Comedy, in fact, though it is surely one of the two or three canonical modes in which the human imagination has made sense of the human condition, has never yet been accommodated by the Cambridge mind, happily as that mind can lend itself to the really quite disparate mode of dry and pungent wit. And so, unlike the Amises and the Burgesses and the Levins, we Cantabrigian Jeremiahs, who have the gift of comedy only fitfully or not at all—we are all too often pompous and boring, and self-pitying too.

It is thus that I reflect with dismay, reading over these lacklustre pages that I have devoted to Cambridge, and to the years of my early life there. How stale I have made it seem! Were there no exaltations, no transports? There were; and it is only the insidiously habitual rhetoric that makes me pass over them. Let me single out one at least. I think of the English Faculty Library at Cambridge, in the rear of the Old Schools. I remember as magical the first visits that I paid to it. So many books! Other freshmen may have been daunted by them, but I exulted in their number. They were all mine if I chose to make them so, every one of them guaranteed to bear in upon and enrich the proclivity that I knew to be, and had declared to be, my own. Therefore there was no question of choosing. Any shelf, chosen at random, would do as well as any other. And, as I recall vividly, the shelf I chose was given over to seventeenth-century pulpit oratory. Why not? One tome after another, the histories and critical commentaries were lugged out to my bicycle-basket, and conveyed to my cramped and cluttered digs in Marlowe Road. (And what wickedly exact fun, I now remember, Arnold Edinborough made of how my West Riding accent handled the vowels of 'Mar*lowe* R*oa*d'!) I was never disappointed. No book of scholarship could disappoint me then. The more recondite the information, the more it entranced me. And so it is still, or would be if I could clear enough time around me; the romance of scholarship is in its exoticism, not in its rigour. The only trouble was when to stop; and it was a real trouble, the worst trouble of student life —today I feel for those of my students who are going to be scholars, as time after time I have to wrench their heads around, jarringly, from one subject or theme or field of interest to what the curriculum declares to be the next in order.

Education! I have no thoughts about education; or else I have too many thoughts, all of them jeremiads. Sometimes, certainly, it happens in classrooms: at Barnsley Grammar School, in the classroom of 'Fiery' Evans, an intense diminutive Welshman whose irascibility, though it was all a pedagogue's tactical histrionics, drove the structure of the French language into my consciousness at a level where nothing will root it out; and in the classroom of Frank Merrin, whose tactic on the contrary was suavity, as he supplied a skeletal history of French literature. But mostly education, the sort that I care about, happens in libraries. And I am grateful to every library I have known: to Barnsley Public Library, especially its reference room, where I read with delight how the battle of Brunanburh, subject of an Old English poem that I have never read and never shall read, may have been fought somewhere between Barnsley and Rotherham; to a weirdly dusty and unpeopled library in Archangel, North Russia, where afternoon sunlight in the summer of 1943 slanted on Tauchnitz editions of F. Marion Crawford; to the library of St Catharine's College, which yielded me a splendid edition of Fanny Burney's *Evelina*; to the library of Caius, where I annotated through much of a long vacation the Sidney Psalter along with John Ruskin's exultant comments upon it; to the neglected but still handsome and surprising library of the Union Society in Cambridge; even the Cambridge University Library, unfriendliest of all; the public library of Plymouth, destroyed in the blitz on Devonport, healing itself slowly through long years after the war; and certainly the library of Trinity College, Dublin, housed incomparably in and below the barrel-vaulted Long Room that is one of the noblest rooms in the world, its symbolically long perspective enforced by matching lines of white marble busts—some of them by Scheemakers, some by Roubiliac.

From the moment I got to Cambridge, nothing did I hear from my teachers but 'tradition'. It was represented as something problematical, hard to get hold of, easily confounded with impostures. In particular it was supposed that I began with a prejudice against it, against the cloudiest concept of what it might be. But had Marlowe not lived in Corpus, James Shirley in St Catharine's, Wordsworth in St John's? Did I, then and there among the colleges, having won my way there out of the benighted provinces, need T. S. Eliot or F. R. Leavis or later Richard Hoggart to tell me on what terms to accept incorporation in the tradition there offered me, physically extant in the disposition of buildings and in book-stacks? Preaching at me, these authorities preached to the converted; and the long-converted grew to resent them. Now, in retrospect, I recognize how I must thank my parents for having saved me from the sterile class-rancour that got in the way of so many of my contemporaries, and impedes their successors to the present day. Since disputatiousness was in Cambridge a sign of 'integrity', and since it came happily and naturally to my cast of mind, I indulged it—to good and profitable effect. But it never truly mirrored my temperament or my sensibility, by which I knew that the tradition was *there*, in Cambridge; and that the custodians of it were not pedagogues and critics, but poets, librarians, and the builders of libraries.

The builders. . . . It was years later, after the war was over, that a student of the Bartlett School of Architecture took a group of us round the colleges, and expatiated on the audacity of Wren's library in Trinity. I have always been grateful to him; but grateful also to Norris Jubb, who returned from South America to be art master in Barnsley Grammar School, whom in his last decline I visited in his semi-detached, two doors away from my parents' house. For it was Norris Jubb, organizing excursions to Romanesque and Gothic churches in the West Riding and down into Lincolnshire, who did more than any one else to open up for me the other art that I respond to fervently outside of the literary arts—that is to say, architecture. What a gift that has proved to be! Bookish as I am and am proud to be, my response to the semblance that architecture creates—what Susanne Langer calls 'the ethnic domain'—is what has enabled me time and again to declare myself a man *pour qui le monde visible existe*. Few of my literary contemporaries at Cambridge could declare as much; and, lacking that sort of purchase on the physically present and manifest, they have been the more vulnerable to the beguiling abstractions of the behavioural scientists and the cheap indignations of professional humanitarians, for whom 'tradition' is a formulaic manoeuvre of the enemy, a danger-signal. Cromwell's iconoclastic roundhead destroyed not architecture so much as the 'graven images' of sculpture; and after my first visit to Italy in 1952 it came home to me that, however Cromwellian I might be by virtue of my sectarian upbringing, this was one area in which I was not Cromwellian at all. In the 1950s Douglas Brown came to stay with us in Dublin, and I realized then that—conscientiously well-informed as Douglas was on sculpture, painting and architecture as on other matters—the moments when I interrupted our animated discussions to ask him to *see* such and such a coign or portico were endured by him as dutiful divagations from what were to him matters of real import—which is to say, literature and music. And so I came to recognize how an education in literature, so far from being an introduction to the world of artistic endeavour generally, could be on the contrary a way of evading the challenge presented to us by artifacts in stone or in pigment; and how a specifically Cambridge way of putting privileged emphasis on the *verbal* arts could lead to just that ultimately philistine conclusion. I see now that a course of lectures regularly given by my St Catharine's tutor, T. R. Henn, on Painting in relation to Literature, was designed to obviate just that depressing condition; but in my own case it didn't work that way, and Henn's lectures did nothing to elevate painting, for me, above the level of knowledgeable connoisseurship at best.

So far what I have recalled has been my freshman year, 1940–41. After five years away, with the Royal Navy, I returned in 1946, having acquired in the interim a young wife and an untimely baby. The four Cambridge years which then ensued, I find it hard to deal with. For we speak of looking down the vista of the past, as down a prospect between banks of trees, their dark lines converging until, at the far bottom of the perspective, they seem to meet at what must be the day of our birth. But we all feel that our past is made up of successive phases; and so it seems that we discern, stretching across the vista of our past, fences or hedges or thin screens of trees which divide the long reach into three or more, perhaps many more, intermediate fields of view. These fields are, or they seem to be, wider than they are deep; hence the impression every one has of how over quite long stretches of our experience time seems to have stood still, our childhood was one long summer's day, or a particularly bad time comes back to us as a night that it seemed would never end. To me, however, in recent years, the past has seemed to be not one vista but many, radiating away from the knoll on which I stand, at liberty, as I turn my head or pivot on my heels, to gaze now down one vista, now down another. This can only mean that I have stopped being able to make sense of my past as successive phases building towards, or for that matter crumbling towards, my present and what I can foresee of my future. In other words, I have lost my sense of direction. If instead of 'direction' I say 'destiny', no one need wonder what that destiny was, or what I believed it to be. Like every ambitious poet, I believed I was destined to be the soul and conscience of my nation. It is a conviction I have lately lost.

And so I have lost, when I think of my past, the sense of consequence, indeed of sequence at all, of succession. My eighteen wartime months in North Russia mostly seem nearer to me now than times of my life which came later. If I turn my head from that Russian vista to the time of my life which succeeded it, I see little but blurs and shadows, or else scenes and figures which stand out sharply enough but disconnectedly, casting no shadows at all. In fact, this stretch of my Cambridge life comes back to me not as a vista at all, but simply as broken ground, inchoate and tumbled. I do not mean that it was an unhappy time, for mostly it wasn't. But it was a time of casting about, of making fresh starts, some of them false ones.

The bald record shows none of this. Did I not, when the war was over, return to Cambridge, picking up smoothly enough where I had left off? I picked up indeed, but not smoothly. We all, all of my generation, perhaps in some sort the whole nation, got into harness again. How perverse it must seem, to phrase in this way the switch from war to peace! Was there not on the contrary a feeling of release and relief, of freedoms regained and restored? I suppose there must have been. But in fact, as is tediously well known, the British in those post-war years were exhorted and compelled by Stafford Cripps and the Attlee government to draw in their belts, to 'buckle to'. The metaphors of harnessing seem inescapable. In my case, as I think for many of my Cambridge contemporaries, the harness was 'your career'. Snaffled and bridled, the bit between my teeth, career indeed was what I did, headlong, self-blinkered and at a furious pace, to fetch up, winded and in a lather of sweat, only within the last few years from this present time of writing.

No one compelled me to this. It was what I chose for myself, and everything in my character and my Barnsley conditioning made the choice inevitable. Moreover—and this is why I risk seeming to write egotistically—my case must be representative of us 'scholarship boys' in general. Others may have shared with me an additional reason why the harness was welcome—namely, the discovery under wartime conditions of alarmingly unruly proclivities in one's self. For during my sailor's years, in Russia and the Far East and at sea, I had sympathized quite ardently with that 'way of excess' which I saw pursued by some of my mess-mates. I liked the imprudent ones far more than the reliable and responsible. I could see myself going along with a desperado of the lower deck, not indeed as an equal ally but as an admiring and mostly loyal lieutenant. There was that in me which was anarchic and fatalistic; the war had shown it to me, and it frightened me. Already at that time, as over the years since and even in post-war Cambridge when I could afford it, I used for these anarchic potencies the safety-valve of heavy drinking.

But this did not prevent me from being still the youthful prig that had been Douglas's friend. And Douglas came back into my life when we each returned to Cambridge in 1946. According to George Eliot, or perhaps to a character in one of her novels, 'A prig is a fellow who is always making you a present of his opinions.' From that mordant indictment I think that both Douglas and I could just about scrape free. But the Oxford Dictionary gives an eighteenth-century sense for 'prig' which I'm afraid fits our case all too neatly: 'A precisian in speech or manners; one who cultivates or affects a propriety of culture, learning, or morals, which offends or bores others; a conceited or didactic person.' And yet if in the late 1940s that was a true bill so far as Douglas and I were concerned, it fitted no less accurately every one in the university who responded to the presence and the ideology of F. R. Leavis in Downing. To be a member of what Leavis promoted as 'a minority culture' one had to be indeed a precisian in speech and, for the most part, in manners also; one had to cultivate a propriety of culture which meant necessarily, so the doctrine went, propriety of morals; one had to be a didactic person; and one had to be prepared for others to be affronted, or bored, by one's pretensions. Now, a quarter-century later, I get the impression that the personality thus delineated is still the distinctive product of the Cambridge English School. And nowadays, if the type and its pretensions are among the things that exacerbate me in and about Cambridge, that doesn't mean in the least that I have achieved a position of principled antagonism to that type, or to my own earlier self which conformed to it. On the contrary, though I want to disown that earlier self, I cannot see in good conscience how to do so. I am exhausted by the to-and-fro of my sentiments on this issue, and exasperated at my inability to resolve it. To put it another way, though I sympathize very promptly and warmly with the angry dislike that the prig provokes, I cannot for long trust or respect the heartily permissive common sense that is proposed as an alternative. In politics I can deal with the prig, that is to say, the doctrinaire; I can oppose him and rule him out of court angrily, consistently, and with a good conscience. But this is because I take politics to be in any case a realm of more or less soiled accommodations and approximations, in which the coarse-grained principle of 'live and let live' seems on the whole to do less harm than any other. But in the areas of personal morality and the arts, realms where I expect (wrongly perhaps) principles more rigorous and absolute, I cannot see, much as I should like to, how to rule the prig, the precisian, out of court. And indeed this dilemma was, I now recognize, predictable and inescapable; son of a Baptist deacon and grandson of a Baptist lay-preacher, how could I not have felt some sympathy, however sneaking, with the prig as the eighteenth century defined him? According to the Oxford Dictionary again, 'prig' in the late seventeenth and early eighteenth century was 'applied to a precisian in religion, *especially a nonconformist minister*' (italics mine). The dissenters' conception of 'a gathered church', gathered *from* the world and in tension with it, cannot help but be the model for Leavis's minority culture. But it was some years later that I worked this out for myself, and documented it in a handful of poems. And although what guided me were the writings of a Cambridge historian of the dissenting churches, Bernard Manning of Jesus, the reading was done in Dublin, where the disestablished Church of Ireland satisfied the need, bred in me as a child, to envisage my church as in tension with the state, by no means coterminous with it as the Church of England must pretend to be. Years later again, after I had myself bandied about the expression 'the Establishment', in its cant sense as referring to what sustains an inert consensus in intellectual and artistic life, I realized that properly speaking there is only one Establishment in English life, and that is the Established Church.

At any rate, between 1946 and 1950 my sympathy with the prig was not sneaking at all, but fervent and militant. Those were the years when *Scrutiny* was my bible, and F. R. Leavis my prophet. It is very hard now for me to be fair to my self of those years. Perhaps the best that can be said for him is that, for good and pressing reasons, he was no longer the young man of 1940 who could dream of reading, in time, along every shelf in the English Faculty Library. Subsisting on a student's grant in four draughty and mouse-infested rooms over the village store in Trumpington, my wife and I could not fail to see that I had to become a breadwinner as quickly and efficiently as possible; and since, thanks to taking good classes in the Tripos, it seemed that my livelihood was to be that of a university teacher, the sheer bulk and expanse of accredited literature even in our native language was no longer, as it had been in Marlowe Road, an endless series of enticing vistas, but on the contrary presented itself as a daunting and unmanageable field through which I must somehow cut a few narrow swathes. And for this *Scrutiny* was irreplaceable. Every issue of the magazine made me a present of perhaps a dozen authors or books or whole periods and genres of literature which I not only *need* not, but *should not* read. To be spared so much of literature, and at the same time earn moral credit by the exemption—no wonder that I loved *Scrutiny*, and Leavis's *Revaluation*, and his *New Bearings in English Poetry*! Of course it was not what Leavis and his collaborators had in mind, nor did I have it consciously in mind myself. But looking back, I can have no doubt that this was one great attraction for me, perhaps the greatest, in the sort of criticism associated with Leavis's name. And indeed at some stage of his education every student needs, and even deserves, to be presented with a rigorously narrow canon of approved reading such as Leavis, not altogether fairly, was widely held to be providing. An immersion in *Scrutiny*, even an infatuation with it, is no bad thing if only one can be sure that the student will in due course pull out of it, or pass beyond it. But of course there is no way of ensuring this; and there's the danger.

There are other dangers. It is by thinking myself back into the person I was then, that I can enter imaginatively into the thoughts and feelings of the fanatic, for instance the committed revolutionary, the persecutor, the gauleiter, the commissar. Perhaps I should be grateful. Certainly, without having undergone this relatively innocuous experience of fanatical commitment, I should have no experiences of my own to call upon, to understand in imagination the appeal for a Nazi or a Communist of the image of a band of embattled brothers, or the psychological security of having, for the assessing of each new experience, a body of scriptural texts to refer to. I could elaborate: for instance, ruthlessness as a virtue, blind obedience as another. . . . But I do not want to be, or to seem, unfair and disproportionate. Simply I put it on record that, however it may have been with others, introspection after the fact assures me that in my case my *Scrutiny* allegiance was fed from sources as deep and as dubious as these.

At this time when I most venerated Leavis—always from a distance, for I was not of his college, and only once was I ever in his house—there stood behind him, so far as I was concerned, a figure of even greater authority, T. S. Eliot. This was to change, and indeed in those very years it was changing, as Leavis, more and more fully convinced of the moral genius of D. H. Lawrence, uncovered evidence of how consistently Eliot had blocked the rating of Lawrence's writings at what Leavis took to be their true worth. To champion Lawrence, Leavis was to have increasingly harsh things to say about what he saw as the humanly constricted nature of Eliot's Anglo-American achievement. But in the 1940s Leavis's second thoughts about Eliot were only just beginning to show themselves; and our respect for him rested in part, and quite properly, on his claim to have been one academic critic of literature who showed himself abreast of the most distinguished creative breakthrough of his time, Eliot's *The Waste Land.* For me, and those of my friends who like me were committed to poetry rather than other forms of literature, it was the young Leavis's championing of the poet Eliot that still carried weight. Eliot, as critic even more than as poet, dominated our horizon. It is hard to convey the virtually unchallenged eminence that Eliot continued to enjoy, in literary circles in Cambridge as elsewhere, through the 1940s and well into the 1950s. Those who did not experience it are right to be sceptical, for it is surely very rare for a poet, still writing and publishing as Eliot was, to enjoy the sort of pre-eminence that he had. The first of my all too many manifestoes about poetry, printed in those years mostly in Cambridge magazines, characteristically genuflected towards the author of *The Waste Land* and *Four Quartets*, and staked out whatever position they timidly sought to maintain, by veering a very few points away from something that Eliot had said in print.

In 1958, when I embarked on my third stint of Cambridge residence after eight years absence in the US and Ireland, things were already very different. The tide of sentiment had turned against Eliot. On the one hand this had to do with what I saw as an unconsidered and sentimental movement towards the political Left. The Left of course had already had good reason to be suspicious of Eliot in the 1930s, and friends of mine like Matthew Hodgart and Ian Watt, who in the 1930s had come up just long enough before me to be influenced by the Popular Front and the immediate aftermath of the Spanish Civil War, had, and doubtless still retain, reservations about Eliot which I can respect and understand. My generation came up to the university in the time of the Molotov-Ribbentrop pact; thus there was no excuse for us if we were starry-eyed about the Stalinist Left, and, since we weren't, Eliot's undoubtedly reactionary politics did not disconcert us. What worried and annoyed me in 1958, as it does now, was the way in which the sentimental Left occupied all the same positions and rehearsed all the same arguments, that I was just old enough to remember from twenty years before. Such manifest inability, on the part of students and their teachers, to learn the plain-as-a-pikestaff lessons of recorded recent history certainly cast a queer and mocking light on the discipline that supposedly we all professed, vowed—so we told ourselves—to 'tradition', to the preserving and handing on of the accumulated and tested experience of previous generations. However, though the positions and the arguments had not changed, the vocabulary had. Where Eliot had been assailed by the Left of the 'thirties in overtly political terms, now, in the 1950s, the animus against him was expressed in a more general, an apparently non-political fashion—he seemed not to like *people* very much, in particular he didn't like or celebrate joyous sexuality. It wasn't hard to see here the Cambridge Left taking over for their own purposes the vocabulary of a man who wasn't at all of their way of thinking—Leavis in fact, in his polemics against Eliot on behalf of Lawrence. The duplicity of that manoeuvre offended me. And if '*people*' ('the people') was one English word that the 1960s was to so besmirch by tendentious usage that it has had to be expunged from the vocabulary of responsible persons, the potent keyword of the decade was—I came to recognize—'class'. From 1959 to 1964, as a Director of Studies at Caius, I exerted myself to recruit young Northerners such as I had been myself twenty years before. But alas, they had all read Richard Hoggart's *The Uses of Literacy*; and that division between North and South which I had interpreted as a *cultural* divide, and a challenging one, they interpreted as a *class* distinction, and a non-negotiable one, therefore not challenging in the least. What's more, their 'North' was not metaphorical at all, but literal; and so they wasted the time when they could have been reading, weeping into their beer-mugs and accusing themselves of being class-traitors because there they were, in the Little Rose or the Baron of Beef, whereas they ought to have been carousing with the South Shields football team. About this time I began to realize that my habits of thought were so alien to those of my countrymen that my future, if I had one, would have to be spent out of England altogether.

If I ask myself what particular responsibility Cambridge has for this state of affairs, I find myself acquitting my old university with a virtually clear slate. It fought for instance, tenaciously and well, to refuse recognition to the baleful non-science called 'sociology'. What went wrong with its students and its teachers in the 1950s and 1960s was something that was going wrong with the national life in those years, as I discovered to my cost when I left it in 1964 to help found the ill-starred University of Essex. Every instance of elegance or propriety, in the university's social arrangements as in its architecture, was to my Caius undergraduates an affront, since it would be either unnoticed or else misconstrued by a rugby-player from South Shields. Was Trinity College therefore to wear sackcloth and ashes for having been so 'elitist' as to employ, once upon a time,

Christopher Wren? The question is absurd; but it is a sort of absurdity that the characteristic polemics of that time pointed towards, and landed themselves in. Because I am myself a man from the West Riding, and count in my family West Riding proletarians as authentic as any that Hoggart takes account of in *The Uses of Literacy*, I feel bitterly that, in that book as in others it has spawned, a real claim that should be made on behalf of such persons has been deflected to serve a rancorous and politically tendentious purpose. The really influential disseminators of this nonsense are not those like Hoggart or Raymond Williams or myself, who know the provincial proletarian and shopkeeper classes from the inside, but the parlour pinks of Hampstead and the Home Counties who, feeling cheated by and guilty about the secure middle-class homes they grew up in, dream up a non-existent alternative, frank and warm, close and earthy, from which they can contrive to feel themselves excluded. Such aberrations were if anything less common in Cambridge than elsewhere in the country, but the fashion for them penetrated the university, and balked the potentialities of more of my pupils than I care to remember.

It was I suppose one day in 1960 or '61 that, about one o'clock, the 'phone rang in the turreted polygonal room in Caius which I had taken over from Charles Brink. I was just finishing a supervision, and got rid of my pupils in a hurry when the voice on the 'phone identified itself as Kingsley Amis, in Cambridge for the day and asking me to lunch with him. Kingsley was one of several people I had hurried to get acquainted with, some years before, when our names had been linked together by commentators in a literary manifestation of the 1950s which got itself called The Movement—itself, I am convinced, an important phenomenon for historians of English society and culture, since it represented the first concerted though unplanned invasion of the literary Establishment by the scholarship-boys of the petty bourgeoisie. Kingsley I liked and had always liked, as I like him still: and in fact, if our relations have always been slightly constrained, it's because there is no British writer among my contemporaries whom I admire more, and the consciousness of that is a little embarrassing to both of us. We lunched together in the University Arms—of all places! (So the old Cambridge hand will exclaim; and yet to those who have read Amis's novels, it will seem the one right Cambridge locale.) He pumped me about what it was like to teach English in Cambridge, and I was eloquently jaundiced about it, along the lines of my preceding paragraph—only to have to back-pedal, lamely and unconvincingly, when he revealed that that very day he had accepted an invitation from Peterhouse to move there from the post he had held for many years in Swansea. Thus began the brief but eventful and unhappy period when Kingsley Amis was a member of the Cambridge English Faculty. Before long John Holloway and I, who had appeared in anthologies along with Kingsley, had to protest in a Faculty meeting when F. R. Leavis, incensed at the fellows of Peterhouse for making the appointment without consulting the English Faculty, described Kingsley as 'a pornographer'. On the contrary of course he is and always has been a very severe moralist, as one sees from his shocked repudiation of both Philip Roth and Vladimir Nabokov. On the other hand he is a master of comic caprice—a perfectly legitimate and entertaining garment for the moralist to appear in, but one that Cambridge has never been able to account for and acknowledge. Ineffectually wise both before and after the event, I saw the outcome as inevitable. In a justifiably bitter essay that he published afterwards in *Encounter*, Kingsley writes of lunch-time sessions in Miller's Wine Bar in King's Parade; sometimes I was of the company, and enjoyed it.

On another occasion he came to a Caius dinner as Joseph Needham's guest, when my guest was his and my friend, Robert Conquest. Also there, I seem to remember, was the Scottish–Polish poet Jimmy Burns Singer who, incurably ill and moving frailly to an untimely death, was to be seen in those years, mostly in Newnham, drinking a quiet and careful pint of beer, a small dog lying at his feet. This memoir would be a more humane document if more of it were taken up with glimpses of such persons, once familiar apparitions in the perspectives of Newnham or Lyndewode Road or Trinity Street. In such a gallery there would certainly appear, for instance, the stooped figure of H. J. Chaytor, the great scholar of the Romance Languages who was Master of St Catharine's when I went up, who after the war was to be seen in Lyndewode Road or Glisson Road, a shabby shopping bag trailing from his left hand. Is it something about Cambridge, or only something about myself when I am in Cambridge, which brings it about that, whereas my memories of Dublin naturally cluster about particular personalities, my Cambridge memories on the contrary take forms that are unpeopled, polemical, and abstract?

One figure at least cannot be allowed to pass from the scene without being established as something more than a peg for a polemic. This is Douglas Brown, who died after a long and crippling illness in 1964. He was out of Cambridge by then, and had been teaching for several years in the English department at Reading. By then I had long grown out of the bemused if also rebellious awe with which I regarded him when he, the brilliantly accomplished and intense Scholar of the college, and I the Exhibitioner, were taught together by Joan Bennett. Over the years I had made as it were a case-study of him, as representing the Cambridge moral ethos in its purity. And though I made my study for compelling and urgent reasons, since I desperately needed to know for the sake of my own identity when to resist that ethos and when to accede to it, nevertheless when Douglas died I had a painful sense, which I have not lost since, of having *used* him and so betrayed him. Douglas himself never made use of men or women in that way, not me nor any one else, at any rate not consciously. And isn't it just this, in the true-blue Cambridge personality, that makes it so woefully alarmed and at a loss before the comedian —in all the senses of that word? The comedian—whether on the stage or off it, on the television screen or in Miller's Wine Bar—necessarily lives and acts by manipulating his audience, and to that extent *using* it. In that sense Tom Henn, my St Catharine's tutor, was a comedian, as I would guess any Anglo-Irishman has to be. Because of that I imagine that Cambridge was the wrong place for him to be, and that he was not happy through the many decades he spent there, any more than was that comedian of a different stamp, George Rylands. For the purely Cambridge cast of mind, if I knew it (as I think I did) in Douglas, does not know what to make of any striking of attitudes, any provisional trying out of postures towards experience, any donning or doffing of alternative masks, any switchings of viewpoint, except as insincerity, lack of seriousness. To this Cambridge mind, with its blade-like directness, any of these more or less histrionic manoeuvrings before experience is profoundly distasteful. And yet to personalities of another cast, just these obliquities of provisional assent are the natural ways by which to arrive, in all seriousness, at sincerity, identity, truthfulness. Douglas was gentle and self-critical, and he would have readily enough agreed with this last contention; and yet his temperament was such that, though he would have given conscious assent, his heart would not have been in it. And thus, though he recognized my badinage when I plied him with it—even, I think, he quite liked the feel of it—of the affecting images which rise to my memory when I think of him, not one presents him as laughing, even less than heartily. He was in earnest, always—he could not help it, that was his nature. He had a sense of humour, right enough; but he did not like it, nor trust it—it seemed irreverent, as of course it is.

It is a long time since I was in Cambridge except on very brief visits; and as I write I contemplate for the first time in many years spending some time there during the coming Michaelmas term. It may be that I shall find the Cambridge I have described utterly changed and vanished. But I do not think so—habits of mind thereabouts do not change lightly, nor fast. And that is not a reproach; on the contrary, it is one of the things that I like about the place—more and more, if the truth be known, as I grow older.

Raymond Leppard

Raymond Leppard was born in 1927, and went up to Trinity as a choral scholar in 1948. He had previously been at the City of Bath Boys' School. He did his National Service before starting, at the age of twenty-one, to read Music at Cambridge. He stayed for five years as a student, returning in 1958 as University Lecturer in Music, a position he held for ten years, working simultaneously as conductor, harpsichordist, composer and arranger. He has published several realizations of Monteverdi and Cavalli. From 1960 he was Musical Director of the English Chamber Orchestra and in 1972 he became Principal Conductor of the BBC Northern Symphony Orchestra. In 1976 he announced his decision to settle in the United States.

From the amount of time that I have spent in Cambridge, it might quite reasonably be deduced that my attachment to the place would prove overly strong for any sort of detached consideration. Not only was I there for five years as a student but, later on, returned for ten more as a don. Yet both times I left because I knew I had to get away and neither now, nor in the period between my student and more senior days, did I find myself dwelling for any length of time, or in any sentimental way, on the place or the people I knew there. I suspect and dislike nostalgia, so that it is quite an exercise of memory and intellect to recall my student days and put such construction as I can upon them, which is the brief of this memoir.

I failed little-go in 1945 as a result of a wilful refusal to learn Latin, something of which I am now ashamed. In the event it was among the most fortunate things that ever happened to me, as it meant I first had to do National Service before coming up, three years later, to spend my time with as unusual a vintage of undergraduates as Cambridge had ever seen.

While I wouldn't wish the wasted years of service in the armed forces on anybody, I do think it was valuable, at least for me, to have spent time in a totally different world from home and school before entering that of Cambridge. Almost all undergraduates in the late 'forties were in the same boat, and the odd ones out were those who came up directly from school. I think they may have suffered as a result. The majority of us, after the inanities of service life at that time, were intellectually starved, and eager for learning and intelligent company. The fact that we were older meant that many of the tiresome hang-ups, emotional and sexual, had at least been encountered if not resolved, and we were a good deal more experienced in meeting and getting on easy terms with a much wider array of people than school or home could ever have provided. Many of our fellow-students were older and more experienced still in the darker horrors of war, but they never spoke of them and we all surely profited from their deeper maturity.

You might think that such a generation would be lawless and fiercely revolutionary in a Cambridge whose rules for running its own society were still much the same as in 1939. But it was not the case. We were all perfectly happy to be in college by midnight, or to climb in if not. The fines for being late and the rebukes if caught climbing were cheerfully accepted as necessary restrictions of a society designed for the general good. There was very little in the way of love affairs; we all knew, by then, how socially disruptive they could be, and term was so busy there really wasn't time. Those who did fall were generally objects of some sympathy, for it kept them out of general circulation; more their loss, we felt, than ours. There was, too, an amused tolerance of the more idiosyncratic features of Cambridge life—like the wearing of gowns and the attentions of the Proctor and his 'bulldogs'—which, of course, we knew were of no actual importance, but acceptable, even enjoyable, because they were symbols of the society we were enjoying and felt fortunate to be part of. Society at large did not then owe us an education. We had to prove ourselves—arrogant as it may sound in these egalitarian days—worthy of it, even to the extent of knuckling down and learning Latin, *quod in tempore perfecti*. Cambridge terms were periods of tremendous and intense high spirits, and the activities that we all managed to cram into those eight weeks were so many and so varied that there seemed little time for sleep. When we weren't involved in concerts, theatre, Footlights, meetings, lectures, study or supervisions, we were discussing them and anything else that came to mind in the gradual process of making contact with the friends who were to remain so and become an integral part of life.

The way our society was ordered meant that the colleges led a more separate corporate existence than they do now, and gained, I think, in character as a result. Their particular characteristics and qualities, it was generally agreed, rubbed off on their undergraduates who then had to deal with their foregone reputations as best they were able. Such generalizations were, of course, foolish but amusing to make and sustain. As they reflected the period and have, doubtless, since then changed, it might be worth recounting how the colleges looked to a Trinity man in the late 'forties.

The college I would most liked to have belonged to, had I not been a member of Trinity, was King's. It had a special aura about it and King'smen always gave the impression of having been, like the twelve, chosen—often, we thought, more for their looks than for intellectual or social talent. Within the college there was a delightfully titillating undercurrent of homosexuality, man-about-townery, café-society sophistication that we didn't necessarily want, but envied nevertheless. The high-table—now rendered sadly low—was full of people who remembered Rupert Brooke and knew the Bloomsbury group; Keynes, Lytton Strachey, the Woolfs, a world that has of late been so wearisomely over-sung. There was enough glamour in it for returning servicemen to be dazzled, and, I suppose, it was good for us to have been dazzled. King's was headed by Provost Sheppard, old long before his time but nimble enough at selecting the best-looking undergraduates for his blessing as they left chapel services. He was a confirmed gambler, and I remember seeing him at the beginning of term in London (from the labels on his luggage, just returned from Monte Carlo), fast asleep on the inner circle, presumably going round and round until he had recovered sufficiently to get off at Liverpool Street and catch the train for Cambridge. The literary jewel in King's crown was E. M. Forster who was kind to the better known or bred undergraduates, and used to give parties and occasional readings of chapters from his overtly homosexual novel, *Maurice*, which finally proved disappointing when published in its entirety after his death. I rather think he knew it wasn't very good. He was aware, though, of being one of the figures of Cambridge, and bore it with a charmingly exaggerated modesty that deceived no one.

My experience of King's was largely through music and theatre, which were much cultivated there. Boris Ord and Philip Radcliffe, of whom more later, both lectured in the Music Faculty and Boris was in charge of Chapel music. Donald Beves acted well; I remember particularly an excellent Monsieur Jourdain in Molière's *Le Bourgeois Gentilhomme*; better, I thought, than Miles Malleson's more famous interpretation, because more real, and so more touching. He entertained with a distant friendliness in his rooms which housed his very fine collection of glass. He used also to perform a memorable, portly Puritan in the various pageants that Pop Prior used to direct during long vacation terms, in which we all took part in one way or another at least once. Each pageant set out to illustrate different aspects of history—Queens of England, Cambridge through the ages, Kings of England—but ended up much the same each time, with the celebrated 'Prior step', the only one she knew to give a semblance of corporate dancing, much in evidence, as well as the inevitable Cromwellian sequence.

Apart from Boris Ord, perhaps the most influential figure in King's, as far as the university was concerned, was Dadie Rylands, the epitome for many of theatrically-orientated sophistication. He always seemed to know so much and, as we gradually found out, did; much more than we used to give him credit for at those moments of extreme exasperation at his bland, devastating demolition of our more pretentious views.

Lovable and maddening at the same time, he was, I think, a true educator and the majority of our current theatrical talents owe him something; or would vehemently deny it, which comes to the same thing. I certainly count my life the richer for having continued to meet and, occasionally, collaborate with him.

Architecturally, King's is a misshapen college, but with a chapel immeasurably greater than any other in Cambridge. And, though the majority of choral scholars have subsequently done very little except live on their memories, they represented then the most exclusive musical society in Cambridge; but one I now count myself fortunate in not having belonged to.

If King's was a college we envied, John's, our nearest neighbour, was not. It wasn't as big as ours, and most of the people there came from places we didn't care to talk about. The chapel was a joke, architecturally, and the courts generally had a grim, unfriendly aspect which seemed reflected by the members of the college. Quite a lot of wild parties went on in the Wedding Cake, but it wasn't generally an hospitable place and, I must say, I found it no different when I went back as a Fellow of Trinity. I don't think I ever dined there in fifteen years of Cambridge life, and the small number of people I am fond of who belonged there seemed to prefer to entertain elsewhere rather than risk, I suppose, a collegiate chill on the proceedings.

I didn't know anyone at Christ's, and if I did know someone from Sidney Sussex he never admitted to it. Fitzwilliam House was another place we looked down on, though I came to sympathize with its excluded condition during the two very happy years I spent, out of college, living with Erika and Stefi Bach—he was a senior member of Fitzwilliam—and was glad for his sake when it achieved full collegiate status.

Caius was, for me, dominated by the figure of Paddy Hadley, our Professor of Music who, I suspect, was happier with the chaps in his chapel choir than in his Faculty. He was wonderful with them, composing pieces and arranging the most surprising things, like scenes from *Boris Godunov*, for them to sing at college concerts. So great was the fervour he brought to the music he loved that they came off amazingly well in performance. Something to learn from that. He was not cut out for the chair of music. Something to learn from that, too. Such musical techniques as he had were locked firmly away in his mind, and could not easily be transmitted. His musical tastes were strong and quite irrational, but we were very fond of him. He drank a lot. It was charitably said to be on account of the pain in his wooden leg, whose mechanism occasionally gave out and left him stranded, immobile, in the middle of Cambridge—I saw him once being wheeled home by the Caius porters in a wheelbarrow, wearing full professorial academic dress—but I believe the drinking was much more to hide from his own failure to fulfil in music the creativity within him. There was a lost generation of English composers—Warlock, Lambert, Moeran, Ireland—who, nervous of academicism, eschewed technical training and finally took to drink for lack of it. Paddy was one of them. Thinking about those days, I remember him in his rooms at composition seminars, which frequently came upon him too suddenly for him to be dressed in anything but pyjamas, and those often in some disarray of which he was quite oblivious. One day a prissy little virginal Girton miss ventured a know-all musicological point which maddened Paddy by its total disregard for the expressive ends of the music under discussion—'Baroque? Fuck Baroque!' he shouted. It wasn't much of an intellectual point, but I bet she never forgot it.

Magdalene was a stuffy college with a very high social rating; Emmanuel was practically non-conformist, and had an annual free-for-all sing-through of the Messiah. I tried it once and left during 'And the glory of the Lord'. Selwyn was non-conformist, but had a lot of good concerts including quite a few professional ones, which irritated Mrs Hackforth (who ran the professional Thursday concerts) and those who believed, as, on the whole, I did, that Cambridge should do most of its entertaining itself.

Pembroke, Trinity Hall, Peterhouse and Corpus were my most visited colleges. They all boasted flourishing musical societies and there was a good deal of helping out at each other's concerts, which meant that we got to know each other's societies and, to some extent, were accepted into them. Corpus was the most urbane, in some ways more than King's, to which it felt, but was not, superior. Quite a lot of Footlights people belonged there and gave sophisticated parties, for which we were supposed to dress well and talk intelligently. One of my closest friends, Malcom Burgess, who used to design all that period of Footlights shows, and is now a Fellow there and University Lecturer in Russian, I met after one of these, wrapped elegantly round a lampost in King's Parade; he was tall and slender in those days, and apt to wear somewhat exaggerated dress. He also stole umbrellas. There was a move to go on somewhere to dinner, probably at the KP, but we had not been introduced at the party. 'Gracious,' he said, when we were; a remark I took to be predatory, but it was only curiously appreciative, and set the tone for banter that has gone on ever since.

We were all jealous of Peterhouse food. In winning the war, it seemed England won the right to starve, and things were worse in the 'forties than at any other time, especially in Cambridge, where a miscalculation in the allocation of rations meant that sometimes we really went hungry. I think the Master of Trinity eventually went to see the Minister of Food about it and, I suppose, though I don't remember, the bad-tempered old harridan who grudgingly doled out our meagre rations of butter, bread and sugar for private consumption in our rooms, gave us a little more as a result. Peterhouse kitchens were subsidized by a handsome bequest, so they ate more and better than any other college.

Pembroke and Trinity Hall were smaller colleges, full of quiet, companionable people. I was a member of a regular string quartet and our leader, Martin Chadwick, was at Trinity Hall and our cellist, Ki Bunting, at Pembroke, so we were frequently to be heard rehearsing in either college.

St Catharine's was a sombre place, and the people there seemed to take on the depressed character of the dark red-brick buildings. It was said that the buildings had never stopped blushing for shame over the scandal of a dishonest Mastership election earlier in the century, on which C. P. Snow based his novel *The Masters*. They—the buildings—have subsequently been cleaned. Downing had some pretty eighteenth-century buildings and some horrid ones in twentieth-century bankers' Georgian, which you saw on the way to the railway station. It housed F. R. Leavis, of whom we became heartily sick on behalf of the friends who read English and had all their enthusiasm dampened by his powerful, ascetic critical theories.

Queens' had a lot of serious-minded theatrical people who knew, or pretended to know, a lot about Ionesco and Genet. People at Clare rowed. Girton and Newnham didn't count very much—especially Newnham. The care that was taken to preserve the girls' virginity was, with a few notable exceptions, far in excess of any threat they were likely to encounter. A few of the female dons indulged in a little gentle match-making, but we were, mostly, well past the stage of coy innuendo and found all that a waste of time. Women in the university were welcome to join in most activities on an equal basis with us. It was, nevertheless, an essentially male society.

Trinity, the largest of the colleges, was far from being the amorphous microcosm of all types and classes it was sometimes accused of being. You had to live in its society to discover that its character was based on the recognition of two important distinctions, more clearly made there than in any other college, largely, I think, because of its size. First and foremost there was the concentration on intellectual matters. Ordinary social levels played no part in this and the appreciation of intellectual achievement and exchange was in no way affected by background or personality. Beyond that point, every sort of distinction was drawn. If you hunted or beagled, you had usually done it before and would surely do it again. If you played badminton, you tended to play it with people who came from places where badminton was played. The same went for all sports: squash, real tennis, rowing, football, hockey, rugger. You played with your type. In various ways and degrees of emphasis this applied to all the societies in the college. They were exclusive, and made no bones about it. Everyone understood, and the larger and smaller distinctions were rigorously maintained. You mixed freely with your intellectual equals when intellectual matters were foremost, and with people who shared your other interests when not. It was a very good way of making a society work, though somewhat unfashionable in these days when every sort of distinction, real and imaginary, is being ironed out.

Crucial to the scheme of things was the participation of the senior members, and my memory is that the Fellows of Trinity were, at that time, a good deal more conscientious about it than in later years. They were almost all readily available, and many of them entertained regularly in their rooms. The most regular meetings were, of course, in the weekly supervisions or seminars, but the extra-curricular meetings were often just as rewarding, and, in retrospect, I think the Fellows I knew were very generous with their time.

Trinity High Table really did have the most distinguished history of any college in virtually all the disciplines and, though it was beginning to fade after the war, the reputation of its intellectual standard was still very high, and deservedly so. G. M. Trevelyan was Master and the shades of G. E. Moore, Bertrand Russell and J. J. Thompson were in evidence everywhere. Bertrand Russell came to dine sometimes, and I remember being invited to meet him after hall by, I think, Harry Holland, who didn't much like him. I can't remember anything he said, only the beak-like nose, the hair, the nasal voice and the physical movements remarkably agile in one so old.

The point about High Table was that you saw its members constantly about the college, and could very easily see and speak with them more intimately whenever the need arose. They, almost all, felt an obligation to be available and take an interest in the undergraduates with whom, for one reason or another, they came in contact. Nor did they overdo it—they were just there and part of the place.

The ones I saw most of were interested in and involved with college music. Principal among them was Hubert Middleton, a much loved but underestimated man. I owe him and his wife, Dorothy, a very great deal. He directed my studies, but generally, in college, he was in charge of chapel and college music, which he looked after with a wisdom and consistency of practice that taught us much beyond the events themselves, and helped to order and develop our various enthusiasms. He had been organist for many years before I met him, and only lately a Fellow of the College, which we felt did not reflect much credit on the Fellowship, though, it must be said, his modesty was as much reason for this late appointment as any lack of appreciation of his worth in the college. At home he and Dorothy were tireless in entertaining numbers of us to memorable evenings of talk, food and drink with, occasionally, a little music; but not often, for Hubert was a thinker about music with a marvellous ear and a warm enthusiasm for what was valuable. Its practice was something he loved to encourage in us, but was not good at himself. He was one of those people who said unforgettable things which influence you for the rest of your life. As a teacher, he had that greatest gift of all of making you feel that he thought you so much better than you knew you were; and you loved him, so you couldn't let him down by not being so.

College music flourished and the place was large enough for us to undertake quite large ventures. There were chamber concerts each Sunday evening, and the college orchestra met on Sunday mornings. Various Fellows' wives joined in, a few friends as well from colleges that had no orchestra of their own, and there was Nellie Naylor who had been turned out of CUMS by Boris Ord. She was not, perhaps, very much of a violinist but, together with her sisters, Glad and Doll, daughters of a former mayor of Cambridge, she was in the world class at croquet, and many an eccentric afternoon was spent in their garden with other friends—Neil, Philip, Brian—learning some of the skills and marvelling at the passions aroused in those otherwise gentle maiden-ladies. Doll was small and did the cooking; Glad gardened and was on various local committees; Nellie was the racy one and, apart from playing the violin, taught ballroom dancing in a little studio at the bottom of their garden. It was not much patronized as far as we could see. Her dismissal from the university orchestra was something of a legend. Boris Ord, searching for a clearly audible mistake in a rehearsal of the slow movement of Beethoven's Choral Symphony, narrowed it down to the second violins and, finally, resolved it altogether by saying firmly, 'Miss Naylor, stop playing.' CUMS's loss was Trinity's gain.

I was a choral scholar, and this meant regular attendance at two week-day evensongs and one on Sundays—not an intolerable burden, even though it was a dreary business musically. Hubert went on valiantly but unenthusiastically with choir practices at which there was, irregularly, a motley collection of boys bribed in from the highways and byways. Some had been there so long they seemed biological miracles. It was all a sad echo of the days when Stanford and Alan Gray had a choir-school to draw from for a table of services that would have graced a cathedral. When I returned to Trinity some years later, we sacked the boys and established a male-voice choir along the lines of Caius, which has gone from strength to strength ever since.

Congregations were abysmally small, even on Sunday evenings, but, occasionally, a sermon would lift a service out of its habitual drabness into something memorable. I recall several by Harry Williams, whose concentration on life and the fruitful living of it seemed to me so much more meaningful than the usual dosage of guilt the church seemed to minister. I remember, too, one foggy November evening—Remembrance Sunday—and F. A. Simpson preaching about the gift Trinity men had made of their lives in the First World War. I shall never forget that, for once, full chapel, the dim lights made dimmer by the encroaching fog, the closing words marvellously delivered—a quote from a head-stone, 'not in vain, my darling, not in vain'. Simpson, perhaps the most selfish man I ever met, arrogant and formidable, published the sermon under the title 'A last sermon' and, reading it again, it still seems to me very strong and moving in a way that need shame no one. The publication eventually occasioned a characteristic bit of Trinity sparring at High Table. Simpson had not preached for some years, but, when he did, another Fellow of Trinity had the temerity to suggest it might be thought odd that Simpson should preach again having already published his last sermon. 'Do you not yet know, B——, the difference between the definite and the indefinite article?' Unanswerable, as any such thrust should be.

Finally, of course, it was the undergraduates who counted most, and the foundation of friendships by now too long established, too intimate, and two involved for any public reckoning. The years, in confirming things, also complicate them so that they go beyond powers of description and analysis; they are simply a part of life.

Official university studies were carried on at the University Music School in Downing Place, a converted church hall with bits added on. It was early days of the Music Tripos; I think I must have been on the second or third wave of undergraduates able to read for an honours degree in Music. The importance of this for the status of music in the university was great, if difficult to explain, and it was largely the work of Hubert Middleton and R. M. Rattenbury, another Fellow of Trinity and Registrar of the university. The whole Faculty was not much above a hundred, and the music school was just about adequate to house us and the Pendlebury Music Library, which, though not comprehensive, did contain an amazing variety of things, and the voracious exploration of unknown music was a feature of those years.

Lectures varied greatly in quality, and the bad ones were less and less well attended as term went on. It could be disastrous to leave it too late before giving up, as you might be among the last two or three and forced, out of charity, to complete the course. Henry Moule lectured well and precisely on subjects like fugue and sixteenth-century counterpoint, giving us to understand that music could be observed with a cool intellect as well as with a warm heart. This thesis underlay the whole Tripos, and the aim was a synthesis of intellect, heart and sensibility. I still believe in this as a way of approaching music, but I did not find it possible, as I had hoped, to live the double life of teacher and performer. The rival claims of each were too strong. Hubert Middleton understood this and was very sympathetic when I decided to throw up my Ph.D. thesis and remove to the profession in London.

Boris Ord's time was largely taken up with King's Chapel, so that he lectured infrequently and not often well. He was at his best in practical seminars on continuo playing and score-reading, at both of which he was superb. We learnt much in watching his work in CUMS rehearsals—I led the violas in the orchestra—and in the University Madrigal Society, in which I sang. I first encountered the reality of Monteverdi's madrigals with this small, select choir which met every week in term, gave infrequent concerts during the year, and also the celebrated Madrigals on the River which, as an occasion, always had more of sentiment about it than serious musical achievement. It worked, though, as an entertainment, and thousands came each year to see us float down the Cam singing 'Draw on, Sweet Night'. Boris could occasionally be persuaded to play in the University Music Club, of which I became President, and his sense of standard helped us greatly to become aware of such things. Perhaps best of all were the parties he used to give in his lovely set at the top of Gibbs building, above Jumbo

Arch. He had two pianos which could safely be played at all hours. Improvising with him, in between ministrations of drinks and 'blotting paper' (biscuits) to his guests, into the small hours and, on occasions in May Week, through the night, remains among the most enjoyable of undergraduate memories.

Philip Radcliffe was also a Fellow of King's, and had an encyclopaedic knowledge of music. His lectures always carried the implication that we should further explore the unknown territories he was showing us; not that we needed much pushing. The illustrations he gave at the piano were famous, for he didn't play well and, quite undaunted, would set out on a most difficult piece—a Scriabin sonata maybe—and after a few bars the brakes would seem to fail and the music increase in speed, until the inevitable tumble in a flurry of notes. Hands would fly into the air and the illustration end with a somewhat disdainful 'and so on'. Example, illustration and illustrator became, in this way, quite memorable.

Robin Orr, who had returned to Cambridge from the war only a short while before we came up, lectured with a dry humour, but we thought of him principally as a composer, and went to hear the new pieces he was writing for the choir at John's. I remember, too, playing some very striking music he wrote for the Greek play—a triennial production at the Arts. The play was *Oedipus at Colonnus*, and must have been among the last of their productions in Greek.

There were other major productions, usually under the aegis of CUMS, at either the Arts or the Guildhall, but most of the really interesting theatre went on at the ADC where many of the productions needed music composing or playing. Peter Hall, Peter Wood, Toby Robertson were actively directing plays, and the current professional stage is peopled with Cambridge actors of that time, too numerous to attempt any sort of list that would not be invidious in its selectivity. It is amazing to consider what a high percentage of the major talent in the entertainment world, to speak of no other, was around in Cambridge and Oxford during those years.

The other society that occupied a fair amount of time was the Footlights. Every generation of that Society thinks its own the best, which probably says more about changes in style of humour than much else. Ours was certainly a very lively vintage. The smokers—social evenings for which, symptom of the times, we used to dress, where new material was tried out—were well attended, and the standard of writing and performance was high. Peter Tranchell was musical director, surely the most original one in the Society's history, and put the music of the May Week revues together with great skill and wit. The intention at that time was to produce a sophisticated, elegant revue rather on the lines of Hermione Gingold's *Sweet and Low* series, though, if anything, ours were more barbed, aimed at a more intelligent audience and, with Peter in charge, far superior musically. Occasionally the Society was invited to perform for a week or two in London. Some thought it a great thing, but in my view it was a mistake, for London management diluted the wit and, eventually, insisted on including women—which changed the style, and the Society lost at least as much as it gained.

If all this was not enough, there were still open lectures to attend, the *Cambridge Review* to read—except for that wretched university sermon which, it was said, could be heard in pulpits all over England the Sunday following its publication. There were *Varsity* and *Granta* to giggle over, college committees to sit on, dinner parties, and occasional walks alone or with friends.

There scarcely seemed time to draw breath and yet, somewhere within the frenetic energy of term, there lay the essence of the paradox that is the strength of the Oxbridge system. While we stretched ourselves to the limit, there was still time to find out about ourselves, our minds, our capabilities and failings—not all, but enough, at least, to make a good start. It was not a system for everyone, nor was it designed to be. You had, in due course, to find within you the determination to get down to work on your own, for no one would make you. The time was there for you to do what you had to do with it. A term or two in the wilderness didn't matter; you could go to pieces; you could try out all manner of eccentricities; you could sport your oak and be in undisturbed quiet for as long as you needed, but, eventually, you had to recognize and accept some responsibility for the life that was in you.

I do hope the sadly mean, jealous spirit that seems to pervade much of our present-day society will not prompt Government to standardize university education in the ridiculous name of equality or fairness; two principles which apply at no point in life. People are all manner of things worth caring about but they are not equal, and life is always worth the living, but it is certainly not fair. Cambridge has shown for over five hundred years that it can adapt to almost any social climate; the lack of any serious undergraduate troubles in recent times is present evidence of that; but it could be destroyed by the disenfranchisement of the colleges, and, I'm sure, there are those in power who would do it to catch a vote, or appease their own wretchedly misguided sense of injustice. I pray the university has enough sense to shout very loud if the need arises.

John Vaizey

John Vaizey was born in 1929, and went up to Queens' to read Economics in 1948. He had previously been at Queen Mary's Hospital School. He worked in Geneva for the United Nations from 1952–3 before being appointed to a Fellowship at St Catharine's. From 1956–60 he lectured at Oxford. After two years as Director of a Research Unit at London University he went back to Oxford as Fellow and Tutor at Worcester College. He is now Professor of Economics and Head of the School of Social Sciences at Brunel University, London. He became a peer in 1976.

People from big cities who go to Cambridge realize what it is like to live in the country. Each Cambridge winter day began with the river smell, mixed with the scent of damp leaves and, as often as not, bonfire smoke, hanging in the tall bedrooms, windows ritually open. Then a quick run to the outside lavatory. It was the time when running water and gas fires were gradually coming in; coal was still rationed to a sack a term. My first two sets of rooms had coal fires and no water; my last set had running water and a gas fire in the study. Then I spent a couple of terms four miles out at Madingley Hall, which had central heating, running water and bed-sitters with Dunlopillo mattresses. It was a time of change from hard to soft, from pre-war to post-war.

The atmosphere of a broken-down country house was made more powerful by the survival of college servants with East Anglian accents; old women who made the bed and shifted the dirt about a bit; mice; and extraordinarily bad food—it was rationed for fourteen years—served in surroundings of some grandeur by waiters, amateur and elderly, but still clearly servants. This was the end of an era when many of the young men came from country houses and rectories; within a decade it would be self-service of hygienically cooked, nourishing and appetizing food, prepared under the watchful eyes of trained catering officers, and the centrally-heated bed-sitter would be hoovered once a week by a young person from a council estate; and the young men came from the prosperous suburbs.

'Any more for Jesus?' the porters at the station cried, evangelically, as they loaded taxi after taxi, mine bound for Queens', with my heavy borrowed suitcases. My sister's old college trunk was waiting in the Lodge, together with a bicycle borrowed from a cousin, and I found myself surrounded by public schoolboys a head taller than I, talking in loud, self-assured voices. They may have been as shy and nervous as I was, but I doubt it.

I knew nobody at Cambridge. I was, I believe, the second boy from my school to go to Cambridge, a university known only to the geography master, and I had picked my college with a pin in the Hither Green branch of the Metropolitan Borough of Lewisham's libraries. St Mildred's Road, Lee, SE12, was a row of semi-detached mock-Tudor houses, fronted with a few bedraggled laburnum trees. Our front windows faced down Milborough Crescent, with a slight rise that only partially obscured the broad vista of similar houses, and behind us was the Southern Railway shunting yard. The incessant clanging and banging of the steam trains in the night was said to be comforting. To get anywhere entailed a lengthy wait for the 75 bus under the railway arch, by the pigeon droppings, or a long walk to Hither Green or Lee station for the quarter-hourly service to Charing Cross.

To move from St Mildred's Road, Lee, SE12, to surroundings so self-consciously soaked in history and narcissistically bathed in beauty was perhaps in itself not extraordinary, though to me it came as a great shock. I had been mostly in hospital since I was fourteen, and when out I had been in a plaster jacket that covered my torso. It was with some apprehension that I went away from home, and the apprehension became a reality when a combination of illness and the difficulties that attend it intensified as the terms went on. A certain amount of loneliness dissipated itself in a choice of acquaintance based purely on propinquity. I clung to that which was nearest. And to this must be added boredom. My chosen subject was Economics. It was taught, not by some magical don, but by a carpet-bagger who came down once a week from London, while the lectures were dull, with no revelation of the mysteries I had longed to penetrate.

Three characteristics which have remained were probably deeply embedded in my character from the earliest time. The first was a self-pitying immobility. This showed itself chiefly in the vacations, spent partly from lack of money but chiefly from lack of enterprise, at St Mildred's Road, Lee, SE12. The excuses—health, indigence—were ample; the experience of six weeks and more of tedium was my own fault. I have a tendency to monumental, overwhelming boredom, and as I have grown older, *ennui* has become my major difficulty. I see it clearly established from the first Cambridge vacation, when I saw nobody from Cambridge and knew nobody worth knowing.

The next characteristic was a timidity in moments of crisis. People take you at your own valuation. Boldness pays. Even at nineteen, some people are making plans for what they will be doing at forty-nine. It never crossed my mind. Disillusion with Economics led me to think of an alternative. Law was interesting, exciting, non-mathematical, well taught. Had I taken up Law I would have enjoyed it immensely; I would have been successful at it. But my college said no and I accepted their refusal. And how, I asked myself, would I finance myself at the bar in those early years? Everybody else had some money. I had none. Even so, a policy of boldness would have paid off. I could not believe, however, that my future did not lie in an office reached from St Mildred's Road, Lee, SE12. So my self-denying masochistic impulses had full play and I stayed out of the law.

The third characteristic is the obverse of the timidity. It is compulsive activity. The way to stave off boredom, to alleviate the depressive timidity, is to do a great many things.

These three impulses were overlaid at Cambridge by instant nostalgia. The phrase 'It won't last, you only have eight more—seven more—six more—terms' was repeated to myself every day. For me, the physical beauty of Cambridge, its chapels, the trees by the river, the little eminence on the walk to Grantchester, the river smell, were part of an instant nostalgia that I would feel, actually feel, in the reality of St Mildred's Road, Lee, SE12, from which there would be no escape and to which, like a ticket-of-leave man, I went back in the vacations. That was reality, Cambridge was fantasy. That was the beginning of the complexity of my love affair with Cambridge. I think that if I had not had the six weeks of residence in July and August every long vacation, I would have gone mad every summer.

The first magic of Cambridge was that it was not a south London suburb. There were other elements in the magic too, of a more positive kind. But I want to emphasize the isolation, the loneliness and the shyness which dominate the Cambridge lives of those who are not from one of the bigger schools and who lack some important inner resources. I knew I was clever; I supposed I was ambitious; but I had no model for my conduct; no expectations that could be judged realistic or unrealistic. I had only the present—eight and a half weeks, alternating with six weeks of excruciating boredom.

The defence that some took was to sleep. People took to their beds till lunch-time or later, like a man in my college called David Stone, who boxed. My reaction was of intense organization: a regular time to get up, a bath, first in to breakfast; the papers in the Junior Common Room, for the first time *The Times* and the *Manchester Guardian* instead of the *Daily Telegraph*, but quick enough in those days of six- and eight-page newspapers. Then lectures and a cup of coffee with people from my college who went to the same lectures; lunch at one, after the last lecture, then a walk, and several hours in the Marshall Library, then early hall (6.30 in the Erasmus Room, proper hall reserved for the senior men) and then an evening free; no work after dinner. In short, I was organized to be busy.

One excitement sprang from the privileged position that Cambridge enjoyed in the world of politics. I went up a convinced, ardent Labour supporter. The Labour Club met often, and on Friday nights and Sunday afternoons it had visiting speakers, usually Cabinet or other ministers. The year 1948–9 was the high tide of Labour enthusiasm, while the ex-servicemen were keen to learn from the leaders, and from their *Keep Left* critics, what the issues of the post-war reconstruction were. The National Health Service began three months before I went up; the Berlin airlift was on; the future Israelis were 'at war' with the 'oppressive' forces of Bevin's colonialism. The Labour Club had a number of prominent Zionists at the top and consequently the visitors were harangued about the Palestine policy. In parenthesis it was not till my first term at Cambridge that I spoke to my first Jew and met my first black man (from Blackpool and Jamaica respectively).

Perhaps my lack of contact with the great world was not as unusual as I thought it. When the college required three testimonials from people of standing who were not connected with my school, only the doctor and the vicar were qualified in something, and even then not proper graduates at that. I had been to a few political meetings and heard Herbert Morrison. At Cambridge, you could not only see them close to, but by a kind of mass propulsion, you could sit in the bar with them after the meeting and, eventually, be expected to dine with them before. The process from total anonymity to dining with a Cabinet minister took fifteen weeks. Small wonder that politics seemed exciting.

It was the great days of the Union Society. Every Tuesday night, at 8.15, the white-tied, tailcoated President led a procession of the eminent through a packed hall. Rarely before and never since have the audiences been so big, and the guests so eminent. Speeches were occasionally brilliant—especially by Percy Cradock, now the Ambassador to China. I spoke only once. I never sought office either in the Union or the Labour Club; and when I ask myself why, I can only reply that politics and debating excited me so much that I became anxious and ill. Politics for me was strictly a spectator sport.

What the Union did for me was to introduce me to the pleasures of a club. You could lunch on pigeon pie, as the red-bearded President, George Pattison, lived in the country and shot. At a press of the bell, a youth in a white coat would bring tea and toast. All the weeklies to read, and unlike the Hither Green public library, the Union library had big shelves of newly-published books. By dint of constant borrowing I was put on the library committee, eventually ending up as librarian, when I became a don. Club life at the Union was the life of Riley for the working class. The Union nobs were rude to the servants.

This political activity must be imagined against the background of a Cambridge, beautiful as ever, far from tarted up after the war, in fact in places rather seedy—the glass was still being put back into the King's Chapel windows—and not overwhelmed by motor cars since there was hardly any petrol. To get to the Union we criss-crossed the City, going into bookshops and teashops. All the amenities of a university city, with its small rituals, were suddenly available, despite austerity. You could buy a cake at Fitzbillies, for example, only if you inherited a paper bag which entitled you to stand in a queue.

As I got into the habit of work I ignored first-year Economics, which was for the most part absurd, and took myself off to second year lectures which were immensely exciting. This was partly because what is now misleadingly known as Keynesian economics was still being invented, and partly because the intellectual division in the Faculty was highly personalized. D. H. Robertson, bald, elegant, feline; Joan Robinson, in battle-dress dyed navy blue, brilliant and ferocious. I arranged to be taught by her; my tutor, who denounced her as a Communist, refused to pay her. I went to read her my essays, which she dismissed with contempt in supervisions that lasted two hours or more. I walked back through the dark and occasionally cried myself to sleep. I have never thought so hard as in trying to write those essays.

It would be unfair to attribute all my enthusiasm for economics to Mrs Robinson, though it was she who was on the verge of a major intellectual breakthrough. Stanley Dennison, the Senior Tutor of Caius, who also taught me, was the Senior Treasurer of the Marshall Society. This undergraduate economics club met on the top floor of the Marshall Library every Tuesday night, at eight. On the first occasion, Ian Little, a dashing man from Oxford, spoke; not one word was understood. On the next occasion, Mrs Robinson had a fearful row with Paul Samuelson, the Nobel Prizewinner and, for reasons unclear, annihilated him. On the next, Sir Hubert Henderson, the Warden of All Souls, carried forward by his own argument, advanced into the middle of the audience and addressed it from behind.

Before the meetings, the Committee met at 6.30 for sherry in Stanley Dennison's rooms, and then for dinner with the speaker at the Arts Theatre restaurant. The country's best economists came to Cambridge, week by week, and talked informally. The dinners, and Mr Dennison's courteous hospitality, taught me how to wine and dine and order in a restaurant. This is the opening of a chapter of adult life that seems to have begun far earlier for the more sophisticated.

Economics took up two other evenings a week. On Mondays, Professor Robertson's Political Economy Club, which he had inherited from Keynes, met in his ice-cold rooms in Great Court. Dennis Robertson was all etiolated Etonian elegance. He wore mittens to keep the cold out, and crouched over the small fire. An undergraduate read a paper; a large kettle was boiled to make tea; lots were drawn, and six undergraduates had to comment on the paper. At 11.30 or so we walked back to Queens' along Trinity Street, arguing about the paper in the glacial chill. On Thursdays we organized the Queens' Economics Group where our long-suffering favourite dons—Dennis Robertson, Joan Robinson, Stanley Dennison, Maurice Dobb, Ruth Cohen—came and talked to us.

I cannot imagine a life where some central intellectual interest was not dominant. Only rarely has economics wholly occupied my mind; but a central concern for some idea has never been absent, and, at the end of my third year, it would have been true to say that, apart from extremely abstruse mathematical theory, I knew all the economics that was then known. That seems to me a comment on the subject—it was almost ideal for an undergraduate course, in that it was extremely difficult, yet limited in scope; wildly divergent views were held with great passion; and it seems to me a comment on a great university that it could produce such enthusiasm and such high training in so brief a time. In short, I have known what it is to be excellently educated.

That, then, is five nights of the week—the Union, the Labour Club, and three nights of economics. Then there was culture. The Arts Theatre and Cinema, and the ADC, were astonishingly cheap. If you stayed on, as I did, the programmes had a certain sameness. Nevertheless, the Marx Brothers, *The Battleship Potemkin*, what I now recognize as the standard repertoire, were all available, and so were productions of Shakespeare by directors and actors who were later to be extremely famous—to transform the English stage. It was the tail-end of the Dadie Rylands revolution, the age of beautifully-spoken uncut texts, with lots of beautiful bronzed male thighs; but already the next revolution was upon us, most obviously in the Footlights, with Jonathan Miller, but soon with the producers of straight plays.

There were thus no evenings left. But there was still plenty of time. My musical life was desultory, though I did hear Myra Hess and the St Matthew Passion; my sporting life was confined to occasional visits to big matches; my love life was sparse. So there was time to go to the Fitzwilliam, time to go to lectures by Bertrand Russell and F. R. Leavis; above all, time to talk continually to highly disparate friends—socialists, Blues, lechers, monks, the clever, the stupid, Christians and Jews. And time to read and read, especially in the vacations.

What did we talk about? Chiefly economics and politics. Books and the cinema. I had read a great deal but I had never discussed a book with anybody else. It was the undamming of a torrent.

This brings me with some embarrassment to the church; it was what, without embarrassment, brought me to the church. Just as the college was like what I was later to know well, a somewhat dilapidated country house, so it was a country house surrounded by a country town, and at the heart of the town was, alive and vital, the church. In this idealized country village, which was the college, with its squirearchy, its young squires, and its peasants, with the porters, in their bowler hats, as villagers with a special status, like the miller, and with inn-keepers, like the undergraduate barmen and the landlords of neighbouring pubs, the idyll of rural England had its George Herberts. The Dean and Chaplain were scholars of considerable rank. They gave liberally of their time to the undergraduates. And there was the daily round of services.

The late 1940s and early 1950s marked a high point of religious revival in Cambridge and the university responded splendidly. It was a generation that asked fundamental questions, answering them in the affirmatives of Christian belief. Perhaps the most influential cleric was Canon Charles Raven, a striking Vice-Chancellor, red-robed, handsome, with a shock of white hair. In the pulpit, to crowded congregations at Great St Mary's, in the college chapel packed to overflowing, his rhetoric matched the hour. His overt concern, already slightly outdated, was the reconciliation of science with religion—clearly quite irreconcilable because dealing with different languages and topics—but his main message was how to live, why to live. And the younger generation of theologians and scholars, led by Ramsey, later Archbishop, and including Harry Williams and John Robinson, were clearly people of intellectual eminence who had already invented—or at least interpreted—the new theology which was exciting, and difficult and appropriate.

I was prepared for confirmation by Henry Chadwick—a formidable course equivalent, in some respects, to Theology Part I, perhaps the most difficult Tripos—and confirmed by the Bishop of Ely. The Book of Common Prayer made, perhaps, the deepest impression, especially the now highly-disregarded Evensong. But, as I look back, what I see is a private experience of catching up with those who had been conventionally educated at a good public school. I raised myself, as it were, from the Remove to the Upper Sixth, sat at the Prefects' Table, and read grace (as a Scholar), gowned in hall. By the time I graduated, I had become an Old Boy, ready to rebel, but overwhelmed by the nostalgia that my contemporaries felt for their public schools, for the Etons, the Sherbornes, even (as Kingsley Amis shows) for the City of Londons; I had made up for the missed rituals, the missed intimacies, the missed intensities of school. Religion gave me an adolescence I had never had; by force of will I put myself through a proper education.

This does not affect, I think, the view of the world that I acquired—for after all, I am a Cambridge man, and the truth matters above all—but it does alter the style of the truth that I acquired. Though our clergy were modern in their theology, though their scholarship—as it happens in Hebrew and patristic history—was superb, their interests, which they shared liberally with their pupils, were old-fashioned, even for Cambridge—tinged with an affected, conscious air of nostalgic antiquarianism. With a degree of play-acting—and all learning is to a degree mimetic—I cultivated the manners of the Dean and the Chaplain, and their interests. But I think I recognized despite all my genuine affection for them that I was in effect irredeemably committed by my admittedly utterly frustrated and unconscious ambition to another way of life and another set of interests, and that growing up represented an abandonment of an intimacy that ultimately was not genuine. But not an abandonment of a residual conviction.

Cambridge did not make me. The pattern of neurosis I

brought with me was not altered. I brought, too, the habit of work from hospital. But Cambridge formed me. It made me determined to be a don in order not to lose the way of life. That way of life was my introduction to adult life. Certainly, in the eight years that followed my going up, it changed only in small ways. I moved my college. I stopped being a student and became a teacher. Each year there was an efflux of friends—most noticeably, of course, when my own generation went down at the end of my second and third years (the ex-servicemen did a two-year course), but friendships bridged the generations.

When I say that Cambridge formed me, I speak of a pattern of responses, a life-style, that exploded most dramatically in my first summer term, progressed through the long vacation residence, and became most dominant in my second year, and emerged fully when I was a young don.

In October, 1951, the Labour government fell. The atmosphere altered almost at once. As building licences became easier to get and were then abolished, the place was spruced up and there was some new building. Rationing ended and the shops filled. The young men changed. In place of the fatherly ex-servicemen who had packed the halls where the Labour Club met, flat caps and checked suits clambered out of little red MGs. The chinless wonder from the peace-time army was there again with the evening dress, May balls, backless gowns—a conscious revival of a mythicized 1920s. They read English and voted Tory. The Labour Club disappeared, submerged by the flood of unrationed petrol. We were all well off compared with what we had been—and indeed compared with what we were to become. The high-living and plain-thinking years replaced their obverse. Partly, in my own case, this was due to a rise in my position: dons, even junior dons, do better than undergraduates, even senior ones; but it reflected a general change in the university.

These then were my circumstances. My circles of acquaintance were at first a chance collection—people I was taught with, people I sat next to in lectures, people I met at the Labour Club. They were overwhelmingly from my own college. But then my horizons spread, mainly in economics, to the clever boys and girls who were reading Economics in other colleges. And, in turn, they were members of circles that overlapped with mine in other respects: the Labour Club, for example, the Union or the casual world of those who went into the theatre purposefully. That is a word that repays attention. As I grew to know people, they fell into three categories. The largest, by far, was that of the don't know, don't cares—those who kept themselves to themselves and were doing nicely, thank you. They had their own interests, their own circle, and they were not interested in extending them or it. One knew such people purely by chance, if one's interests coincided by chance with theirs. The next largest group was of those who knew where they were going, exactly. It was only gradually that it dawned on me that some Labour Club zealots were making a fuss of a Cabinet Minister not because he fascinated them, or they thought he was fun, or for any other reason except that he could help them on their way to a safe Labour seat. The same was true of people in all walks of Cambridge life. They had their eye firmly on the main chance. And that included knowing me, or not knowing me. As I was revealed as one of the clever young men of the Economics Faculty, which justifiably stood high in the academic pecking order, and as a friend of the dons, I became worth cultivating.

Here a contrast with Oxford reveals itself. Careerists abound there, too, but emphasis is put on general interest rather than on particular achievement. There, however, the dons assume that it is their job to help everybody up what I like to think of as the Ladder of Life (as one businessman I know used to call it, evoking images of Bath Abbey with Jacob's ladder going up the west front). At Cambridge, except at King's, the Great World was none of their business, which was to cut you down to size. At Oxford, it was thought that the Glittering Prizes were yours for the asking the moment you went down, whereas at Cambridge it was solid success in late middle age that was the objective. Such young men were already exceedingly middle-aged, or perhaps I was there at a middle-aged time. It is extraordinary, nevertheless, how accurate their predictions of themselves have proved.

Then there were the free souls, who had no idea what they were to do, or how they would live in five, let alone fifty, years' time. In my own case there was a complex of reasons for this attitude. I had never met anyone else as clever as I was until I went to Cambridge, though intelligence had not seemed to me an asset, but rather something to be hidden. I knew, for example, that I was potentially a powerful public speaker. Had I known what I know now I should not have hesitated to go into politics. But I was panicked by the thought that the sheer pleasure of Cambridge, which I identified with its freedom, would be followed by years of the prison house, based on Lee, SE12.

When I was offered a job in the Bank of England which would have led to the heights, the salary was £400 a year. It would have meant living at home for a lengthy period. The assumption was that the young had little value; that they did not marry; that they had a private income, or at least parental financial backing. There was also the belief, exemplified by the Civil Service, in whose competitive entry I was also successful, that the first few years should on principle be exceptionally dull. A year at twenty-one is a very long time, especially if you are a young twenty-one.

My firm belief was that the true value of Cambridge lay in the opportunity to taste as widely as possible in the bowls of experience, laid out like some enormous *hors d'oeuvre*. There may have been a psychological basis for this, notably my unwillingness or inability to commit myself to a deep sexual relationship. Not only were there men who were married, there were men who lived as though they were married, the girl arriving with the milk and leaving at the locking of the gates. What they saw of Cambridge I cannot imagine; a bedroom in Stoke-on-Trent would have done just as well. But, the obverse of a deep relationship is a series of shallow ones. And it was on this basis that I lived my life. I had close friends whom I saw every day. There were people I regularly lunched and dined with. There were people to whom I bared my soul. They were an extraordinarily disparate group.

What I chiefly regret is the absence of any set of clear goals, and I feel that this sprang from some deep fear of discovering my ability and ambition, a fear that Cambridge reinforced. The emotional coldness, the emphasis on distance and reticence, left a vast amount of unexplored emotional stuff, which erupted volcanically from time to time. For that I blamed myself. But it was at least in part the fault of the system that this was so. The Oxford colleges, I later discovered, were more intimate, their dons more accessible, emotional warmth cultivated, the inexpressible more encouraged to be expressed.

A university, above all Oxford University, exists partly to express emotion; to lay bare ability and ambition and foster it. In my case Cambridge did not—for one very good reason and one very bad one. The bad one was that the intellectual tone of my Faculty was devoted not to enhancing the careers of its students, but rather to war to the knife, and consequently the Faculty, which is extremely important, did not look after its own. To this must be added my college's remoteness from the centre of power, and its inability to help anybody in this way, except in the law, a career already closed to me by tutorial edict. If a Faculty and a college are not an employment exchange, a psychological clearing station, half their manifest function is missing. My own complex love affair with Cambridge prevented my going to, say, Nuffield College, Oxford, or to the London School of Economics, which would have played just this role, so I added my own defensive mite to the lack of concern about the future.

The good reason was that Cambridge's main contribution to the tone of intellectual life has been a ruthless, forthright intellectual honesty, of which the Puritan revolution is the exemplar. Not for them any soft Carolinian ways. I think that this intellectual ruthlessness has appalling effects on the manners and emotions, but excellent results on the intellectual morals of the Cambridge young. Of course, it has its destructive effects on morals in the wider sense, too. Leavis, who may be seen as the representative of this great tradition in a lean period, became a cult figure during the heyday of English, in the mid 1950s; a movement I was on the fringe of, since the people whom I much admired and liked included some of his pupils. St Catharine's, my second college, was under the beneficent sway of Tom Henn, who shrewdly sent his tougher and cleverer pupils to a Leavisite supervision, in order to get them good results in the Tripos. I have watched their marriages, intensely entered into, intensely wobble and crash, as the necessity to bare feelings, to analyze motives, to tell the truth without fear or favour has put the marital structure of compromise and accommodation to the test. I would have been a nicer but a wobblier man if I had gone elsewhere. It is the wobblies who get on.

The other consequence of Cambridge is a complex network of acquaintance and shared experience without which I would have remained in Lee, SE12. Any kind of higher education would have opened various doors for me, and the current cult of equality has put a label of gilded youth on those who after all have Firsts from a famous university and no other string to pull. Nevertheless, at crucial moments, it has been of some help to know some people, though not ever, as it happens, the people whom I knew as an undergraduate. I find this question of influence operates, not through direct patronage, but chance, accidental encounters; and here what counts to some extent is the superficial ease of manner, the acceptability that Cambridge gives. It is irritating, I think, to find gaucherie among those one assumes should be men of the world and, paradoxically, it was my belief that self-education and self-improvement demanded a breadth of experience, of acquaintance, that covered my extreme shyness with an easy manner in most situations.

Indeed, looking back on it, I would put a continuous raw edginess and wariness, tinged with an ever more frantic nostalgia—'what shall I do, what will become of me'—as the dominant mood of my days in Cambridge, a mood that grew more acute towards the end of my time as a don there, since it was clear that a permanent appointment was out of the question. To this was added a growing lack of intellectual self-confidence, that was masked by the easy manner, so that the way of life in Cambridge was an end in itself, rather than a means to a further end—intellectual achievement, or a deeper personal relationship. Neither of these was achieved till I had left Cambridge. It is impossible for me, therefore, to look back on Cambridge calmly, or without a sense of its having in some sense been a limiting as well as a supremely liberating experience.

What I brought to Cambridge was an iron will and a high ability, and I found them insufficient since what I most lacked—confidence, and a sense of direction—it was determined not to give. Instead, what the training as an undergraduate gave was a series of hurdles over which to so superbly jump; and life, on that model, becomes a series of ever more bizarre hurdles built in the same manner, but not serving at all the same purpose. By its deliberate cultivation of the manners and values of the lower-upper-middle class of an earlier generation (Repton and Rugby, on the science side, were its dominant social origins)—for it is always twenty years behind the metropolitan values—it created, in me at least, a feeling of gross social and educational inadequacies without any obvious means, other than by one's own efforts, of overcoming them. Cultivation was a matter of the will.

How distant it all seems now. Above all is the gap of feeling; the gap that separates a life that held fear and hope in unequal and uncertain alliance from a life that knows the certainties of what has recently been and what now is. I still have the feeling that I shall get into the car and drive to Cambridge and the action will still be going on, that the pattern of life lived there so intensely, of depression and elation, of work and of daily participation in what seemed the smartest, the serenest of life styles will recur. The intensity of feeling that Cambridge causes has to do with the end of adolescence, and in my case of the simultaneity of adolescence with maturity.

Those to whom the climacteric came later or earlier see nothing of this side of the Cambridge experience; to them it has none of the splendour, tragic and comic, of a first experience of life. But there is, secondly, the character of the university itself. Above all its Puritan concern with the truth, which is perfectly compatible with a series of faculties that are not particularly good—History, Classics, Modern Languages—but which are nevertheless of the same style, hard and rude, as those faculties that are excellent. In one of the vignettes I see the *Eagle*, where I used to lunch (two shillings and threepence, including white coffee and bread, with three courses) with my closest friend, and the beer-stained trousers of a boisterous research student, drinking at the bar, a daily annoyance. 'Watson,' said my medical friend, 'winning the Nobel prize.' In economics, Mrs Robinson was doing work of no less importance; only political prejudice and male chauvinism has stopped her Nobel prize. To be part of, or even adjacent to, such efforts was an incomparable experience.

The sheer beauty of the place in contrast with St Mildred's Road, Lee, SE12, cannot be over-emphasized. Cambridge had the air of a run-down country estate, where great events were taking place; it was, perhaps, a year-round Aldeburgh Festival, with its hierarchies of dons, students and servants, its round of entertainments in the damp and cold, its slightly uncomfortable arrangements for sleeping and eating; its daily informal combination of privacy and a public life.

But, above all, there was the high seriousness of work. The

place existed for learning and the study of matters of supreme importance. The work came first ('Do your people keep up Christmas?. . . . Pity, interferes with the work'—Joan Robinson) and everything else a long way after; and the high seriousness of work affected one's attitudes to everything else—drama, politics, debates, sport—because the touchstone was excellence and the supremacy of the intellect. One's feelings were engaged, one's whole being; and if one's feelings and one's being suffered in consequence, that was a misfortune.

Nostalgia, reminiscence, forgetfulness, despair—these are the emotions conjured up and, as with a conjuror's trick, there is a feeling that, in a flash of movement too quick for the eye to register, the true experience has been missed. I wish it had been other than it was; I would like to have been more flamboyant, more successful, more prepared to leave; but the fact remains that I grew up there, bringing what, deeply flawed, I had, and it made me what I am, a deeply-flawed Puritan, dedicated to work, self-improvement, the cultivation of the intellect, goodness and truth.

Thom Gunn

Thom Gunn was born in 1929, and went up to Trinity to read English in 1950. He had previously been at University College School, London, and done his National Service in the army. Since 1954 he has lived in California, where he has been an Associate Professor in the English Department at Berkeley. His books of poetry include Fighting Terms *(1954),* The Sense of Movement *(1957),* My Sad Captains *(1961),* Moly *(1971) and* Jack Straw's Castle *(1976).*

I almost didn't go to Cambridge. My headmaster thought I should, and I thought I should, but my father wasn't sure. I wasn't bright enough to get a college scholarship and my father wasn't poor enough for me to apply for a state scholarship. So while I did National Service there was the possibility that I might not actually get there: it was in any case dreadfully distant, an escape from the drudgery of the army into the bright and tranquil life of the mind. I wrote a poem addressed to Cambridge. 'Shall I ever rest on your learned lawns?' I enquired. That was my image of it, a lot of serene young men sitting around on the Backs reading serious books.

So when, during a first roll-call of freshman in Great Hall at Trinity, a student answered his name with 'Here Sergeant', and I joined the general titter, it was from relief. We were here at last in Cambridge, actually on the site of learned lawns, we had entered the tradition.

I certainly didn't perceive the snobbery involved. I would have warmly denied it indeed, because my expectation of the place was largely based on the picture given of it in E. M. Forster's *The Longest Journey*. I expected a lot of Ansells and Rickeys, and exciting talks about ideas.

And Cambridge itself collaborated with my expectations. The Master of the college, G. M. Trevelyan, who was by then a very small bent old man, had all the new boys to tea early in that first term, and told us sweetly and learnedly about the buildings and history that we were now the latest instalment of. He showed us an Elizabethan ceiling with great pendulous decorations like stalactites which had been discovered in this century above a false ceiling of a later date, put up when Tudor things had become unfashionable. And he described how one Master, Bentley, had locked all the Fellows in a room until they gave in to his requirements for palatial alterations to his Lodge.

Meanwhile for us there were bedmakers to bring up our shaving water, there were meals in the big shadowy Hall, there was the crisp beauty of the buildings—Neville's Court for perfection, Great Court for show, and Whewell's Court for living in. And even Whewell's Court, where I was for all three years, was a fine example of heavy Victorian Gothic.

One of my contemporaries arrived at Cambridge with a broad Yorkshire accent. But this was 1950, and he made it his business to reform it, so that by the end of the year he was talking through his teeth as affectedly as any of the young gents at the Pitt Club. I wonder if he has since changed it back again.

I was reading English, and shared supervisions with a wonderful Manxman called Seth Caine. We were studying *Piers Plowman* when we found that as members of Trinity all we had to do was ask the librarian and he would show us the fifteenth-century manuscripts in the Wren Library. So we went. He was kind to us and perhaps slightly amused, since we had come not so much to satisfy scholarly curiosity as to test our power.

But historic elegance, detached enlightenment and the life of the mind just about summed up my first year at Cambridge. I read Chaucer and discovered Donne. My supervisor, Helena Shire, worked me hard, and I liked her very much. I tried to smoke a pipe, but kept on coming across a residue of bitter juices from former attempts which was most unpleasant. This was in my first term, when I also toyed with the idea of buying a blazer, and wrote a series of poems about dejected old men walking through dead leaves. Then I became a pacifist. Then I read aloud from left-wing poetry of the 'thirties at meetings of CUSC, the socialist club, with John Mander, an Etonian Marxist two or three years younger than I, who was writing poetry that seems good to me even today. I couldn't help noticing that his poetry had a vigour somewhat lacking in mine. And as I got toward the end of the academic year I couldn't help feeling, also, that perhaps rather more might have happened to me than the life of the mind. It certainly did seem that there could be parties a bit more exciting than CUSC meetings: one saw dashing undergraduates hurrying *somewhere*, gowns flapping in the wind, and it was evidently toward parties one wasn't asked to. The truth was, I had the desire to be a social climber, but not the talent. I couldn't even find the bottom rung of the ladder, if there was one.

But just at the end of my first year, something did happen. I had a poem published in an anti-war issue of an undergraduate magazine, *Cambridge Today*. The poem was written after seeing the Lewis Milestone film, *A Walk in the Sun*, and was predictably Audenesque in idiom. But people reacted to it, another magazine's editor mentioned it in print, and I felt very encouraged. I tore up the poems about the old men and decided to work hard at writing poetry all summer.

The summer vacation was in fact as important as the whole of the preceding year. I read the whole of Shakespeare, and doing that, Helena Shire later remarked, adds a cubit to anybody's stature. And one day, hitch-hiking along a long narrow dusty road in France, I experienced a revelation of physical and spiritual freedom that I still refer to in my thoughts as the Revelation. It was like the elimination of some enormous but undefined problem that had been across my way and prevented me from moving forward. But now I suddenly found I had the energy for almost anything. And wherever I was, working in a farm camp, hitch-hiking through France, and later studying my books at my aunt's in Kent, I pushed myself through an apprenticeship in poetry. I was greatly influenced by Auden still—in one poem I even addressed Picasso as 'Sir', imitating Auden's Hopkinsey invocation to God, 'Sir, no man's enemy . . .' And Donne gave me the license both to be obscure and to find material in the contradictions of one's own emotions. But I wrote steadily, averaging about a poem a week, and was to continue doing so without stop for at least another year and a half.

Right from the start the second year was busier than the first. Apparently that single, derivative poem had had the authority to get me taken seriously by the other poets. That autumn a group of us would get together every week to discuss each other's work—Norman Buller and Harold Silver, I think, and maybe I knew John Coleman that early, and John Mander, who was still a communist but was soon to be come an Anglo-Catholic and amaze me with talk of heresies, a word I had seen in print but had never heard spoken before. They were good practical little meetings, as I remember, in which we tried to suppress our own vanities and be of help to each other.

One windy autumn night I was walking along Jesus Lane from one of these meetings. Coming to the corner of Sidney Sussex Street, I could see my own window above. Friends would shout up to me from this street corner, to save themselves climbing two flights of stairs to find if I was in. I noticed that I had left my light on and found myself imagining that I had called my name aloud and could now see my own head stick out of the window above. There were times when anything seemed possible.

Meanwhile I was going to all of F. R. Leavis's lectures, though it was earlier, at the end of the previous year, that I had discovered him. He attracted me as few other teachers at Cambridge did: it is true that his lectures were prepared monologues like everybody else's, but they seemed to have the improvisatory character of discussions. And he was frank about his passion for literature—it was for him important because of its bearing upon experience, no less. If the passion sometimes made him argumentative or undignified, so much the worse for those he argued with, it all helped to validate his approach. I could see it all, this commitment to literature, as neither pastime nor occasion for scholarship, it was after all the reason I had wanted to read English in the first place. And his discriminations and enthusiasms helped teach me to write, better than any creative writing class could have. His insistence on the realized, being the life of poetry, was exactly what I needed. His perceptions about language and verse movement in discussing the first lines of *Burnt Norton*, of Wordsworth's 'Surprised by joy', of 'If it were done when 'tis done', for example—by going directly to the texture of poetry, by showing how the reader's halting and attentive voice is an equivalent to the poet's act of exploration, by risking close scrutiny that entered into the terms of creation—brought me right to the hearth of my own activity. I was the victim of large, vague, diffused emotions. Seeing them as too diffused I had tried to turn my back on them, and had written my poems about old men who possessed only minimal emotions. But Leavis's lectures helped me to deal directly with my own, by reducing their diffusion, by concentrating them.

Yet there was an orthodoxy. I had to learn without becoming a disciple, for disciples have a tendency to turn observation into doctrine. But I was not after all one of Leavis' students and indeed met him only once personally, and then it was in my third year. So I learnt what I could and then ran off with it. Which is not to say that I don't look back upon his lectures with gratitude and love.

I was to have several close friends who read English at Leavis's college, Downing, but they were all in some way a bit alienated from the master himself. It was in fact about this time, at the beginning of my second year, that I met a brilliant young freshman from Downing, a Scot named Karl Miller.

Argumentative, inquisitive, imaginative, he seemed to have no preconceived ideas of what he might find at Cambridge and he wasn't going to accept anybody else's. His very abrasiveness was part of his charm. And he charmed me off my feet, as he did everybody whom he didn't irritate, and I stuck by his side, all admiration, for the next year.

When I wrote a new poem I would give it to him for criticism, and he would pin it to the wall above his desk for several days before he told me what he thought of it. He helped me in other and greater ways. He matured my mind amazingly, and I learned from his habit of questioning, of questioning everything. There was always something rather childish about the way I submitted to the enthusiasms of others. If I learned to argue with them a little, it was from him.

I no longer wanted to be a social climber. The people I knew now were much too exciting for me to want to go beyond them. Another friend from Downing was John Coleman, a poet and reviewer. He was so wise and worldly that I was once heard to say, 'Five minutes with John Coleman and all my problems are solved.' His affectionately witty manner struck me as the last word in sophistication. I wrote a poem to him beginning 'You understand both Adolphe and Fabrice'. And he did, too, though he was not to be without his problems. Some time after I first knew him he was walking one evening with a girl on a Cambridge street, neither of them in the black gowns students were then supposed to wear after dark. Proctors appeared to question them; they answered with assumed voices and farcical accents, for which they were sent down from Cambridge.

Meanwhile, independently of my friends, I was trying to develop certain thoughts. They amounted to a rather crude theory of what I called 'pose', based partly on the dramatics of John Donne, somewhat perhaps on Yeats's theory of masks, and most strongly on the behaviour of Stendhal's heroes. I was to find support for it from other sources, notably from some of Shakespeare's characters, like the Bastard in *King John* and

Coriolanus, and later from Sartre. It was, as you can see, literary in character, but its principal source was the Revelation on the road in France, with its intimations of unbounded energy. The theory of pose was this: everyone plays a part, whether he knows it or not, so he might as well deliberately design a part, or a series of parts, for himself. Only a psychopath or a very good actor is in danger of *becoming* his part, however, so one who is neither is left in an interesting place somewhere in between the starting point—the bare undefined and undirected self, if he ever existed—and the chosen part. This is a place rich in tensions between the achieved and the unachieved. I thought of Julien Sorel with Madame Rénal, the counterpoint a man's vulnerable emotions made upon his seduction timed by the clock.

To tell the truth, I don't remember doing much about my theory in the actual living of my life, but viewing myself as an actor trying to play a part provided rich material for poetry. It also provided opportunities for falling flat on my face once I forgot the more ridiculous possibilities implicit in the whole theory. One of the poems I wrote during this year was called 'A Village Edmund', referring to Edmund in *King Lear*. It concluded thus:

> '*When it was over he pulled his trousers on.*
> "*Demon lovers must go,*" *he coldly said.*
> *And she stared at the pale intolerable moon.*'

Toward the end of my second year I met Tony White, another student from Downing. I had been aware of him for a long time, as many others had, for he was a rising local actor. He had played, or shortly was to play, Aufidius, Astrov, Gaveston, Mark Antony (in *Julius Caesar*), Petruchio, Romeo, and Cyrano, among other parts, as romantic-existentialist characters. The similarity between the parts is not great, perhaps it was an error that he made it so, but the vigour of the interpretations amounted to a unifying style. If his Aufidius was slightly more sensititive than one would have expected, one might almost say more alienated, then his Romeo was also more of a tough than he is usually seen to be. For his interpretation of Romeo, indeed, Tony took as a guiding hint the scene with the apothecary near the end—a certain callousness qualifies the romantic obsession, but maybe also makes his absorption in it possible. But in all the parts, as he played them, there was a kind of athletic defiance of the gods.

We first met at a party, where we joyfully discussed Stendhal for about two hours. We were later to find many other shared enthusiasms. But, well as I came to know him at Cambridge, I think I took him at face value at this time, and it was easy to do so, his surface was so finished, so lively and delightful in itself. He was a man of courtesy, and I mean courtesy not merely in a social sense, it was a giving of himself, in all his strength and sweetness, to others, whom he admired more than he could ever admire himself. His courtesy was a direct result of the deep unease in him, a defiance of it. And ultimately he wasn't able to keep up the kind of self-regard which would have been necessary for him to continue as an actor.

Anyway, from the time I met him till his death as the result of a football accident at the age of forty-five, he was one of the most important people in my life. If I was not yet to learn the real vulnerabilities in him for a while (and they were vulnerabilities that in others would have seemed like strengths), we were still becoming tied to each other by mutual enthusiasm. He seemed to articulate in a bolder way than I ever could the kind of personal freedom that I had glimpsed on the road in France: he was a model as well as a friend. He helped me to shape my thoughts. It was he who first got me to read Sartre's plays and Camus' novels. (They were not yet taught in universities.) He introduced me to his friends who had already left Cambridge. We formed projects together, we studied books together, we even found, to our amusement, that we both affected the same check shirts, which we had bought on Charing

Cross Road, making us look, we hoped, more like Canadian loggers than Cambridge undergraduates.

I have a card from him which must date from a bit later, the beginning of 1954:

All my best wishes for
panache, logique, espagnolisme,
l'imprévu, singularité and
MAGNANIMITY
in the New Year
from one Étranger
to another.

He was certainly fully aware of the comic implications of our home-made philosophy, the mélange of Rostand, Stendhal, Shakespeare, and Camus.

Cambridge had not before seemed so rich in its fulfilment of possibilities. I had a lot of exciting friends, I was doing well in my exams, and there was the summer. The winter of Cambridge is so bleak, so unremitting, that the early summer always seems like a gift; it is even greater than anything one could possibly have *earned* by suffering through the other seasons. I have memories of charming idylls such as every undergraduate has always had: of sitting on the Backs in early evening listening to the long calls of the birds as they went to their nests, of bicycling out past the fields to supervisions at Conduit Head Road and once of clearing the orchard there with a billhook, and of a time very close before exams when some of us took off the afternoon and punted down to Grantchester and back, Karl Miller improvising ballads about the people in the boat, particularly about Geoffrey Strickland, in stanzas that started 'Now old Sir Geoffrey . . .'

And a play was put on, *The Taming of the Shrew*. Toby Robertson directed it, his sister Toppit played Katherine, Tony White played Petruchio, and other friends like Sasha Moorsom were in it. I was persuaded to play First Servant, and as Second Servant almost never turned up to rehearsals I got his lines too. It was played during May Week, three nights in Trinity Fellows' Garden and three nights in King's Fellows' Garden. In the last scene as night came on, the servants held up flaming torches. It was Cambridge at its sweetest—Shakespeare, the moonlit summer night, the park-like private gardens of wealthy colleges, friends I hoped would be friends for life—different kinds of happiness rolled into one.

Yet there was no fixed Cambridge. There was instead a number of beautifully kept-up old buildings and a core of teachers and retainers. This was a background against which a lot of intelligent young people improvised their fantasies of what 'Cambridge' might be. The fantasies could be sporty or scholarly, they might be about artistic community or gilded youth, but they were all essentially derivative, and it was the derivativeness that provided continuity. My Forsterian fantasy had been brought up to date but also enriched and extended by the fantasies of my friends. And apparently, whether we were conscious of it or not, our fantasies—which we speedily fulfilled—had to do with success.

I conclude this, not because I can remember making my bid for local fame, but because in my third year I got it and people seldom become successful without wanting to be. There was always a niche for the Cambridge Poet (as for the Cambridge Politician, the Cambridge Editor, and the Cambridge Actor), and I was indeed happy to occupy it now that John Mander had given up writing. I edited an anthology of student poetry. I was now president of the English Club, with Karl doing the hard work, as secretary. As such, I gave embarrassed introductions to Angus Wilson, Henry Green, Dylan Thomas (sober and punctual), W. W. Robson, Kathleen Raine, Bonamy Dobrée, William Empson, and other writers who came to speak to us. And Mark Boxer (the cartoonist Marc) asked me to help with the magazine *Granta*, of which he was editor, but that worked out only for a short time, even though I continued to publish in it.

Looking back on that time, I can see it all as a bit incestuous: we promoted each other consistently. For example, the university newspaper *Varsity* featured a profile of a local celebrity each week, and it seems to me that we all wrote each other's profiles, thus creating and perpetuating each other's celebrity.

I now went to as many chic parties as I wanted to, but I wanted to less and less. I had a sense of the whole thing stiffening, there was less of that fine feeling of flexibility that there had been the year before.

I do remember one remarkable party, or rather Karl told me about it because I passed out from drinking about a half-gallon of sherry. It took place at Newnham, and a don had to be specially brought from her bed, in her nightdress and dressing-gown, to open a side gate, normally locked, so that I could be carried more easily to a waiting taxi. She stood there in pained silence, waiting to give permission for the closing of the gate, and it seems that as I was being hauled past her my unconscious body gave a terrific fart, as if adding the sin of ingratitude to that of gluttony. I do not remember this personally, but I have Karl's word for it.

There was later a memorable escapade. About six of us, three boys and three girls, decided to go to Paris for a week. So after my yearly Christmas job with the post office, I went over to stay with John Coleman, who was now teaching in a school near there. The place he had borrowed from a gym teacher was far too small, so we all moved to a cheap hotel on the Rue Jacob, sleeping in two rooms. Paris was iron-cold, and we had a wonderful time, though I can't remember the order in which things happened very well. The group kept separating, reforming, and separating again. We ate horsemeat steaks and black sausage on the Boulevard St-Germain. Tony had met a French girl on the boat and she asked him and me round to dinner with her family, where the father kept putting down Shakespeare as a barbarian who couldn't observe the unities. We saw

Phèdre at the Comédie Française, done in much the same style as in the seventeenth century. One of us, John Holmstrom, bought some books by Genet, which he intended to smuggle back into England, these being banned books. And I found myself somehow spending the end of New Year's Eve alone in someone else's room at the top of a smelly tenement. I opened the windows before I went to sleep and drunkenly watched the big damp snowflakes as they fell through the patch of light. A couple of days later Tony and Bronwyn O'Connor and I returned across the Channel together, sitting on the deck singing music-hall songs so that we wouldn't think about being sick.

Then we went back for our last two terms at Cambridge. The best thing about being an undergraduate at Oxford or Cambridge was that you were trusted to do the work more or less in your own time and to feed on what authors you would. I now went to almost no lectures in English, but to some in the French and History Faculties. And it must have been around this time that I realized I was getting more education from my contemporaries than from my teachers. Moreover I don't think I met any teachers at Cambridge in the whole of my first two years, apart from my supervisors. In my third year I did meet a few, but largely because I went to the right parties.

Meanwhile Mark Boxer was sent down for 'blasphemy', because *Granta* published a poem uncomplimentary to God. Its sophistication is sufficiently indicated by the lines 'You drunken gluttonous seedy God,/You son of a bitch, you snotty old sod.' It is hard to believe that such a poem should have caused a scandal, and in fact the scandal was caused only for the Proctors. But it was the Proctors who had the power to send Mark down and to ban *Granta* for a year. However, some undergraduates, graduates, and dons revived the magazine under the name of *Gadfly*, of which the format and contributors were identical. It even contained drawings by Mark.

One morning I read in the *News Chronicle* of Dylan Thomas's death. Karl had taught me to love his poetry. I went round to

Karl's room and, not finding him there, left a solemn little note on his mantelpiece: 'This is a black day for English poetry', so that he should know I was feeling the proper grief.

And from around this time I find an issue of a mimeographed periodical called *Broadsheet*, in which a reviewer ends his piece with these words: 'Since writing this article I have met E. J. Hughes, of Pembroke, who is trying to bring writers of poetry in Cambridge together at the Anchor, where the landlord has set aside a room for the display of poetry.' E. J. Hughes of Pembroke was very retiring. I am not sure if I even knew him to speak to while I was at Cambridge, though I did know what he looked like. We did not become friends until years later, after he had, as Ted Hughes, published his first book.

As the year went on, I withdrew more and more from the 'Cambridge' I had helped create. I had fallen in love, but that is another story. In any case I felt a pull away from the place.

In the summer I hung on after the term was over, deciding for indefinite reasons to take my degree in person, in wing collar, bow tie, and rented suit. Most of my friends did it by proxy and it was already tourist season, the Backs and the river covered by straying families with cameras and sandwiches. But I was still a part of it for a few more days before I joined the families as one who had no place here.

What I was to realize more clearly after I had gone down was that, for all who go there, whether rich or poor (or, most likely, middle-class), Cambridge is a place of privilege, and things are usually made easier for those who have been there. My first books were reviewed more kindly than they deserved largely, I think, because London expected good poets to emerge from Oxford and Cambridge and here I was, somebody new with all the fashionable influences and coming from Cambridge. I am not implying that those who treated me so well when I started publishing were consciously playing favourites, but I know that they were mostly from Oxford and Cambridge themselves and that *I got a hearing* more readily than if I had just graduated from the University of Hull.

Many of my contemporaries went on to become well known —as directors of plays, actors, editors of magazines, historians, reviewers, novelists, dramatists. London received them warmly, and being talented they flourished in the warmth. Only Tony White, among my close friends, became an exception: he joined the Old Vic company, and had got so far after a few years as to play Cassio in *Othello* when he dropped it all, for a life of odd jobs and translating, barely making ends meet as a handy man, plumber, house painter, or translator of some lengthy anthropological work from French into English. He dropped out, coolly and deliberately, from the life of applause, having come to see how the need for it complicates one's existence quite unnecessarily.

So I am grateful to Cambridge for many things. It enriched my life enormously, it give me the security and advantages that everybody ought to have, but it also brought me up against someone who could eventually teach me that the real business was elsewhere completely.

Simon Gray

Simon Gray was born in 1936, and went up to Trinity to read English in 1956. He had previously been at Westminster School and at Dalhousie University, Canada. From 1960–65 he worked as a supervisor in English. He has written five novels, several television plays and a number of highly successful stage plays which have been acclaimed on both sides of the Atlantic, including Butley *and* Otherwise Engaged. *He is now a lecturer in English for London University at Queen Mary College.*

When I was three I was evacuated to Montreal with my slightly older brother, to live out the war with our grandparents, then in their late sixties. Our grandfather was a businessman who spent the weeks in Toronto and only the weekends at home. My grandmother, an alcoholic, was mainly confined to a large, musty room at the back of what remains in memory a large, dark house. Occasionally she emerged, smelling strongly of peppermints. There was also an aunt, in her early forties, who had long before resigned herself to looking after our grandmother—her only child, so to speak. It was an unhappy household. My father told me, many years later, that his father remained passionately in love with his mother, who had never loved him. Thus, his weekly absences; thus also, perhaps, her addiction to drink; and our aunt's servitude. Whatever their feelings about each other, their interdependence was so complete that when my grandmother died—some twenty years ago—my grandfather and my aunt followed within a few months. The causes of their deaths were medically different, of course, but in reality they had long since come to form one organism.

However these three actually viewed their responsibilities to the two children that war had thrust upon them, they quickly simplified them into catering arrangements. They fed us with all the foods that were to remain unobtainable in

England for another decade. They made sure we had clothes, clean sheets and were well shod. They made sure we went to bed at night and got up in the mornings. But they never played with us and only rarely spoke to us. In other words, they treated us as members of the family.

As soon as we were old enough, we were sent to a local school where, after an introductory month during which we were beaten up when we arrived in the morning, beaten up in the first break, beaten up at lunchtime, beaten up in the second break, and beaten up on the way home, we were accepted into one of the gangs, and joined in beating up less adaptable children. After school and in the holidays we hung about street corners, or went down to the drug store for sodas and cokes, beat up the sons of the two French Canadian families in the street, and three Jewish brothers, one of whom was called Harvey. We read and exchanged comics and smoked fairly heavily. By my eighth birthday I was on ten cigarettes a day. Our grandparents gave us pocket-money, but not enough for our style of life, so we stole more from them, or from the parents of other members of the gang. I also practised on my own a form of begging. I would write on an envelope an address in England I'd copied from one of the letters that arrived for my grandparents, take up a position by a post-office, and cry. On being asked what was the matter, I would explain that I'd lost the stamp money for my letter to Mummy and Daddy, and so would collect in the course of a session anything up to two dollars. I only stopped when a middle-aged plain-clothes policeman told me that if he hadn't been on his way home, he'd have taken me down to the station. He said that from then on he would have me watched by other men in plain clothes. There are moments in my life now when I believe he still does.

We had left England with the moppet hairstyles, the piping accents, the submissive feelings and no doubt manner, of the nanny-trained, middle-class infant. We were returned to it with crew-cuts, harsh North American accents and (in my case—I can't speak for my brother, a lawyer) criminal habits. In our grandparents' house there had been several photographs of our father, their son, whom we failed to recognize from our own past. I don't recall any photographs of our mother. We were therefore as horrified by the powerfully-built man and the tall, vivid woman who claimed us from the ship at Southampton as they were by their two over-fed sons, with their cropped heads, jug ears, and cunning eyes. We were far too old to be the children of such young parents, and they, who had no doubt often dreamt of clutching again the mere children who had left them, were ashamed of us. I don't recall the trip from Southampton to Hayling Island, where my father had become a GP before the war, and where he had now settled again to become a pathologist, but I do recall our bath, that first night. We were put in together, and our mother washed us. She had us nude and defenceless, but we were no babies of hers. At least, not yet. This was known on both sides.

Our re-education began at once. Our mother gave us elocution lessons (the key words were 'water', 'tomatoes' and 'laugh') and we were sent to the only girls' school on the Island. I suppose that if our mother was to achieve that hold on her two sons that is the inalienable right of middle-class Englishwomen, she had at short order to induce the correct sexual confusions. Two years there were followed by three at a boys' boarding school in Portsmouth, which were followed by two at a prep school in London, where we'd moved after the Portsmouth contribution and at which I was alternately fondled and caned by an extremely possessive pederast; which were followed by five at a famous public school—Westminster for me, St Paul's for my brother—as day boys. At eight and nine we had been acceptable, indeed dominant, members of a Montreal street gang. At thirteen and fourteen we appeared to be acceptable, indeed dominant—because we were both good at sports—members of our years at our respective London public schools. At seventeen my brother had decided on Sandhurst and a career in the British army; at sixteen I had settled for Oxford and the intellectual life. I remained, however, something of a thief (at fifteen I'd been almost expelled for a sustained fraud on the London underground, which had led to an appearance in Juvenile Court) and a total liar. I was determined never to fuse my life at school with my life at home, and so told lies in each about the other, and told lies in each about everything else as well. I can't explain, of course, what it was I was protecting, but the habit of fluent evasion (my lies not being simple denials of actuality, but complicated alternatives to it) marked me out at school as a clear scholarship candidate.

The intellectuals at Westminster in my time had been comprehensively prepared in Latin, Greek, English and English manners. My Latin and Greek were feeble, my English essays designed to conceal that I'd only partially read, if at all, in the subject on which I was writing authoritatively, and my English manners, being acquired by observation and imitation, could be rapidly adjusted to circumstances. My little peroration at the Juvenile Court hearing elicited more than one appreciative nod, for instance, just as my General Paper essays in the History Sixth were acknowledged as models of that cultivated but not disturbing originality that wins scholarships.

While in the History Sixth I had a passionate friendship, which never became quite an affair, with a more clever and daring boy who was frequently and romantically ill (he died at Oxford in his early twenties) and I dramatically renounced all games and corps, in order to devote myself more fully to an intellectual life that was all the more shapely in form and epigrammatic in expression for being barren of content. I really did know *almost* nothing, which was exactly enough to spread through the Oxford scholarship papers. If my performances were confidence tricks, then my expensive schooling had given me the confidence to pull them off. I had infiltrated Westminster, in the decreasing though continuing expectation of being found out. Through Westminster I would infiltrate Oxford. It was all quite easy.

Unfortunately my expensive education had drained my father's finances. Just as I was poised to slide out of Westminster and up into Christ Church, the means test, the hospital politics that evolved out of the National Health Service, and a new set of taxes, compelled him to emigrate back to Canada. My distress at having to sacrifice my heritage was alleviated by the realization that I would at least be escaping National Service. I had long suspected that nothing in my nature or education had prepared me properly for that.

Nobody who came across me during my four years in Halifax, Nova Scotia, would have had reason to believe that this was, for me, a return visit. There was anti-semitism in Halifax, and a general dislike of French Canadians, but there were no street gangs that, for safety's sake, I needed to join. It was a coastal town, clean of air, with vast beaches and a pervasively moral atmosphere. Along the main street there were almost as many churches as there were banks. I allowed my hair to hang to the nape of my neck—in my first week a policeman stopped traffic in order to wonder aloud at its length—and my Westminster drawl contrasted pleasingly, to my ears anyway, with the nasal Scotian twang. The irony of a chap destined for the Oxford quads actually finding himself on the Dalhousie campus was one that I further enjoyed by bringing it pointedly to the attention of the natives. I sauntered about the college (which now houses the largest collection of Rudyard Kipling in the world) with the poems of T. S. Eliot in one pocket and a pencil and a pad of verses in the other. I saw myself as a boulevardier fallen among provincials, and only discovered after I'd left that I'd been seen in my turn as the campus pansy. My career as a student was a succession of triumphs. I was treated by Anglophile professors and associate professors and assistant professors of English with reverence. Quite a few of them were New Zealanders; others were underqualified Englishmen, or mere Canadians even; too nervous of being seen through themselves, to dare to see through me. My essays were passed about the department, and sometimes on into other departments. Once a Professor (or Assistant, or Associate) of Economics searched me out in the library, where I held court by isolating myself in a far corner, to congratulate me on a slimy pastiche of James, borrowed from an equally slimy but more skilful pastiche by Beerbohm. In seminars I could force abdications with a phrase. Fellow students scribbled my rehearsed throw-aways into their course note-books. Those teachers in whose eyes I caught any glimpse of the sardonic, I boycotted for fastidious reasons that helped guarantee my reputation while satisfactorily undermining theirs.

I also made two close friends, one the son of a rabbi, the other of the principal of a Baptist theological college, with whom I read Shakespeare, Plato, Aristotle, Kant, Heidegger, Sartre, Camus, and one or two medium-to-light weights; with whom I went to Westerns and gangster films, discussed life and sex (we took them to be synonymous), and to whom I showed my poems and various novels; in collaboration with whom I founded a literary magazine in which we published my more major works and anonymously, for fillers, some of my minor ones; and from whom, therefore, I received whatever in Halifax, Nova Scotia, I did receive of an education.

I also had one or two experiences with girls—those who were of an intellectual bent themselves, and therefore thought there was some cachet in cuddling the campus pansy (who also, by the way, had a weight problem, owing to a secret addiction to candy bars, hamburgers and coca cola); but on the whole kept sex down to those conversations about life, or firmly back in the head from which I frequently expressed it into socks and handkerchiefs, in the usual manner of adolescents, which I no longer was. The Campus pansy/intellectual was in one or two respects, perhaps, a mite regressive, though in fact heterosexual enough for two—the penalty, I now see, of insisting on remaining an English public school boy (which, you must remember, I'd never properly been).

But otherwise I grew, and not only fat. I'd started my career at Dalhousie by presenting myself as an English boulevardier.

I concluded it as a citizen of all civilization, known as France. As soon as I'd taken my degree (a most distinguished one romantically marred only by a couple of failures in compulsory courses that demanded, along with application, knowledge), I departed for Clermont-Ferrand to teach as an 'assistant' in its College-Technique. I was going there to be, not just a Frenchman, but (from the Anglo-Saxon point of view) a thorough-going frog, which would entail losing some inches in height, changing the colour of my eyes, wearing a beret, stinking of garlic, despising the English (this I'd managed in advance), acquiring a mistress a decade older than myself and, if necessary, picking up some of the language. By the end of my first week I realized, as I sat in a café puffing Gauloises and sipping marcs with the five or six other outcast English students who infested the educational institutions of that magnificently provincial city, that I was already on the right lines. But during my year I didn't advance much beyond that first circle, except into several official *vins d'honneur*, from one of which, through an excess of wine, I only failed by inches to make it out of the door over which I vomited, and thus had the honour of hearing myself described by one of the thorough-going frogs at the back of the room as a 'sale cochon anglais'.

At Clermont-Ferrand I became close friends with the English *lecteur* at the university, a man of twenty-six who had been doing the French circuit since coming down from Downing three years before. He introduced me to the novels of D. H. Lawrence and the critical writings of some Cambridge don called Leavis, about whom I'd once read an article in the *New Statesman*, I think it was, by J. B. Priestley, it must have been, and of whom I therefore also had the measure (as, by the way, I had of J. B. Priestley, having read a Leavis or Leavisite reply the following week). I spent the next two months on the bed reading Lawrence, and then Leavis on Lawrence, and then Leavis on George Eliot, Henry James and Conrad (the Great Novels course had included *Adam Bede*, so I'd got the measure of her; and *Lord Jim*, so I'd got the measure of him; and *The*

Ambassadors, the victim of my plagiarized pastiche, so I'd got the measure of him), and then I read George Eliot, and then Henry James, and then Conrad; and then Leavis on all of them, all over again. My real introduction to English literature was thus made in a bed-sitter in Clermont-Ferrand, with five years of an English public school education, and three years of a Canadian university already behind me. And my introduction had come through an accidental encounter with a teacher whose writings showed me I still hadn't learnt to read. It became a matter of great importance to get to Cambridge as quickly as possible, for Cambridge—in English studies at least—was evidently Leavis.

One brilliant winter's morning, four years after I'd arrived in Cambridge, I walked as a research student beside my current supervisor through one of the colleges on the river. My supervisor was a celebrated literary critic, a national reviewer, with an easy, anecdotal manner. He'd always treated me with consideration, never bullying me for work (I wasn't doing any) and ready to pour me in his study as many glasses of sherry as he poured himself. As we passed over the river he raised, for the first time in our relationship, Leavis's name. What did I think of Leavis? I tried to tell him, going back to the first acquaintance in Clermont-Ferrand, and on through the lectures and seminars as an undergraduate. He listened, with his customary inattentive courtesy. 'Yes,' he said fretfully, when I'd nearly finished, 'I do wish he'd hurry up and die.' This may, of course, have been from impatience with my labouring literalness. I had, after all, answered in detail a question that was perhaps intended, in the Cambridge fashion, to answer itself. Even so, I didn't doubt that he had betrayed himself into a literalness of his own. He hated Leavis, as did many members of the Faculty who, if they didn't as a whole take literature seriously, took seriously any of their colleagues who did. Not that Leavis was yet as isolated as he was to become. He still had his Fellowship at Downing, still gave his weekly seminars and lectures, and had a self-appointed coterie of Downing graduates and a girl or two who had fallen in with Downing graduates. It must be admitted, however, that these chaps and their girls weren't, except when viewed from a distance, much fun. They spoke in almost inaudible voices (the girls didn't speak at all) and were masters of what I can only describe as moralizing *longueurs*—i.e. sustained passages of silence which were boring even though one knew that adverse judgements on oneself were being formed in and expressed through them. Febrile personalities (such as mine) could be panicked into hysterical utterance, by which they stood further condemned. In my first year as an undergraduate I bumped into one of the Leavisites in a pub (but what was *he* doing there? Unless waiting for someone like me). He was a chunky fellow, broad of shoulder with a broken nose and the characteristic mumble of profound seriousness. He greeted my greeting with a small movement of the mouth, which inevitably impelled me into an extravagant dilation on some film or other I'd seen that week—it might even have been that day; there were long periods of my life when I went to the cinema twice a day; one week, by a judicious use of taxis, I got it up to three times. When I'd come to my throbbing conclusion, he regarded me for an hour or two with an expression of pondering or ponderous humility, muttered 'I see' and departed. I later heard, as one always did hear these things in Cambridge, that he'd finally forced me, in some pub or other he'd caught me in, to expose myself as a 'brute'. A brute. The campus pansy had found his balls, at last.

The only time the Leavis circle—in which, by the way, I never saw Leavis himself—came to life was when it was debating such matters as whether it was the cleaning woman, or Dr Q. D. Leavis, or Leavis himself who'd hung up the washing that had been observed flapping from the garden line shortly after breakfast, but which had been taken down (by whom?) some time before lunch. Inaudible or even silent on so many topics, they were dreadful gossips—in the double sense—on any aspect of the Leavises' domestic arrangements. They were, not to mince words, a pretty grisly gang; but time, thank God, has wreaked its usual shapely havoc. I've heard reports of one who, famous for his scathing silences from which he fired questions so remorselessly personal that they can only have been intended to elicit angry stammers from men and tears from women, or both from both; who shrouded his own movements in such mystery but to such seemingly sinister purpose that his was the face I always conjured up when asked to imagine the traditional knock on the door, at three in the morning, in Kafka and other police states; who seemed so totally without warmth, or even intellectual sympathy, or any but the vilest curiosity—I've heard reports that he has long since sunk cosily into a provincial nook, where, a gentle but bonhomonous homosexual, he dispenses hospitality and kindly advice to all who need it; and doubtless to quite a few who don't.

I myself started at Cambridge as a post-graduate. I concocted in Clermont-Ferrand, with my Downing friend's help, a specious outline for proposed research on Henry James, which was accepted by whatever board was responsible for those matters; then, having gained my entrée, insinuated myself back to undergraduate status—I was anyway only twenty—and settled down at Trinity to my two years (my three at Dalhousie being assessed by Cambridge as worth one of Cambridge) of life and literature. Of life through literature.

Those two years, of the in fact eight I spent altogether in Cambridge, ended in the usual unnatural fashion with the Tripos examination. In preparation for it I had only one supervisor, who did me no harm and almost certainly meant me none. We walked in the Fellows' Garden in good weather, or sipped coffee in his college rooms in bad, and we gossiped of this or that great writer, soothingly. He was intellectually versatile, with a grasp of different disciplines—law, philosophy, modern languages, classics, even mathematics—and also an elaborate traditionalist. When I once turned up for a supervision without a gown, he sent me back—a matter of a mile or two—to get it; and on another occasion, when I confessed I was desperate for a cigarette, he pointed out to me that I was having a supervision, and was therefore obliged to wear a gown; and that undergraduates were not allowed to smoke while wearing gowns; then resolved the problem by informing me that he was about to leave the room, and that as long as he was out of the room the supervision was not taking place; and that therefore as long as I took my gown off, and kept it off while he was out of the room, I could smoke my cigarette. He may, of course, have been something of a comedian as well as a traditionalist.

The only lectures and seminars I went to were those given by Leavis. This was not because I was unduly discriminating, but because in the gap between being a child and having children I found it difficult (having little reason) to get up before lunch; on top of which we weren't allowed to smoke in lectures, a prohibition less disabling to my career as a student than it is now to my career as a lecturer.

As for Leavis's teaching—well, whatever I learnt from it, I carefully refrained from summoning forth during the examinations, for which I trained myself up on the side, so to speak, of my interest in literature and in which I employed the techniques I'd acquired at Westminster, in the History Sixth, with the Oxford General Paper in view. I suppose that my predictable success (I'd predicted it, anyway) was an agreeable late return to my father for the money he'd invested in my Public School education, but I mustn't completely disclaim my own contribution—that part of my nature which had combined smoothly with circumstances to make me, from an early age, an accomplished liar. I wrote all my papers with a fraudulent fluency that could only have taken in those who were bound by their own educations to honour a fluent fraud—at least to honour him more highly than any churlish Leavisite whose sense of the texts depended on close and therefore uncertain readings. The rewards were considerable. A first class degree, and the pleasure of knowing that if I hadn't got the measure of Leavis himself, I'd got the rest of the Faculty dead right.

My moral and social education (they were, in important respects, synonymous) proceeded along the same lines as my intellectual one, to this extent at least: that in public I was a fraud, of ever-increasing fluency. I had polished opinions on novels, poems, plays, films and all pieces of music, including those I hadn't read, seen or heard (I am almost tone deaf). These opinions, however phrased—and the phrasing was all—could be reduced to one uncomplicated formulation: *over-rated.* Everything was over-rated. Except by me, of course. I went of an evening to the rooms of friends in their colleges, and drank whisky, and curling my voice as a way of curling my lip, delivered my opinion for two hours or so. Then, with the air of a man with more stimulating assignations to keep, I made my exit on a valedictory sneer, then slunk anonymously through the dark streets to the cinema where I sat completely rapt before films that nobody, including their writers, their directors, or the rest of the audience, would ever over-rate, or rate at all. After the film, I would go to the rooms of friends in their colleges, with an air of having kept some stimulating assignations, and join in a poker game that often lasted until two or three in the morning. We played for sums we couldn't quite afford, and so frequently ended up, all our cultivated urbanity corroded by whisky and fatigue, in squalid squabblings over our winnings and losings. I remember that one night a man who had lost hand after hand to the tune of ten pounds or so, collected two shillings and sixpence on a straight flush. I drew no conclusion from this, or indeed from any other event in my nightly life, which in retrospect seems to have been one long night, although the routine must quite frequently have been broken by circumstances, if never by inclination. After the poker game, my mouth burnt out with cigarettes, my head aching with whisky, and my stomach dipping from both, I went to bed. At least I suppose I did. I have little recollection of the period between the last dead hand and the first cup of tea in the morning.

Being a sort of alien, with a distastefully complicated background, I wasn't offered rooms in college. I lived in a boarding-house with a couple of aspirant politicians from Ghana or Tanzania; an extremely old mathematical historian of twenty-six or seven who was engaged on a work so comprehensive and detailed that he couldn't see his way to begin the actual writing of it for another decade, at least; and a straight up-and-down sort of open-faced chap who was doing one of those fringe courses set up by the Colonial Department a year or so before the Department was wound up, along with a large part of our national history and influence, for ever. We were, in other words, and in our different ways, all aliens. As was our landlord, an extravagant Pole who dressed and spoke as if he ran a tenement in the Bronx. His wife, however, was a sweetly plump, soft-spoken little Englishwoman whom one from time to time suspected of spooning rat-poison into the sugar bowl. She served the breakfasts we all ate together, uncommunicatingly; and she made the beds we never shared; and she made sure the water was hot only between 7 and 7.13 in the evenings, as it was her boast that her lodgers could have baths as often as they liked—which, under the circumstances, wasn't anything like as often as they needed them. I have no inclination to go into the room now, small and dreadful as it was, having had to go into it when it was my home, with such despairing regularity, twenty years ago.

My daily life, those long stretches of it that weren't spent with my supervisor or at the Leavis seminars, or lying in bed with a hangover, passed in a kind of blank fretfulness. I did some reading, of course, in my calculatingly selective way, dully, with a pencil to hand for the notes that would (and did) recall it all in the week before the Tripos, but many of my afternoons drifted by in the cinema, or as I tramped and tramped the Cambridge streets. I went to Boots a great deal, passing aimlessly between the counters, or mulling listlessly through the books in its subscription library, turning the pages of the identically spined and coloured volumes in its Western, Thriller and Romance sections, following fragments of the different stories until they cohered into one dully lunatic, unconcludable epic. Sometimes I went to Lyons, and sat over a cup of tea, reading the *Evening Standard* and the Cambridge *Daily News*. Once I stood in the Market Place, in the rain, for about an hour, unable to decide where to go until I became so wet I had (thank God) no choice but to return to my room and sit shaking before my meter-operated gas fire. It seems now, in recounting it, like a kind of madness, and perhaps it was. I have no idea what my soul was up to, although its sporadic yearnings were not unlike the continuous, unassuaged yearnings of my body. Perhaps I was just waiting, getting through the hours until my first public appearance and the first airing of my single opinion.

I was saved by the vacations, part of which were spent back in Halifax, Nova Scotia. In the summer I swam in its great cold harbours, and worked with undistracted if cynical clarity for the Tripos. The winters were bitterly cold, and yet I could trudge the almost snow-bound streets with a dizzying sense of purpose and even a future, as if Cambridge had only been a long, dull dream from which I had awakened at last.

To which I inevitably returned. But as the Tripos loomed nearer, so did my concentration achieve a focus. I still put in my opinionated public appearances, still played poker, went to the cinema, and did my Boots-Lyons circuit, but for shorter periods, and always with a redeeming sense of something that had to be got back to. In the last weeks of my second year, in the general atmosphere of examination terror, I came to terms with Cambridge for a brief spell at last, positively enjoying even its beauty, which I seemed to see for the first time as I walked to the examination hall in the bright morning, and away from it in the soft afternoon. When the examinations were over, I lay on the Backs in the sun and celebrated my imminent triumph, while simultaneously swearing that when I left Cambridge in a few weeks it would be for ever, and that I'd never open another book; except from interest, disinterestedly.

Next year, lodged as a fraudulent research student (I'd resubmitted my Henry James piece) I organized, in a magazine I edited with a friend, an examination of the examinations. We debated whether the questions they contained could successfully provoke anything but fluency and fraudulence. It's a tradition of English life that though we might sometimes be compelled to bite the hand that feeds us, we never bark at it in public places. Among elderly Faculty members we were dismissed as 'bounders' (the word was actually used), while in the *Cambridge Review*, edited by younger Faculty members whose primary qualifications we had denigrated, we were described as 'psychopathic hoodlums' which my co-editor, a mild-mannered man of disinterested intelligence who'd anyway read History, could well have been; and which I, in spite of my most secret inclinations, had so far found myself unable to be. *The Listener* took up the matter of examinations, as did the *T.L.S.*; and found against us, as did the *T.L.S.* I should like to claim that from then on my life as a research student was made insupportable by vindictive dons of all ages, but it wasn't so. I was allowed to stay on, and on; and long after I could stand it, on. I had early been alerted to the fact that by changing my research subject every year, I could jostle back to the beginning all over again. When I finally managed to leave, eight years after arriving as a first-year research student, I was still in my first year of research, which I still hadn't begun.

But of the six years that followed my degree I remember little more than the little I've already recorded. Often, when I lie sleepless at night, I need to invoke certain scenes from my past (a late cut executed in the middle of my fifteenth summer, say; or a coolly-taken goal, lifted with the toe over the heads of the backs and into the left-hand corner of the net—that, in my great Junior Colts season) in order not to be invaded by those many other scenes I wish absolutely to revoke. But of the new or ancient shames that bring me out of bed and downstairs for tea, cigarettes and monotonously unconvincing justifications, none belongs to or points back to my Cambridge years—not even my undergraduate ones. This eery infertility may be the result of my having written two novels about being in Cambridge while I was still there, so that I'd seen the experience not only published but in part remaindered before being completed. Or it may simply be that those eight years contained nothing of any consequence, except in their inconsequential passing. From the brightest perspective eight years can be judged as no time at all, especially if one doesn't remember noticing them going by; and could therefore be described as a period of unruffled calm, or happiness perhaps.

But here are some facts. Having begun by not being offered rooms in college in my two years as an undergraduate, in all subsequent years, as I became more deeply habituated to the seedy bed-sitters from which I could conduct my furtively independent existence, I declined them. In my last years, and from a panicky sense that loneliness had become an unendurable addiction, I moved into a cold little warren of rooms above a coffee shop which I shared with two other outcasts, one of whom, a Classical research student from King's, was a friend with whom I could eat, for instance, a Christmas dinner of sardines on bread. One winter it was so cold that we wore overcoats in the sitting-room, and I had to take two blankets to my favourite cinema—at which, on mid-week evenings, I was the only patron. Back in my first bed-sitter I used to be kept awake by two young men from Trinity, I think, who quarrelled shrilly beneath my window. One of them committed suicide by tying his head into a plastic bag. The other then went down, or was sent down, or possibly simply followed suit. There was a man from Sidney with alopecia, three tufts of hair growing from a thin blotched head, whom I saw on the streets regularly every year except my last when, instead of dreading the sudden sight of him, I found myself eagerly looking out for him. There was another man, from Trinity again I think, an asthmatic whom prescribed drugs transformed in a matter of months from youthful slenderness to bloat decadence. He also took his life. There was a small, elderly Scots tramp who ran about the town shadow-boxing (like so many of the rest of us) until one term I realized that he too had gone. There were May Balls, to which I always seemed to go in the company of girls who'd waited until the last minute to be invited by other men, with whom they nevertheless succeeded in meeting up after about the third dance of the ball itself, and on my ticket so to speak, and danced my dances with them before allowing themselves to be led off by them (while still morally on my ticket, so to speak), just before dawn, to somewhere that was far beyond the reach of my glaring eyes and acquiescent smile. There were quite nice afternoons on the river with friends, but far better ones alone in the cinema. I drank more and more as the terms succeeded each other with less and less definition. After taking my own degree, I supervised undergraduates. I wrote two novels and began a third, which I concluded after I'd got away at last, to London. And yes, of course, the bells. The bells rang incessantly, tolling my terms in, pealing to my departures, from which they tolled me back again. The winter light always seemed to dim by three in the afternoon, just as the crocuses on the Backs invariably came up earlier that year. Those are some facts. But even recording them doesn't help me to remember them, except thinly.

I have an abiding impression, though, that something was continuously, undiagnosably unpleasant all the time I was there—apart, that is, from myself. An impression that becomes vivid on those occasions, (as few as I can make them) when I go back. There is the moment, as the London train slides along the interminable Cambridge platform, when my stomach lurches, and I violently wish I were visiting somewhere else I used to live; or even better, somewhere I've never lived at all.

Eleanor Bron

Eleanor Bron went up to Newnham College in 1957 to read French and German, and on leaving Cambridge eventually joined former Footlights colleagues John Bird and Peter Cook in London's 'First Satirical Nightclub—The Establishment' in Soho. After a tour of the United States and an extended stay in New York with the 'Establishment', she returned to England to appear in Ned Sherrin's 'Not So Much A Programme More A Way Of Life' on BBC TV, and has since performed and written several television series which have run parallel with leading roles in such plays as A Day in the Death of Joe Egg, The Prime of Miss Jean Brodie, Major Barbara, Hedda Gabler, The Merchant of Venice *and* Private Lives. *Her films include* Help, Alfie, Bedazzled, Two for the Road *and* Women in Love. *She has written several plays for television, and a book about her bicycling experiences, as well as a song cycle with John Dankworth and new verses for Saint-Säens' 'Carnival of the Animals'.*

For no apparent reason everyone in my family supported Oxford in the Boat Race so I supported Cambridge, and by the time I came to take the Oxford and Cambridge Entrance exams that long-standing contrariness had developed into a strong preference, totally unfounded. Yet already at the interviews I felt happy in the freezing Cambridge air, and welcome; at Oxford though more snug I was ill at ease. They said: 'Your German is not as good as your French, is it? And your French isn't up to standard.' Why drag me here then? They can't be so short of contenders. In almost all cases they obviously know before they see you whether it's yes or no, and that is what you feel through the careful courtesy and the glasses of sherry. Here was a new world indeed—all those bottles and bottles of ritual sherry being consumed. I can't dissociate the mental odour of those rooms from the sherry—those golden glasses of liquid civilization.

I have to think about what I expected and find that nothing could have been vaguer than my anticipations, founded chiefly on the Boat Race and the Footlights, a world that had nothing to do with mine and of which I had no knowledge at all.

At school Cambridge and Oxford had been presented as absolutes, almost tangible values. Each word seemed to contain continuing and complex experience, to be almost as big as the big insufficient words like Marriage, Pain, Death, Birth—rickety bridges between abstraction and reality. In fact, as I see now, what my teachers were holding out to me were the golden globes of Opportunity. Cambridge, they insisted, would be a Unique Experience. It was. So much so that I never really crossed that particular bridge to fuse my few preconceptions with what I actually found. In my very first term, cycling across Silver Street Bridge one misty autumn evening, I remember being moved by the eery beauty of the mill and the water, and I found myself wishing quite desperately: 'I hope I get in, oh I do hope I get in', and feeling afterwards rather foolish. In that sense I never did get in. I never conclusively fused the idea with the fact, not even in restrospect.

Years and years later I went on a visit to Cambridge with some friends and was persuaded to go back to Newnham, chiefly to look at the new library. I can't now remember the new library but I do remember vividly the strange null sensation of walking again down those endless Newnham corridors, past the familiar busts that lurk in the gloom at night outside the library, the flowing beard of Henry Sidgwick, and Dante's polished head just inside the swing doors. What was so strange was that I could not believe that I had ever been there. I went into the old library, up the first level along the metal walk and past the shelves to sit in the favourite alcove, a bay window-seat, romantic, peaceful, with a view across the walled yard to the outside world passing up and down the road whose name I can't even remember any more. I must have spent weeks and months sitting up there. In my mind I knew it and yet seeing that table and the view and looking down into the library where people came and went and the doors clacked to and fro with little quickening and diminishing explosions, I could not believe that I had ever sat there reading books, trying to think. It was like having spare memories, an uncanny sensation and not a very pleasant one: *not* seeing a ghost. Not seeing a ghost because you are the ghost.

In Cambridge itself the feeling is different. Here spectres

abound and the situation becomes more clear. Here there are streets and corners haunted forever: an unexpected meeting in the fog, a chase by the Proctors in full cry one dark gownless night after the Footlights—the first intimation of the possible uses of relative fame. We spotted them, nipped down a side street by Queens'. They spotted us and lay in wait, cutting us off. He peered at me: 'You've just been working very hard. Go on, off you go.' And off we went.

There is the corner by Bowes and Bowes, remembered for André Schiffrin's observation that all the Jewish girls went off with non-Jewish men and vice-versa; The Whim, where Bill Wallis introduced me to the Footlights heroes Joe Melia and Michael Collings; The Coffee Pot in Green Street, with the flat above, shared by Andrew Sinclair, John Bird, and Timothy Birdsall, its line of unwashed milk bottles stretching along the grimy corridor up the stairs to the kitchen. At the end of one term someone forgot to cancel the standing grocery order and by the start of the following term box upon weekly box of butter, cornflakes, bread, soup and Oxford marmalade had been piled high beside the bottles by the insouciant grocer's boy.

But I don't have to go back to Cambridge to remember those things. I did drive through recently, diverting to pick up a fellow actor on the way to Nottingham, and experienced acute suffocation and shock. I take that route and my heart sinks—there is a particular oast house I pass that does it, and it's worst in the autumn, with the leaves turning, reminding of the start of the new year. It is a strange combination of nerves—the claustrophobia comes from the awful Kafkan feeling that some unknown thing is expected of me; the shock, from the thought that I spent three thoughtless years of unparalleled pampering and privilege in this place, and that still it goes on after all this time. I am astounded, and shocked, by the lavishness and luxury of it. Very puritanical. Very Cambridge. All of which may relate entirely to the fact that what I do is almost precisely what I was persuaded not to do in order to go up to Cambridge; and which may explain why I haunt Newnham and why Cambridge haunts me.

My headmistress was a quietly impressive person and certainly one of the most distinguished women I have ever met. She it was who took me aside one day and talked me out of going to Drama School—that, she said, was what all young girls want to do. It was astute of her to say this since, in a totally unimaginative and uncritical way, I have never liked the idea of doing what everyone else wants to do. She said that it would be a waste of a good mind for me not to try for university, and I was very flattered. This was the first I had heard of my having a 'good mind'. I liked the sound of it.

Now, although the existence of other places was acknowledged—specific credit being accorded to, say, the French Department at Manchester, or the English at Reading—by 'university' Oxford and Cambridge was what was meant and what everyone's hearts and their good minds were set on. Looking back now I resent very strongly the emphasis on this particular academic achievement which prevailed in the school, but I do so on behalf of the other girls, and perhaps groundlessly. I cannot complain for myself, nor feel anything but gratefulness to Dr Anderson (as she then was) or to the teaching staff at North London Collegiate, since I, with a few chosen others, reaped every advantage of it. For years the teachers at my school had fought battles we knew nothing about to gain admittance to any form of higher education, let alone university. They were continuing the fight and any good minds they came across were eagerly plucked up as ammunition to hurl at the battlements. Other things did go on—Art, Music, Games, Decency, standards were high all round and yet. . . . It has troubled me since to think that the Unchosen Many must often have wondered what there was for them, what valuable fulfilling lives to compare with our assured and gilded futures.

For me, however, at that time, there was not much option or desire but to bask in the exhilarating glow that was being generated by this new possibility and the heightening unfamiliar sense of unexpected things being at stake. Attendance at university was by no means a family tradition. Both my parents left school at fourteen, my mother to help her father, who had himself left Poland as a young boy, inspected New York and Liverpool and then settled on and in Glasgow, where he became a bristle merchant. My father at fourteen took a job in the counting house of a firm that made trimmings for millinery. His father, who had a few shops in Stoke Newington, decided that he would like to try his hand at becoming a bookmaker, and having observed my father's aptitude for figures and calculation took his son away from his first job to act as his bookie's clerk on the racecourses, where he spent a large amount of his time and shirts. In spite of his passion and gift for maths and the sciences, the elder of my two brothers had had to leave school to learn the family business, by now metamorphosed into music publishing. The younger studied medicine at Guy's Hospital. By the time my future had to be mapped out I could be afforded the luxury of having no clear and immediate prospects of earning. It was an odd reversal of custom that I, the youngest child and a girl, should have the opportunity to continue a glossy unfocused education, but it was vaguely supposed that it would be a good thing, would broaden, deepen and somehow render me fit to mingle with The Best. Whether or not my three years did for me what it was hoped they would—I cannot judge—they certainly made me unfit to live with my family any more. I was too clever, my new friends were too clever. Even now I suspect that Cambridge has left me with, or encouraged, a drive towards cleverness for its own sake which is as difficult to throw off as a nervous tic. At that time in spite of determined but belated attempts to cut me back down to size, I was like Alice. My broadened mind could scarcely squeeze between the door-jambs, and vacations were uncomfortable.

These preliminaries to going up seem to me inevitably to have conditioned the experience itself. Not only in my case but in every case, so much of the response was governed by the expectation. What of the experience itself? It falls for me into three areas: Newnham, Work and Everything Else. While I was there the areas were by no means as distinct as they now seem, and in retrospect their relative balance has certainly shifted. For my first two years Newnham loomed very large, chiefly as a place to grumble about and get away from. My room, though far larger than my tiny bedroom at Edgware, was a rather gloomy one and it took me almost a year to appreciate the subtle charm of its location, which cut me off from the sun but provided an exit to the World—a rooftop under my window and a short drop into waiting arms in the street whose name I forget. I still have a scar on my wrist where I caught it on the spike of the railing. Worth it, though. Climbing out made me feel I had got through some kind of test. Climbing in, to King's for a party, was even better, like getting the equivalent to the Advanced Motorists' Certificate.

At Newnham we grumbled about the food and the various complex rules for signing in and out which were curiously conceived: if on going out you had not remembered to sign on the list to indicate that you would be back after eleven, and then after all you did come back after eleven, you were accorded some sort of black mark. It was therefore simpler on those occasions to stay out altogether. Perhaps they reckoned that if you were not bright enough to have worked this out you did not deserve any better, and that if you were you could look after yourself. We sat for hours in front of gas fires in each other's rooms, sharing shillings and matches and coffee. We grumbled about our essay subjects, our parents, our minds, other people, Life. It was not until my third year that I recognized that this communal grumbling was the unspun stuff of friendship. My head mistress had made a point of telling us that the friends we made at school and the friends we made at university would last our lives, a little as if that would be it —afterwards no more friends to be had. Fortunately I have since made friends as firm and as fast, but in some ways it has been true, and as will be seen there was possibly an irony in this admonition of hers, since ultimately my Cambridge friendships came to outweigh so heavily my academic goals, and were the real gift, for me, of Cambridge. But certainly the friendships made were something she heavily stressed and it may be that my assumption that in the eyes of my teachers Cambridge's importance lay in things of the mind, was a total misreading. In my final year I began to appreciate far more the instantly available companionship that Newnham offered and the place generally acquired an appeal that had escaped me before. I spent a lot more time there. I don't think that this was just because I had a larger room, or that, because by now so many of my friends had gone down, I was not so tempted to rush out for relief, or that the approach of Tripos was concentrating my mind. I suddenly realized that in less than a year I should probably be some unknown where in a bed-sitting room cooking for myself on a gas-ring with no friends a mere corridor away to call on and moan to. In this building friends and food and immediate future were now contained and secure and more valued because I saw that it would not always be so.

Some aspects of Newnham did bother me and continued to bother me. Clearly the college had modelled many of its procedures on the men's colleges. The College Feast seemed to me a bizarre and lamentable affair, with all of us pointlessly wearing evening dress shrouded by black gowns, no men in sight, a failed banquet and an array of speeches delivered by women who were not at ease to women who were not very interested. By now all this must certainly have changed, with the advent of approximate equality, but the fact is that such a gathering was not natural in the way that an assembly composed of men is natural, or has at least acquired a naturalness from sheer custom—they have been doing it for so long that even the air of boredom does have a kind of grace about it. This dinner summed up for me a lot of what seemed at the time to be amiss with Newnham—our hearts were not in it. Reality and Life were elsewhere. I was certainly in part reacting against school and the evils of separate education for boys and girls. The teacher/pupil barrier, acceptable perhaps at early stages of tuition, seems never to be broken through at a girls' school and this, I think, has the unfortunate effect of maintaining false authorities. Good manners and respect for certain territorial rights may be desirable socially but when carried over into the realms of thought they are not useful or stimulating and I was disappointed to find at Newnham that the old habit died hard and that the barrier continued as great as ever. When I went to school I accepted segregated education as the norm. It now seems to me a destructive and totally pernicious practice setting up and maintaining all kinds of artificial situations and intellectual deprivations.

In this respect Cambridge was some sort of beginning, though regrettably few tutorials were mixed. What Newnham did offer in total contrast to school was another kind of freedom that I failed to appreciate while I was there. If I was aware of it at all I mistook it and dismissed as indifference what I would now interpret as a brand of sophistication riddled with integrity. Where school had continually insisted on the corporate allegiance, the importance of shining in order to reflect glory, pointing with a natural but irksome pride at Old Girls who had achieved, Newnham was what can only be described as cool; not a parent but a godparent, mature and detached, with nothing to prove and who, in your interest, threw you untaught into the sea to swim or not. Any achievement, academic or otherwise, was basically your own affair; credit, if any there was, would reflect on you, not on your mentors, tutors or supervisors. They were there to provide possibilities, you were there to use them as and if—within reason—you wished. Of course if you did not use them at all you might get sent down.

It is hard now to judge how much I was involved in the ostensible purpose of my Cambridge stay—getting a B.A. I still have most of my notes and essays, including those with the small claim to fame of having been borrowed by Peter Cook for the German Tripos. Many, I know, slung what notes they had made into the nearest bin as soon as the results were posted, or ceremonially put a match to them. I have hung on to mine and why? Partly for sheer wonder that I once knew so many of those things. It is a sad enactment of the reality, which is that whatever is written on them has not become a part of me, but remains outside. I did go to lectures, I did make notes, I did write essays. I read a lot of what was prescribed and yet I feel as if I learned nothing. I loved Montaigne in spite of his appalling attitude to women, I can remember a line or two of Maurice Scève, I have accents instead of fractions on my typewriter. So I have not even the excuse that I wasn't trying, I really did work quite hard—because of my grant and for fear of failing and because I simply was not clever enough to be cavalier about it all, tossing off essays like pancakes while getting on with the main task of appearing to have fun. Somewhere there was a grain of the academic in me, though not anything like enough to keep me alive in the wilderness. I did occasionally become intoxicated with pieces of work and research I embarked on. Perhaps it has all long since become what Montaigne called 'sang et nourriture' but if so, it is a layer of me that is buried deep down.

Harder to bear than that lost knowledge, which is in theory recoverable, is the fact that I still find it so incredibly hard to think, to order my thoughts in a way that does not lead me into whirlpools of confusion. Lucidity, or some means, however slow, of reaching it, is what I should have wished to come away with after three years. Writing articles today is still as horribly painful as writing essays was twenty years ago. I am forced to conclude that this is because of a temperamental slackness, a simple lack in me, but for some years I blamed it on my choice of subject and this is one of those unknowable possibles I still mull over in more aggressive moments. It always seemed to me that the approach to literature in the Language Schools was so much less rigorous and initiated a less lasting, less stimulating and useful discipline than that of, say, the English, History or Anthropology Schools. I still find that friends who have read English stun me with their lucidity, but who knows, perhaps my very reasons for settling on French rather than English, the fascination with the sound of the surface as much as the content, are at the root of an inborn fuzziness. I remember being surprised to discover a multitude of subjects I didn't know existed, that I might have chosen to read, and being annoyed that I had made the discovery too late, as I saw it; but it would have been perfectly possible to change. Several friends did.

The study of foreign languages and literature may have allowed for individual scholarship and purely academic work—eminent scholars abounded in the Faculty; but there was no sense of any need to relate these studies to anything outside themselves, or to place them in any wider context. There was no tension. I went to one or two lectures outside my subject, by F. R. Leavis and Professor John Wisdom. The presence of such charismatic figures obviously did create the kind of tension I mean and which I feel is necessary to any enterprise. Leavis supplied this for English students. Whether they were for or against what he stood for, his presence obliged them to define and question the purpose of their studies. The Anthropologists had a tension of excitement that came from their relative youth as a Faculty, their subject was still under definition. The Moral Scientists (who anywhere else would be 'reading' or rather, studying Philosophy) were inventing their subject as they went along, and perhaps their tension came from the thought that they might one day invent it out of existence. (In fact I think this is what has happened.)

So the feeling persists that reading languages was for me an aesthetic indulgence and not an intellectual discipline. Yet this was not a feeling which made me uncomfortable—I didn't have it at the time. I arrived like so many others full of trepidation, and fears that after the false security of being in the top layer at school I was now to be thrown among the cream and would be shown up for what I was. It was both a relief and a disappointment to find that this was not so. I was neither too thin nor too rich but somewhere in the pasteurized homogenized bulk of students. Rumours would go about that this or that student was brilliant (by which was meant that he or she was tipped for a First). No one in my Faculty had that reputation; but even if you could track the others down, they always appeared on the surface to be agreeable and human, like Margaret Drabble, and to enjoy gossip and tea and crumpets. On the whole ordinariness was most in evidence and interestingness was what you looked for, not perhaps consciously, but because theoretically ordinariness was where you had come from and what you were supposed to be leaving behind.

A sense of escape, of release seems, looking back, to have been very strong, but this is interpretation. I did not feel it as release. At the time I think all was acceptance. Everything that happened was new, there were no comparisons to make and any expectations had been of the vaguest. So that though in fact I think I was thrown among a group of individuals who really were brilliant, not necessarily each by each but certainly as a massed event quite amazingly original and creative, I was not then aware of it as something exceptional. They happened to be the people I liked and had most fun with. They seemed special to me and do still, but I am too fond of them and then to judge of my judgement. It happens that the year I went up fell roughly in the middle of a roughly ten-year span which seems to have been golden, or glittering if you prefer. A recent television series followed the lives of a number of undergraduates who must have been up at the beginning of the curious decade and the few episodes I was able to catch left me feeling that I had had a narrow escape and great good luck in finding myself at Cambridge at my particular moment and among those particular people.

That fictional world bore strong resemblances to ours, with first experiences of all kinds for so many of us, emotional entanglements, a period of a sifting and sorting; and with a hefty emphasis on extra-curricular activities. Two differences struck. Firstly that, possibly in rosy retrospect, I cannot remember the smell of ambition being quite so strong, or such a strong sense that everyone was out to carve a ruthless professional career for himself; and secondly, we all seem to have liked each other so much. Both these impressions require qualification: I would not deny the existence of crude ambition in many Cambridge circles, nor that it was often at its blatantest in the theatrical world. Restricted though it was financially and physically that world did manage to reproduce quite closely the rivalries and disappointments of the professional theatre; but the involvement, though intense, was chiefly local.

I did not even bother to audition for the ADC (the Amateur Dramatic Club, which had its own little theatre) because I found the ambiance over-intense and self-conscious, and joined instead the Mummers (the Avis of Cambridge Dramatic Societies) which was not quite so serious, and less exclusive, with a membership drawn, to its advantage, from Town as well as Gown. Cambridge 'actors' and directors abounded as a type and many of them did go on to become professional—the list just of those I knew personally during my three years is very long indeed considering that we were all there to take degrees. It was always clear that very many of these would become professionals because they were so good at it and so dedicated. (In fact it was drawing a comparison between their dedication and my own uncertainty that made me initially reject the stage as a career when I came down.) But amongst all the earnest professionals there was always a leavening of true amateurs. In John Bird's cast for N. F. Simpson's *A Resounding Tinkle* were several undergraduates who did not aspire to be actors at all, not even amateur, such as Timothy Birdsall, the cartoonist, Jonathan Spence, who was reading History at that time, but is now a leading Sinologist at Yale, James Cornford, who went on to become a lecturer in politics, Geoff Patti, now a Conservative M.P., and John Tydeman, the director. It happens that N. F. Simpson himself came down to see it, with Bill Gaskill from the Royal Court. The play had been produced at the Court in a one-act version, because George Devine, the theatre's Director, had considered it unstageable. They were curious to see how we had got through it all in one evening and were astounded by our speed, if not by our pace. Even if the play had been put on with such a visit in mind, which I doubt, this was certainly not what we were thinking of while we worked on it. It was one of the happiest productions I have ever been in. But apart from the broad mainstream everyone else kept darting off to explore tributaries. I did not do much else besides acting but John Bird, having given up rugby after his first year, wrote as well as designing and directing. (He actually wrote a review of a play directed by Clive Swift for which he had himself designed the sets—Sartre's *Les Mouches*—with the headline: 'No Zip in Clive Swift's Flies'.) Timothy acted occasionally as well as designing and illustrating and cartooning.

It may all have been ambition but if so it was adulterated by a lovely exuberance and a perhaps sneaking desire to make things good and interesting and if possible enjoyable. There was an assumption, very arrogant, that if you were any good things would happen. I think it's true too, since Cambridge is on my mind, that we felt able to make this assumption just because we were at Cambridge and not somewhere else. I remember being furious when Andrew Sinclair, back from London having had his first novel picked up by Faber, said very very kindly to Timothy: 'I put in a good word for you, Timmy.' If Timothy thought about it at all it must have made him laugh but I was outraged—how dare he imagine, I thought, the great condescending oaf, that someone with Timothy's talent needed any spokesman?

Timothy and John and William Plowden edited together several editions of *Granta*, a magazine which in its heyday was a good thing. *Granta* introduced another broadening element in the triumviral form of three post-graduate Americans at Clare (I think they were all at Clare). Together with an

Englishman, Jonathan Spence, they edited *Granta* for a term. André Schiffrin, now Managing Director of Pantheon Books in America, Roger Donald and Dick Gooder faced the revelation of the famous tutorial system of education with great charm and good humour—a basically serious-minded trio who manifested in all things a wonderful contrast to the outwardly flighty approach of their undergraduate colleagues. These three were only a few among many compatriots, some of them at Newnham. The Americans were powerful contributors in every sphere to the Cambridge scene and an important counterbalance to the parochialism and inwardness of Cambridge. Many of these poor scholars suffered a good deal for their taste of tradition. They suffered from the cold and from the initial coldness of the English who did not always go to great lengths to make them feel at home. Inhospitality to strangers is not peculiar to Cambridge but it is sad that having found our feet in a new environment we instantly sloughed off any memories of being fresh and apart, and made so little effort.

Perhaps I underrate the ambitions of my chums and my own, and the extent of our calculation; or perhaps at the time hot aspiration seemed more like wishing and it is only in the cold backward glance that they harden to primitive flints. Where ambition existed, it was plain to see. It was stark naked for instance in one contemporary, now famous, who succeeded in raising mediocrity to dizzying heights through sheer determination and stamina and insensitivity of an enviable kind. He set his sights from the start and never strayed from them, an attribute I by no means undervalue; but there it always seemed out of place and laughable.

There were certainly rivalries and feuds and general loathings but there was probably more liking and affection, and some mutual respect and admiration as well as a certain amount of overcoming of prejudice. For the whole of my first year I shared a washing cubicle with a haughty upper-class girl who had the next room to mine. If I were at my ablutions she would tap on the door and having made her presence felt would not then go away but waited outside until I emerged. Then, with a flashing overhead smile, she would utter: 'Splendid!' and sail in. In spring and summer she would leave large bunches of lilac to 'drink' in our mutual wash-basin. At breakfast she always looked immaculate; made-up, hair in a neat bun she would speak to no one, but absorbed herself heart and soul in the *Daily Express*—not, as I later discovered, her own, but the one delivered to the Junior Common Room. If by chance I passed her in the corridor and she were in her nightdress, with her long hair streaming, she ignored me. One of us, I was never sure which, became automatically invisible because she was improperly dressed. One night, however, attired thus, she did speak. She knocked on my door and actually uttered the classic: 'Some of us are trying to sleep.' It was not until I got to know her—she was also in *A Resounding Tinkle*—that I found she was nothing like my view of her. Cambridge had been forced upon her and she was not happy there, and lonely. During the production her hair metaphorically tumbled down and we all became good friends.

When John Bird asked me to play Middie Paradock in *A Resounding Tinkle* he mentioned that he had just met the funniest man in the world, and asked him to play Bro—Peter Cook. They were comically and temperamentally and in every way different but sparked one another and continued to spark one another long after we had all gone down, working at the 'Establishment' nightclub which Peter started in Soho. Peter and Timothy and John wrote a number of ludicrous and hilarious sketches under the collective name of e. e. duncansson, which are sadly lost to us now. They were probably too far ahead of their time, judging by the reception of one which did receive a public performance in the Footlights of 1959, *Last Laugh*. This sketch, in which I played the role of a Miss Rigby, was cut after the first night and together with all the other works of duncansson has never been seen or heard since.

I was not the first girl to appear in the Footlights (though I was the first to be in a Footlights Smoker, a claim to fame that I owe to Bamber Gascoigne who didn't know the rule about women in Smokers and wrote a part for me into one sketch); but it was still not their policy. I suppose that if I had any ambition at all on going up that was it—to be in the Footlights. Revue had always attracted me as much as the idea of becoming a dramatic actress—I still fail to see why that supposed boundary has to be so difficult to cross. The legend of the Footlights had spread as far afield as my home suburb and had been enhanced by the London triumph of *Out of the Blue* starring Jonathan Miller, and a year or two later, when I went up, by the emergence of Joe Melia in *Springs to Mind.*

I owe very much to Joe, including at least two classic moments of heart-stopping romance, first when meeting me by chance he discovered that I had not been asked to a May Ball. 'I suppose you wouldn't want to go to one with me?' he said, and transformed the term. So I was able to wear my only evening dress, bought in December for £3 for the Twickenham Ball. I had not worn it however, except to sit about like The Heiress waiting for my escort—a nice man who might still go scarlet at the memory so I will spare his blushes. He stood me up, as he later confessed, in sheer terror that I would make nasty remarks all evening, so the story doesn't say much for me either. The John's Ball itself was the other, very extended moment, classically romantic at that point where story-book is about to spill over into woman's magazine, with lavish food, happy young people on the Threshold laughing and calling irreverently in settings of antithetic dignity, passing under archways, over bridges—the river—wafting across lawns to the sound of a steel band, the first I had ever heard. I mention all this because the physical beauty of Cambridge, the historic buildings of great grace and elegance, the river, the backs, smothered with daffodils in spring, all this, combined with the closeness of the society, could not help but contribute to the powerful impact of the place on its inmates. So many of them, inevitably, were at a particularly open moment of their lives, momentarily poised like passengers in an unusually well-appointed transit lounge. It is a moment that must have come in their lives wherever they were, at drama school, in their first job, in the army. The fact that they spent it at Cambridge was for most of them—not all—their great good fortune, and perhaps for many the brightest time of their lives, when anything and everything still seems possible. I have a photograph (taken at a Twickenham Ball I actually did get to—always Balls, never Dances) of a foursome of us looking bright-eyed and self-conscious in the direction of the camera with glasses in our hands. Timothy parodied our wet expressions with a perfect inscription, that has since so sadly gathered yet another irony, because he died only a few years afterwards, but still does catch the mood of that moment:

> '... We were happy in those days, young and beautiful, life stretching ahead of us golden with opportunity, and all our evenings were gay with music and laughter. Then the war came and with it the realization that all this must end. So this is to remind us.'

We did go on knowing each other, liking each other, working together and following each other's work and the circle of our acquaintance was not limited to our direct contemporaries. Cambridge was like a sea with new waves constantly arriving, receding, meeting and flowing over the outgoing waves so that, for example, on coming down I met and worked with John Fortune and with Christopher Booker, both of whom I had known only very slightly at Cambridge, and with Michael Frayn and Jonathan Miller, who had left some years before I went up. Amnesty International organized a concert recently to raise funds, and assembled a throng of performers largely drawn from Oxford and Cambridge graduates, and spanning the generations from *Beyond the Fringe* to the Monty Python teams. Charity concerts are usually sprawling disjointed affairs. Each performer is interested only in his or her spot and intent on making that as long as possible to demonstrate audience demand. The Amnesty concert had an atmosphere that was unique for such an occasion. Rehearsals were not seen just as marking time until your own bit but as a lovely opportunity to watch friends and colleagues working; and in performance each one did what he had to do and then came off. It was an atmosphere of mutual regard and pleasure in each other's skills which does exist among musicians but is rare in showbiz.

All this points up another effect of the Cambridge experience. People who were only nodding acquaintances while I was up have become close friends since we have found ourselves out in the cold world. I do not think I am alone in feeling a distinct and favourable prejudice when I meet someone of whatever age who has been at Cambridge. This phenomenon no doubt gives rise to the accusations about Varsity networks, jobs for the boys. They are probably very often true. There are very few who have such strength that they can resist the desire to surround themselves with like-minded people, or the feeling that people from their own university are likely to be just that. I have tried for years to justify a feeling that Oxford and Cambridge types are distinct and very different though it is not easy to substantiate. The very colours seem to suggest them, the rich dark blue and the pale ascetic blue, the highly political worldly Oxford of social veneer and savoir-faire, the chill, puritan, inward, Arts and Science Cambridge of savoir pure and simple, with occasional bursts of self-conscious frivolity. Even the physical settings reinforce these images, Oxford warmer, lusher, mingled in with the town and the decaying fumes of real life; Cambridge in the flat lands, bleak, spartan, separate, immediately accessible, obviously pretty, tarty and heartless like Paris, where Oxford, like London, is grander, more mixed, harder to know but richly repaying exploration.

I have a theory which is always shouted down, especially in Oxford, but I will repeat it, since I can never remember for more than two minutes anyone else's disproving arguments.

It is that, while both places in many ways made Class redundant, it was obliquely and differently done by each: Oxford people level up (in the social sense) whereas at Cambridge people level down. Almost all the Oxford graduates I meet really know and really care, for example, about wine and food and like it to be known that they do. Friends and acquaintances who went to Oxford all acquired a veneer of upper or upper middle-classiness, while at Cambridge the upper classes simmered down to a vague middle and lower-middleness. Cambridge, whatever else, was a great melting pot whose ingredients, though not representative, were certainly very various. I think it did fulfil what those who encouraged me to go there hoped it would—it lifted me right out of my environment without finally estranging me from it, and plunged me into new worlds. It did not qualify me to do any job, as I found when I started looking for one—one reason why I decided to give the stage a whirl after all; but it did make me far more capable of mingling with the 'Best', the real as well as the mere mock, because whatever it stood for in *their* minds, it reduced my areas for apology by one. I did not have to wonder whether things would have been different for me if I had not gone to Cambridge, a question I sometimes sense at the back of some people's minds and sympathise with. Whether it actually effected any transformation in me I cannot tell, or whether the fact of being able to say that I had been to Cambridge made any difference. Probably more doors spring automatically open to television personalities than to Cambridge graduates—the B.A. Hons (Cantab) just added a certain curiosity value.

I go to Oxford a lot these days since my brother has moved there, and I really enjoy it: the students, the bookshops, the bustle, the quintessential atmosphere of university life is distilled for me there. I have been promised a tour of all the new buildings at the Other Place and I suppose one day soon I shall go and take a look at them. But it's no use pretending I can ever go back to Cambridge again because Cambridge was never a place. It sent me away into the hurly-burly by an indirect and devious route, via London's Soho and Winnetke, Illinois, and sadly it did not teach me to think; but it did light up new forks in the road and, directly and indirectly, gave me some of the people I love most in the world.

Piers Paul Read

Piers Paul Read was born in 1941, and went up to St John's College in 1959 to read Moral Sciences (he later changed to History). The son of Sir Herbert Read, he had previously been at Ampleforth College in Yorkshire. After graduating he worked in Germany, where he wrote his first novel, Game in Heaven with Tussy Marx. *Back in England, he worked for a year on* The Times Literary Supplement. *In 1967 he married and spent a year in the United States on a Harkness Fellowship. He is the author of six novels and of* Alive, *the best-selling account of the Andes survivors.*

My father never sat an examination for a university degree. He went to Leeds University for one year before leaving to fight in the First World War. Later in life he was made Professor of Fine Art at Edinburgh University. It was there that he met my mother who had studied under Tovey and was then a lecturer in Music. In spite of this background they both wanted me to go to Oxford or Cambridge and like most children I absorbed my parents' ambition. At the age of sixteen I left school and went to London where I was tutored for three months in History. I sat the examination for St John's College, Cambridge and was offered a place for October 1959, which meant waiting two years to go up.

I went abroad, first to Paris and later to Germany. In Paris I became involved in the political chaos which marked the end of the Fourth Republic. The streets were filled with demonstrators who at each corner faced clusters of armed police. At one time I was seized and thrown into a Black Maria. I mention this only to explain the state of mind in which I finally arrived at Cambridge. I felt moved and excited by the idea that men could march and fight for heroic causes, though I was vague as to what the causes should be. Neither Catholicism nor History, the faith and discipline which I had taken from school, seemed adequate for the understanding of life. I became fascinated by the idea of Philosophy. I read Plato and

Rousseau, and when I returned to England wrote to the Senior Tutor at St John's to ask whether I could change my field of studies from History to Philosophy.

The reply came that this could be done, but that Philosophy at Cambridge was not called Philosophy but Moral Sciences. This redoubled my enthusiasm. A 'moral scientist' was just what I wanted to be. I imagined myself in a laboratory wearing a white coat, examining specimens of good and evil.

For the six or eight months I still had to wait before going up to Cambridge I worked in London for the publishers Thames and Hudson. I rented a room in Sloane Street and would call on various friends of my parents who, because of my isolated upbringing in Yorkshire, I had never met before —Magouche Gorky, the widow of Arshille Gorky, who had four beautiful daughters; Willy and Clothilde Peploe, who had two. These drawing-rooms in Kensington and Belgravia were light, comfortable and civilized—filled with beautiful furniture, paintings and *objets d'art*. The conversation was intelligent, witty, flattering, affectionate. I basked in an atmosphere of femininity and friendship. I mention this because one's impressions of a place are so influenced by what one has known before.

My rooms in my first year at St John's College were under an eighteenth-century roof in the Third Court. They consisted of a bedroom, a kitchen with no running water, and a sitting-room with a gas fire, which was the only form of heating. There went with these rooms a man-servant called a 'gyp' who made one's bed, washed up coffee cups and complained about the tax on cigarettes. The obligation to employ this grizzled relic to do things one was used to do for oneself and the denial of proper facilities to keep oneself warm were my first intimation that at Cambridge form mattered more than content. The pattern was repeated in almost every other aspect of college life. We dined in a magnificent hall, wearing our black gowns, eating disgusting food served by clumsy, sullen servants. As a special privilege the new undergraduates were invited to drink a glass of sherry on an autumn evening in the candle-lit Senior Combination Room. The dimness of the light did not conceal the dimness of the dons, nor their lack of interest in the class of '59.

A second and more serious area of disillusion was with the subject I had chosen to study—Moral Sciences. The Professor at that time was John Wisdom—a kindly, eccentric man who gave lectures dressed in riding breeches. At one of the first of these, he asked me, almost rhetorically, for an example of a metaphysical question.

' "Does God exist?" ' I suggested.

He blushed at my naiveté. 'The kind of question I had in mind,' he said, 'was "does this desk exist?" ' And he continued his lecture, and the lectures which followed, on questions of this kind.

For weeks I grappled with the existence or non-existence of the desk. I struggled through A. J. Ayer's *Language, Truth and Logic* and *The Problem of Knowledge* in search of 'the necessary and sufficient condition for knowing that something is the case . . .' I tackled Russell, Ryle, Moore and Wittgenstein without understanding more than a fraction of what they were talking about. If, before my tutor or among my fellow students, I mentioned Plato, Kant, Nietzsche, Marx or Sartre, I was treated with a pained smile or a scoffing laugh as if I had dropped the name of Walt Disney in a class on the Quattrocento. Such speculative, Continental fun-philosophies were considered quite outside the bounds of serious study. How could you talk about Man, God, Destiny, History or Despair until you could be sure that your pen or your desk or you yourself had a provable existence?

After two months of this intellectual torment I went to my moral tutor and asked him if I could change my subject. He was sympathetic. He said that many young undergraduates came up to Cambridge full of self-confidence because they had been top of their class at school, only to find themselves out of their depth among the much cleverer boys from the rest of the country.

I returned to History, a subject I had always found interesting and worthwhile. For a week or so I considered English, but was advised against it both by Hugh Sykes Davies, the English tutor at St John's, and by my father. My father, who was knowledgeable in a wide range of disciplines, rarely gave advice—preferring to let his children learn from their mistakes: but he knew by then that I was interested in writing and he thought that a writer should not study English because it clogs his mind with criticism.

The more I write, and the more I study other writers, the more convinced I am that he was right. When he gave advice it was usually sound: he was kind, wise and unpretentious. This was another source of disappointment with Cambridge: I had expected to be taught by men of the same stature but found none. If I had been a more outstanding student, I might have drawn more from them. As it was, I was always aware of their boredom and haste. The 'unique' tutorial system, always said to be the envy of the world and the justification for the high fees at Cambridge, seemed to me to be squeezed in by busy dons whose minds were elsewhere—on the train they had to catch to do a broadcast in London; or on some vexed question of college or university politics—an election, perhaps, or the vintage to be laid down in the Senior Combination Room Cellars.

I had been told that academic studies should not be considered the most important aspect of a Cambridge education. It was the 'life' which was supposed to be so exceptional, and like all first year undergraduates I went out in search of it. I joined the Union (for ten guineas) and the United Nations Association, hoping to be drawn into some whirlpool of idealistic enthusiasm: but I found that I was trapped in the company of my contemporaries who were all just as timid and immature as I was. Here again, my 'home background', and my life between school and university, were a disadvantage. There had been more wit and intellectual stimulation in those London drawing-rooms, or sitting around the breakfast-table at home with my parents, brothers and sister, than I found in the Junior Combination Room. Nor was I impressed by my surroundings. My home was certainly simpler than those palaces on the Backs, but in its way it was as beautiful and certainly more comfortable. Nor did the flat countryside around Cambridge compare to the landscapes of my native North Yorkshire.

The College Authorities, so punctilious about the payment of one's bill, did nothing to draw their undergraduates out of the swamp of their own immaturity. We were left to learn from our contemporaries which was the blind leading the blind. I made very few friends in my first year. My most constant companion was John Procopé, a classics scholar at King's College, who was a neighbour in Yorkshire. We would meet most days for a picnic lunch in our rooms, where he would recount with a delighted *frisson* how there was a miner's son with rooms in the same building as his own. Since Procopé's family had a large fortune which had originated in coal, the situation presented many possibilities to young men still obsessed by class distinctions. We were both impressed by those we knew who dared to lose money at poker, go out with the black Princess Elizabeth from Uganda or make some outrageous remark such as 'I never dine in hall because I might find myself next to the son of a worker.'

In reality this would not have been easy. The sons of workers were hard to find. The only undergraduate I ever met who came from the so-called working classes—viz. a council flat in south London (I do not count Brian Pollitt, son of the wartime Secretary of the Communist Party)—was also the only other first-year student in St John's to study Moral Sciences and as such became my friend. He had won a scholarship to St Paul's School in London and then another to Cambridge. He was both practical and brilliant. He could grasp the riddles of logic and metaphysics, and at the same time amass a variety of scholarships and grants by the judicious exploitation of his background. He avoided his college bills and of course he was treated leniently because the college was as eager to cultivate this proletarian seedling as were American colleges to cultivate black students in the 1960s. He got a two-one in the first part of the Tripos and was groomed for a First; but he was determined to resist the bourgeois embrace, and a week before his final examinations he left Cambridge and went to ground in his native Lambeth.

My image of myself when I arrived at Cambridge was of someone radical, even revolutionary, who would change the world. My misfortune was that others did not see me in the same way. I used to wear riding-boots instead of shoes, cavalry twill trousers and a hacking jacket because I had read (in Evelyn Waugh) that one should dress for university as for a country house weekend. An undergraduate who did not know me reported to a friend that I was 'obviously someone whose father had a title'.

All the same I continued to think of myself as 'un ami du peuple' and despise the Old Etonians at the Pitt Club. At the same time I was gradually won round to a kind of dandyism. I squandered a large slice of my allowance on trousers with no turn-ups, and a suede jerkin. Every time I passed the window of a certain clothes shop in Green Street, I would linger over its displays. I had my eye on a particularly exotic overcoat of check tweed with a 'Pomeranian' collar. It cost twenty-three pounds—a sum quite beyond my means until a friend in King's lost money at poker which he could not pay. He needed fifty pounds for a fortnight and offered fifty per cent interest. I lent it to him and a fortnight later he paid up. I bought the coat and wear it still.

My neighbour from Yorkshire, John Procopé, introduced me in the course of my second year to his friends in King's. Before coming to Cambridge I had naively imagined that a place at the university represented some sort of absolute achievement: I only gradually realized that each college had its own character, and that St John's was large and nondescript. I had no friends at that time from the smart colleges such as Trinity or Magdalene, only two friends in my own college—a gammy-eyed Catholic comic and a double-barelled *bon viveur*—and in retrospect think myself lucky to have been taken into the exotic intellectual circle at King's. For I was invited by Procopé to a party in his rooms which he had done his best to transform into something from Beardsley or Huysmans. The walls were painted black, the windows shrouded in black curtains. The room was lit by candles and filled with the fumes of a sickly incense. Our host served oysters and whiskey and played Wagner on his gramophone. I never saw the denouement of this entertainment but left to be sick in the lavatory at the end of the corridor.

Through Procopé I met Jonathan Benthall, a scholar in English from Eton—clever, frail, superior but stylish in his aesthetic idiom. I never said much in these circles because I never quite knew the rules of the game—what to scoff at or what to admire. I felt remote from the nervous jokes about the homosexual dons, or from the drama when one of our friends tried to kill himself with a shotgun because he had fallen in love with another. I do remember that at the end of my second year I felt embarrassed when some young undergraduates wanted to discuss the existence of God. I had made some progress.

At the same time my faith in the Roman Catholic religion survived all the ridicule of the Moral Scientists or the scepticism of my clever friends in King's. It existed on another plane. I went regularly to church but did not take much part in the life of the Chaplaincy. I liked the Chaplain, Monsignor Gilbey, but always felt that if I got to know him better, I would disappoint his social and political if not his spiritual expectations. I also used to visit the Dominicans but felt ill at ease as I often do in the company of priests.

For those brought up as Catholics, faith can have this strange life of its own; and you can no more abandon it than change the colour of your skin. You can pursue a course of action that might seem incompatible with the principles of your belief—most notably at that age a search for experience which by its nature includes sin. And certainly it was not because of my purity or virtue that I spent three years in Cambridge without any sexual experience. When I first arrived I was in love with a fifteen-year-old girl who lived near to us in Yorkshire. She went to a boarding school in Sussex and in the middle of my first term I took a train to Brighton and there hired a taxi to take her out. She told her headmistress that I was her grandmother. We had lunch in Brighton, then went to a cinema where we kissed in the back row. In the dark I caressed her bosom—the first I had touched since my lips left my mother's breast. Perhaps this alarmed the girl because she wrote to me afterwards breaking things off. I was sad for a while but also relieved: the trip to Brighton had cost a lot of money.

My mind turned to girls at Cambridge but I found myself trapped. Those who appealed to me were timid. They smiled when I smiled but could not respond to my diffident desire. The others—those strapping girls from progressive, co-educational schools, who bore down from Newnham or Girton on their bicycles, frightened me so much that I fled to the easier company of my male friends from any opportunity they presented. Only once did I go with a girl to her rooms. She was very pretty, very thin and so shy that she never spoke. I talked about her parents and her poetry and eventually the curtains were drawn and she was undressed in front of the gas fire. I looked at her naked figure, but whatever feelings I should have had in that situation were smothered by my horror at the sight of her emaciated figure. Her bones and pubic hair protruded like those of a corpse. I thought only of the photographs of Belsen and was paralysed. She dressed again without anything taking place between us. I said nothing to explain my behaviour and she never spoke anyway.

Though I did not then have a conscious ambition to become a writer—partly because it had been drummed into me since I was a child that it was impossible to make one's living as an author—I did write while I was at Cambridge. The themes of religion, revolution, history, love and sex were much the same as those which have preoccupied me ever since. I was still at that time acutely self-conscious as a public schoolboy and vexed by the whole question of the public schools, which now seems to be less important. I tried to write a play in which a 'Labour revolutionary, very talented and with a keen sense of justice', is seduced by 'the establishment as personified by Annabel, the daughter of the Earl of Languor'. And that theme, mixed with the life of Eleanor Marx, which I had stumbled on while reading for my special subject, the History of Political Thought, made up my first novel, which I wrote when I went down. All that I had published in Cambridge was a short, absurdist play entitled *Miss Harriet* which was included in *Granta* by the editor, Tom Lowenstein.

During the summer before my last year at Cambridge, Jonathan Benthall, who had stayed for the long vacation term, wrote that he had met and liked one of the so-called 'ice-cream set' called Alexander Chancellor. This set—a group of rich Old Etonians, members of the Pitt Club—embodied everything I still thought I despised. I wrote a sharp letter to Benthall, regretting his choice of friends, but when I returned to Cambridge in the autumn and met the affable, unaffected Alexander Chancellor I found myself slipping easily into his circle. The millionaires who had led the set had gone down at the end of the previous year, and the rump of this *jeunesse dorée* would meet on most afternoons in a café called The Whim. The richer, who were always in debt, would eat bacon and poached eggs; the more cautious and middle-class like myself had tea and toast. Afterwards we might go to a film or talk in one another's rooms about people or films—never about Art or History. Benthall, the scholar, intellectual and aesthete, saw himself as the young Proust and Alexander Chancellor or John

Sebastian McEwen, the youngest member of the group, as a kind of St Loup. He was irritated when it turned out that I was the one to write a novel.

It was a pleasant, undemanding life which went well with the scenery of lawns, bridges and elegant architecture. Real life was postponed: girls and revolution remained peaceably in my imagination. It was only towards the end of that year that I became impatient to leave. I had no real idea of what I wanted to do when I went down—my father wanted me to be a publisher, and my tutor suggested the job of a newscaster on commercial television—but I felt sure that something more dramatic and demanding must be waiting outside the bounds of the town and university.

On my very last night at Cambridge I went to the May Ball at my own college, St John's. Quite courageously I had invited a pretty girl from London whom I hardly knew. Over dinner in the candle-lit Senior Combination Room she told me that she was in love with a young man who could no longer see her because he was dying from an incurable brain disease. We ate 'Cygne St Jean', which tasted like turkey. There was not enough to drink. The girls in their long dresses and the men in their white ties and tails seemed to me absurd—a tableau of everything fraudulent and pretentious about life at Cambridge. None of my Etonian friends was there: instead it was the bright boys from the grammar schools and minor public schools, intoxicated with this mirage of their success. As they danced and capered, aping the aristocracy of the nineteenth century, I listened to my partner's compulsive confessions about her dying boy-friend. Dawn when it came was not romantic but damp and cold. I took my partner back to her lodgings and barely kissed her good-night. When I finally left Cambridge, I was glad to go.

Looking back over fourteen years I am grateful for the history that I managed to absorb, and for the three years of leisure in those pleasant surroundings. I am quite conscious that a Cambridge degree helped me obtain certain posts and scholarships; and that the prestige of the university did much to build up my self-confidence. I still feel, however, that its pretensions amount to fraud—a confidence-trick played on the nation and the world. Its pseudo-aristocratic ideals of idiosyncratic scholarship and convivial Epicureanism are, especially at this moment in our history, another instance of 'la trahison des clercs'. Succeeding generations of able, intelligent and idealistic young men are turned into intellectual narcissists as dons, or narrow, complacent careerists as diplomats or civil servants.

I have never willingly gone back to Cambridge and I am sorry for the most brilliant among my contemporaries who stayed behind. John Procopé is still there. Jonathan Benthall wanted to stay but in the event did not: he is now director of the Royal Anthropological Institute. Alexander Chancellor is editor of *The Spectator*; John Sebastian McEwen is his Art Critic, and Henry Keswick, one of the ice-cream set, is the proprietor. The editor of *Granta* who printed my play is collecting Eskimo legends on Cape Hope in Alaska. My working-class friend has disappeared. The girl I took to the May Ball married David Dimbleby, had three children and has now written a cook-book. Her dying boy friend is still alive.

Arianna Stassinopoulos

Arianna Stassinopoulos was born in Athens in 1950, and went up to Girton to read Economics in 1969. She had previously been at the Hill Memorial High School in Athens. In 1971 she became President of the Union. After graduating she started on a career of journalism and broadcasting. Her first book, The Female Woman, *was published in 1973, and it has since been translated into eleven languages. She recently completed her second,* The Hungry Sheep Look Up, *a study of political leadership.*

We were all collected in the Junior Common Room. All graduating Girtonians—'69 vintage. Miss Duke, Senior Tutor, classical scholar, and perfectionist, was inspecting us to make sure that we were each up to the vineyard's specifications before we could be allowed to proceed to the Senate House, kneel in front of the Vice-Chancellor, and be solemnly proclaimed a B.A. Cantab. It looked as though we were—all in plain black dresses with long sleeves ('of such a length that your elbows are well covered when your arms are outstretched in front of you'), white cuffs and collars, black shoes ('sandals are not permitted'), and black hired gowns with furry white hoods. I longed for a touch of loud, vulgar orange. I smiled. Miss Duke half-smiled.

'Your nails are painted red.'

'Yes?'

'You cannot of course receive your degree with painted nails.'

Of course? Of course.

'We must get hold of some nail varnish remover very quickly.'

I wondered if Matron kept some in her special little cupboard in the sickbay. What, Matron, a closet nail varnisher? No, not possible.

'Do you have your family with you?'

Do I have my family with me! She, a Greek scholar and

lover of modern Greece, should know that it was only through extraordinary good luck that I didn't have my entire Greek village—Athens—with me. A member of 'the family' was dispatched, and an hour later, with virginal white fingernails, I was kneeling in front of the Vice-Chancellor, and a couple of hours later, in Lofty Latin, the deed was done. On the lawn outside the Senate House, the ceremony over, I chuckled to myself: the painted toenails could breathe again.

On a similar June day, in the year of Queen Victoria's Diamond Jubilee, on the same spot where I was standing, Cambridge undergraduates and Cambridge B.A.s and Cambridge M.A.s, under a shadow of confetti, squibs and crackers, and surrounded by placards screaming 'Get thee to Girton, Beatrice, get thee to Newnham, this is no place for you maids' had ceremoniously burnt a big-footed Girtonian and a red-haired Newnhamite. The effigies had been burnt so that what had just happened between the Vice-Chancellor and a few hundred graduating females could not have happened. But it did happen, and so there I was on Saturday, 24 June 1972—fully, properly and generally admitted to the university, just as I was about to leave Cambridge for the Capital.

In the book that I've been keeping ever since I was nine, a kind of Narcissus commonplace book, with my own haphazard, commonplace thoughts, dreams and impressions, there is no entry for 24 June 1972. Occasions are not the stuff of indelible memories—that's why they have to be preserved in scrapbooks. Senate House ceremonials, gowns, robes and Latin High Mumble belong to universal Cambridge—not to *my* Cambridge. My Cambridge is really my Cambridges: two of them. The one lasted longer and the other meant more. My first Cambridge was the talking Cambridge, the Cambridge of the Union, the Cambridge of 'the bumbling McTaggart chattering about the Absolute', of easy profundities and profound self-congratulation, of esoteric name-dropping and gargantuan speculations. My second Cambridge was the Cambridge of withdrawing into Girton and myself, of reading by the gas-fire and thinking by the pond at the bottom of the Honeysuckle Walk—of holding up 'the grain of sand' and occasionally seeing it catch the light. It lasted for the two final terms and it included the three weeks leading up to Tripos—a mixture of frenzy, sleeplessness and exultation that could well have proved combustible.

It was then that I discovered Girton and fell in love with it—a love affair that was very belated, fairly intense and unavoidably short. C. S. Lewis called Girton 'The Castle of Otranto': massive, solid, tenacious-purpose, rather than simply purpose built. And yet full of Gothic arches, turret staircases, haunted spots and very unmassive smug corners. But these I didn't discover until my second Cambridge. My first impression was of corridors, endless, echoing, freezing corridors, leading to my 'fresher's' room after what seemed like a few miles' walk from the Porter's Lodge. I had read somewhere the proud claim that no two rooms at Girton were made to exactly the same measurements. All I could think of when I first saw mine was that in the interests of variety and having exhausted all possible permutations of rooms for human habitation, our founding mothers designed at the end of corridor A in the Old Court, a room for a particularly sedate stuffed squirrel—and this was where I was to spend my first year at Cambridge. Or to be more accurate, this is where I was to spend a few sleeping hours before rushing back to the Bustle and the Life—the muddles and the chaos and the panics. So I have no waking memories of my first-year room, or my second-year room. But when I'm old, tired and memory-mongering, I'd like to go back to my third-year room, secluded at the end of a little passage, and looking over the lacrosse field, the yew hedge and the lawns with the glades and the thickets beyond. I remember, in the summer term, moving my bed next to the open window, and being woken up around six by the Mistress, unintentionally serenading me with Elizabethan poems during her morning walk.

But at the beginning was not the Serenade, but the Word—buzzing insistently and at times gloriously in the ears. If there ever was a battle between Economics, Education and the Union, I didn't even notice it being fought. It was an intensely political period. War-on-Want lunches and world-saving, bring-a-bottle parties and breast-beating, were the most conspicuous—and the most heady, they told us—cocktail on offer. I bought the politics at once, but I was saved from relevant, and meaningful and passionate commitment: maybe it was the 'suspecting glance' that protected me from that particular evil eye. Nothing could protect anyone from the noise of intellectual self-laceration. It drowned all others: a drum-and-fife band led by social descenders with a sense of purpose.

I can't remember a time when politics left me cold. But it was at the Union that what were political instincts gradually became political convictions. The political debate is basically the same whether you are in Athens, in Cambridge or in Timbuctoo, in Plato's Greece or in Harold Wilson's England —the issues of the day whether introducing the Industrial Relations Act, or subsidizing the tomato growers of Northern Macedonia, are equally good testing ground for principles and ideas. I threw myself into the Union: my maiden speech was made at the first debate on the traditional Michaelmas term motion of no confidence in Her Majesty's Government, a motion which according to the records and irrespective of what Government is in power, has never once failed to be carried. My one great advantage was that I hadn't been weaned on the two Unions' mythology—fighting for King and Country, the breeding-ground of the great, the toughest House to speak in, the nursery of statesmen. . . . So although I was fascinated, I was not overwhelmed. My one reservation was my accent. Would I be clearly understood? I listened attentively to the sparring politicians in that first debate and my fears were put to flight—I became convinced for the first, though not for the last time, of the immense value in British public life of total incomprehensibility.

If I wasn't overwhelmed by the Union—neither was the Union by me. I can't say that the night of my maiden speech was one of those nights when new men are discovered and new reputations forged—in fact the Chief Clerk told me later that one of the secretaries, having listened to my speech, was overheard breathing a very deep and very audible sigh of relief: 'Thank God! At least I won't have that funny name to learn to type.' But the apprenticeship had begun. Every Monday night became Union night. I would stay until the end. And I would wait to be called to speak from the floor, even when the only members left in the chamber were those whose inertia had momentarily got the better of their judgment.

There was a lot of contemptuous talk against speech-makers and Union careerists—with, as it happens, an intellectually impeccable pedigree going back to Socrates and Montaigne: 'Away with that Eloquence that so enchanted us with its Harmony, that we should more study it than things.' 'Foul. No rhetoric,' cried Rosencratz; but I wallowed in it—in the rhetoric, and in the eloquence, and in the 'cultured insolence', and even in the verbal savagery, in the whole magic of people's minds moved by words. These were of course rare moments, but I would sit through all the acres of slogans, far-fetched allusions, platitudes, idiotic puns and sub-Wildean witticisms, to live through them again.

One of these moments came in my second term. The motion was one of those omnibus Union motions that sometimes led to the best debates: 'The House believes that Technological Advance Threatens the Individuality of Man and is becoming his Master'. At least it wasn't going to be an occasion of my Family Income Supplement Statistics are better than your Family Income Supplement Statistics. I had been given my first paper speech in a major debate—the Union careerist's dream. It meant that I would be proposing the motion, seconded by George Steiner, with C. P. Snow and Lord Mountbatten opposing and Prince Charles speaking from the crossbenches. There was enough drama in the packed House to satisfy even the most theatrical. And the moment came during George Steiner's speech: he stood up after Lord

Mountbatten had sat down, a small man with a withered arm but a face which could express every emotion from hatred to amusement and then invent some more. There was only the occasional gesture and very little emphasis. But there was inspiration and there was movement, a touch of unconscious magnetism and plenty of conscious strength. He got a standing ovation from a House which, unlike our younger sister at Oxford, is very sparing with them, and naturally won the debate for our side. When in the Committee room after the debate, he asked the Prince and the Earl to sign the order paper 'for his children', I felt uneasy, almost let down. He had after all for thirty-five minutes only an hour before transcended all earthly princes—a speaker transformed into a poet and an orator. It was they who should have asked him to sign the order paper—'for their children'.

George Steiner was in fact the nearest we had to a Guru Don. Spurned by the academic establishment, he was an Extraordinary Fellow of Churchill, in much more than the technical sense. At a time when our self-appointed spokesmen were campaigning to abolish lectures, there were long queues outside Lady Mitchell Hall for his. And it wasn't just the English Faculty that was queueing. All the disciplines—and many of the congenitally undisciplined—were there. And George Steiner on his feet is George Steiner at his best. All the rococo obscurities of his writing, the gallicisms, the 'counterfactualities' and the 'hermeneutics' go, and there he stands, wearing the full Grand Old Lecturer panoply of eccentricity, quotability, formidability, irony and great themes *sub specie aeternitatis*.

All the rest of my forays across the commanding heights of learning proved disastrous. Especially over the border into what is still called out of academic inertia rather than any good reason I can think of, the Philosophy Department—peopled by logicians with razor-sharp minds with which they slash the air. Logic may be a many-splendoured thing, but personally I've never found the splendours of crossword puzzles and executive parlour games difficult to resist. And there was little else on offer. All the problems that I naively expected to be the Department's main preoccupations—ethical values, moral judgments, free will and determinism, the meaning of life—were in fact the great untouchables. Cambridge philosophers, tired of thinking, had 'invented a doctrine which would make such an activity unnecessary'.

At least economists were never meant to do any serious thinking. So Economics could quietly go on making giant strides at the frontier and collapsing at the centre. Formal models, statistics and intricate mathematics were the new gods. Pigou had said that these methods would act as a barrier to charlatans. Instead they turned out to be very effective barriers to reflection and understanding. Some of the most important factors affecting economic behaviour and economic performance—aptitudes, attitudes, religious beliefs and institutions—were relegated to the *ceteris paribus* category and cavalierly ignored. Then the lecturer would proceed to make on behalf of his pet model claims of such naked hubris that I fully expected any moment some Greek god to strike him down. It was often like listening to an extremely sophisticated biological discussion on the respective merits of models based on the assumption that children were brought by storks compared to those assuming that they were found under gooseberry bushes—and then proceeding to draw important policy conclusions from the results.

Lectures could be given up, but not supervisions. Once upon a time no Girtonian could be supervised without a chaperon. *Autres temps, autres moeurs*. In my first week, I found myself sitting in the dashing Dr Mitchell's oak-panelled room in Trinity, glass-of-*dry*-sherry in hand, trying to concentrate on the Repeal of the Combination Acts. I did so hope that if Miss Maynard could see me, she would say again as she had said about another Girtonian a few decades ago: 'My dear, she was such a nice girl, with rosy cheeks and nice manners and nicely dressed, and you wouldn't have thought she knew anything!'

Except that in my case the impression wouldn't have been too far from the truth—by the end of the three years, my weekly essays had become masterly exercises in evasion and bluff. Unbeatable training for Fleet Street. More difficult to master was the art of dignified retreat when the bluff was called. What is the correct exit line, for example, when having produced just such a prize essay on Gunnar Myrdal's 2221-page epic *Asian Drama*, and having been asked 'How much of it have you read?', and having smugly replied 'All of it of course,' you are wryly told 'That's certainly more than he's read himself!'?

Cambridge was still basking in the sunset of the 'effortless superiority' cult. It had learnt to accept enthusiasts, but had nothing but undisguised contempt for plodders. Even in our uncertain world, full of gloomy statistics about rising graduate unemployment, we still went on as if the whole apparatus of lectures, text-books, supervisions and weekly essays was something to be put up with, but not what Cambridge was all about. Yes, we had heard the Pagliaccio cry '*La commedia e finita*,' but we didn't want to believe it. Yes, everyone knew very well that there was no longer a direct apostolic succession from Cambridge to the Lord Chancellorship, or the Headmastership of Eton, or the Governorship of the Ionian Islands, or even the merchant bank of one's third choice and the advertising firm of one's fourth, but there was still a touching confidence whenever two or three gathered together at The Whim, The Copper Kettle or the Sidgwick Site Buttery, that the Cambridge gods would not abandon us. Somewhere in our midst, we felt, must hover a few soul-driven geniuses, waiting to spread their wings to the light. We knew not where, but when we indulged in our favourite sport of forecasting our friends' and our enemies' future, we always erred on the side of extravagance—nobody wants to belittle an angel unawares. If only we could remember the forecasts, what lovely long lists we would compile in a few years' time, as our golden boys and girls start to join the ranks of the ex-future Prime Ministers, ex-future greatest novelists since Tolstoy and ex-future greatest con-men since Stavisky.

Most of the important contenders for that last title would be found amongst those aesthetes of the 'seventies who, like their patron saints of the 'twenties, arrived at Cambridge intent on nothing but lifemanship: cultivating the art of living, perfecting their assumed personalities and elevating exhibitionism to an art. Some of them arrived already perfect. Robert Fraser was one of them. In appearance, he was a combination of Cyril Smith and Miss Pears Soap 1955—massive, round and baby-pink, dressed in striped trousers, stiff collar and black jacket, nearly correct and definitely outlandish. His fame preceded his exploits—the only Trinity fresher (how monumentally absurd the word sounds when applied to Robert!) with a room at Great Court. His dinner parties confirmed the fame. At the end of dinner, when the port was circulating and the cigar smoke rising, he would tell us with that marvellously round voice of his, that made you convinced he had a liqueur chocolate in the back of his mouth, exactly how many pints of double cream—specially sent from the country—he had used in the cooking. If the perfect host is one who himself says nothing of interest but acts as a catalyst for others to show off, then he was the most perfect imperfect host. His only contribution to other people's conversation was as a stimulant *in absentia*. At his dinners, his guests were there to admire, gape and consume. His erudition was immense and immensely visible. So was his snobbishness.

He tried the Union—but he was forty years too late. We were the committed generation. So he gave us up. My own Union career had taken a rather unexpected turn. Two weekends before the end of my first term, I went down to London and while I was away, my name was put down in the Candidates' Book for Standing Committee by Barbara Scott (now Kaplan and mummy), a Girtonian in her second year, who had plenty of other opportunities during my time at the Union to act as a combination between guardian angel and *deus-ex-*

machina. When I was told, I tried to withdraw my name but the ballot papers had been printed. It was not a case of reluctant philosopher-kings, but of straightforward, common or garden vanity—I simply did not fancy the idea of seeing my name at the bottom of the greasy pole. As it happened, I didn't. 'And it was at the Union Society on 26 November 1969, as I sat musing amidst the election results of the Michaelmas Term, while the bejeaned undergraduates were singing rock vespers in the Round Church, that the idea of becoming President of the Union first started to my mind.' And it seemed to be coming to pass until suddenly on 23 October 1970, something happened which convinced me that the idea was Wromantic but Wrong, and Wrong because Unrealizable.

The occasion was the debating equivalent of Ali v. Fraser—G. K. Galbraith v. William Buckley on 'The Market is a Snare and a Delusion', televised by NBC, with two undergraduates opening the debate and two closing it. I was making the closing speech on G. K. Galbraith's side, against the free market (it was before I had taken the road for Monetary Damascus), and as fate would have it, actually sitting next to him. He spoke—badly, very badly, in fact—and sat down. Buckley, dripping smoothness, ease and self-assurance proceeded to tear him to elegant little pieces. The Professor was becoming visibly agitated. He leaned and whispered in my ear, 'Can you please stand up and interrupt him—tell him that the conditions he's describing only apply to the Stock Exchange, and that all other Markets are far too imperfect to bear out his case.' Perhaps. Maybe. Still, this was a debate, not a seminar. And Bill Buckley is a real pro, as they say where he comes from. But the venerable Professor, prophet, poseur, and licensed Jeremiah of the 'Affluent Society', 'The New Industrial State' and all enemies of The New Paradise on Earth, was nudging me on. So I stood up. Buckley gave way—and, incidentally, a new meaning to 'reculer pour mieux sauter'—and 'Well, Madame,' he said, 'I do not know what market *you* patronize.'

You may think that the Union has a weak sense of humour,

but he brought the House down. I can still feel my cheeks burning as I sat down, bidding as I thought a final farewell to the idea that 'had started to my mind'. Need I say that after a comedown of that magnitude, my closing speech was not a success? The final nail was put in the coffin by one of my closest friends then and even more so now, Christie Davies, a 'mature' ex-President, who kept popping back on his way from London to Leeds, where he was teaching. Well, he had popped back that evening, and he popped up immediately after me and gave a virtuoso Union performance—light, paradoxical, effortless, brilliant. He clinched the devastation of our side and, I was sure, of my Union career. But even the Union forgets, and a month later I had recovered sufficiently to attempt a comeback, speaking with Trevor Huddleston and Denis Healey against sales of arms to South Africa. At the end of term I was elected Secretary against the then Chairman of the Conservative Association, who had been the *Varsity* favourite. Bang went my trust in opinion polls—for ever.

If Sitwell got his education 'in vacation from Eton', I got mine 'in vacation from Economics', and in preparation for my Union speeches. Just looking around my bookshelves at the moment, I can relive the debates I spoke in—Religion and Education, Critics and the Arts, Trade Unions and the State, Censorship and Literature, Racialism and Communism. Every speech acted like a base camp for exploration. I would start on a reading jaunt around the subject, the more unfamiliar the better, trying to relate the 'burning' issues of the debate to the fundamental ideas, to the past, to what was perennial rather than merely topical. Most of the discoveries were of course totally useless for the debate. But 'Ithaca set you on the beautiful journey. Without her you would never have taken the road'. Gradually the skeleton of what I believed and what I hazily sensed began to emerge—and debate by debate new reactions would get into the bloodstream, the bones would become fleshier, almost corpulent.

The most important thing the Union gave me was not the

Presidency but the opportunity to 'connect, always connect'; to realize that everything—political ideas, religious beliefs, social systems, personal lifestyles—ultimately hangs together; that there really does exist a sympathy of all things, 'one common flow, one common breathing'. The Union gave me the framework. The Presidency—through the national publicity and the debate on Women's Liberation—gave me a book commission. The decision to give up my place at the Kennedy School of Government at Harvard, and with it any idea of graduate work in America, followed naturally, almost inevitably, as did the desire and the decision to make my home in London.

From Secretary to Vice-President, to President, that was the chain, too often broken to provide any guarantees. The evening that the results of the Vice-Presidency were coming out, Shirley Williams was giving the Founders' Memorial Lecture at Girton. As Secretary of the JCR, I had been invited to the dinner the Mistress was giving after the lecture. I was sitting next to her. She knew about the election. And if it had been a General Election with herself leading the Labour Party, I doubt if she could have shown more concern. Finally somebody came in and passed a piece of paper with the result to the Mistress. That evening solved for me the mystery of why Shirley Williams is the most popular politician in Britain—across parties. Her ability to empathise with someone else's anxiety and someone else's happiness is astounding, total and totally real.

One of my inflationary pre-election promises was that there would be two debates a week instead of one, and something happening at the Union every evening. There was. But only after a delirious summer holiday on the beaches of my Union office, and a weekly routine walk-out by the Union permanent staff. The day that I opened one of the desk drawers for some writing paper, and found instead a pile of greaseproof paper with the compliments of the Standing Committee, I also realized that well, yes, perhaps that third letter to John

Mortimer comparing him to the rising sun and the aurora borealis simultaneously, could, maybe, be toned down. Still, he did finally agree to speak against Mary Whitehouse and Lord Longford, only to be greeted by the Chief Clerk when he arrived with 'Good evening, Lord Longford. I say, you have put on a little bit of weight.'

I wonder whether other people's Presidencies were as studded with gaffes as mine was, right down to the cook choosing pork as the main course when the Israeli Ambassador was speaking, which coupled with the fact that members of the Arab delegation refused to sit at the table with the Israelis and sat in the billiard room eating Mars bars instead, gave a new twist to the art of imaginative mixings at dinner parties.

The big success of the term was our record recruitment figures, and the big flop the 1971 Cambridge Teach-In on Higher Education. Sir Eric Ashby, the Vice-Chancellor, was to open the weekend proceedings after lunch on the Friday; the list of participants reads still today as a more or less complete Who's Who in the world of Higher Education. Cambridge was plastered with posters, leaflets and programme cards. Walking with the Vice-Chancellor from the dining-room to the Chamber, I had to explain why in that case he was about to trumpet the opening in the presence of three unhappy-looking undergraduates and two very superannuated LEA officials—at least that's how many they seemed against the massed ranks of empty benches. Over the weekend I had to explain the same thing to John Vaizey, and Lord Boyle, and Baroness Lee, and Professor Gareth Williams, and Sir Desmond Lee, and Lord Beaumont. . . . In between, I was running about desperately trying to find someone to explain it to me. *Varsity*'s headline gave the verdict: 'Flop-In at the Union'. All we had to do at the post mortem was provide the moral. 'Eels in the process of being skinned,' murmured the Assistant Clerk, 'are clearly not interested in a three-day Teach-In on Higher Skinning.' We decided that that would do.

In between debates, three line whips, replacements, 'members' queries', 'Films at the Union', crisis runs on the billiard chalk, and 'Concerts at the Union', the official skinning was going on. I knew about Keynes, Keynesian Economics and the Economics of Keynes, the world of Keynes and the post-Keynesian world. I also knew—some graduate student had mentioned him at some optional class—that there was somebody called Milton Friedman who hadn't understood Cambridge Economics. I had listened to Professor Kaldor beam away about Selective Employment Tax and Regional Employment Premiums, and read in my *Financial Times* that grown-up politicians were impressed.

I had also heard Professor Joan Robinson, and I had seen those extraordinary blue eyes of hers set in a face made all the more striking by every deep etched wrinkle, light up at the mention of China and Chairman Mao. She was a China-addict right down to her Chinese tunic, and a people-addict right down to announcing that she would be available to meet the undergraduate-people in the buttery of the Faculty every Tuesday at five, for a chat and a cup of tea. The first Tuesday six of us turned up. She talked about Mao's 'proletarian road' to industrialization, about the peasantry being absorbed into socialism and the production of food being ahead of the growth of population. The second Tuesday three of us turned up and she talked about Chairman Mao's love of paradox. The third Tuesday, I dropped out. Watching Joan Robinson go into ecstasy about China and Mao was one of the most depressing sights at Cambridge—a one-woman re-enactment of the Passion of the intellectual in search of a secular creed. Would she, I wondered, be around long enough to hate unutterably what she now praised unstintingly? To realize that she, and many much less brilliant than herself, were displaying an imbecile credulity that an African witch-doctor would have found enviable?

The BBC had wanted to film one of her lectures for my television programme, 'One Woman's Week', but she would never agree. I was in fact amazed when Mr-Crisis-of-Capitalism-Marris accepted. The filmed lecture was the first one of his I'd been to. The two weeks we spent filming my week were full of such moments of truth. By the end I felt less like 'one woman', and more like an extra on the *El Cid* set.

But I was learning. About truth and television. About changing in loos—however small and into however eleborate an evening dress. About rumours, allegations and how to deal or not to deal with them. There was only one other Greek undergraduate at Cambridge, apart from me. Connoisseurs of Greek politics from Alcibiades to Papadopoulos will instantly know that we were therefore inexorably bound to each other by all the traditional bonds of suspicion, rivalry and resentment. His reaction when I was elected President was to spread brotherly rumours of my undying support for the Greek junta. By the day of the first debate of my term, the rumours had become a front page story in *Varsity*, complete with all the dramatic props—calls for my resignation, confession, retraction, execution. The Standing Committee met, issued a suitably melodramatic statement on the lines of 'fully behind our President', and advised me to do nothing. I did in future have many opportunities to regret disregarding their advice. But not on this occasion. The Chamber was absolutely crammed and so was the gallery, when I walked in with the guest speakers. And there are few more exciting sights. There was all the hush and expectancy of a first night, and my sense of theatre—in this case the theatre of the absurd—rose to it: 'Good evening. Before we proceed to the motion before the House tonight, I propose to. . . . I believe. . . . Members have the right. . . . I therefore call on the Vice-President to take my seat and myself to answer members' questions.' I had arrived with four pre-Watergate tapes of my Union speeches in the last two years against the Greek regime, in favour of the expulsion of Greece from the Council of Europe, against the Garden House celebrations. And by the end of the cross-examination, it was clear that only those for whom evidence is a fetish of the bourgeoisie, remained unconvinced. It seems touchingly childish now, but it was one of my happiest moments at Cambridge.

And at least as dramatic as my Farewell Debate, when walking into the Union with the guests after dinner at Trinity, I was practically lynched by what looked—and felt—like crowds of Leeds United supporters whose team has lost an away match, but in fact turned out to be Union members who after queueing to get in had discovered the Chamber full and the gate shut.

The night of my Farewell Debate was also the last night of my first Cambridge. For my second Cambridge, the scene moves to Girton, and the action stops. Our founder had insisted not only on privacy but on remoteness. Emily Davies was convinced that Girton should be at least two and a half miles away from town, so that there would not be 'the morning calls, and the dropping in and the servants coming with notes to wait for an answer, and the general victimization of idle ladies'. She would have had trouble recognizing today's servant problem, but how right she was about 'this great boon—the power of being alone—perhaps the most precious distinctive feature of college life'.

I had before then felt that real excitement of absorption and discovery usually associated with mad professors with butterfly nets and an air of poetic absentmindedness. But I had in a way, fought against it—it seemed an ersatz kind of excitement, an abdication from life. My second Cambridge and Emily Davies's remote Girton, made me realize—more, it made me feel—that it is just as real and that the only problem is achieving that most elusive of all combinations: 'between stillness and the stream of the world'.

The stream of the world was only very occasionally allowed in during that period. But on one such evening, just before I went into exam quarantine, a fairly large stream was being entertained in my room with stuffed vine leaves and Greek wine that made one guest take back everything he'd ever said against *vin ordinaire*. Ten of us, four men and six Girtonians stayed behind after hours, that is after 11.30 pm, chattering away, no doubt, about what would happen if one fell through a hole that went through the centre of the earth. There was a knock on the door and the porter's voice. Quick, quick . . . quicker. . . . We pushed the men out of the window, shut it, sat down demurely and opened the door. It was not to be. A second porter had been placed outside the window—Girtonians in the nineteen-seventies being clearly about as inventive as Girtonians in the eighteen-seventies. The men were caught, and I was summoned to the Senior Tutor's office and fined £10 for having four men in my room after hours. I reckon that £2.50 per head, even taking into account the shortage of supply due to the public school system and all that, was slightly excessive. 'And I am assuming that *Varsity* will not hear of this fine,' were the Senior Tutor's menacing parting words. 'Machiavelli's theory on the control of information available to the masses was the precursor of the modern public relations industry. Discuss.'

Exams were imminent. And for three weeks to the day before the first paper, even a furtive glance across the Arts Pages of the *Financial Times* was classified as a venal sin. I still in fact get that extra twinkle of the transgressor's pleasure from the Arts Pages of the *FT*.

And then came the results (two-one—'you really were amazingly lucky, my dear'), and May Week, and floating ribbons and deep pillows on slow-moving punts, and white necks, and india-rubber faces, and organza dresses, and blinking eyes, and Pimms on Trinity lawn, followed by Pimms on Pembroke lawn, followed by Pimms No. 3 at Magdalene. The men would buy a bottle of *Moet et Chandon* and a box of cigars and set up as *bon viveurs* and the women would borrow mummy's Ascot hat and set up as *femmes fatales*. Being in love was *de rigueur*. 'Peu importe l'objet, c'est une passion.' So was tennis, croquet, dripping with sweat and plunging in the river—'from the heat to the cold with the gourmandise of a tingling curry eaten with chilled white wine'. The occasional suicide would be ascribed to exam tension.

And then The End.

To Mr Isaac Newton I am indebted for the details of Cambridge Life during May Week, to Professors Khan and Kaldor for my mastery of the monetary roots of inflation, to Lord (Bertrand) Russell for my conversion to the joys of chastity, to Mr E. M. Forster for my passions, to Mr Rupert Brooke for my astringency, to Lord (Maynard) Keynes for my dislike of hobnobbing with the powerful, to Mr Wittgenstein for my rigid moral principles, to Mr G. E. Moore for my intellectual frivolity. . . .